Zola's Introduction to Hebrew

עִבְרִית לְמַתְחִילִים

I V R I T   L E M A T C H I L I M

THIRD EDITION

Zola's Introduction to Hebrew
עִבְרִית לְמַתְחִילִים

Zola Levitt Ministries, Inc.
P.O. Box 12268
Dallas, Texas 75225

by John Jeffrrey Parsons

בָּרוּךְ הוּא הָאֱלֹהִים אֲשֶׁר נָתַן־לָנוּ
תְּשׁוּעָה נִצַּחַת בְּיַד יֵשׁוּעַ הַמָּשִׁיחַ אֲדֹנֵינוּ

1 Corinthians 15:57

This work is thankfully dedicated to the LORD Jesus,
the Jewish Messiah and great King.
May His great Name be exalted forever and ever.

תֹכֶן

Contents

Part I: Mechanics

Hebrew Consonants

Hebrew Vowels

Part II: Selected Readings

ב"ה

Acknowledgements

Without Mark Levitt's constant encouragement and love, this book never would have been completed. Ms. Karen Risch spent many hours diligently proofing the text to ensure accuracy. Mr. Aaron Eby helped with some Hebrew translations and provided quiz ideas. To each of these precious friends I extend a hearty *"Todah!"* Dr. Yigal Levin of Bar-Ilan University, Israel, provided invaluable assistance with Hebrew phonetics, transliterations, and scholarly exhortation. Additional thanks to Mr. Don Day, Mrs. Dorothy Richter, Olga Krasnenkova, Rabbi Ed Rothman, Mr. Irv Davis, Dr. Danny Ben-Gigi, Dr. Lee Martin, and Sandra Levitt. Special thanks to Dr. Zola Levitt, editor-in-chief, for his unswerving commitment to the truth of God and his faithful proclamation of the good news of our redemption through Jesus, the Jewish Messiah.

Works from several sources were used to verify the accuracy and content provided in this book, though all errors are the responsibility of the author. See the bibliography at the end of the book for a list of works consulted. The fonts used in this book are all copyrighted by international law and are listed in the colophon. The text, artwork, and pedagogy of this book are all subject to international copyright. Please contact John J. Parsons (info@hebrew4christians.com) or Zola Levitt Ministries for permission to use any part of this material.

Foreword

Hebrew is God's first language, one could say, because He chose this language to communicate His first divine revelations to the world. From Genesis to Malachi, God spoke to His Chosen People—and ultimately to all the peoples of the earth—in a language both beautiful and sacred.

John Parsons, author of the monthly Hebrew Lessons in our national newsletter, has carefully laid out a plan of study for those wishing to learn Hebrew for the very first time.

As someone schooled in the Hebrew language both in America and in Israel, I am confident that this introduction to the language will equip you with practical and Biblically-oriented tools for reading and interpreting the Hebrew Scriptures.

Applying yourself to this course of study may seem daunting at first, but it quickly becomes easier and more enjoyable as you go along. Stick with it. The value of what you learn and then put into practice in Bible study will last for all of eternity.

And as you progress in this study, keep in mind the fact that the ability to read correctly a single verse from a 3,500-year-old text is something no human being can do in any other language.

I applaud you for your decision to study the sacred language of the Bible. May God grant you wisdom and insight as you apply your mind to His Word.

Zola Levitt
Dallas, Texas

מָבוֹא

Shalom and Welcome to Hebrew!

Basic Features of Hebrew

Before beginning to study Hebrew, it is important to get an overview of the basic features of this fascinating language.

- **Letters**—There are twenty two letters of the Hebrew alphabet, with five letters having additional "final forms" when they appear at the end of a word. There are no capital letters in Hebrew.

- **Vowels**—Hebrew is normally written without vowel letters. Today, vowel marks are used to facilitate learning the language.

- **Right-to-Left**—Hebrew is written and read from right to left, rather than left to right as in English.

- **Letter Styles**—Modern Hebrew uses square script (*ketav meruba*) for printed materials (such as books, newspapers, road signs, etc.) and cursive script (*ketav yad*) for handwriting. For sacred writings such as the Torah scroll, a type of calligraphy is used.

- **Transliterations**—The process of writing Hebrew words in the English alphabet is known as "transliteration" and is as much an art as a science. In this book we have attempted to follow a consistent transliteration scheme.

- **Pronunciations**—Ashkenazi Jews (those of Eastern European descent) tend to pronounce the alphabet differently than Sephardic Jews (those of Spain, Northern Africa, and Israel). In this book we will use the Sephardic pronunciation since it is the one used in the land of Israel.

Qumran Hebrew
2nd Cent. BCE

Gezer Calendar
10th Cent. BCE

Pictograph
15th Cent. BCE

Torah Hebrew
7th Cent. C.E.

Modern Print
20th Cent. C.E.

IC

Modern Cursive
16th Cent. C.E.

Did you know?

Like other ancient writing systems, the Hebrew alphabet originally was written using a pictographic script. The earliest Hebrew script (sometimes called Paleo-Hebrew) resembled the ancient Phoenician alphabet. Examples can be found on coins and clay fragments (called *ostraca*). Later, this script was replaced by the Aramaic alphabet (called *Ketav Ashuri* or *Ketav Meruba*) by Ezra the scribe sometime during the Babylonian exile. Today, both the *Torah* and newspapers use modernized renditions of this same script, though everyday correspondence is written using cursive.

Why Study Hebrew?

In case you need some motivation to begin your study of Hebrew, consider the following:

- **The Holy Language**—Hebrew is the original language of the Bible. It is the language in which the Almighty spoke forth the *Torah* to Moses and it is also the language in which the prophets expressed their revelations. If you want to know the Bible better, you will want to study Hebrew.

- **The Lord Jesus Knew Hebrew**—Jesus both spoke and read Hebrew (Matt. 5:18, Luke 4:16-20, Acts 26:14).

- **The Foundation of the New Testament**—All of the original authors of the New Testament were Jews who spoke and read Hebrew (Acts 21:40, 22:2; John 5:2; Luke 23:28; Acts 15:13-21). Studying Hebrew will give you new insight into the meaning of the New Testament writings.

- **The Language of the Synagogue**—At the time of Jesus, the *Torah* was regularly read at the synagogues (Acts 15:21). In fact, throughout the nearly 2,000-year Diaspora, the study and recitation of Hebrew has helped unite the Jewish people with a common form of expression and worship. Jews have been praying the same blessings, chanting the same Scriptures, and studying the same texts for literally thousands of years. Studying Hebrew will help you appreciate the Jewish roots of Christianity and make you a sensitive witness to God's Chosen people.

- **The Language of Modern Israel**—Hebrew is the only ancient language to have been revived as a modern spoken language. Today Hebrew still serves as the language of Judaism, and is also the official language of the state of Israel. Your study of Hebrew will help you better appreciate modern Jewish culture and the people living in Israel.

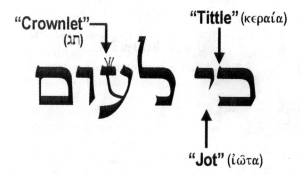

Knowing the "Jots" and "Tittles"

The Lord Jesus told his disciples that not one "jot" or "tittle" will pass away from the Law until all is fulfilled (*see* Matt. 5:18). The word translated "jot" (ιωτα in the Greek New Testament) refers to the smallest Hebrew letter ("Yod"), and the word translated "tittle" (κεραια in Greek) refers to the "horn," or smallest stroke of a Hebrew letter, probably something like a "serif" in our modern English typefaces.

The smallest stroke of the smallest letter of the Hebrew text was important to the Lord Jesus, and, if we esteem the Scriptures as He did, we likewise will pay attention to the details of the Sacred Writings. But how can we determine what a "jot" or a "tittle" is without having a knowledge of the original Hebrew text? It is our hope that this book will help you to both read and write basic Hebrew words and sentences, and thereby become aware of the "jots" and "tittles" that "shall in no way pass until all is fulfilled" (Matt. 5:18).

מָבוֹא

The Structure of this book

Unlike many tools for learning Hebrew available today, *Zola's Introduction to Hebrew* teaches you Hebrew step-by-step, in a logical and consistent way. You can proceed at your own pace, though normally you will want to try to work through a lesson a week.

The book is essentially broken down into two basic parts: Hebrew Mechanics (Part I) and Hebrew Readings (Part II). Part I (Lessons 1–12) presents the Hebrew language in a deductive manner, giving you a manageable set of letters or vowels to study in progressive increments. Part II (Lessons 13–19) presents the Hebrew language in an inductive manner, reinforcing the learning of the letters and vowels you studied earlier.

Part I: Mechanics

Part I consists of a methodical study of the Hebrew letters and vowels. Each lesson builds on the preceding lesson and provides the following components:

- **Introduction**—Lesson learning objectives are clearly presented along with a "Lesson at a Glance" overview.

- **Lesson Content**—The presentation of new material is provided in a logical, step-by-step manner.

- **Lesson Review**—The presentation of new material is reviewed and practice exercises are given.

- **Lesson Summary**—The material is succinctly summarized to reinforce learning. Flash cards and summary tables are provided.

- **Writing and Transliteration Practice**—Both writing and transliteration practice exercises are given to further consolidate learning.

- **Lesson Quiz**—At the end of each lesson, a short quiz is provided to help you gauge your progress.

Part II: Guided Readings

Part II consists of guided readings of the most sacred Jewish prayers and scriptures. We start with the Shema and the Ten Commandments, and progress through Shabbat prayers, Havdalah prayers, Siddur Prayers and Blessings (i.e., common synagogue prayers), the *Tanakh*, the *Brit Chadashah*, and the Hebrew Names of God. Throughout the guided readings, a unique format is used to facilitate comprehension:

אֵל	מֶלֶךְ	נֶאֱמָן.
ʼel	**me**·lekh	ne·ʼe·man
God (is)	*King*	*faithful*

God is a faithful King.

At the end of Part II, there is a Hebrew Glossary with some key Messianic terms, information on the Jewish calendar and holidays, and a weekly Torah reading schedule.

Suggestions for the Student

Although Hebrew can be a difficult language to study, we have made every effort to present the fundamentals of the language in a clear, step-by-step manner. Here are a few tips to help you master the material presented in this book:

- **Pray**—This study of Hebrew is not intended to be an academic exercise, but to deepen your awareness of the greatness and glory of the God of Israel. Ask the Lord to help you master the material in order to know Him better.

- **A Lesson a Week**—For Part I of the book, it is recommended that you proceed through a lesson a week for 12 weeks. Part II may be studied and reviewed for months to come.

- **Review Every Day**—Set aside some time every day to review the material. Studying 30 minutes a day is generally more effective than studying once a week for a few hours.

- **Use Graph Paper**—Although we have provided grids for you to practice forming the Hebrew letters, you may want to purchase additional graph paper to use while learning the new scripts.

- **Make Flash Cards**—Flash cards are quite helpful as you are trying to recall the shapes and sounds of new letters, vowels, and words. Besides the exercise involved in creating them, they can be carried with you anywhere to quickly reinforce your learning.

A Note to the Teacher

As a self-study tool with the adult learner in mind, certain concessions were made to ensure consistency of approach. For example, vowels are not directly introduced until Lesson Seven, so the first few weeks of study center strictly on the mechanics of the consonantal text, i.e., letter formation and recognition. Vowels are introduced according to phonetic class, with a separate lesson on each of the primary vowel classifications. Since most beginning students struggle with the Sheva more than other diacritical marks, a separate chapter is devoted to its mastery. The dagesh, syllabification, furtive patach, and Hebrew dipthongs are all integrated into the lesson on the Sheva in order to make a smooth transition to the guided readings of Part II

This book does not formally introduce grammatical concepts, apart from the basic syntactical rules of the sheva, the dagesh, syllabification, and the notion of the shoresh. Transliteration, as much an art as a science, tends to follow the more common Anglicized conventions. Therefore, to ensure proper vocalization skills, proper phonetics will need to be demonstrated as the student begins recitation of the guided readings. The Hebrew for Christians web site (http://hebrew4christians.com) provides audio support for the basic contents of this book.

Lesson One

THE FIRST FIVE LETTERS

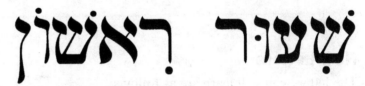

Lesson Introduction

In this lesson you will learn the first five letters of the Hebrew alphabet. In particular, you will learn:

✓ The names of the Hebrew letters

✓ How to write the letters in both square (block text) and in modern script

✓ How to properly pronounce the letters

✓ How to accurately transliterate the letters

✓ How to recite the letters in the correct order

✓ How to correctly identify the letters in a string of Hebrew text

New Letters

The letters you will learn are as follows:

ה	ד	ג	בּ	א
Hey	**Dalet**	**Gimmel**	**Bet**	**Aleph**

Right to left!

Lesson at a glance

After you have studied this lesson, the following information should be clear:

#	Name	Book	Block	Cursive	Pronounced	Trans.	Hebrew Name
1	Aleph	א	X	IC	silent letter	'	אָלֶף
2	Bet	בּ	בּ	כּ	**b** as in **boy**	b	בֵּית
	Vet	ב	ב	כ	**v** as in **vine**	v	
3	Gimmel	ג	ג	ۿ	**g** as in **girl**	g	גִּמֶל
4	Dalet	ד	ד	ʒ	**d** as in **door**	d	דָלֶת
5	Hey	ה	ה	ה	**h** as in **hey**	h	הֵא

The first letter of the Hebrew alphabet is called "Aleph" (pronounced "**ah**-lef"). Aleph has no sound of its own, but usually has a vowel associated with it.

In modern Hebrew, the letter Aleph can appear in three forms:

א	X	IC
Book Print	Manual Print	Cursive

Manual Print (Block)

Notice that the manual print form of Aleph resembles the book print version—except that the strokes of the lines are all even. You will learn manual print in order to recognize the printed Hebrew letters as they appear in Hebrew texts. You write the manual print version of the letter Aleph according to the following pattern:

The numbered arrows show the order and direction for drawing the lines (the gray rectangle indicates the letter proportions in a graph paper cell).

Hebrew Cursive

Manual print is important to learn to help you recognize printed Hebrew type; however, handwritten communication is normally written using Hebrew cursive. You write the cursive version of the letter Aleph according to the following pattern:

Write the letter from right to left, beginning with the stroke labeled 1 and then to the stroke labeled 2.

Practice

Write the letter Aleph (from *right to left*) in both manual print and script several times:

X **Manual Print**

IC **Cursive**

The second letter of the Hebrew alphabet is called "Bet" (rhymes with "mate") and has the sound of "b" as in **boy**.

In modern Hebrew, the letter Bet can appear in three forms:

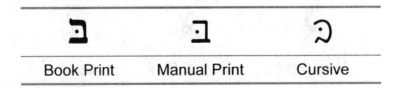

Book Print	Manual Print	Cursive

Manual Print (Block)

Write the manual print version (or "block" version) of Bet as follows:

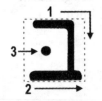

Note that the second line extends past the vertical line to the right.

If no dot appears in the middle of the letter (called a dagesh mark), Bet is called "Vet" and is pronounced as a "v" as in vine.

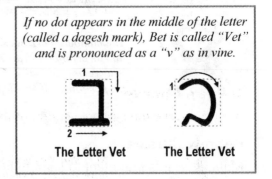

The Letter Vet   **The Letter Vet**

Hebrew Cursive

And the cursive version:

Note that the cursive version of Bet is formed using a single stroke.

Practice

Write the letter Bet (from *right to left*) in both manual print and cursive several times:

בּ **Manual Print**

ב **Cursive**

Note: The sole difference between the letter Bet and the letter Vet is the presence or absence of the dot in the middle of the letter (called a *dagesh mark*). When you see the dot in the middle of this letter, pronounce it as a "b"; otherwise, pronounce it as a "v."

The third letter of the Hebrew alphabet is called "Gimmel" (pronounced "**geeh**-mel") and has the sound of "g" as in "**g**irl."

In modern Hebrew, the letter Gimmel can appear in three forms:

ג	ג	ג
Book Print	**Manual Print**	**Cursive**

Manual Print (Block)

Write the manual print version of the letter Gimmel according to the following pattern:

The numbered arrows show the order and direction for drawing the lines (the gray rectangle shows the letter proportions in a graph paper cell).

Hebrew Cursive

You can write the cursive version of the letter Gimmel as follows:

Note that the cursive Gimmel is formed using a single stroke.

Practice

Write Gimmel (from *right to left*) in both manual print and cursive several times:

ג **Manual Print**

ג **Cursive**

Note: Like Bet, Gimmel can also sometimes have a dot in the middle of the letter, but today this does not affect its pronunciation: with or without the dot it is still pronounced as "g" as in **g**irl (historically, Gimmel without the dot was pronounced "gh'). We will explain the use of the dot (dagesh mark) in Lesson Twelve.

The fourth letter of the Hebrew alphabet is called "Dalet" (pronounced "**dah**-let") and has the sound of "d" as in "**d**oor."

In modern Hebrew, the letter Dalet can appear in three forms:

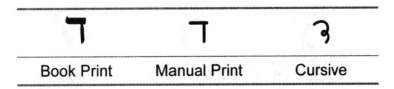

Book Print	Manual Print	Cursive

Manual Print (Block)

Write the manual print version of the letter Dalet according to the following pattern:

Note that the first line extends past the vertical line to the right.

Hebrew Cursive

And write the cursive version as follows:

This is a bit difficult to write at first, but practice makes perfect!

Practice

Write the letter Dalet (from *right to left*) in both manual print and cursive several times:

Manual Print

Cursive

Note: Like Gimmel, Dalet can also sometimes have a dot in the middle of the letter, but this does not affect its pronunciation: with or without the dot, it is still pronounced "d" as in **d**oor (historically, Dalet without the dot was pronounced "th'). We will explain the use of the dot (dagesh mark) in Lesson Twelve.

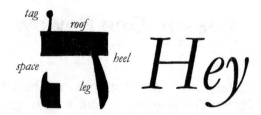

The fifth letter of the Hebrew alphabet is called "Hey" (pronounced "**hey**") and has the sound of "*h*" as in "*h*ay."

In modern Hebrew, the letter Hey can appear in three forms:

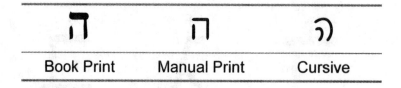

ה	ח	ה
Book Print	**Manual Print**	**Cursive**

Manual Print (Block)

Write the manual print version of the letter Hey according to the following pattern:

Note that there is a gap between the top of the horizontal line and the second vertical stroke.

Hebrew Cursive

And write the cursive version like this:

Note that there is a gap between the two lines.

Practice

Write the letter Hey in both manual print and cursive several times:

ה **Manual Print**

ה **Cursive**

Notes: Hey is known as a **guttural letter** since it used to be pronounced in the back of the throat. Other guttural letters are א, ע, and ח. Note also that when Hey appears at the end of a word, it is normally silent.

Lesson One Review

Reciting Order

Mazal tov! If you have studied Lesson One carefully, you have learned the first five letters of the Hebrew alphabet. You are now on your way to learning Hebrew in earnest!

Manual Print

Practice writing each of the first five manual print letters in the order shown. Say each letter name out loud as you write it:

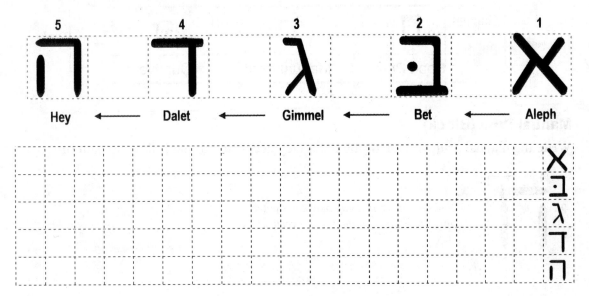

5	4	3	2	1
Hey ←	Dalet ←	Gimmel ←	Bet ←	Aleph

Hebrew Cursive

Now do the same with the Hebrew cursive letters:

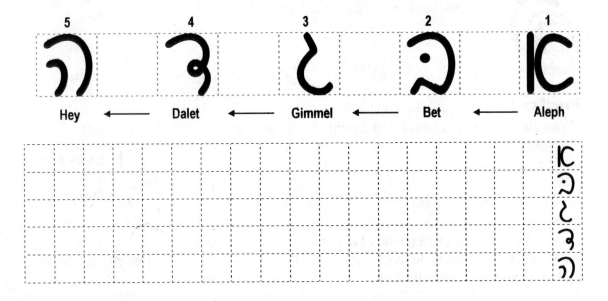

5	4	3	2	1
Hey ←	Dalet ←	Gimmel ←	Bet ←	Aleph

Lesson One Summary

Reciting Order: the first five letters

The following table should make sense after studying this lesson:

Book Print	Name	Block	Cursive	Pronounced	Transliteration
א	Aleph	✗	Ic	silent letter	' (or none)
בּ	Bet	בּ	ɔ	**b** as in **b**oy	b
ב	Vet	ב	ɔ	*no dot*: **v** as in **v**ine	v
ג	Gimmel	ג	ʒ	**g** as in **g**irl	g
ד	Dalet	ד	ʒ	**d** as in **d**oor	d
ה	Hey	ה	ɔ̃	**h** as in **h**ey	h

Notes:

- The manual print letters resemble the book print letters—except that the strokes of the lines are all even. You learn manual print merely to recognize the printed Hebrew letters as they appear in Hebrew texts; for handwritten communication you use Hebrew cursive (called *Ketav Yad*).

- If there is no dot in the middle of the letter, Bet is called "Vet" (and is pronounced as "v" as in vine). Other letters that can take a dagesh mark are Gimmel and Dalet (though today there is no change to the pronunciation for these letters, however).

- Aleph (א) and Hey (ה) can sometimes function as vowel letters (more information is provided in Lesson Seven). They are also called *guttural letters*.

Additional Information:

Before the Aramaic "square script" developed (called *Ketav Ashuri* or *Ketav Meruba*), Hebrew was written using pictographs, like other ancient languages.

Name	Numeric Value	Hebrew	Pictograph	Meaning
Aleph	1	אָלֶף	 𓃾	Ox / strength / leader
Bet / Vet	2	בֵּית	𓉐	House / "In"
Gimmel	3	גִּמֶל	�	Foot / camel / pride
Dalet	4	דָּלֶת	 𓂧	Tent door / pathway
Hey	5	הֵא	 𓀠	Lo! Behold! "The"

Note: The numeric values (and ancient pictographs) are sometimes used by Kabbalists to infer mystical meaning from the Scriptures and certain Hebrew words. While this practice may occasionally offer some interesting insights, it is to be avoided since it often leads to speculations and doubtful interpretations.

Lesson One Writing Practice

Each lesson will provide a section for you to practice what you have just learned. As much as is possible, try to do the exercises from memory, not looking back on the previous material. If you mix up print and cursive letters, don't be discouraged! Practice makes perfect! And remember to write the letters from right to left!

Review Drill: First 5 Letters (manual print)

From memory, write the first five letters in manual print in the squares below (write Bet and Vet on the same line). Say each letter aloud as you write it in the squares below:

1

2

3

4

5

Review Drill: First 5 Letters (cursive)

From memory, write the first five letters in cursive in the squares below (write Bet and Vet on the same line):

1

2

3

4

5

Did you know?

A Hebrew scribe (called a *Sofer*) is trained to faithfully reproduce the exact lettering of the Torah text, even including textual oddities such as enlarged letters, small letters, inverted and even broken letters. The rules for writing a Torah are very complex, and to become a certified Sofer requires much study. And, depending on the size of the Torah, it can take about a year to write a Torah scroll!

Certified soferim are sometimes called "**STaM**," an acronym for three of the sacred Jewish scribal items—**S**ifrei Torah (Torah scrolls), **T**efillin (phylacteries) and **M**ezuzot—parchments on which portions of the Shema are written, and which Jews are commanded to place on their doorposts.

Transliteration Examples

The following Hebrew letters are transliterated into English. The Hebrew is read from right to left, but the transliterations are written from left to right.

ד	ג	בּ	ב	א	**1.**
d	g	b	v	' (or none)	

בּד	דה	בּה	בב	ה	**2.**
bd	dh	bh	vv	h	

בּג	דאב	גב	בא	בּא	**3.**
bg	d'b	gb	v'	b'	

אכאו	אוגל	כהה	אגל	אואג	**4.**
'b'	g'd	vhd	dg'	d'd	

גּהד	אואג	בכ	היאו	היה	**5.**
dhv	'gd	bv	hy'	hyh	

From our Sages...

The first letter of the Hebrew Bible is a Bet rather than an Aleph, and certain Jewish sages have puzzled over why this is the case. One sage thought that this is because the letter Bet connotes power because of the force of air (*ruach*) being spoken forth; another thought that by starting with a Bet rather than an Aleph, the Almighty was in effect revealing that man did not know the first principles about the creation; yet another thought that since Aleph is a silent letter, it represents God in His unspeakable glory and life, which forever precedes all things (see Isa. 44:6, cp. Rev. 22:13). Jesus described Himself as the "Aleph and the Tav," and the Aleph, humble and lowly, gives out its strength (Aleph) before the house (Bet) of creation in sacrificial love.

Transliteration Practice

Hebrew to English

Transliterate each row of Hebrew letters into English. Read the Hebrew from right to left, but write the transliterations from left to right. Say the name of each letter out loud.

בֹּה   דגדה   אב   אדה   בגד   .1

הד   גבדה   הא   בּאה   בבד   .2

כֹּב   בּככ   הכ   הכו   הכ   .3

בֹל   כּובּדה   כו   בֹל   היה   .4

English to Hebrew

Transliterate each row of English letters into Hebrew cursive. Read the English from left to right, but write the transliterations directly beneath from right to left. The first exercise is done for you.

vb	'h	dg	vd	dv	.5
				בֹל	

bv'	d'g	gdg	vg	db	.6

hv	bg	b'	v'	bgd	.7

Lesson One Quiz

Each lesson will provide a short quiz to help you reinforce your learning.

1. Write Letter Names

Write the name for the following Hebrew letters. The first exercise is done for you.

בּ	א	ב	ג	ה	ד	Book Letter
					Dalet	Name
					d	Transliteration

ל	ﬣ	כ	א	ב	ה	Cursive Letter
						Name
						Transliteration

2. Write Hebrew Letters

Write the Hebrew letter for the letter name. The first exercise is done for you.

Hey	Dalet	Gimmel	Vet	Bet	Aleph	Name
					א	Hebrew
					'	Transliteration

3. Transliteration

Transliterate each row of Hebrew letters into English. Read the Hebrew from right to left, but write the transliterations from left to right. Say the name of each letter out loud.

.a   אב אדה גב דאדה בה אב בה הגב

'v

.b   בבד אבא הא בנד דג אדא אנה דאג

.c   אד בגדה הב גבדה הד אנא אהג דגד

4. Recognition

Circle the correct answer.

What letter is this? רֹ

1. Hey
2. Vet
3. Gimmel
4. Dalet
5. Aleph

What letter is this? בֹ

1. Hey
2. Vet
3. Gimmel
4. Dalet
5. Aleph

What letter is this? גֹ

1. Vet
2. Hey
3. Gimmel
4. Dalet
5. Bet

What letter is this? כֹ

1. Gimmel
2. Vet
3. Hey
4. Dalet
5. Aleph

What letter is this? בֹ

1. Vet
2. Hey
3. Gimmel
4. Dalet
5. Bet

What letter is this? הֹ

1. Hey
2. Vet
3. Gimmel
4. Dalet
5. Aleph

What letter is this? אֹ

1. Aleph
2. Vet
3. Gimmel
4. Dalet
5. Hey

What letter is this? גֹ

1. Gimmel
2. Bet
3. Aleph
4. Hey
5. Dalet

What letter is this? הֹ

1. Bet
2. Hey
3. Gimmel
4. Dalet
5. Aleph

5. Completely fill in the alphabet table you have studied:

Book Print	Name	Block	Cursive	Pronounced	Transliteration
א					
בֿ ב					
ג					
ד					
ה					

"A b b a"

Lesson Two

THE NEXT FIVE LETTERS

שָׁעוּר שֵׁנִי

Lesson Introduction

In this second lesson you will learn the next five letters of the Hebrew alphabet (and also review the previous letters you have learned). In particular, you will learn:

✓ The names for five new Hebrew letters

✓ How to write the letters in both square (block text) and in modern cursive

✓ How to properly pronounce the letters

✓ How to accurately transliterate the letters

✓ How to recite the letters in the correct order

✓ How to correctly identify the letters in a string of Hebrew text

New Letters

The letters you will learn are as follows:

י	ט	ח	ז	ו
Yod	**Tet**	**Chet**	**Zayin**	**Vav**

Right to left!

Lesson at a glance

After you have studied this lesson, the following information should be clear:

#	Name	Book	Block	Cursive	Pronounced	Trans.	Hebrew Name
6	Vav	ו	ו	ı	**v** as in **v**ine	v	וָו
7	Zayin	ז	ז	ʓ	**z** as in **z**ebra	z	זַיִן
8	Chet	ח	ח	ת	**ch** as in Ba**ch**	ch	חֵית
9	Tet	ט	ט	ც	**t** as in **t**ime	t	טֵית
10	Yod	י	י	ʾ	**y** as in **y**es	y	יוֹד

The seventh letter of the Hebrew alphabet is called "Vav" (pronounced "**vah**v") and has the sound of "v" as in "*v*ine."

In modern Hebrew, the letter Vav can appear in three forms:

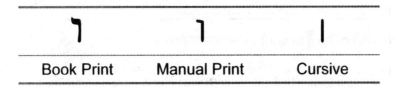

| Book Print | Manual Print | Cursive |

Manual Print

Write the manual print version of the letter Vav according to the following pattern:

Note that there is a slight left-to-right incline in the horizontal stroke.

Hebrew Cursive

You can write the cursive version of the letter Vav according to the following pattern:

A single downward stroke: that's all there is to the script Vav!

Practice

Write the letter Vav (from *right to left*) in both manual print and cursive several times:

Manual Print

Cursive

Note: In ancient Hebrew, Vav was pronounced "w" and is often transliterated as "w"; however, in modern Hebrew Vav is pronounced as a "v" sound. Vav can also function as a "**consonantal vowel**" in Hebrew texts. More information is provided in Lesson Seven.

The seventh letter of the Hebrew alphabet is called "Zayin" (pronounced "**zah**-yeen") and has the sound of "z" as in "zebra."

In modern Hebrew, the letter Zayin can appear in three forms:

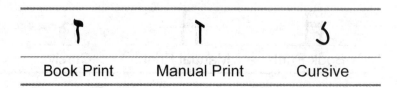

| Book Print | Manual Print | Cursive |

Manual Print

Write the manual print version of the letter Zayin according to the following pattern:

Note that the first stroke slightly descends from the left to right.

Hebrew Cursive

You can write the cursive version of the letter Zayin according to the following pattern:

The script version of Zayin looks somewhat like a backwards "c."

Practice

Write the letter Zayin (from *right to left*) in both manual print and cursive several times:

Manual Print

Cursive

Note: The cursive version of Zayin is sometimes written as a "**descender**," that is, with the bottom of the stroke descending below the baseline. Be careful not to confuse the print version of Zayin (ז) with Vav (ו).

 *Chet*

The eighth letter of the Hebrew alphabet is called "Chet" (rhymes with "let") and has the (light scraping) sound of "ch" as in "Ba**ch**."

In modern Hebrew, the letter Chet can appear in three forms:

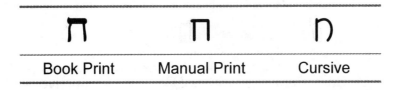

ח	ח	ח
Book Print	Manual Print	Cursive

Manual Print

Write the manual print version of the letter Chet according to the following pattern:

Note that the first stroke "overhangs" the vertical second stroke.

Hebrew Cursive

You can write the cursive version of the letter Chet according to the following pattern:

Note that the second stroke extends slightly above the first stroke.

Practice

Write the letter Chet in both manual print and cursive several times:

Manual Print

Cursive

Note: Chet makes a light, scraping sound in the back of the throat while making an "h" sound. Chet is known as a **guttural letter** since it is pronounced in the back of the throat. Other guttural letters include א, ה, and ע. Chet is sometimes transliterated as ḥ, which is why you sometimes see the word "Chanukah" spelled as "Hanukkah" in English.

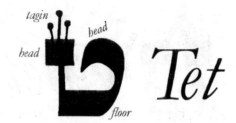

The ninth letter of the Hebrew alphabet is called "Tet" (rhymes with "met") and has the sound of "t" as in "*t*all."

In modern Hebrew, the letter Tet can appear in three forms:

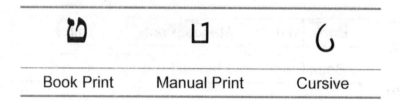

Book Print	Manual Print	Cursive

Manual Print

Write the manual print version of the letter Tet according to the following pattern:

Note that the initial horizontal stroke slightly ascends from the left to right before descending.

Hebrew Cursive

And you write the cursive version according to the following pattern:

Note that the stroke ascends above the top of the line (an "ascender" letter).

Practice

Write the letter Tet in both manual print and cursive several times:

Manual Print

Cursive

Note: Some academic Hebrew books use ṭ to transliterate Tet (in order to distinguish it from the letter Tav, which we will study later). In this book, however, we will transliterate Tet using the letter "t."

Yod

The tenth letter of the Hebrew alphabet is called "Yod" (rhymes with "mode") and has the sound of "y" as in "**y**es."

In modern Hebrew, the letter Yod can appear in three forms:

י	י	י
Book Print	**Manual Print**	Cursive

Manual Print

Here is the manual print version of the letter Yod:

Note that the stroke descends only about halfway toward the baseline.

Hebrew Cursive

And the cursive version:

Some people make this stroke simply as a small vertical line.

Practice

Write the letter Yod in both manual print and cursive several times:

Manual Print

Cursive

Note: Yod can also sometimes function as a "**consonantal vowel**" in Hebrew texts (more information is provided in Lesson Seven). Yod is also sometimes (erroneously) pronounced "Yood."

Lesson Two Review

Reciting Order

Tov Me'od! (very good) You're making progress! If you have studied Lesson Two carefully, you have learned the next five letters of the Hebrew alphabet.

Manual Print (Block)

Practice writing and reciting each of the five manual print letters in the order shown:

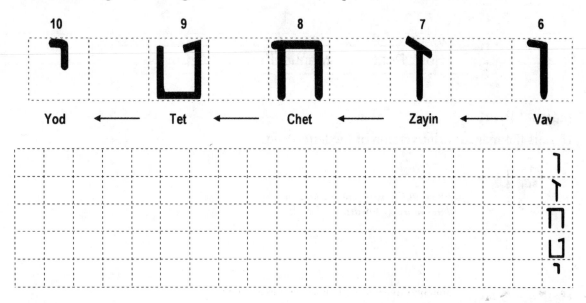

Hebrew Cursive

Now do the same with the Hebrew cursive letters:

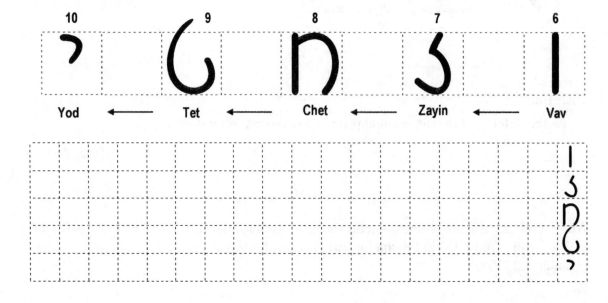

Lesson Two Summary

Reciting Order: the first 10 letters

Book Print	Name	Block	Cursive	Pronounced	Transliteration
א	Aleph	X	ℐC	silent letter	' (or none)
בּ	Bet	בּ	ב	**b** as in **b**oy	b
ב	Vet	ב	כ	*no dot*: **v** as in **v**ine	v
ג	Gimmel	ג	ᒷ	**g** as in **g**irl	g
ד	Dalet	ד	𝟹	**d** as in **d**oor	d
ה	Hey	ה	ᕼ	**h** as in **h**ey	h
ו	Vav	ו	I	**v** as in **v**ine; "consonantal vowel"	v
ז	Zayin	ז	Ⴝ	**z** as in **z**ebra	z
ח	Chet	ח	∩	**ch** as in Ba**ch**	ch (or ḥ)
ט	Tet	ט	Ꮯ	**t** as in **t**ime	t (or ṭ)
י	Yod	י	ᒥ	**y** as in **y**es; "consonantal vowel"	y

Caution:

- "Look Alike" Letters:

| Chet | Hey | | Vav | Zayin |

Additional Information:

Before the Aramaic "square script" developed (called *Ketav Ashuri* or *Ketav Meruba*), Hebrew used pictographs, like other ancient languages.

Name	Numeric Value	Hebrew	Pictograph	Meaning
Vav	6	וָו	Y	Nail / peg / add / "And"
Zayin	7	זַיִן	⌐	Plow / weapon / cut off
Chet	8	חֵית	⊞	Tent wall / fence / separation
Tet	9	טֵית	⊗	Basket / snake / surround
Yod	10	יוֹד	⊔	Arm and hand / work / deed

Lesson Two Writing Practice

Each lesson in this book will provide a section for you to practice what you have just learned. As much as is possible, try to do the exercises from memory, not looking back on the previous material. If you mix up print and cursive letters, do not be discouraged! Practice makes perfect!

Review Drill: First 10 Letters (manual print)

From memory, write the first ten letters in print in the squares below (write Bet and Vet on the **same** line):

1
2
3
4
5
6
7
8
9
10

Review Drill: First 10 Letters (cursive)

From memory, write the first ten letters in cursive in the squares below (write Bet and Vet on the **same** line):

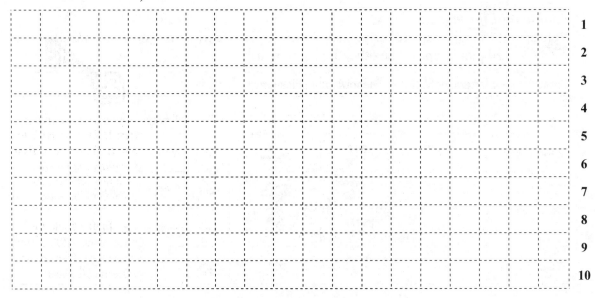

1
2
3
4
5
6
7
8
9
10

Transliteration Examples

The following Hebrew letters are transliterated into English. The Hebrew is read from right to left, but the transliterations are written from left to right.

י	ט	ח	ז	ו	**1.**
y	t	ch	z	v	

יד	אוט	חי	בזד	ואד	**2.**
yd	'vt	chy	bzd	v'd	

גוזה	טבה	הזה	גבה	יוד	**3.**
gvdh	tvh	hzh	gbh	yvd	

אוחד	טוב	אבא	דודי	בו	**4.**
'chd	tvv	'b'	dvdy	v'	

Preview: the Shoresh (שֹׁרֶשׁ)

Many Hebrew words are built upon a **three-consonant root** (called the "shoresh") that contains the essence of the word's meaning. Vowel patterns and other changes are added to a shoresh to give a Hebrew word a more determinate meaning (you will learn about vowels beginning in Lesson Seven). Following a common convention, we designate a root using the three consonants separated by three dots. For example, the Hebrew root for **love** is:

א.ה.ב

Circle the **root letters** in the following words and phrases (ignore the other marks):

English	Hebrew
Love	אַהֲבָה 'a·ha·**vah**
Love of God	אַהֲבַת הַשֵׁם 'a·ha·**vat** ha·**shem**
"Love the Lord!" (Psalm 31:23)	אֶהֱבוּ אֶת־יְהוָה 'e·he·**vu** 'et-ha·**shem**

A key to understanding a given Hebrew word is to identify the root and then to identify the function of the letters and vowels attached to the root.

Note: In this book, the divine name, יהוה, is not pronounced. Instead, we substitute "*hashem*" instead.

Transliteration Practice

Hebrew to English

Transliterate each row of Hebrew letters into English. Read the Hebrew from right to left, but write the transliterations from left to right. Say the name of each letter out loud.

טִי	אהבה	חִי	דוד	אח	.1

זאת	בּוֹאִי	בָּא	בדא	דודי	.2

הִיה	יוֹדֵה	בֵּאֵ	הֹוֹח	בֵּאֵ	.3

חַן	בֵּאֵ	בִּי	טֵבֵב	טוֹבה	.4

English to Hebrew

Transliterate each row of English letters into Hebrew cursive. Read the English from left to right, but write the transliterations directly beneath from right to left. The first exercise is done for you. For this exercise, transliterate "v" as a "Vet" (rather than as "Vav").

zvt	'hvh	dg	yvd	'ch	.5
				אח	

chg	gdb	zh	z'	ch'	.6

'b'	vch'	bvg	vy	tzch	.7

Lesson Two Quiz

Each lesson provides a quiz to help you reinforce your learning.

1. Write Letter Names

Write the name for the following Hebrew letters. The first exercise is done for you.

ט	ר	ז	י	ח	Book Letter
				Chet	Name
				ch	Transliteration

ן	י	ת	ל	ע	Cursive Letter
					Name
					Transliteration

2. Write Hebrew Letters

Write the Hebrew letter for the letter name. The first exercise is done for you.

Yod	Tet	Chet	Zayin	Vav	Name
				ו	Hebrew
				v	Transliteration

3. Transliteration

Transliterate each row of Hebrew letters into English. Read the Hebrew from right to left, but write the transliterations from left to right. Say the name of each letter out loud.

a. אוי אב יה יהוה ואדה חגב
’vy

b. והבידו טדי־אדה באה אדוי זה

c. הזה הגבדה הד אהג חגדה וזה גטח

4. Recognition

Circle the correct answer.

What letter is this? ח

1. Hey
2. Yod
3. Vav
4. Chet
5. Tet

What letter is this? ה

1. Chet
2. Yod
3. Hey
4. Tet
5. Aleph

What letter is this? ﬥ

1. Tet
2. Yod
3. Zayin
4. Chet
5. Gimmel

What letter is this? ﬧ

1. Vav
2. Yod
3. Tet
4. Chet
5. Zayin

What letter is this? י

1. Vet
2. Yod
3. Vav
4. Chet
5. Zayin

What letter is this? ו

1. Tet
2. Zayin
3. Vav
4. Hey
5. Yod

5. Completely fill in the alphabet table you have studied:

Book Print	Name	Block	Cursive	Pronounced	Transliteration
א					
ב					
ג					
ד					
ה					
ו					
ז					
ח					
ט					
י					

מָה־אָהַ֫בְתִּי תוֹרָתֶ֑ךָ

O how I love thy law (Psalm 119:97a)

mah 'a·**hav**·ti to·ra·**te**·kha

Lesson Three

THE NEXT FIVE LETTERS

שִׁעוּר שְׁלִישִׁי

Lesson Introduction

In this lesson you will learn five more letters of the Hebrew alphabet (and also review the previous letters you have learned). In particular, you will learn:

✓ The names for five more Hebrew letters

✓ How to write the letters in both square (block text) and in cursive

✓ How to properly pronounce the letters

✓ How to accurately transliterate the letters

✓ How to recite the letters in the correct order

✓ How to correctly identify the new letters in strings of Hebrew text

New Letters

The five new letters you will learn are as follows:

ס	נ	מ	ל	כ
Samekh	**Nun**	**Mem**	**Lamed**	**Kaf**

Right to left!

Lesson at a glance

After you have studied this lesson, the following information should be clear:

#	Name	Book	Block	Cursive	Pronounced	Trans.	Hebrew Name
11	Kaf (*) Khaf	כּ כ	בּ ב	ᴐ ᴐ	k as in kite ch as in bach	k kh	כָּף
12	Lamed	ל	ל	ℓ	l as in look	l	לָמֶד
13	Mem (*)	מ	Δ	N	m as in mom	m	מֵם
14	Nun (*)	נ	ב	J	n as in now	n	נוּן
15	Samekh	ס	▽	O	s as in son	s	סָמֶךְ

(*) = has an ending letter form (sofit)

Kaf / Khaf

The eleventh letter of the Hebrew alphabet is called "Kaf" and has the sound of "k" as in "*k*ite."

In modern Hebrew, the letter Kaf can appear in three forms:

ךּ	ךּ	ꜩ
Book Print	Manual Print	Cursive

Manual Print

Write the manual print version of Kaf as follows:

The Letter Kaf

Hebrew Cursive

Now write the cursive version of Kaf this way:

A single stroke, like a backwards "c" is used to form this letter.

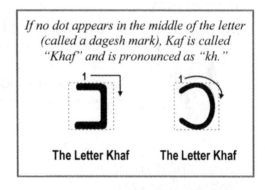

If no dot appears in the middle of the letter (called a dagesh mark), Kaf is called "Khaf" and is pronounced as "kh."

The Letter Khaf   **The Letter Khaf**

Practice

Write the letter Kaf (from *right to left*) in both manual print and cursive several times:

Manual Print

Cursive

Notes: Be aware that Khaf (i.e., כ) has the scraping sound of "ch" as in Ba**ch** and is sometimes transliterated as "ch" rather than "kh" (in this book we consistently use "kh" for Khaf). Kaf/Khaf also has a different form when it ends a word (called **sofit form**), which we will study in Lesson Six.

The twelfth letter of the Hebrew alphabet is called "Lamed" (pronounced "**lah**-med") and has the sound of "l" as in "**l**ook."

In modern Hebrew, the letter lamed can appear in three forms:

Book Print	Manual Print	Cursive
ל	ל	ל

Manual Print

Write the manual print version of the letter Lamed this way:

Note that the first stroke extends above the line and inclines from left to right.

Note: The letter Lamed is called an "ascender" because it ascends above the top of the line (above the "x-height" of the text).

Hebrew Cursive

And write the cursive version as follows:

Note that the stroke hooks to the right and ascends the line.

Practice

Write the letter Lamed in both manual print and cursive several times:

Manual Print

Cursive

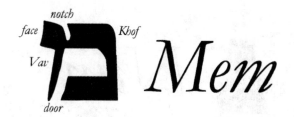

Mem

The thirteenth letter of the Hebrew alphabet is called "Mem" and has the sound of "m" as in "*m*om."

In modern Hebrew, the letter Mem can appear in three forms:

מ	ג	N
Book Print	Manual Print	Cursive

Manual Print

Write the manual print version of the letter Mem according to the following pattern:

Note that there is a gap at the bottom left of the letter.

Hebrew Cursive

Now write the cursive version of the letter Mem according to the following pattern:

The script form of Mem looks a lot like an English capital "N" but is written from right to left.

Practice

Write the letter Mem in both manual print and cursive several times:

Manual Print

Cursive

Note: Mem has a different shape when it ends a word (called **sofit form**), which we will study in Lesson Six.

The fourteenth letter of the Hebrew alphabet is called "Nun" (pronounced "noon") and has the sound of "n" as in "*n*ow."

In modern Hebrew, the letter Nun can appear in three forms:

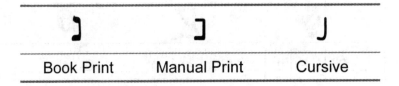

Book Print	Manual Print	Cursive

Manual Print

Write the manual print version of the letter Nun as follows:

Nun is about half the width of the letter Kaf.

Hebrew Cursive

The cursive version looks like this:

The script version looks somewhat like an English lowercase "j" (but it does not have a dot and does not dip below the line).

Practice

Write the letter Nun in both manual print and cursive several times:

Manual Print

Cursive

Note: Nun has a special shape when it ends a word (called **sofit form**), which we will study in Lesson Six.

Samekh

The fifteenth letter of the Hebrew alphabet is called "Samekh" (pronounced "**sah**-mekh") and has the sound of "s" as in "*s*on."

In modern Hebrew, the letter Samekh can appear in three forms:

ס	‬ע	O
Book Print	Manual Print	Cursive

Manual Print

Here is the manual print version of the letter Samekh:

Note that the top stroke has an "overhang" on the left.

Hebrew Cursive

And the cursive version:

The script form of Samekh looks like an English capital "O."

Practice

Write the letter Samekh in both manual print and cursive several times:

Manual Print

Cursive

Note: Be careful not to confuse the book print shape of Samekh (ס) with the letter Mem (מ), and especially Mem Sofit (see Lesson Six for more information). In some scholarly works, Samekh may be represented using a letter other than "s."

Lesson Three Review

Reciting Order

Tov Me'od! Only seven more letters to go! If you have studied Lesson Three carefully, you have learned the next five letters of the Hebrew alphabet. You are making progress!

Manual Print (Block)

Practice writing and reciting each of the five manual print letters in the order shown:

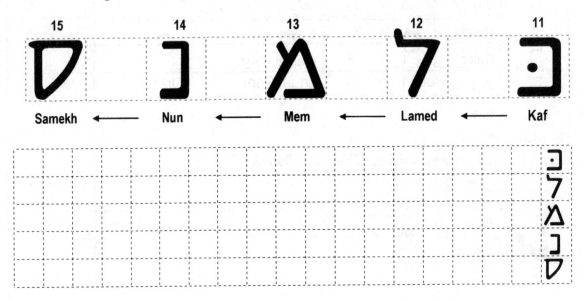

Hebrew Cursive

Now do the same with the Hebrew cursive letters:

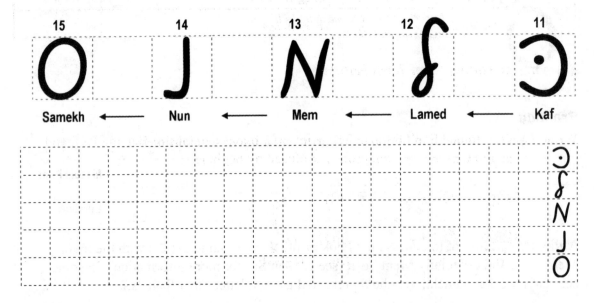

Lesson Three Summary

Reciting Order: the first 15 letters

Practice writing and reciting the first fifteen letters of the Hebrew alphabet as shown:

Book Print	Name	Block	Cursive	Pronounced	Transliteration
א	Aleph	X	IC	silent letter	' (or none)
בּ	Bet	בּ	כּ	**b** as in **b**oy	b
ב	Vet	ב	כ	*no dot*: **v** as in **v**ine	v
ג	Gimmel	ג	८	**g** as in **g**irl	g
ד	Dalet	ד	ड	**d** as in **d**oor	d
ה	Hey	ה	ற	**h** as in **h**ay	h
ו	Vav	ו	I	**v** as in **v**ine; "consonantal vowel"	v
ז	Zayin	ז	ऽ	**z** as in **z**ebra	z
ח	Chet	ח	॥	**ch** as in Ba**ch**	ch (or ẖ)
ט	Tet	ט	৬	**t** as in **t**ime	t (or ṭ)
י	Yod	י	י	**y** as in **y**es; "consonantal vowel"	y
כּ	Kaf (*)	כּ	Ɔ	**k** as in **k**ite	k
כ	Khaf	כ	C	*no dot*: **ch** as in ba**ch**	kh
ל	Lamed	ל	৷	**l** as in **l**ook	l
מ	Mem (*)	מ	N	**m** as in **m**om	m
נ	Nun (*)	נ	J	**n** as in **n**ow	n
ס	Samekh	ס	O	**s** as in **s**on	s

(*) = has an ending letter form (sofit)

Caution:

- **More "look-alike" letters:** The print (and book) versions of Bet and Kaf, and Nun and Gimmel are sometimes confused by beginners:

Bet   Kaf   Nun   Gimmel

Additional Information:

Before the Aramaic "square script" developed, Hebrew was written using pictographs, like some other ancient languages.

Name	Numeric Value	Hebrew	Pictograph	Meaning
Kaf	20	כַּף		Palm of hand / to open
Lamed	30	לָמֶד		Staff / goad / control / "toward"
Mem	40	מֵם		Water / chaos
Nun	50	נוּן		Seed / fish / activity / life
Samekh	60	סָמֶךְ		Hand on staff / support / prop

Hebrew Numbering (Introducing Gematria)

In some cases, especially in dates and in Bible references, the Hebrew letters can function as numbers. For example, Aleph can stand for the number 1, Bet for 2, and so on. For numbers such as 19, Yod (10) and Tet (9) are combined; for 27, Kaf (20) and Zayin (7) are combined, and so on:

9	8	7	6	5	4	3	2	1	Multiples of 10	
ט	ח	ז	ו	ה	ד	ג	ב	א		
יט	יח	יז	טז	טו	יד	יג	יב	יא	י	10
כט	כח	כז	כו	כה	כד	כג	כב	כא	כ	20
לט	לח	לז	לו	לה	לד	לג	לב	לא	ל	30
מט	מח	מז	מו	מה	מד	מג	מב	מא	מ	40
נט	נח	נז	נו	נה	נד	נג	נב	נא	נ	50
סט	סח	סז	סו	סה	סד	סג	סב	סא	ס	60

Note:

The numbers 15 and 16 are not written as you might expect (i.e., as י + ה and י + ו, but rather as ט + ו and ט + ז) in order to avoid irreverently writing the sacred Name of God:

(See Lesson Eighteen)

Lesson Three Writing Practice

Review Drill: First 15 Letters (manual print)

From memory, write the first fifteen letters in print in the squares below (write Bet/Vet on the same line; do the same for Kaf/Khaf):

1
2
3
4
5
6
7
8
9
10
11
12
13
14
15

Writing Errors?

A *Sefer Torah* (Torah Scroll which contains the first five books of the Bible) is composed of several pages of kosher parchment (called *yeri'ot*) that are painstakingly crafted to ensure the utmost adherence to *halakhah* (legal) standards. Special ink recipes are used for the Sofer's ink quill (usually a feather).

It is sometimes thought that a Sofer cannot make a mistake when writing a Torah scroll, but this is not true. If a mistake is made, the ink is scraped off the yeri'ah (parchment page) with a piece of sharp glass or pumice stone.

However, if a mistake is made while writing one of God's holy names, the scroll cannot be corrected, and the flawed yeri'ah must be stored in a special holding container (called a *genizah*) until it is buried with other unusable holy texts.

No mistakes in a finished Sefer Torah are permitted. If someone detects an error while reciting in the synagogue, the scroll is considered invalid (*passul*) and has to be returned to the Sofer for repair (called *tikkun*). *Tikkun 'olam* is an important concept that means "repair of the world" by means of trusting in the Lord.

שִׁעוּר שְׁלִישִׁי

Review Drill: First 15 Letters (cursive)

From memory, write the first fifteen letters in print in the squares below (write Bet/Vet on the same line; do the same for Kaf/Khaf):

Did you know?

The Hebrew of ancient times used a different written script than that used in modern Torah scrolls. This script is sometimes called *paleo-Hebrew* and greatly resembles ancient Aramaic. For example, the sacred Name of God has been found in a Dead Sea Scroll fragment (1 QpHab 10.9-15) looking like this:

It is commonly believed that Ezra the Scribe transliterated this original Hebrew into the Aramaic square script sometime around 450 B.C. Today this script is sometimes referred to as *Ketav Ashuri*, and the sacred Name of God appears as: יְ-הֹ-וֹ-הֹ.

For more information about ancient Hebrew, consult a good book on the history of ancient Semitic languages (see the bibliography at the end of this book).

Transliteration Examples

The following Hebrew letters are transliterated into English. The Hebrew is read from right to left, but the transliterations are written from left to right.

נ	מ	ל	כּ	כ	**1.**
n	m	l	k	kh	

לא	כִּי	כבוד	טוד	ס	**2.**
l'	ky	kvvd	tvd	s	

כל	ילד	הנה	אני	סכה	**3.**
kl	yld	hnh	'ny	skh	

גבדה	מנה	למה	אי	מה	**4.**
gvdh	mnh	lmh	my	mh	

Preview: Another Shoresh (שֹׁרֶשׁ)

As mentioned in Lesson Two, many words in Hebrew are built upon a three-consonant root called the "shoresh" that contains the essence of the word's meaning. Vowel patterns and other changes are added to a shoresh to give a Hebrew word a more determinate meaning (you will learn about vowels beginning in Lesson Seven). For example, the Hebrew root for **trust** is:

$$\text{ב.ט.ח}$$

Can you identify the **root letters** in the following words and phrases? (ignore the other marks):

English	Hebrew
Trust, confidence; security	בִּטָחוֹן bi·ta·**chon**
Safety	בְּטִיחוּת be·ti·**chut**
"Trust in the LORD and do good" (Psalm 37:3)	בְּטַח בַּיהוָה וַעֲשֵׂה־טוֹב be·**tach** ba·Adonai va·'a·seh-tov

A key to understanding a given Hebrew word is to identify the root and then to identify the function of the letters and vowels attached to the root.

Note: In this book, the word "Adonai" is often used in place of the sacred name for God.

Transliteration Practice

Hebrew to English

Transliterate each row of Hebrew letters into English. Read the Hebrew from right to left, but write the transliterations from left to right. Say the name of each letter out loud.

כִּי	הָיָה	חַי	טוֹב	חָבֵד	.1
אָז	מוּכָּה	לֹא	סוּסָה	סוּס	.2
חָסָף	אַבָּא	כִּי	טוֹבָה	אוֹהֵב	.3
נוֹדָה	אֵמָא	לִג	אֵמָא	כְּסַ	.4

English to Hebrew

Transliterate each row of English letters into Hebrew cursive. Read the English from left to right, but write the transliterations directly beneath from right to left. For this exercise, transliterate "v" as a Vet (instead of a Vav) and "kh" for Khaf.

svs	'khv	my	mh	l'	.5
				לָא	
mkh	l'b	ky	m'	'l	.6
tchd	mkh'	lvg	nyk	tkh	.7

Lesson Three Quiz

Each lesson provides a short quiz to help you reinforce your learning.

1. Write Letter Names

Write the name for the following Hebrew letters. The first exercise is done for you.

כּ	כ	מ	ל	נ	ס	Book Letter
					Samekh	Name
					s	Transliteration

N	C	כ	O	נ	ו	Cursive Letter
						Name
						Transliteration

2. Write Hebrew Letters

Write the Hebrew letter for the letter name. The first exercise is done for you.

Samekh	Nun	Mem	Lamed	Kaf	Khaf	Name
					כ	Hebrew
					kh	Transliteration

3. Circle the "look-alike" letters

For each row, circle the letters that look alike.

.a ס נ מ ל כ כ י ט ח ז ו ה ה ד ג ב א

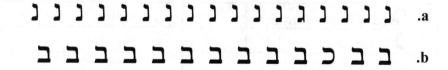

.b O נ N ו ל ל י ו ה ה ו ה ל ל כ כ

4. Which letter is out of place?

Circle the letter that is different:

.a נ נ נ נ נ נ נ נ נ נ ג נ נ נ נ

.b ב ב ב ב ב ב ב ב ב כ ב ב

5. Recognition

Circle the correct answer.

What letter is this? כ

1. Hey
2. Khaf
3. Chet
4. Vet

What letter is this? ס

1. Mem
2. Nun
3. Samekh
4. Tet

What letter is this? א

1. Nun
2. Mem
3. Bet
4. Aleph

What letter is this? ƒ

1. Dalet
2. Lamed
3. Kaf
4. Samekh

What letter is this? נ

1. Vet
2. Nun
3. Lamed
4. Khaf

What letter is this? ב

1. Kaf
2. Khaf
3. Bet
4. Vet

What letter is this? כ

1. Vav
2. Khaf
3. Vet
4. Chet

What letter is this? כ

1. Bet
2. Lamed
3. Kaf
4. Chet

What letter is this? מ

1. Samekh
2. Nun
3. Mem
4. Vav

6. Completely fill in the alphabet table you have studied:

Book Print	Name	Block	Cursive	Pronounced	Transliteration
א					
ב					
ג					
ד ה					
ו ז					
ח ט					
י					
כ					
ל					
מ					
נ					
ס					

Lesson Four

THE NEXT FIVE LETTERS

שִׁעוּר רְבִיעִי

Lesson Introduction

In this lesson you will learn five more letters of the Hebrew alphabet (and also review the previous letters you have learned). In particular, you will learn:

✓ The names for five new Hebrew letters

✓ How to write the letters in both square (block text) and in modern cursive

✓ How to properly pronounce the letters

✓ How to accurately transliterate the letters

✓ How to recite the letters in the correct order

✓ How to correctly identify the new letters in strings of Hebrew text

New Letters

The letters you will learn are as follows:

ר	ק	צ	פ	ע	
Resh	**Qof**	**Tsade**	**Pey**	**'Ayin**	**Right to left!**

Lesson at a glance

After you have studied this lesson, the following information should be clear:

#	Name	Book	Block	Cursive	Pronounced	Trans.	Hebrew Name
16	'Ayin	ע	ע	צ	silent letter	‘	עַיִן
17	Pey	פּ	פּ	ə	**p** as in **p**ark	p	פֵּא
	Fey	פ	פ	ə	**ph** as in **ph**one	ph / f	
18	Tsade	צ	צ	3	**ts** as in nu**ts**	ts / tz	צָדִי
19	Qof	ק	ק	ף	**q** as in **q**ueen	q / k	קוֹף
20	Resh	ר	ר	ꝛ	**r** as in **r**ain	r	רֵישׁ

The sixteenth letter of the Hebrew alphabet is called "Ayin" (pronounced "**ah**-yeen"). Like Aleph, 'Ayin has no sound of its own, but usually has a vowel associated with it.

In modern Hebrew, the letter 'Ayin can appear in three forms:

ע	v	צ
Book Print	Manual Print	Cursive

Manual Print

The manual print version of the letter 'Ayin looks like this:

Note that the second stroke descends to the right of the end of the first stroke.

Hebrew Cursive

You can write the cursive version of the letter 'Ayin according to the following pattern:

A single looping stroke is used to form this letter.

Practice

Write the letter 'Ayin in both manual print and cursive several times:

Manual Print

Cursive

Note: 'Ayin is known as a guttural letter since it is pronounced in the back of the throat (other guttural letters are א, ה, and ח). Like Aleph, 'Ayin is often *untransliterated* in English (e.g., *Ayin* instead of *'Ayin*).

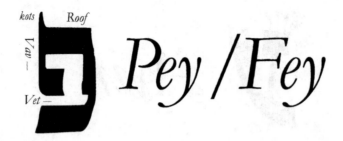

The seventeenth letter of the Hebrew alphabet is called "Pey" (rhymes with "pay") and has the sound of "p" as in "*p*ark."

In modern Hebrew, the letter Pey can appear in three forms:

Book Print	Manual Print	Cursive
פ	פ	∂

Manual Print

Write the manual print version of Pey as follows:

Most people form this letter using two separate strokes.

> *If no dot appears in the middle of the letter (called a dagesh mark), Pey is called "Fey" and is pronounced as a "ph" as in phone.*
>
> **The Letter Fey**   **The Letter Fey**

Hebrew Cursive

And the cursive version:

A single curling stroke is used to form this letter.

Practice

Write the letter Pey in both manual print and cursive several times:

Manual Print

Cursive

Note: When no dot appears in the middle of the letter, Pey is called "Fey" and is pronounced as a "ph" as in *ph*one (or "f" as in *f*ood). Pey also has a special form when it ends a word (called **sofit form**) which we will study in Lesson Six.

tagin
head
kots
Nun *Yod*

Tsade

The eighteenth letter of the Hebrew alphabet is called "Tsade" (pronounced "**tsah**-dee") and has the sound of "ts" as in "nu*ts*" (or "tz" as in "pizza").

In modern Hebrew, the letter Tsade can appear in three forms:

צ	צ	3
Book Print	Manual Print	Cursive

Manual Print

Here is the pattern for the manual print version of Tsade:

Note that the second stroke descends from the right and meets the first stroke about halfway.

Hebrew Cursive

And here is the cursive version of Tsade:

This letter looks a little like the number "3."
Note that the top of the letter sometimes may extend slightly above the upper line.

Practice

Write the letter Tsade in both manual print and cursive several times:

Manual Print

Cursive

Note: In the past, Tsade sometimes was transliterated using "z" (producing spellings such as "Zion" for צִיוֹן) and in some academic work you might see it transliterated as ṣ. In this book, we will transliterate Tsade with "ts" (as in nu*ts*). Tsade also has a special form when it ends a word (called **sofit form**), which we will study in Lesson Six.

The nineteenth letter of the Hebrew alphabet is called "Qof" (pronounced "**kof**") and has the sound of "q" as in "**q**ueen."

In modern Hebrew, the letter Qof can appear in three forms:

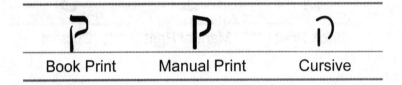

Book Print	Manual Print	Cursive

Manual Print

Here is the manual print version of the letter Qof:

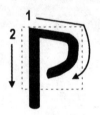

This letter looks like the English letter "p." Note that the second stroke descends below the letter's baseline. Note the "gap" between the end of the first stroke and the second stroke.

Note: The letter Qof used to be pronounced at the back of the throat, but in modern Hebrew sounds like a Kaf.

Hebrew Cursive

And the cursive version:

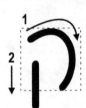

The second stroke descends below the letter's baseline. Note the "gap" between the end of the first stroke and the second stroke.

Practice

Write the letter Qof in both manual print and cursive several times:

Manual Print

Cursive

Note: Qof is quite often transliterated using a "**k**" (as in "kaddish"), but in this book, we have followed academic convention and used "**q**," reserving "k" for Kaf.

שִׁעוּר רְבִיעִי

roof

leg

The twentieth letter of the Hebrew alphabet is called "Resh" (pronounced "**raysh**") and has the sound of "r" as in "*r*ain."

The letter Resh can appear in three forms:

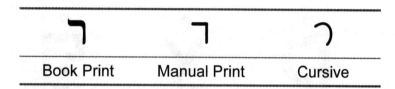

Book Print	Manual Print	Cursive

Manual Print

Write the manual print version of the letter Resh according to the following pattern:

This letter looks a little like a backwards English letter "r." Note that the second stroke descends below the letter's baseline.

Hebrew Cursive

And write the cursive version according to the following pattern:

The script version is simply a more curved version of the manual print letter.

Practice

Write the letter Resh in both manual print and cursive several times:

Manual Print

Cursive

Notes: Try pronouncing the "r" sound with the back of the tongue using a "rolling" sound. Resh is usually transliterated as "r" in English. Resh sometimes functions as a **guttural** letter in Hebrew. Be careful not to confuse Resh (ר) with the book print form of Dalet (ד).

שָׁעוּר רְבִיעִי

Lesson Four Review

Reciting Order

You are almost through the alphabet now! Only two more letters to go! If you have studied Lesson Four well, you have learned the next five letters of the Hebrew alphabet.

Manual Print (Block)

Practice writing and reciting each of the five manual print letters in the order shown:

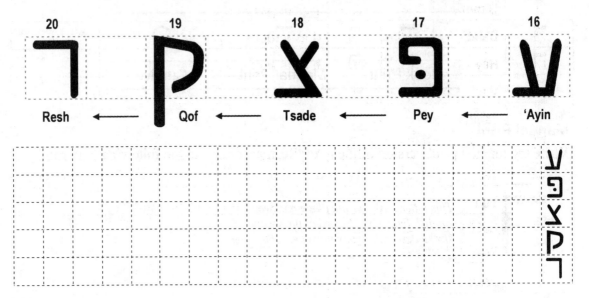

Hebrew Cursive

Now do the same with the Hebrew cursive letters:

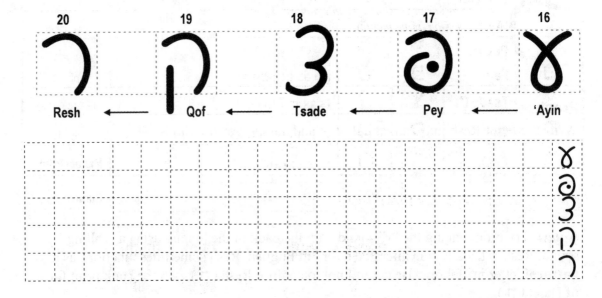

שִׁעוּר רְבִיעִ

Lesson Four Summary

Reciting Order: the first 20 letters

Book Print	Name	Block	Cursive	Pronounced	Transliteration
א	Aleph	X	IC	silent letter	' (or none)
ב	Bet	בּ	ב	**b** as in **b**oy	b
ב	Vet	ב	ב	*no dot:* **v** as in **v**ine	v
ג	Gimmel	ג	ε	**g** as in **g**irl	g
ד	Dalet	ד	ς	**d** as in **d**oor	d
ה	Hey	ה	ה	**h** as in **h**ay	h
ו	Vav	ו	I	**v** as in **v**ine; "consonantal vowel"	v
ז	Zayin	ז	ς	**z** as in **z**ebra	z
ח	Chet	ח	ת	**ch** as in Ba**ch**	ch (or ḥ)
ט	Tet	ט	G	**t** as in **t**ime	t (or ṭ)
י	Yod	י	׳	**y** as in **y**es; "consonantal vowel"	y
כ	Kaf (*)	כּ	ב	**k** as in **k**ite	k
כ	Khaf	כ	כ	*no dot:* **ch** as in ba**ch**	kh
ל	Lamed	ל	∫	**l** as in **l**ook	l
מ	Mem (*)	מ	N	**m** as in **m**om	m
נ	Nun (*)	נ	J	**n** as in **n**ow	n
ס	Samekh	ס	O	**s** as in **s**on	s
ע	'Ayin	ע	X	silent letter	' (or none)
פ	Pey (*)	פּ	∂	**p** as in **p**ark	p
פ	Fey	פ	∂	**ph** as in **ph**one	ph / f
צ	Tsade (*)	צ	3	**ts** as in nu**ts**	ts / tz (or ṣ)
ק	Qof	ק	ק	**q** as in **q**ueen	q / k
ר	Resh	ר	ר	**r** as in **r**ain	r

(*) = has an ending letter form (sofit)

Notes:

- New look-alikes:

Dalet   **Resh**   **Tsade**   **Ayin**

Additional Information:

Before the Aramaic "square script" developed, Hebrew was written using pictographs, like some other ancient languages. Here are the new letters and their associated meanings:

Name	Numeric Value	Hebrew	Pictograph	Meaning
'Ayin	70	עַיִן		Eye / to see / experience
Pey	80	פֵּא		Mouth / word / speak
Tsade	90	צָדִי		Man on side / desire / need
Qof	100	קוֹף		Sun on horizon / behind
Resh	200	רֵישׁ		Head / person / first

More Hebrew Numbering (Gematria)

In some cases, especially in dates and in Bible references, the Hebrew letters can function as numbers. For numbers such as 125, write ק (100) then כ (20) then ה (5); 125 = קכה.

9	8	7	6	5	4	3	2	1	Multiples of 10	
ט	ח	ז	ו	ה	ד	ג	ב	א		
יט	יח	יז	טז	טו	יד	יג	יב	יא	י	10
כט	כח	כז	כו	כה	כד	כג	כב	כא	כ	20
לט	לח	לז	לו	לה	לד	לג	לב	לא	ל	30
מט	מח	מז	מו	מה	מד	מג	מב	מא	מ	40
נט	נח	נז	נו	נה	נד	נג	נב	נא	נ	50
סט	סח	סז	סו	סה	סד	סג	סב	סא	ס	60
עט	עח	עז	עו	עה	עד	עג	עב	עא	ע	70
פט	פח	פז	פו	פה	פד	פג	פב	פא	פ	80
צט	צח	צז	צו	צה	צד	צג	צב	צא	צ	90
קט	קח	קז	קו	קה	קד	קג	קב	קא	ק	100
רט	רח	רז	רו	רה	רד	רג	רב	רא	ר	200

Lesson Four Writing Practice

Review Drill: First 20 Letters (manual print)

From memory, write the first twenty letters in the squares below (write Bet/Vet on the same line; do the same for Kaf/Khaf and Pey/Fey):

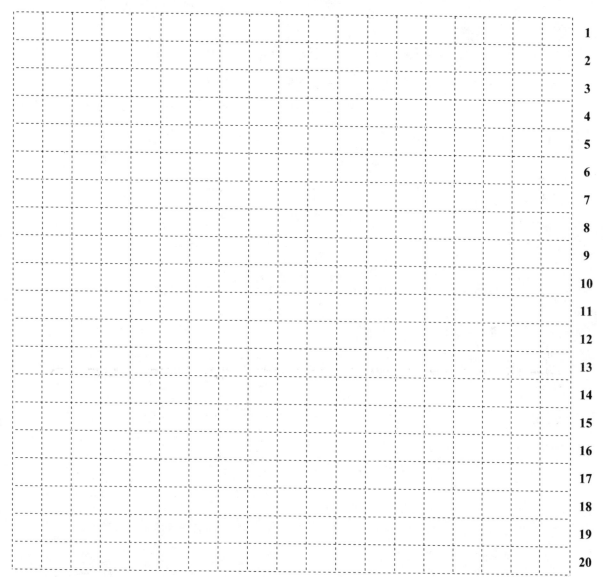

1
2
3
4
5
6
7
8
9
10
11
12
13
14
15
16
17
18
19
20

Did you know?

The LORD gave Moses two tablets of stone containing the Ten Commandments (in Hebrew, עֲשֶׂרֶת הַדִּבְּרוֹת, *ʿa·se·ret had·di be·rot*) and that these tablets (luchot ha'edut) were inscribed by the very "finger of God?" (*see* Exodus 31:18 and Lesson Thirteen).

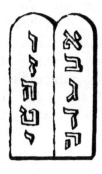

luchot ha'edut

Review Drill: First 20 Letters (cursive)

From memory, write the first twenty letters in the squares below (write Bet/Vet on the same line; do the same for Kaf/Khaf and Pey/Fey):

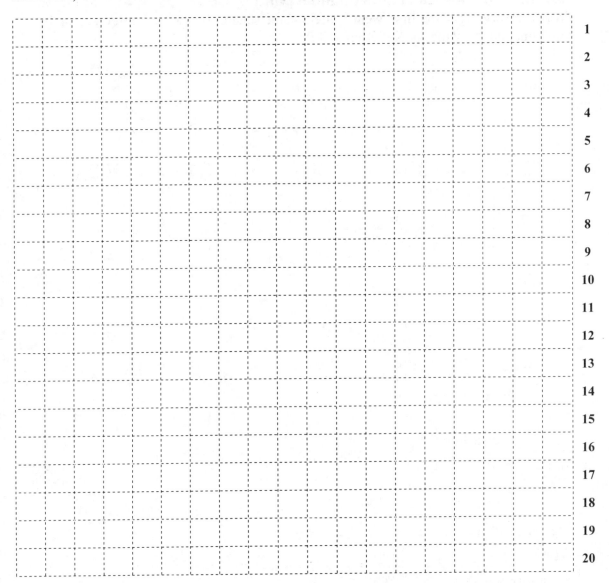

1
2
3
4
5
6
7
8
9
10
11
12
13
14
15
16
17
18
19
20

Did you know?

In most synagogues the *Sefer Torah* (Torah scroll) is stored in a holy place (called the *Aron haqodesh*) and is "dressed up" in a manner resembling the apparel of the High Priest during the temple days? A crown for its head, a breastplate, a tunic, and other specialized decorations all mark the Sefer Torah as the most precious possession of the Jewish people.

Aron Haqodesh

Transliteration Examples

The following Hebrew letters are transliterated into English. The Hebrew is read from right to left, but the transliterations are written from left to right.

ר	ק	צ	פ	ע	1.
r	q	ts	p	' (or none)	

רבִּי	רב	רע	קדו	צבא	2.
rby	rv	r'	qdv	tsv'	

אוזר	פִי	צדק	חו	רוֹפה	3.
'vzr	phy	tsdk	ch'	rvfh	

עיר	פּרִי	קִימן	אוֹנִינו	צדִי	4.
'yr	pry	kymnv	'vnynv	tsdy	

Preview: Another Shoresh (שֹׁרֶשׁ)

The three-consonant root ("shoresh") for **righteous** is:

$$צ.ד.ק$$

Can you identify the root letters in the following words and phrases?

English	Hebrew
Act of righteousness	צְדָקָה tse·da·**qah**
Righteousness	צֶדֶק **tse**·deq
The thirty six (lamed = 30 + vav = 6) righteous persons in the world.	ל״ו צַדִּיקִים Lamed-Vav tsad·di·**qim**
"Righteous art thou, Adonai" (Psalm 119:37)	צַדִּיק אַתָּה יְהֹוָה tsad·diq 'at·tah 'Adonai

Note that the double quote mark (″) is called a *Gerashim* and is used to indicate that the letters (of a string) are to be pronounced *as letters* (and not as part of a word). Thus ל״ו is pronounced "Lamed-Vav."

Transliteration Practice

Hebrew to English

Transliterate each row of Hebrew letters into English. Read the Hebrew from right to left, but write the transliterations from left to right. Say the name of each letter out loud.

.1   חבד   טוב   חי   היה   כי

.2   סוס   סוסה   לא   מוכה   אז

.3   כסכד   טוכה   חי   סוכ   חיי

.4   סככ   אוככ   לול   אבכ   לודה

English to Hebrew

Transliterate each row of English letters into Hebrew cursive. Read the English from left to right, but write the transliterations directly beneath from right to left. For this exercise, transliterate "v" as a Vet (instead of Vav) and "kh" as a Khaf.

.5	l'	m'	my	'khv	svs
	לא				

.6	'l	m'	tsdk	l'	mch

.7	tkh	nyk	lvg	mch'	tchd

Lesson Four Quiz

Here is your short quiz to help you reinforce your learning.

1. Write Letter Names

Write the name for the following Hebrew letters. The first exercise is done for you.

פּ	ע	פ	צ	ר	ק	Book Letter
					Qof	Name
					q	Transliteration

ק	צ	3	ר	פ	ס	Cursive Letter
						Name
						Transliteration

2. Write Hebrew Letters

Write the Hebrew letter for the letter name. The first exercise is done for you.

Resh	Qof	Tsade	Pey	Fey	Ayin	Name
					ע	Hebrew
					'	Transliteration

3. Transliteration

Transliterate the Hebrew letters into English. Read the Hebrew from right to left, but write the transliteration from left to right. Say the name of each letter out loud.

a. צדיק יהוה בכל דרכיו

4. Circle the "look-alike" letters

For each row, circle the letters that look alike.

a. א ב ג ד ה ו ז ח ט י כ ל מ נ ס ע פ צ ק ר

b. C כ ב ה ו ן ח ל ס ט י כ ל נ ו ר צ ס ק ר

5. Which letter is out of place?

Circle the letters that are different:

צ צ צ צ ע צ צ צ צ צ צ צ צ צ ע צ צ צ **.a**

ר ר ד ר ר ר ר ר ר ר ר ר ד ר ר ר ד ר **.b**

6. Recognition

Circle the correct answer.

What letter is this? ד

1. Hey
2. Vet
3. Gimmel
4. Dalet
5. Aleph

What letter is this? ר

1. Dalet
2. Resh
3. Gimmel
4. Vav
5. Zayin

What letter is this? ב

1. Hey
2. Vet
3. Gimmel
4. Dalet
5. Bet

What letter is this? ט

1. Vav
2. Yod
3. Tet
4. Chet
5. Zayin

What letter is this? פ

1. Bet
2. Kaf
3. Fey
4. Chet
5. Pey

What letter is this? ה

1. Tet
2. Zayin
3. Vav
4. Hey
5. Yod

What letter is this? צ

1. 'Ayin
2. Aleph
3. Tsade
4. Resh
5. Qof

What letter is this? כ

1. Hey
2. Vet
3. Gimmel
4. Dalet
5. Aleph

What letter is this? ח

1. Hey
2. Chet
3. Gimmel
4. Dalet
5. Aleph

What letter is this? ע

1. Tsade
2. Aleph
3. 'Ayin
4. Resh
5. Qof

What letter is this? ק

1. Resh
2. Pey
3. Dalet
4. Qof
5. Tet

What letter is this? נ

1. Nun
2. Resh
3. Gimmel
4. Dalet
5. Aleph

7. What three letters can take a "dot" to make them sound differently?

1.

2.

3.

8. **Completely fill in the alphabet table you have studied:**

Book Print	Name	Block	Cursive	Pronounced	Transliteration
א					
ב					
ג					
ד					
ה					
ו					
ז					
ח					
ט					
י					
כ					
ל					
מ					
נ					
ס					
ע					
פ					
צ					
ק					
ר					

צַדִּיק יְהוָה בְּכָל־דְּרָכָיו

The LORD is righteous in all his ways
(Psalm 145:17)

tsad•dik Adonai be•khol de•ra•khav

Lesson Five

FINISHING THE ALPHABET

שִׁעוּר חֲמִישִׁי

Lesson Introduction

In this short lesson you will learn the last two letters of the Hebrew alphabet (and also review all of the previous letters you have learned). In particular, you will learn:

✓ The names for the last two Hebrew letters of the alphabet

✓ How to write the letters in both square (block text) and in modern cursive

✓ How to properly pronounce the letters

✓ How to accurately transliterate the letters

✓ How to recite the Hebrew alphabet in the correct order

✓ How to correctly identify the new letters in strings of Hebrew text

New Letters

The letters you will learn are as follows:

ת	שׁ / שׂ
Tav	**Shin / Sin**

⇐ Right to left!

Note:

- The letters Shin and Sin are counted as a single letter in this book.

Lesson at a glance

After you have studied this lesson, the following information should be clear:

#	Name	Book	Block	Cursive	Pronounced	Trans.	Hebrew Name
21	Shin	שׁ	שׁ	*e*	**sh** as in **sh**y	sh	שִׂין / שִׁין
	Sin	שׂ	שׂ	*e*	**s** as in **s**un	s	
22	Tav	ת	ת	ת	**t** as in **t**all	t	תָּו

The twenty-first letter of the Hebrew alphabet is called "Shin" (pronounced "**sheen**") and has the sound of "sh" as in "**sh**y."

The letter Shin can appear in three different ways:

שׁ	שׁ	℮̇
Book Print	Manual Print	Cursive

Manual Print

Write the manual print version of the letter Shin according to the following pattern:

Two strokes are used to create this letter.

> *If the dot appears in the left of the letter, Shin is called "Sin" ("seen") and is pronounced as "s" as in sun.*
>
> **The Letter Sin**　　**The Letter Sin**

Hebrew Cursive

Now write the cursive version of Shin this way:

This letter looks a little like an English cursive lowercase "e."

Practice

Write the letter Shin (and Sin) in both manual print and cursive several times:

Manual Print

Cursive

Note: If a dot appears to the upper right of the letter, pronounce "**sh**"; if it appears to the left, pronounce "**s**." Note also that some academic Hebrew books use š for Shin and ś for Sin (reserving **s** for Samekh). In this book, we transliterate *both* Sin and Samech as "s."

The last letter of the Hebrew alphabet is "Tav," which has the sound of "t" as in "*t*all."

In modern Hebrew, the letter Tav can appear in three different ways:

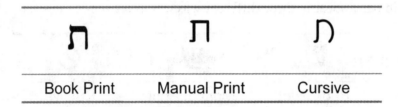

Book Print	Manual Print	Cursive

Manual Print

Write the manual print version of the letter Tav this way:

Note that the first stroke overhangs the second stroke, and that the second stroke has a small "foot" that goes to the left.

Hebrew Cursive

And write the cursive version as follows:

This letter is similar to the print version except that the first stroke slopes down from the top right to the baseline.

Practice

Write the letter Tav in both manual print and cursive several times:

Manual Print

Cursive

Note: The letter Tav can also take a dot, or dagesh mark (i.e., תּ). In ancient Hebrew, a Tav without the dot (i.e., ת) was pronounced "th" (e.g., as in Sabba*th* for שַׁבָּת). In the Ashkenazi tradition, (ת) is pronounced "s" (as in "Shabbos"). In modern Hebrew, both ת and תּ are pronounced as "t." We will explain the use of dagesh marks in Lesson Nine.

Lesson Five Review

Reciting Order

This has been a shorter lesson because we want to give you a chance to review the entire alphabet in this lesson. If you have studied Lesson Five carefully, you have learned the last two letters of the Hebrew alphabet.

Manual Print (Block)

Practice writing and reciting the manual print letters in the order shown:

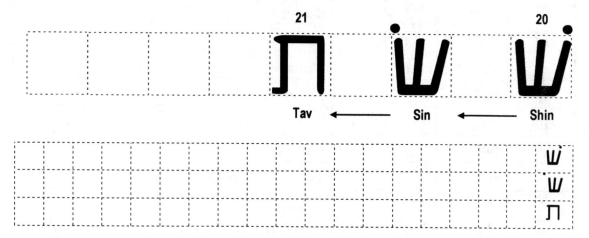

Hebrew Cursive

Now do the same with the Hebrew cursive letters:

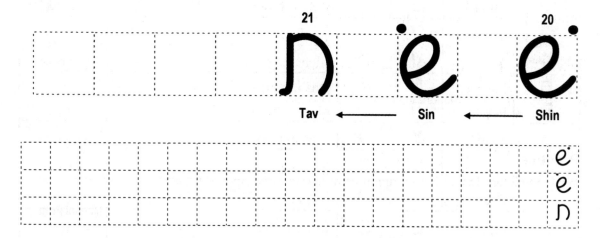

שִׁעוּר חֲמִישִׁי

Lesson Five Summary

Reciting Order: the Standard Alphabet (medial letters)

Book Print	Name	Block	Cursive	Pronounced	Transliteration
א	Aleph	X	IC	silent letter	' (or none)
בּ	Bet	ב	ב	**b** as in **b**oy	b
ב	Vet	ב	כ	*no dot*: **v** as in **v**ine	v
ג	Gimmel	λ	ﻉ	**g** as in **g**irl	g
ד	Dalet	ד	ʒ	**d** as in **d**oor	d
ה	Hey	ה	ה	**h** as in **h**ay	h
ו	Vav	ו	ı	**v** as in **v**ine; "consonantal vowel"	v
ז	Zayin	ז	ʃ	**z** as in **z**ebra	z
ח	Chet	ח	ת	**ch** as in Ba**ch**	ch (or ḥ)
ט	Tet	ט	G	**t** as in **t**ime	t (or ṭ)
י	Yod	י	ʾ	**y** as in **y**es; "consonantal vowel"	y
כּ	Kaf (*)	כ	C	**k** as in **k**ite	k
כ	Khaf	כ	C	*no dot*: **ch** as in ba**ch**	kh
ל	Lamed	ל	ʃ	**l** as in **l**ook	l
מ	Mem (*)	ﻣ	N	**m** as in **m**om	m
נ	Nun (*)	נ	J	**n** as in **n**ow	n
ס	Samekh	ﬡ	O	**s** as in **s**on	s
ע	'Ayin	ﬡ	Ɣ	silent letter	' (or none)
פּ	Pey (*)	פּ	ⱻ	**p** as in **p**ark	p
פ	Fey	פ	ⱻ	**ph** as in **ph**one	ph / f
צ	Tsade (*)	צ	3	**ts** as in nu**ts**	ts / tz (or ṣ)
ק	Qof	ק	ק	**q** as in **q**ueen	q (or k)
ר	Resh	ר	ר	**r** as in **r**ain	r
שׁ	Shin	שׁ	ẹ	**sh** as in **sh**y	sh (or š)
שׂ	Sin	שׂ	ẹ	**s** as in **s**un	s (or ś)
ת	Tav	ת	ת	**t** as in **t**all	t

(*) = has an ending letter form (sofit)

Similar-looking Letters

When you are first learning the Hebrew alphabet, some letters appear similar to one another and can cause confusion. The most easily confused are listed below.

Gimmel   Nun

Gimmel has a "foot" whereas Nun does not. Note that Nun could also be mistaken for Khaf.

Vet   Khaf

Vet's second stroke extends to the right of the first stroke, whereas Khaf is a single stroke.

Vav   Zayin

Zayin's first stroke extends to the right of the vertical stroke, whereas Vav is a single stroke.

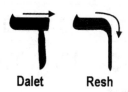

Dalet   Resh

Dalet's first stroke extends across its second stroke, whereas Resh is a single stroke.

Hey   Chet   Tav

Hey has a "window" at the top, whereas Chet does not; Tav has a "foot" the points left.

Tsade   'Ayin

Tsade's second stroke comes from the top right, whereas Ayin's comes from the top left.

Additional Information:

Before the Aramaic "square script" developed (called *Ketav Ashuri* or *Ketav Meruba*), Hebrew was written using pictographs, like some other ancient languages.

Name	Numeric Value	Hebrew	Pictograph	Meaning
Shin / Sin	300	שִׁין	ᚂᚁ	Eat / consume / destroy
Tav	400	תָּו	✝	Mark / sign / covenant

More Hebrew Numbering (Gematria)

In some cases, especially in dates and in Bible references, the Hebrew letters can function as numbers. For numbers such as 342, write שׁ (300) then מ (40) then ב (2); 342 = שמב.

	9	8	7	6	5	4	3	2	1	*Multiples of 10*
	ט	ח	ז	ו	ה	ד	ג	ב	א	
י	יט	יח	יז	טז	טו	יד	יג	יב	יא	10
כ	כט	כח	כז	כו	כה	כד	כג	כב	כא	20
ל	לט	לח	לז	לו	לה	לד	לג	לב	לא	30
מ	מט	מח	מז	מו	מה	מד	מג	מב	מא	40
נ	נט	נח	נז	נו	נה	נד	נג	נב	נא	50
ס	סט	סח	סז	סו	סה	סד	סג	סב	סא	60
ע	עט	עח	עז	עו	עה	עד	עג	עב	עא	70
פ	פט	פח	פז	פו	פה	פד	פג	פב	פא	80
צ	צט	צח	צז	צו	צה	צד	צג	צב	צא	90
ק	קט	קח	קז	קו	קה	קד	קג	קב	קא	100
ר	רט	רח	רז	רו	רה	רד	רג	רב	רא	200
שׁ	שט	שח	שז	שו	שה	שד	שג	שב	שא	300
ת	תט	תח	תז	תו	תה	תד	תג	תב	תא	400

The Hebrew Year

The Hebrew year begins on *Rosh Hashanah* (which occurs on the Gregorian calendar in September / October). When a Hebrew year is written using letters, you simply add the values of the letters. Often the year is written with an implied addition of 5,000. So, for example, the year 5762 is written as 762 rather than 5762:

400+300+60+2 = (5)762

The double quote mark (Gerashim) is used to indicate that this is an abbreviation and not a Hebrew word. Gerashim are normally placed before the last letter in the string.

To calculate the Jewish Year from our Gregorian calendar, you subtract 1,240 and then add 5,000.

Lesson Five Writing Practice

Review Drill: Standard Alphabet (manual print)

From memory, write the Hebrew Alphabet in the squares below (write Bet/Vet on the same line; do the same for Kaf/Khaf, Pey/Fey, and Shin/Sin):

	1
	2
	3
	4
	5
	6
	7
	8
	9
	10
	11
	12
	13
	14
	15
	16
	17
	18
	19
	20
	21
	22

Did you know?

A certified sofer STaM must rigorously study the smallest details of each Hebrew letter in order to form them according to *Halakhic* (legal) guidelines (*halakhah* means "the way to walk" and constitutes rabbinic interpretations of how Torah is to be observed.)

שִׁעוּר חֲמִישִׁי

Review Drill: Standard Alphabet (cursive)

From memory, write the Hebrew Alphabet in the squares below (write Bet/Vet on the same line; do the same for Kaf/Khaf, Pey/Fey, and Shin/Sin):

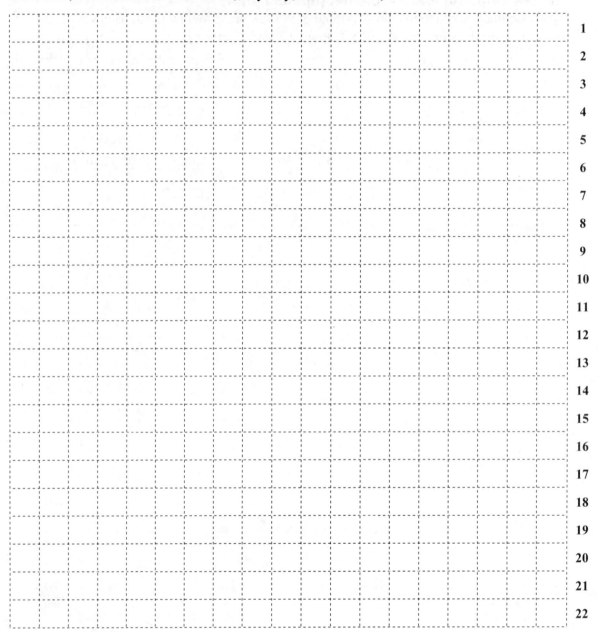

1
2
3
4
5
6
7
8
9
10
11
12
13
14
15
16
17
18
19
20
21
22

From our Sages

Some Torah sages have said there are four basic levels of meaning embedded in the Torah: 1) the **P**eshat, or literal reading of the text; 2) **R**emez, or the allusion of the text; 3) **D**erash, or the interpretation of the text; and 4) **S**od, the mystical meaning of the text. Together, these terms form the acronym "PaRDeS," which is a Persian term referring to paradise or the Garden of Eden. Thus the study of Torah leads the learner back to the God of Israel, and eventually to the paradise of personally knowing God.

פרד"ס

PaRDeS

פְּשָׁט רֶמֶז דְּרָשׁ סוֹד

Mystery   Application   Hint   Literal

Transliteration Examples

The following Hebrew letters are transliterated into English. The Hebrew is read from
right to left, but the transliterations are written from left to right.

שַׁדַּי	ת	ס	שׂ	שׁ	**1.**
shdy	t	s	s	sh	

חסד	אשרי	צבאות	אלהי	צבא	**2.**
chsd	'shry	tsv'vt	'lhy	tsv'	

תלי	עז	מצוה	הוא	אתה	**3.**
tly	'z	mtsvh	hv'	'th	

קרות	ואמות	השמש	ישראל	הזקן	**4.**
krvt	vmvt	hshmsh	ysr'l	hzkv	

Preview: Another Shoresh (שֹׁרֶשׁ)

The three-consonant root ("shoresh") for **book** is:

ס.פ.ר

Can you identify the **root letters** in the following words and phrases?

English	Hebrew
book	סֵפֶר se·fer
Torah Scroll	סֵפֶר תּוֹרָה se·fer to·rah
Torah Scribe	סוֹפֵר so·fer
"Book of the Covenant"	סֵפֶר הַבְּרִית se·fer ha·be·rit

*A key to understanding a
given Hebrew word is to
identify the root and then
to identify the function of
the letters and vowels
attached to the root.*

Transliteration Practice

Hebrew to English

Transliterate each row of Hebrew letters into English. Read the Hebrew from right to left, but write the transliterations from left to right. Say the name of each letter out loud.

.1   ישוע   אדני   שמש   תורה   אמא

.2   תודה   רבה   מצוה   מוכה   אמונה

.3   אותה   שמא   צדק   אומת   מצוה

.4   כסבר   קדשו   תאומ   משה   מנה

English to Hebrew

Transliterate each row of English letters into Hebrew cursive. Read the English from left to right, but write the transliterations directly beneath from right to left. For this exercise, transliterate "v" as a Vet (rather than a Vav) and "kh" as a Khaf.

.5	'dny	mt'	khy	m'	shmsh
	אדני				

.6	tvdh	mtsvh	yshy'	tlmd	shdy

.7	tsdq	chvh	bgd	qdsh	'mdh

Lesson Five Quiz

Each lesson in this book will provide a section that will quiz your knowledge and reinforce your learning.

1. Write Letter Names

Write the name for the following Hebrew letters. The first exercise is done for you.

שׁ	שׂ	ת	Book Letter
		Tav	Name
		t	Transliteration

ת	e͑	e	Cursive Letter
			Name
			Transliteration

נֵר תָּמִיד

"Ner Tamid" – the perpetual lamp burning in the *Mishkan* (Tabernacle). *See* Exodus 27:20.

2. Write Hebrew Letters

Write the Hebrew letter for the letter name.

Tav	Sin	Shin	Name
			Hebrew
			Transliteration

3. Transliteration

Transliterate the Hebrew letters into English. Read the Hebrew from right to left, but write the transliteration from left to right. Say the name of each letter out loud.

a. זמרו ליהוה חסידיו והודו לזכר קדשו

4. Circle the "look-alike" letters

For each row, circle the letters that look alike. Draw a connecting line to letters that sound alike (e.g., Vet and Vav).

a. א ב ג ד ה ו ז ח ט י כ ל מ נ ס ע פ צ ק ר שׁ ת

b. כ

שִׁעוּר חֲמִישִׁי

5. Which letter is out of place?

For each row, circle the letters that are different:

ת ת ח ת ח ת ח ת ת ת ת ת ת ת ה ה ת .a

ה ה ה ה ת ה ה ה ה ה ה ת ה ח ה ה ה .b

6. Recognition

What letter is this? שׁ

1. Samekh
2. Sin
3. Tsade
4. Shin
5. Kaf

What letter is this? ס

1. Samekh
2. Sin
3. Tsade
4. Shin
5. Kaf

What letter is this? שׂ

1. Samekh
2. Sin
3. Tsade
4. Shin
5. Kaf

What letter is this? ת

1. Tet
2. Chet
3. Tav
4. Hey
5. Zayin

What letter is this? ט

1. Tet
2. Chet
3. Tav
4. Hey
5. Zayin

What letter is this? פ

1. Tsade
2. Qof
3. 'Ayin
4. Pey
5. Fey

What letter is this? כ

1. Vet
2. Samekh
3. Resh
4. Chet
5. Khaf

What letter is this? ח

1. Vet
2. Samekh
3. Resh
4. Chet
5. Khaf

What letter is this? ס

1. Kaf
2. Sin
3. Tsade
4. Shin
5. Samekh

What letter is this? ₹

1. Aleph
2. Bet
3. Dalet
4. Gimmel
5. Lamed

What letter is this? ل

1. Fey
2. Zayin
3. 'Ayin
4. Lamed
5. Yod

What letter is this? ٧

1. Yod
2. Resh
3. Tav
4. Tet
5. Vet

7. Name the "sound-alike" letter-pairs.

Write the five pairs of letters that are written differently but have the same sound.

1.
2.
3.
4.
5.

8. Completely fill in the alphabet table you have studied:

Book Print	Name	Block	Cursive	Pronounced	Transliteration
א					
ב					
ג					
ד					
ה					
ו					
ז					
ח					
ט					
י					
כ					
ל					
מ					
נ					
ס					
ע					
פ					
צ					
ק					
ר					
ש					
ת					

בְּטַח אֶל־יְהוָה בְּכָל־לִבֶּךָ

Trust in the LORD with all your heart   (Proverbs 3:5a)

be·**tach** el-Adonai be·khol li·**be**·kha

Reciting Order: the Standard Alphabet (medial letters)

Book Print	Name	Block	Cursive	Pronounced	Transliteration
א	Aleph	X	IC	silent letter	' (or none)
בּ	Bet	בּ	ꜱ	**b** as in **b**oy	b
ב	Vet	ב	ꜱ	*no dot*: **v** as in **v**ine	v
ג	Gimmel	λ	₹	**g** as in **g**irl	g
ד	Dalet	ד	₹	**d** as in **d**oor	d
ה	Hey	ה	ꜱ	**h** as in **h**ay	h
ו	Vav	ו	I	**v** as in **v**ine; "consonantal vowel"	v
ז	Zayin	ז	ꜱ	**z** as in **z**ebra	z
ח	Chet	ח	ꜱ	**ch** as in Ba**ch**	ch (or ẖ)
ט	Tet	ט	ꜱ	**t** as in **t**ime	t (or ṭ)
י	Yod	י	ꜱ	**y** as in **y**es; "consonantal vowel"	y
כּ	Kaf (*)	כּ	ꜱ	**k** as in **k**ite	k
כ	Khaf	כ	ꜱ	*no dot*: **ch** as in ba**ch**	kh
ל	Lamed	ל	ꜱ	**l** as in **l**ook	l
מ	Mem (*)	מ	N	**m** as in **m**om	m
נ	Nun (*)	נ	J	**n** as in **n**ow	n
ס	Samekh	ס	O	**s** as in **s**on	s
ע	'Ayin	ע	ꜱ	silent letter	' (or none)
פּ	Pey (*)	פּ	ꜱ	**p** as in **p**ark	p
פ	Fey	פ	ꜱ	**ph** as in **ph**one	ph / f
צ	Tsade (*)	צ	3	**ts** as in nu**ts**	ts / tz (or ṣ)
ק	Qof	P	ꜱ	**q** as in **q**ueen	q (or k)
ר	Resh	ר	ꜱ	**r** as in **r**ain	r
שׁ	Shin	שׁ	ꜱ	**sh** as in **sh**y	sh (or š)
שׂ	Sin	שׂ	ꜱ	**s** as in **s**un	s (or ś)
ת	Tav	ת	ꜱ	**t** as in **t**all	t

(*) = has an ending letter form (sofit)

Lesson Six

THE SOFIT LETTERS

שִׁעוּר שִׁישִׁי

שִׁעוּר שִׁשִּׁי

Lesson Introduction

Five Hebrew letters are formed differently when they appear as the last letter of a word (these forms are sometimes called "sofit" (pronounced "so-**feet**") forms). Fortunately, the five letters sound the same as their non-sofit cousins, so you do not have to learn any new sounds (or transliterations); however, you will need to be able to recognize these letters when you see them. The five sofit letters are as follows:

ץ	ף	ן	ם	ך
Tsade Sofit: "ts" as in "nu**ts**"	**Fey Sofit:** "ph" as in "*ph*one"	**Nun Sofit:** "n" as in "*n*ow"	**Mem Sofit:** "m" as in "*m*om"	**Khaf Sofit:** "ch" as in "Ba*ch*"

Notes:

- *You already know these letters!* The letter Khaf Sofit, for example, is simply the letter Khaf with an altered shape. The shape of the letter does **not** affect the way the letter is pronounced.

- These letters often served a punctuation purpose, indicating, for instance, the end of a sentence or a pause in the reading.

- Here are the five "regular" (medial) letters with their sofit cousins:

ץ / צ	ף / פ	ן / נ	ם / מ	ך / כ
Tsade / Tsade Sofit	**Fey / Fey Sofit**	**Nun / Nun Sofit**	**Mem / Mem Sofit**	**Khaf / Khaf Sofit**

Tip:

The sofit letters form the mnemonic "KheM•Ne•FaTS," representing the letters:

צ פ נ מ כ

Remember: *Sofit letters appear at the end of a Hebrew word. The changing of the letter's form does not change its pronunciation, only the way the letter appears.*

Khaf Sofit

In Lesson Three you learned that the letter "Khaf" has the (hard, scraping) sound of "ch" as in "Ba*ch*" and may appear in three forms: כ (book print), כ (manual print), and coloured (cursive). When appearing at the end of a word, however, Khaf changes to a "sofit" form, and can likewise appear in three forms:

ך	ך	‍
Book Print	**Manual Print**	**Cursive**

Manual Print

The manual print version of Khaf Sofit looks like this:

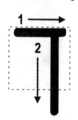

Note that Khaf Sofit resembles a Dalet except that the second stroke descends well below the baseline of the text.

בָּרוּךְ

↑
Khaf Sofit

Hebrew Cursive

Write the cursive version of Khaf Sofit this way:

A single stroke is used to form this letter. Note the letter resembles a cursive Vet but has a long tail that descends below the baseline.

Practice

Write the letter Khaf Sofit in both manual print and cursive several times:

Manual Print

Cursive

Note: The letter Khaf Sofit can also take a dot, or dagesh mark (i.e., ךּ), in which case it is pronounced like the letter Kaf (i.e., כּ).

Mem Sofit

In Lesson Three you also learned that the letter Mem has the sound of "m" as in "*m*om" and may appear in three forms: מ (book print), מ (manual print), and N (cursive). When appearing at the end of a word, however, Mem changes to a "sofit" form, and can likewise appear in three forms:

ם	ם	ם
Book Print	Manual Print	Cursive

Manual Print

Write the manual print version of the letter Mem Sofit according to the following pattern:

Note that Mem Sofit resembles a Samekh except that it is more box-shaped.

Mem Sofit

Hebrew Cursive

Now write the cursive version of Mem Sofit this way:

The script form of Mem Sofit looks somewhat like an English lowercase "p" except that the second stroke does not descend below the baseline.

Practice

Write the letter Mem Sofit in both manual print and cursive several times:

Manual Print

Cursive

Note: Be careful not to confuse the book print shape of Mem Sofit (ם) with the letter Samekh (ס).

tagin
head
leg

Nun Sofit

In Lesson Three you learned that the letter Nun has the sound of "n" as in "*n*ow" and may appear in three forms: **נ** (book print), **נ** (manual print), and **נ** (cursive). When Nun appears at the end of a word, however, it changes to a "sofit" form, and can likewise appear in three forms:

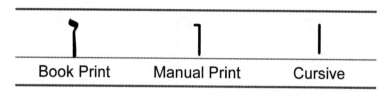

| Book Print | Manual Print | Cursive |

Manual Print

Write the manual print version of the letter Nun Sofit according to the following pattern:

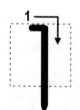

Note that Nun Sofit resembles a Vav except that it descends below the baseline.

Nun Sofit

Hebrew Cursive

Now write the cursive version this way:

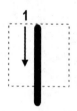

The script form of Nun Sofit looks like a Vav except that it descends from the baseline.

Practice

Write the letter Nun Sofit in both manual print and cursive several times:

Manual Print

Cursive

In Lesson Four you learned that the letter Fey has the sound of "ph" like "**ph**one" (or "f" as in "**f**ood") and may appear in three forms: פ (book print), **פ** (manual print), and ⊃ (cursive). When Fey ends a word, however, it changes to a "sofit" form, and can likewise appear in three forms:

ף	ף	ƒ
Book Print	**Manual Print**	**Cursive**

Manual Print

Write the manual print version of the letter Fey Sofit according to the following pattern:

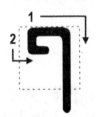

Note that Fey Sofit resembles the standard letter Fey except that it has a "tail" that descends below the baseline.

Fey Sofit

Hebrew Cursive

And the cursive version as follows:

The script form of Fey Sofit is a bit difficult, though it somewhat resembles a cursive English letter "J." Note that it is an ascender letter.

Practice

Write the letter Fey Sofit in both manual print and cursive several times:

Manual Print

Cursive

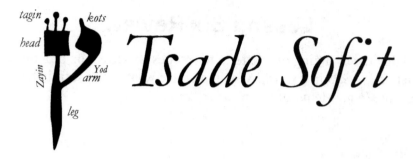

In Lesson Four you also learned that the letter Tsade has the sound of "ts" as in "nu*ts*" and may appear in three forms: **צ** (book print), **צ** (manual print), and **3** (cursive). When it appears at the end of a word, however, Tsade changes to a "sofit" form, and can likewise appear in three forms:

ץ	ץ	$\wp$
Book Print	Manual Print	Cursive

Manual Print

Write the manual print version of the letter Tsade Sofit according to the following pattern:

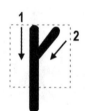

Note that Tsade Sofit resembles the standard letter Tsade except that it has a "tail" that descends below the baseline.

אֶרֶץ

Tsade Sofit

Hebrew Cursive

And the cursive version as follows:

The script form of Tsade Sofit is a bit difficult, though it somewhat resembles a cursive English letter "L." Note that it is an ascender letter.

Practice

Write the letter Tsade Sofit in both manual print and cursive several times:

													Manual Print
													Cursive

שִׁעוּר שִׁישִׁי

Lesson Six Review

Keep in mind that the changing of a letter's form does not affect its pronunciation, only the way the letter *appears* in a word. As you practice writing the sofit letters, pronounce the phonetic value (e.g., Mem Sofit: "m" as in "*m*om").

Manual Print

Practice identifying each letter with its corresponding sofit form:

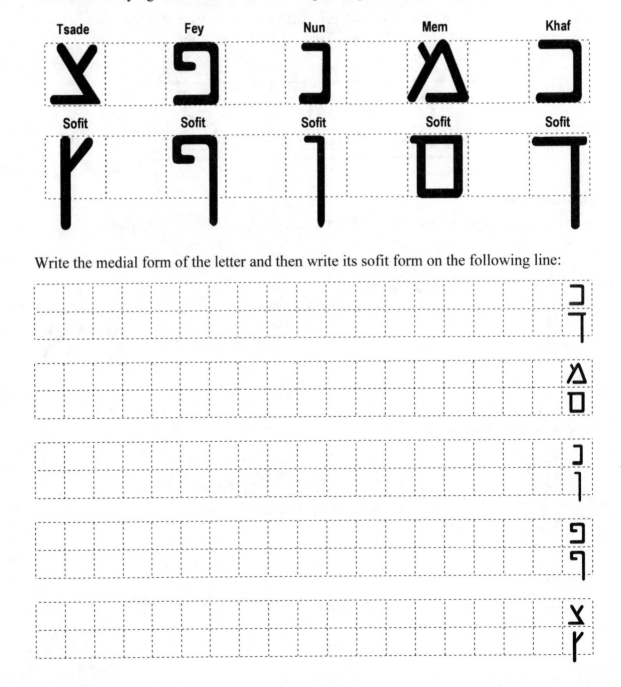

Write the medial form of the letter and then write its sofit form on the following line:

Lesson Six Review

Again, keep in mind that the changing of a letter's form does not change its pronunciation, only the way the letter *appears* in a word. As you practice writing the sofit letters, pronounce the phonetic value (e.g., Mem Sofit: "m" as in "*m*om").

Hebrew Cursive

Practice identifying each letter with its corresponding sofit form:

Tsade	Fey	Nun	Mem	Khaf
3	ට	ل	N	כ
8	8	Sofit	Sofit	Sofit
		١	ව	כ

Write the medial form of letter and then write its sofit form on the following line:

כ
ך

N
ם

ل
ן

ට
8

3
8

The Complete Hebrew Alphabet

Book Print	Name	Block	Cursive	Pronounced	Transliteration
א	Aleph	א	ן	silent letter	' (or none)
בּ	Bet	בּ	ב	**b** as in **b**oy	b
ב	Vet	ב	ב	*no dot*: **v** as in **v**ine	v
ג	Gimmel	ג	נ	**g** as in **g**irl	g
ד	Dalet	ד	₹	**d** as in **d**oor	d
ה	Hey	ה	ה	**h** as in **h**ay	h
ו	Vav	ו	۱	**v** as in **v**ine; "consonantal vowel"	v
ז	Zayin	ז	۲	**z** as in **z**ebra	z
ח	Chet	ח	ת	**ch** as in Ba**ch**	ch (or ḥ)
ט	Tet	ט	ﻻ	**t** as in **t**ime	t (or ṭ)
י	Yod	י	'	**y** as in **y**es; "consonantal vowel"	y
כ	Kaf	כ	כ	**k** as in **k**ite	k
כ	Khaf	כ	⊃	*no dot*: **ch** as in ba**ch**	kh
ך		ך	ך	*sofit form*	
ל	Lamed	ל	ﺭ	**l** as in **l**ook	l
מ	Mem	מ	N	**m** as in **m**om	m
ם		ם	ﻭ	*sofit form*	
נ	Nun	נ	ﻝ	**n** as in **n**ow	n
ן		ן	ﺍ	*sofit form*	
ס	Samekh	ס	O	**s** as in **s**on	s
ע	'Ayin	ע	צ	silent letter	' (or none)
פ	Pey	פ	ə	**p** as in **p**ark	p
פ	Fey	פ	ə	**ph** as in **ph**one	ph / f
ף		ף	ﻝ	*sofit form*	
צ	Tsade	צ	₹	**ts** as in nu**ts**	ts / tz (or ṣ)
ץ		ץ	ﻍ	*sofit form*	
ק	Qof	ק	₱	**q** as in **q**ueen	q (or k)
ר	Resh	ר	ﺭ	**r** as in **r**ain	r
שׁ	Shin	שׁ	ﻉ	**sh** as in **sh**y	sh (or š)
שׂ	Sin	שׂ	ﻉ	**s** as in **s**un	s (or ś)
ת	Tav	ת	ﻥ	**t** as in **t**all	t

Similar-looking Letters

When you are first learning the Hebrew alphabet, some letters appear similar to one another and can cause confusion. The most easily confused are listed below.

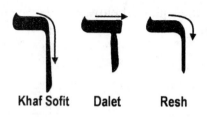

Khaf Sofit Dalet Resh

Vav Nun Sofit Zayin

Dalet's first stroke extends across its second stroke, whereas Resh is a single stroke. Khaf sofit looks like a Resh with a long tail.

Zayin's first stroke extends to the right of the vertical stroke, whereas Vav is a single stroke. Nun sofit looks like an extra long Vav.

Mem Sofit Samekh

Tsade Sofit Fey Sofit

Samekh has a rounded second stroke whereas Mem sofit has a square shape.

Fey Sofit loops downward, whereas Tsade Sofit loops upward.

More Hebrew Numbering (Gematria)

Although not often used, the Hebrew sofit letters are also assigned numeric values:

9	8	7	6	5	4	3	2	1		Multiples of 100
ט	ח	ז	ו	ה	ד	ג	ב	א		
ךט	ךח	ךז	ךו	ךה	ךד	ךג	ךב	ךא	ך	500
םט	םח	םז	םו	םה	םד	םג	םב	םא	ם	600
ןט	ןח	ןז	ןו	ןה	ןד	ןג	ןב	ןא	ן	700
ףט	ףח	ףז	ףו	ףה	ףד	ףג	ףב	ףא	ף	800
ץט	ץח	ץז	ץו	ץה	ץד	ץג	ץב	ץא	ץ	900

Crowning letters

In some Torah Scrolls, eight Hebrew letters are given special adornment by attaching **three "tagin"** or crownlets to them. Collectively these letters are sometimes called "sha'atnezgets" letters. Some people have said that these crownlets are the "tittles" referred to by Jesus in Matthew 5:18, although it is unclear that the *tagin* were in use at the time of the Lord Jesus. It is more likely that the "tittle" refers to the "qots" or "thorn" that projects from a letter.

"Sha'atnez gets" letters

שִׁעוּר שִׁשִׁי

Lesson Six Writing Practice

Review Drill: Complete Alphabet (manual print)

From memory, write the entire Hebrew Alphabet in the squares below.

	Label
	Aleph
	Bet / Vet
	Gimmel
	Dalet
	Hey
	Vav
	Zayin
	Chet
	Tet
	Yod
	Kaf / Khaf
	Khaf Sofit
	Lamed
	Mem
	Mem Sofit
	Nun
	Nun Sofit
	Samekh
	'Ayin
	Pey / Fey
	Fey Sofit
	Tsade
	Tsade Sofit
	Qof
	Resh
	Shin / Sin
	Tav

Lesson Six Writing Practice

Review Drill: Complete Alphabet (cursive)

From memory, write the entire Hebrew Alphabet in the squares below.

	Label
	Aleph
	Bet / Vet
	Gimmel
	Dalet
	Hey
	Vav
	Zayin
	Chet
	Tet
	Yod
	Kaf / Khaf
	Khaf Sofit
	Lamed
	Mem
	Mem Sofit
	Nun
	Nun Sofit
	Samekh
	'Ayin
	Pey / Fey
	Fey Sofit
	Tsade
	Tsade Sofit
	Qof
	Resh
	Shin / Sin
	Tav

Transliteration Examples

The following Hebrew letters are transliterated into English. The Hebrew is read from right to left, but the transliterations are written from left to right (note that the five sofit letters are transliterated just like their non-sofit (i.e., "medial") cousins).

ד	ם	ן	ף	ץ	**1.**
kh	m	n	ph (or f)	ts (or tz)	

בְּרוּך	שָׁלוֹם	בִּטָּחוֹן	אָלֶף	אֶרֶץ	**2.**
brvkh	shlvm	btchvn	'lf	'rts	

שֶׁלְך	שָׁמַיִם	אֶרֶץ	אַף	מֶלֶך	**3.**
shlkh	shmym	'rts	'f	mlkh	

דְּבָרִים	בָּרוּך	קָם	שְׁלוֹמְך	הָרִים	**4.**
dvrym	vrvkh	km	shlvmkh	hrym	

The Messiah Jesus is the Truth

The word for truth, אמת (*emet*), contains the first, middle (if you include the sofit letters) and last letter of the Hebrew alphabet, which seems to suggest that the truth contains everything from Aleph to Tav. The Lord Jesus said that He is both the Truth and the Aleph and the Tav, the Beginning and the Ending.

Identify the Hebrew letters in the following Scriptures:

English	Hebrew
I am the Aleph and the Tav, the first and the last (Rev. 1:8).	אָנֹכִי אָלֶף וְתָו רֹאשׁ וָסוֹף׃ 'a·no·khi 'a·lef ve·tav rosh va·sof

English	Hebrew
I am the way and the truth and the life (John 14:6).	אָנֹכִי הַדֶּרֶךְ וְהָאֱמֶת וְהַחַיִּים׃ 'a·no·khi ha·de·rekh ve·ha·e·met ve·ha·chaim

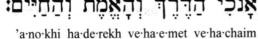

Transliteration Practice

Hebrew to English

Transliterate each row of Hebrew letters into English. Read the Hebrew from right to left, but write the transliterations from left to right. Say the name of each letter out loud.

אף	בבתך	שלום	מלך	ברוך	.1
נשוין	הימים	חדשים	מתן	חסדים	.2
חמץ	כהנים	דין	רבן	הסא	.3
אורל	אל	מתן	אלל	סול	.4

English to Hebrew

Transliterate each row of English letters into Hebrew cursive. Read the English from left to right, but write the transliterations directly beneath from right to left. If "kh," "m," "n," "f," or "ts" appear at the end of the string, use the sofit characters to transliterate.

'rts	'm	kvm	'mn	shlvm	.5
				שלום	
chmts	svf	dyn	'f	ktn	.6
rbn	mtsvh	hshm	shm	sm	.7

Lesson Six Quiz

Here is your quiz to help you reinforce your learning.

1. Write Letter Names

Write the name for the following Hebrew sofit letters.

ם	ן	ף	ץ	ך	Book Letter
				Khaf	Sofit Name
				kh	Transliteration

ן	ם	כ	ץ	ף	Cursive Letter
					Sofit Name
					Transliteration

2. Write Hebrew Letters

Write the Hebrew sofit letter for the letter name. The first exercise is done for you.

Tsade	Fey	Nun	Mem	Khaf	Name
				כ	Hebrew
				kh	Transliteration

3. Transliterations

Transliterate the Hebrew letters into English. Read the Hebrew from right to left, but write the transliteration from left to right. Say the name of each letter out loud.

.a אני יהוה ראשון ואת אחרנים אני הוא

.b שמע ישראל יהוה אלהינו יהוה

.c ואהבת את יהוה אלהיך

4. Which letter is out of place?

Circle the letters that are different:

ס ס ס מ ס ס ס ס ס מ ס ס ם ס ס ס ס .a

ר ר ר ך ר ר ר ר ו ר ר ר ר ר ר ר .b

5. Recognition

Circle the correct answer.

What letter is this? ך

1. Nun Sofit
2. Khaf Sofit
3. Mem Sofit
4. Tsade Sofit
5. Fey Sofit

What letter is this? ר

1. Dalet
2. Resh
3. Khaf Sofit
4. Vav
5. Zayin

What letter is this? ב

1. Hey
2. Vet
3. Gimmel
4. Dalet
5. Bet

What letter is this? ץ

1. Nun Sofit
2. Khaf Sofit
3. Mem Sofit
4. Tsade Sofit
5. Fey Sofit

What letter is this? ם

1. Nun Sofit
2. Khaf Sofit
3. Mem Sofit
4. Tsade Sofit
5. Fey Sofit

What letter is this? כ

1. Nun Sofit
2. Khaf Sofit
3. Mem Sofit
4. Tsade Sofit
5. Fey Sofit

What letter is this? ץ

1. 'Ayin
2. Fey Sofit
3. Tsade Sofit
4. Mem Sofit
5. Khaf Sofit

What letter is this? ץ

1. Nun Sofit
2. Khaf Sofit
3. Mem Sofit
4. Tsade Sofit
5. Fey Sofit

What letter is this? ן

1. Vav
2. Nun
3. Nun Sofit
4. Resh
5. Zayin

What letter is this? ע

1. Tsade
2. Aleph
3. 'Ayin
4. Resh
5. Qof

What letter is this? ם

1. Nun Sofit
2. Khaf Sofit
3. Mem Sofit
4. Tsade Sofit
5. Fey Sofit

What letter is this? ף

1. Nun Sofit
2. Khaf Sofit
3. Mem Sofit
4. Tsade Sofit
5. Fey Sofit

6. What three letters can take a "dot" to make them sound different?

1.

2.

3.

8. **Completely fill in the alphabet table you have studied:**

Book Print	Name	Block	Cursive	Pronounced	Transliteration
א					
בּ					
ג					
ד					
ה					
ו					
ז					
ח					
טִ					
י					
כּ					
ל					
מ					
נ					
ס					
ע					
פּ					
צ					
ק					
ר					
שׁ					
שׂ					
ת					

Lesson Seven

A-TYPE VOWELS

שִׁעוּר שְׁבִיעִי

Introduction to Hebrew Vowels

You may recall from your early school days that the English alphabet includes the vowel letters "A-E-I-O-U" (and sometimes "Y"). Unlike English, however, the Hebrew alphabet is a consonantal one: there are no separate letters for vowels in the written alphabet (though some letters, in particular Vav and Yod, can function as "consonantal vowels"). This does not mean, of course, that vowels are not used in Hebrew. In fact, it is impossible to say anything at all without vowel sounds. But ancient Hebrew contained no written vowels as distinct letter forms: the actual vowel sounds were "added" to the reading by means of oral tradition and long-established usage.

As an experiment, try reading the following:

Lv th Lrd yr Gd wth ll yr hrt

If you were able to "figure out" that the above string of letters reads "Love the Lord your God with all your heart," (Deut 6:5), then you might be able to see how a language could be entirely made up of consonants—with the reader supplying the missing vowels.

In written Hebrew the string of letters might look like this:

ואהבת את יהוה אלהיך

All of the letters in this string are Hebrew consonants you have learned—there is not a vowel in the bunch! In order to properly read this text, you, the reader, must supply the missing "intonations" or vowels.

Adding vowel sounds to a string of letters was not too difficult as long as you were immersed in the oral tradition and regular usage of the day. However, after the Diaspora more and more Jewish people began speaking the languages of their surrounding cultures —and literacy of the written Hebrew text became a more serious issue.

Sometime beginning around 600 A.D., a group of scribes in Tiberias called the Masoretes (*mesora* means "tradition") began developing a system of vowel marks (called *neqqudot)* to indicate how the text was traditionally read. Since these scribes did not want to alter the consonantal text, they placed these markings under, to the left, and above the Hebrew letters. Beside these vowel marks, the scribes also added "cantillation" marks (in Hebrew, *ta'amim*) to indicate how the text was to be chanted or sung.

The "pointed" text of the Deuteronomy passage would now look like this:

וְאָהַבְתָּ אֵת יְהֹוָה אֱלֹהֶיךָ

Notice that the little marks—the dots and dashes and so on—appear mostly below the Hebrew letters. Yes, these marks are the objects of our study in the following lessons, and if you study well, they will soon become indispensable aides as you are learning to read and write Hebrew—especially the Hebrew Scriptures and the prayerbook (Siddur).

"Simple" Hebrew Vowels

Most vowels in the Hebrew are called "simple" vowels (or basic) because they are composed of one Hebrew letter and an identifying vowel mark:

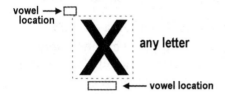

Note that the "**X**" refers to any Hebrew letter (for example א, ב, and so on) and the rectangular boxes below and to the upper left of the letter refer to a possible vowel mark location. This scheme will become abundantly clear as you progress through this lesson.

"Consonantal" Vowel Letters (*Matres Lectiones*)

Before the vowel points were introduced, however, the scribes used the letters ו, י, and ה (and sometimes א) to indicate vowel sounds. These are sometimes called "consonantal vowels," or *matres lectiones* (Latin for mothers of reading), so that when one of these consonants was encountered, the reader understood to make an associated vowel sound:

Note: The *matres lectiones* are traditionally read as follows: **Xה** is for "a" or "o"; **Xי** is for "i"; and **Xו** is for "o" or "u".

In addition, because it is so weak, there are times when Aleph (א) does not accept a vowel. When this occurs, Aleph is said to be "quiescent" and is not transliterated (in modern Hebrew, a quiescent Aleph often fulfills the function of indicating an "a" sound in the middle of a word). All of this should become clear as we proceed in this lesson.

"Full" (or mixed) Hebrew Vowels

After the scribes added vowel points to the texts, the consonantal vowels were often retained with the result that some of the vowels included both "simple" vowel marks as well as consonantal letters. These are now known as "full vowels" (as opposed to the "simple vowels," which are the marks without the additional the letters ו, י, and ה).

To make matters somewhat easier, in this book we will include both simple and full vowels under the classification of the sound they make.

Our approach

As mentioned above, in English we have the basic vowel categories of "A-E-I-O-U," and we will introduce the Hebrew vowels in this same order. In other words, we will show you the "A-type" vowels first, then the "E-type," and so on, each as a separate lesson.

A few additional comments before we begin looking at the actual Hebrew vowels. First, originally each Hebrew vowel marking had its own unique sound, but over time many of these were gradually combined to indicate the same intonation. Thus you will see examples of different vowel marks that make the same sort of sound.

Second, Hebrew vowels are given special names which you may or may not wish to memorize (though it is recommended if you wish to pursue Hebrew studies). In this book, we will provide the names for the vowels, but the important thing is for you to be able to determine the appropriate vowel sound when you see a given Hebrew vowel mark. The emphasis, in other words, is not the academic but the practical: we want you to be able to confidently pronounce the Hebrew words you will be learning.

We will present the vowels slowly and methodically, just as we did with the Hebrew letters. If you take the time and apply yourself diligently, you will soon enjoy the satisfaction of sounding out real Hebrew words. May the Lord God of Israel bless you in your study.

A word of caution

Be patient and go slowly. Each Lesson presents a separate vowel type in sequence. Review the reading exercises until you feel comfortable with what you are learning. It might help to make flash cards with a vowel mark on the front and the name of the vowel and its sound on the back. Examples are provided in the Lesson Reviews.

Lesson Introduction

So far we have been studying Hebrew letters. In this lesson you will begin learning about Hebrew vowels. In particular, you will learn:

- ✓ The vowel marks for the "A-type" vowels
- ✓ How to write the vowel marks with Hebrew letters
- ✓ How to pronounce Hebrew letters and words with vowel marks
- ✓ How to accurately transliterate the vowel sounds
- ✓ How to read Hebrew words using the vowel marks
- ✓ The names of the Hebrew vowels
- ✓ The classification for the vowels (long or short)

Lesson at a glance

After you have studied this lesson, the following information should be clear:

Simple Vowels

The simple (or basic) vowel marks you will learn are as follows:

Vowel Mark	Vowel Name	Sound	Hebrew	Trans.	Class
אָ	Qamets	"a" as in aqua	קָמֶץ	a	Long
אַ	Patach	"a" as in aqua	פַּתַח	a	Short
אֲ	Chateph Patach	"a" as in aqua	חָטֵף פַּתַח	a	Reduced

Full Vowel (Variant)

The following vowel is a variation on the simple Qamets vowel:

אָה	Qamets Hey	"a" as in aqua	קָמֶץ הֵא	ah	Long

Simple A-Type Vowels

The first vowel group you will learn is sometimes called the "A-type" because it indicates an "**a**" sound (as in "**yacht**" or "**aqua**") when combined with a letter. The following table shows the main A-type vowels:

Vowel Mark	Vowel Name	Sound	Hebrew	Trans.	Class
X̱	Qamets	"a" as in **aqua**	קָמֵץ	a	Long
X̲	Patach	"a" as in **aqua**	פַּתַח	a	Short
X̤	Chateph Patach	"a" as in **aqua**	חֲטֵף פַּתַח	a	Reduced

Notes:

- Although these vowel marks look different, they all represent an "ah" **sound**. To simplify things, we will transliterate all three vowels using an "a" in English.
- Note which vowel is **long** (Qamets) and which are **short** (Patach, Chateph Patach).
- The Chateph Patach is sometimes called a "half vowel" and is the shortest of all vowels: it can *only* appear under the **guttural letters**: א, ה, ע, ח.

"Simple" Hebrew Vowels

These vowels are "simple" vowels because they are composed of one Hebrew letter and one identifying vowel mark:

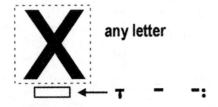

any letter

Note that the "**X**" refers to any Hebrew letter (for example א, ב, ג, and so on) and the rectangular box below the letter refers to a vowel mark location (**important note**: if transliterated at all, the letter Aleph will use (').

Sounding Out the Vowels

To sound out the vowel, *first* pronounce the letter sound and *then* add the vowel sound. Thus you would read בָּ as "ba" (*not* "ab").

דָ	גַ	גָ	בַ	בָּ	אֲ	אַ	אָ	1.
da	ga	ga	ba	ba	'a	'a	'a	

Simple A-Type Syllables

"Open" Syllable Sounds

A syllable is a unit of sound. A syllable is called "open" when it does not end with a "stopping" sound:

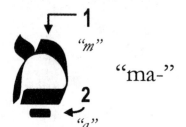

"m"

"a"

"ma-"

This syllable ends with an "a" sound (i.e., Patach), so it is an "open syllable."

Read each open syllable aloud. Remember that the "a" transliteration is an "ah" sound:

דָ	גַ	גָ	בֶ	בָ	אֶ	אַ	אָ	**1.**
da	ga	ga	ba	ba	'a	'a	'a	
זַ	זָ	וַ	וָ	הֶ	הַ	הָ	דַ	**2.**
za	za	va	va	ha	ha	ha	da	
כָ	יִ	יָ	טַ	טָ	חֶ	חַ	חָ	**3.**
ka	ya	ya	ta	ta	cha	cha	cha	
סָ	נַ	נָ	מַ	מָ	לַ	לָ	כֶ	**4.**
sa	na	na	ma	ma	la	la	ka	
צֶ	צָ	פַ	פָ	עֶ	עַ	עָ	סַ	**5.**
tsa	tsa	pa	pa	'a	'a	'a	sa	
תַ	תָ	שֶׁ	שָׁ	רַ	רָ	קֶ	קָ	**6.**
ta	ta	sha	sha	ra	ra	qa	qa	

"Closed" Syllable Sounds

A syllable is called "closed" when it ends with a "stopping" sound:

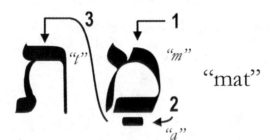

"mat"

This syllable ends with a stopping "t" sound (i.e., Tav), so it is a "closed syllable."

Read each closed syllable aloud. Remember that the "a" transliteration is an "ah" sound:

1.

רָו	פָּת	טַס	שָׁם	חָם	דָּג	גָּר	מַת
rav	pat	tas	sham	cham	dag	gad	mat

2.

דָן	בָּר	יָם	שָׁת	דָּם	לָךְ	בָּם	אַב
dan	bar	yam	shat	dam	lakh	bam	'av

3.

לָהּ	קָם	מָן	מַל	יָד	גָּר	רָב	אַד
lah	kam	man	mal	yad	gar	rav	'ad

Note:

- The last example shows a dot inside the closing Hey (הּ). This dot is called a ***mappiq*** and indicates that the Hey is to be pronounced as a closing stop (if the Hey did *not* have the mappiq (i.e., ה), this would be an open syllable and the Hey would be silent). The dotted Hey has a faint "h" sound.

Did you know?

The Torah Scroll is one of the most precious objects of Jewish worship. To show respect and protect the scroll from dirt and oil from the reader's hands, a *Yad* (Hebrew, hand) is normally used while reading.

Most *yaddim* are made of beautifully wrought silver. The pointing end of the Yad is commonly shaped like a small hand with its index finger extended.

yad

A-Type Writing Practice

Practice: Write the Hebrew Sounds

Write the Hebrew vowel marks for each letter of the alphabet. Use all the possibilities for the "A-Type" vowels you have studied. For example, Aleph can take a Patach, a Qamets, and a Chateph Patach, so there are three possibilities. Use cursive as you write.

1.

ha	da	da	ga	ga	ba	ba	'a	'a	'a

2.

ta	cha	cha	cha	za	za	va	va	ha	ha

3.

na	ma	ma	la	la	ka	ka	ya	ya	ta

4.

tsa	tsa	pa	pa	'a	'a	'a	sa	sa	na

5.

ta	ta	sha	sha	ra	ra	qa	qa

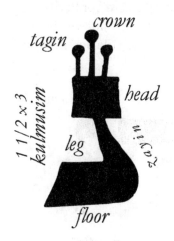

crown
tagin
head
1 1/2 × 3
kulmusim
leg
zayin
floor

Did you know?

The original Torah was written without any vowel points at all. This meant, of course, that in order to read the text properly, the reader was responsible for supplying the missing "intonations" or vowels.

Why is this the case? Why would the Lord provide only the consonants without the vowels? Some sages have said that by supplying the vowels, the reader must be active and do his or her part—that is, the reader must supply the intonation and "exhale" the words that the Lord has so graciously inspired.

The reading of Torah, then, involves two things: the text itself and the reader who brings to the text the willingness to breathe out the divine inspiration. And without the *Ruach* (the Spirit), the text itself is dead, "for the letter killeth, but the Spirit gives life" (*see* 2 Cor. 3:6).

Full A-Type Vowel

In addition to the three simple A-type vowels you have studied, there is a full-vowel variation that you should be aware of:

- Qamets can have a silent Hey (ה) following it (the Hey, a *mater*, is not pronounced but is considered part of the vowel):

Vowel Mark	Vowel Name	Sound	Hebrew	Trans.	Class
הָX	Qamets Hey	"a" as in aqua	קָמֶץ הֵא	ah	Long

Notes:

- This vowel is composed of both a Qamets and a Hey in combination and normally marks the **end of a word**. We will transliterate this vowel mark using an "ah" in English.

- If there is a dot inside of the following Hey (הּ), it is considered a consonant and not part of the full vowel (the dotted Hey is called a *mappiq*).

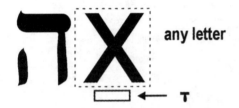

any letter

Before the vowel points were introduced the scribes used the letter ה to indicate a vowel sound.

Note that the "**X**" refers to any Hebrew letter (for example א, ב, ג, and so on) and the rectangular box below the letter refers to a vowel mark location. When the letter Hey follows a letter with a Qamets or Patach, it functions not as a consonant, but as a vowel letter. This is called a "consonantal vowel" and the result is called a "mixed" or "full" vowel.

Sounding Out the Vowels

To sound out the vowel, *first* pronounce the letter sound and *then* add the vowel sound. Thus you would read בָה as "bah" (*not* "abh").

A-Type Reading Practice

One syllable:

שָׁם	רָב	עָם	לָךְ	דָּם	גָּר	בָּא	אָז	1.
sham	rav	'am	lakh	dam	gar	ba	'az	

שָׂר	צָר	פָּם	כַּף	חַג	הַר	אַף	אַל	2.
sar	tsar	pam	kaf	chag	har	'af	'al	

Two syllables:

קָרָא	נָפַל	מָךְ	זָכַר	בָּשָׂר	בָּרָא	אָדָם	3.
qa·ra'	na·fal	ma·kha	za·khar	ba·sar	ba·ra'	'a·dam	

שַׁעַר	שָׁלַח	רַבַּת	מַעַל	דַּעַת	בַּעַל	אַחַת	4.
sha·'ar	sha·lach	rab·bat (*)	ma·'al	da·'at	ba·'al	'a·chat	

שַׁחַר	מָסָה	נָתַן	יָלַד	הָלַךְ	הַבַּד	אָמַר	5.
sha·char	ma·sah	na·tan	ya·lad	ha·lakh	hab·bad (*)	'a·mar	

חֲזַק	עֲמַל	עֲפַר	הֲדַר	הֲבָּא	אֲגַג	אֱל	6.
cha·zaq	'a·mal	'a·far	ha·dar	hab·ba' (*)	'a·gag	'al	

Three syllables:

וַיֵּשֶׁב	הָאַחַת	בָּרָעָב	הָאָדָם	הַנַּעַר	וַיַּעַשׂ	7.
va·ya·shav	ha·'a·chat	ba·ra·'av	ha·'a·dam	han·na·'ar	va·ya·'as	

חֲנָעַד	וַיָּקָם	הַבָּשָׂר	כָּרְשָׁע	הָרָעָב	צָרָעַת	8.
cha·na·'ad	va·ya·qam	hab·ba·sar	ka·ra·sha'	ha·ra·'av	tsa·ra·'at	

Four syllables:

הַצְּלָחַת	בַּצָּרָתָה	הָאֲדָמָה	הָרַחֲמָה	9.
ha·tsa·la·chat	ba·tsa·ra·tah	ha·'a·da·mah	ha·ra·cha·mah	

---

* The dagesh in בּ indicates a "doubling" of the letter, causing the previous syllable to be closed. More information about the dagesh is provided later.

A-Type Transliteration Practice

Hebrew to English

Transliterate each row of Hebrew words into English. Read the Hebrew words from right to left, but write the English transliterations from left to right. Pronounce each word out loud when finished. The first word is done for you.

יָשַׁב	אַחַת	אֶבָל	דָּבָר	אָדָם	.1
				'a·dam	
וַיֵּשֶׁב	הָאַחַת	אַבָּא	הַדָּבָר	הָאָדָם	.2
חָזַק	דָּם	בָּשָׂר	בַּעַל	אֶבֶד	.3
וָחֳדָשׁ	צָדָה	הָרַע	הַגָּדְרה	בָּרָעָב	.4
וַיֵּשֶׁב	הַבָּשָׂר	כְּרֶשַׁע	הָאֲדָמָה	צָרַעַת	.5
מַצָּה	וַיָּקָם	תָּצַד	מַעֲשָׂה	גָּרְפָּה	.6
הָרַחֲמָן	הַשָּׁעָה	כַּלָּה	הַגָּדְרה	שַׁבָּת	.7
פָּרָשָׁה	נַבֵּךְ	מַתָּן	הַמָּשָׁל	מָשָׁל	.8

Lesson Seven Summary

In this lesson you learned the main A-type vowels:

Simple Vowels

Vowel Mark	Vowel Name	Sound	Hebrew	Trans.	Class
אָ	Qamets	"a" as in **aqua**	קָמֵץ	a	Long
אַ	Patach	"a" as in **aqua**	פַּתַח	a	Short
אֲ	Chateph Patach	"a" as in **aqua**	חָטֵף פַּתַח	a	Reduced

Notes:

- Although these vowel marks look different, they all represent an "ah" **sound**. To simplify things, we will transliterate all three vowels using an "a" in English.
- Note which vowel is **long** (Qamets) and which are **short** (Patach, Chateph Patach).
- The Chateph Patach is sometimes called a "half vowel" and is the shortest of all vowels: it can *only* appear under the **guttural letters**: א, ה, ע, ח.

Full Vowel Variant

אָה	Qamets Hey	"a" as in **aqua**	קָמֵץ הֵא	ah	Long

Notes:

- The full vowel variant only appears at the **end of a word**. We will transliterate it using "ah" in English.
- If there is a dot inside of the following Hey (ה), it is considered a consonant and *not* part of the full vowel (the dotted Hey is called a *mappiq*).
- The letters Aleph and 'Ayin are often not transliterated at the start of a word.

Quick Summary:

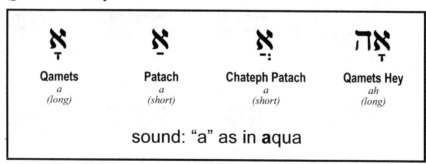

שִׁעוּר שְׁבִיעִי

Lesson Seven Quiz

1. Write the Vowel Marks

In this lesson you learned four vowel marks. Write the mark and its sound in the columns next to its name.

Name	Mark	Sound	Transliteration
Qamets			
Patach			
Chateph Patach			
Qamets Hey			

2. Write the Vowel Names

Write the name for the vowel in the column next to its mark.

Mark	Name	Sound	Transliteration
אָ			
אַ			
אֲ			
אָה			

3. True or False

Circle the correct answer:

1. Chateph vowels can only appear under guttural letters.
    True
    False

2. There is one syllable for each Hebrew vowel mark.
    True
    False

4. Identify the Vowel Class

For each vowel, provide the name and sound and indicate if it is long or short in the column next to the vowel mark (reduced vowels are considered short):

Mark	Name	Sound	Class
אָ			
אַ			
אֲ			
אָה			

5. Completely fill in the vowel table you have studied:

Complete the following table. For extra credit, try writing the Hebrew name for each "A-Type" vowel:

A-Type:

Mark	Name	Sound	Hebrew	Trans.	Class
אָ					
אַ					
אֲ					
אָה					

6. Transliterate the following Hebrew words

Remember there is one syllable per Hebrew vowel. The first word is done for you.

Word		Transliteration	Word		Transliteration
אָדָם	(man)	'a·**dam**	שָׂרָה	(Sarah)	
דָּבָר	(word)		נָתָן	(Nathan)	
דַּעַת	(knowledge)		אַחַת	(one)	
אַהֲבָה	(love)		בָּשָׂר	(flesh)	

Quick Vowel Review

Each Lesson on the vowels will conclude with an essential summary of the vowels you have studied so far. You may want to make **flash cards** using this summary as a guide (write a vowel mark on one side of a card and its sound, transliteration, and class on the other side).

A-Type:

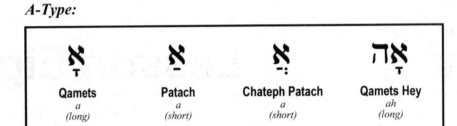

אָ	אַ	אֲ	אָה
Qamets	**Patach**	**Chateph Patach**	**Qamets Hey**
a	*a*	*a*	*ah*
(long)	*(short)*	*(short)*	*(long)*

sound: "a" as in **a**qua

Lesson Eight

E - TYPE   VOWELS

שִׁעוּר שְׁמִינִי

Lesson Introduction

In this lesson you will learn additional Hebrew vowels. In particular, you will learn:

✓ The vowel marks for the "E-type" vowels

✓ How to write the vowel marks with Hebrew letters

✓ How to pronounce Hebrew letters and words with vowel marks

✓ How to accurately transliterate the vowel sounds

✓ How to read Hebrew words using the vowel marks

✓ The names of the Hebrew vowels

✓ The classification for the vowels (long or short)

Lesson at a glance

After you have studied this lesson, the following information should be clear:

Simple Vowels

The basic vowel marks you will learn are as follows:

Vowel Mark	Vowel Name	Sound	Hebrew	Trans.	Class
אֵ	Tsere	"e" as in they	צֵרִי	e	Long
אֶ	Segol	"e" as in they	סֶגּוֹל	e	Short
אֱ	Chateph Segol	"e" as in they	חָטֶף סֶגּוֹל	e	Reduced

Full Vowels (Variants)

The following vowels are variations on the simple vowels shown above:

| אֵי | Tsere Yod | "ei" as in eight | צֵרִי יוֹד | ei | Long |
| אֶי | Segol Yod | "ey" as in obey | סֶגּוֹל יוֹד | ey | Long |

Simple E-Type Vowels

The next vowel group you will learn is sometimes called the "E-type" because it indicates an "e" sound (as in "they") when combined with a letter. The following table shows the main E-type vowels:

Vowel Mark	Vowel Name	Sound	Hebrew	Trans.	Class
X̤	Tsere	"e" as in they	צֵרִי	e	Long
X̤	Segol	"e" as in they	סֶגּוֹל	e	Short
X̤	Chateph Segol	"e" as in they	חֲטֶף סֶגּוֹל	e	Reduced

Notes:

- Although these vowel marks look different, they all represent an **"e" sound** (Segol and Chateph Segol sometimes have a shorter "e" (as in "red") sound). We will transliterate all three vowel marks using an "e" in English.
- Note which vowel is **long** (Tsere) and which are **short** (Segol, Chateph Segol).
- The Chateph Segol is sometimes called a "half vowel" and is the shortest of all vowels: it can *only* appear under the **guttural letters**: א, ה, ע, ח and is pronounced a bit quicker than the Tsere and Segol vowels.

"Simple" Hebrew Vowels

These are "simple" vowels because they are composed of one Hebrew letter and one identifying vowel mark:

 **any letter**

Note that the "**X**" refers to any Hebrew letter (for example א, ב, ג, and so on) and the rectangular box below the letter refers to a vowel mark location.

Sounding Out the Vowels

To sound out the vowel, *first* pronounce the letter sound and *then* add the vowel sound. Thus you would read בֵּ as "be" (*not* "eb").

דֵּ	גֵּ	גֶּ	בֵּ	בֶּ	אֱ	אֶ	אֵ	1.
de	ge	ge	be	be	'e	'e	'e	

Simple E-Type Syllables

"Open" Syllable Sounds

A syllable is a unit of sound. A syllable is called "open" when it does not end with a "stopping" sound:

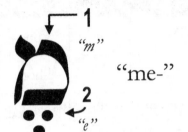

"m"

"me-"

"e"

This syllable ends with an "e" sound (i.e., Segol), so it is an "open syllable."

Read each open syllable aloud. Identify the vowel shown under the letter.

דֵּ	גֵּ	גֶּ	בֵּ	בֶּ	אֶֶ	אֶ	אֵ	1.
de	ge	ge	be	be	'e	'e	'e	
זֶ	זֵ	לֶ	לֵ	הֶ	הֵ	הֶ	דֶּ	2.
ze	ze	ve	ve	he	he	he	de	
כֵּ	יֶ	יֵ	טֶ	טֵ	חֶֶ	חֶ	חֵ	3.
ke	ye	ye	te	te	che	che	che	
סֵ	נֶ	נֵ	מֶ	מֵ	לֶ	לֵ	כֶּ	4.
se	ne	ne	me	me	le	le	ke	
צֶ	צֵ	פֶּ	פֵּ	עֶֶ	עֶ	עֵ	סֶ	5.
tse	tse	pe	pe	'e	'e	'e	se	
תֶ	תֵ	שֶׁ	שֵׁ	רֶ	רֵ	קֶ	קֵ	6.
te	te	she	she	re	re	qe	qe	

"Closed" Syllable Sounds

A syllable is called "closed" when it ends with a "stopping" sound:

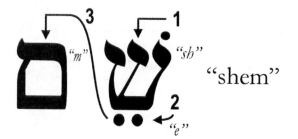

"shem"

This syllable ends with a stopping "m" sound (i.e., Mem Sofit), so it is a "closed syllable."

The following syllables are called "closed" because they end with a "stopping" sound. Read each closed syllable aloud:

שֵׁם	חֵן	אֵל	בֶּן	יֵשׁ	אֵת	הֵם	עֵץ	1.
shem	chen	el	ben	yesh	et	hem	ets	

אֵת	כֵּן	אֵם	תֵּת	שֵׁת	קֵץ	שֵׁשׁ	לֵב	2.
et	ken	em	tet	shet	qets	shesh	lev	

חֵת	גֵּר	אֵת	בֵּת	סֵג	פֵּת	מֵשׁ	רֵשׁ	3.
chet	ger	et	bet	seg	pet	mesh	resh	

The Name of the LORD

The third of the ten *mitzvot* (commandments) is: "Thou shalt not take **the name** of the LORD thy God **in vain**" (Ex 20:7). Many of the Jewish sages taught that the word translated "name" (*shem*) powerfully refers to the character or reputation of the one who bears it.

The Name

The revealed name of the LORD – י ה ו ה – thus can be understood as the invocation for the very presence of God Himself. The word translated "in vain" probably comes from another word that pictures a rushing and destructive storm (*shoah*). One way to understand this *mitzvah,* then, is that we should never invoke Adonai's name in a thoughtless, careless, or "stormy" manner (for this reason, Orthodox Jews never pronounce the literal name of the LORD, but substitute the word "HaShem" instead).

E-Type Writing Practice

Practice: Write the Hebrew Sounds

Write the Hebrew vowel marks for each letter of the alphabet. Use all the possibilities for the "E-Type" vowels you have studied (for example, Aleph can take a Tsere, a Segol, and a Chateph Segol, so there are three possibilities). Use cursive to write your answers.

1.

| he | de | de | ge | ge | be | be | ʼe | ʼe | ʼe |

2.

| te | che | che | che | ze | ze | ve | ve | he | he |

3.

| ne | me | me | le | le | ke | ke | ye | ye | te |

4.

| tse | tse | pe | pe | ʻe | ʻe | ʻe | se | se | ne |

5.

| | te | te | she | she | re | re | qe | qe |

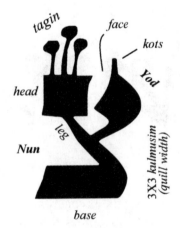

tagin   face
kots
Yod
head
leg   3X3 kulmusim (quill width)
Nun
base

Did you know?

There are 304,805 letters in a Torah scroll, and if even one letter is extra or missing it renders the entire scroll invalid (*passul*). Each letter written in a scroll is given precise specification according to Halakhic (legal) rules.

The word Sofer (scribe) is related to the word for counting, and a qualified Sofer constantly counts lines, letters on each line, and even spaces between letters. Each letter is precious and is a work of art.

The Sofer must also have the proper *Kavannah* (intention) and awe for the holiness of the task of writing sacred texts. The scribe considers himself to be actually reciting the words as given by God to Moses long ago.

Full E-Type Vowels

In addition to these E-type vowels, there are two variations that you should be aware of:

- Both Tsere and Segol may have a Yod immediately following it (the Yod then functions not as a consonant, but as a vowel letter):

Vowel Mark	Vowel Name	Sound	Hebrew	Trans.	Class
אֵי	Tsere Yod	"ei" as in **eight**	צֵרִי יוֹד	ei	Long
אֶי	Segol Yod	"ey" as in **obey**	סֶגוֹל יוֹד	ey	Long

Note:

- Both of these vowel marks represent an **"ey" sound** (we use different transliterations only to indicate that we are reading a different vowel mark).

any letter

Before the vowel points were introduced the scribes used the letter י to indicate a vowel sound.

The "**X**" refers to any Hebrew letter (for example **א**, **ב**, and so on) and the rectangular box below the letter refers to a vowel mark location. When the letter Hey or Yod follows a letter with a Tsere or Segol, it functions not as a consonant, but as a vowel letter. This is called a "consonantal vowel" and the result is called a "full" vowel.

Remember:

- A "full vowel" is a variation only in the way a vowel sound is spelled: you will *pronounce* the vowel in the same way its simple vowel cousin.

Sounding Out the Vowels

To sound out the vowel, *first* pronounce the letter sound and *then* add the vowel sound. Thus you would read בֵּי as "bey" (*not* "eyb").

דֵי	דֶי	גֵי	גֶי	בֵּי	בֶּי	אֵי	אֶי	
dey	dei	gey	gei	bey	bei	'ey	'ei	1.

Additional Variation:

- At the end of a word, both Tsere may have a Hey immediately following it (e.g. אֵה). The Hey then functions not as a consonant, but as a vowel letter.

E-Type Reading Practice

One syllable:

1. אֵת   עֵץ   שֵׁם   אֵל   הֵם   כֵּן   הֵן   לֵב

     'et   'ets   shem   'el   hem   khen   hen   lev

2. פֶּן   בֶּן   מֶה   זֶה   אֶל   בֶּן   אֶת   שֵׁם

     pen   ben   me   ze   'el   ven   'et   shem

Two syllables:

3. אָמַר   הוּא   אֵלָה   אֱנָשׁ   אֱמֶת   חֵמָא   עֱנָה

     'e·mar   he·ve   'e·lah   'e·nash   'e·met   che·ma   'e·nah

4. הַשֵּׁם   מֵעֵץ   הֵחֵל   יֵצֵא   אֶלֶד   מֵעַל   חֶסֶד

     ha·shem   me·'ets   he·chel   ye·tse   'e·led   me·'al   che·sed

5. עֶרֶב   אֶרֶץ   נֶפֶשׁ   לֶחֶם   דֶּרֶךְ   לֶמֶד   עֶשֶׂר

     'e·rev   'e·rets   ne·fesh   le·chem   de·rekh   le·med   'e·ser

6. עֶבֶד   מֶלֶךְ   צֶדֶק   כֶּסֶף   אֶלֶף   רֶחֶם   שֶׁקֶל

     'e·ved   me·lekh   tse·deq   ke·sef   'e·lef   re·chem   she·qel

Three syllables:

7. מֵאֶרֶץ   וַיֶּפֶת   לָלֶכֶת   הֶהָשֵׁב   לֶחָצֵר   יֵאָכֵל

     me·'e·rets   va·ye·fet   la·le·khet   he·ha·shev   le·cha·tser   ye·'a·khel

8. אֵקָדֵשׁ   שֶׁשָׁמֵם   אֶכָּבֵד   הֶעָרֵל   לֶעָיֵף   אֶדָדֵם

     'e·qa·desh   she·sha·mem   'e·ka·ved   he·'a·rel   le·'a·yef   'ed·dad·dem

lovingkindness

שִׁעוּר שְׁמִינִי

E-Type Transliteration Practice

Hebrew to English

Transliterate each row of Hebrew words into English. Read the Hebrew words from right to left, but write the English transliterations from left to right. Pronounce each word out loud when finished. The first word is done for you.

.1   אֱמֶת   אֶרֶץ   צֶדֶק   לֶחֶם   חֶסֶד
ʼe·met

.2   אָלֶף   אֵיכָה   הָאֱמֶת   אַהֲבָה   אָמֵן

.3   בֵּית   בֶּן־אָדָם   גֵת   בָּשָׂר   גֶּבֶר

.4   גֶשֶׁם   דָּגֵשׁ   דֶּלֶת   הֵא   הֶבֶל

.5   הָלְכָה   הַשֵּׁם   זָקֵן   חָבֵר   חֶטֶף

.6   חֵית   חָמֵץ   טֵבֵת   טִית   יֵצֶר

.7   כַּוָּנָה   כֵּס   כַּפָּרָה   כֶּתֶר   לֵבָב

.8   הַמֵאָה   מָגֵן   מֶלֶךְ   נֶגֶב   סֵפֶר

Lesson Eight Summary

In this lesson you learned the main E-type vowels:

Simple Vowels

Vowel Mark	Vowel Name	Sound	Hebrew	Trans.	Class
אֵ	Tsere	"e" as in they	צֵרִי	e	Long
אֶ	Segol	"e" as in they	סֶגּוֹל	e	Short
אֱ	Chateph Segol	"e" as in they	חָטֵף סֶגּוֹל	e	Reduced

Full Vowel (Variants)

The following vowels are variations on the simple vowels shown above:

אֵי	Tsere Yod	"ei" as in **eight**	צֵרִי יוֹד	ei	Long
אֶי	Segol Yod	"ey" as in obey	סֶגּוֹל יוֹד	ey	Long

Notes:

- Although these vowel marks look different, they all represent an "e" **sound**, and we will transliterate the vowel marks using an "e" in English.
- Note which vowels are **long** (Tsere, all the full vowels), and which are **short** (Segol, Chateph Segol).
- At the **end of a word**, both Tsere may have a Hey immediately following it (the Hey then functions not as a consonant, but as a vowel letter).
- The Chateph Segol is sometimes called a "half vowel" and is the shortest of all vowels: it can *only* appear under the **guttural letters**: א, ה, ע, ח.

Quick Summary:

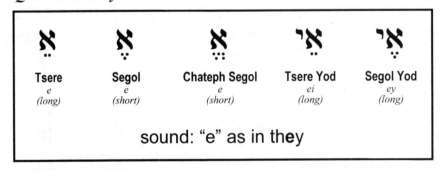

Lesson Eight Quiz

1. Write the Vowel Marks

Write the mark, its sound, and its transliteration in the columns next to its name.

Name	Mark	Sound	Transliteration
Tsere			
Segol			
Chateph Segol			
Tsere Yod			
Segol Yod			

2. Write the Vowel Names

Write the name for the vowel in the column next to its mark.

Mark	Name	Sound	Transliteration
אֵ			
אֶ			
אֱ			
אֵי			
אֶי			

3. Identify the Vowel Class

For each vowel, indicate if it is long or short (reduced vowels are considered short):

Mark	Name	Sound	Class
אֵ			
אֶ			
אֱ			
אֵי			
אֶי			

4. **Completely fill in the vowel table you have studied this lesson:**

E-Type:

Mark	Name	Sound	Hebrew	Trans.	Class
אֶ					
אֱ					
אֵ					
אֵי					
אֶי					

5. **Transliterate the following Hebrew words**

Remember there is one syllable per Hebrew vowel. The first word is done for you.

Word		Transliteration	Word		Transliteration
אֶרֶץ	(earth)	'e·rets	שֵׁם	(name)	
לֶחֶם	(bread)		אֵל	(God)	
שֶׁמֶשׁ	(sun)		לֵב	(heart)	
אֱמֶת	(truth)		בֵּין	(between)	

6. **Review the A-Type Vowels**

Complete the following table for the A-Type vowels you learned in Lesson Seven. For extra credit, try writing the Hebrew name for the vowel:

A-Type:

Mark	Name	Sound	Hebrew	Trans.	Class
אָ					
אַ					
אֲ					
אָה					

7. **Completely fill in the Vowel Table:**

Complete the following table. Note that the table includes both the "A-Type" and "E-Type" vowels. For extra credit, try writing the Hebrew name for the vowel:

Vowel Table:

Mark	Name	Sound	Hebrew	Trans.	Class
אָ					
אַ					
אֲ					
אָה					
אֵ					
אֶ					
אֱ					
אֵי					
אֶי					

אֵל אֱמֶת

G o d   o f   T r u t h

אֵל אֱמֶת

Quick Vowel Review

Here is a list of the Hebrew vowels you have studied so far. You may want to make flash cards for the new vowels you have learned.

A-Type:

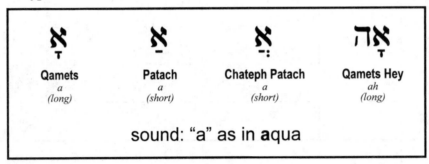

Qamets	Patch	Chateph Patach	Qamets Hey
a	*a*	*a*	*ah*
(long)	*(short)*	*(short)*	*(long)*

sound: "a" as in **a**qua

E-Type:

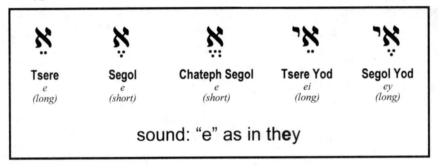

Tsere	Segol	Chateph Segol	Tsere Yod	Segol Yod
e	*e*	*e*	*ei*	*ey*
(long)	*(short)*	*(short)*	*(long)*	*(long)*

sound: "e" as in th**ey**

Lesson Nine

I-TYPE VOWELS

שִׁעוּר תְּשִׁיעִי

Lesson Introduction

In this lesson you will learn additional Hebrew vowels. In particular, you will learn:

- ✓ The vowel marks for the "I-type" vowels
- ✓ How to write the vowel marks with Hebrew letters
- ✓ How to pronounce Hebrew letters and words with vowel marks
- ✓ How to accurately transliterate the vowel sounds
- ✓ How to read Hebrew words using the vowel marks
- ✓ The names of the Hebrew vowels
- ✓ The classification for the vowels (long or short)

Lesson at a glance

After you have studied this lesson, the following information should be clear:

Basic Vowel

The basic vowel mark you will learn is as follows:

Vowel Mark	Vowel Name	Sound	Hebrew	Trans.	Class
אִ	Chireq	"i" as in machine	חִירֶק	i	Short

Full Vowel (Variant)

The following vowel is a variation on the simple vowel shown above:

אִי	Chireq Yod	"i" as in machine	חִירֶק יוֹד	i	Long

I-Type Vowels

The next vowel group you will learn is called the "I-type" because it indicates a **"ee"** sound (as in "machine" or "siesta") when combined with a letter. The following table shows the main I-type vowels:

Vowel Mark	Vowel Name	Sound	Hebrew	Trans.	Class
X	Chireq	"i" as in machine	חִירֶק	i	Short
יX	Chireq Yod	"i" as in machine	חִירֶק יוֹד	i	Long

Notes:

- Although these vowel marks look different, they both represent an **"ee" sound**. To simplify matters, we will transliterate both vowels using an "i" in English.
- Note which vowel is **short** (Chiriq) and which is **long** (Chiriq Yod).

"Simple" and "Full" Hebrew Vowels

The Chireq is a simple vowel and the Chireq Yod is a "mixed" or "full" vowel.

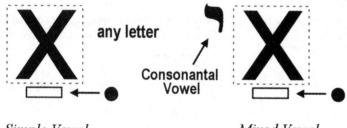

Simple Vowel   *Mixed Vowel*

Note that the "**X**" refers to any Hebrew letter (for example **א, ב, ג**, and so on) and the rectangular box below the letter refers to a vowel mark location. When the Yod follows a letter with a Chireq, it functions not as a consonant, but as a vowel letter. This is called a "consonantal vowel" and the result is called a "mixed" or "full" vowel.

Sounding Out the Vowels

To sound out the vowel, *first* pronounce the letter sound and *then* add the vowel sound. Thus you would read **בּ** as "bi" (*not* "ib").

1.

דִי	דִ	גִי	גִ	בִּי	בִּ	אִי	אִ
di	di	gi	gi	bi	bi	'i	'i

I-Type Syllables

Both of these syllables end with an "**ee**" sound, so they are "open syllables":

The following syllables are called "open" because they do not end with a "stopping" sound. Read each syllable aloud:

דִי	דְּ	גִי	גְּ	בִּי	בְּ	אִי	אְ	1.
di	di	gi	gi	bi	bi	'i	'i	
חִי	חְ	זִי	זְ	וִי	וְ	הִי	הְ	2.
chi	chi	zi	zi	vi	vi	hi	hi	
לִי	לְ	כִּי	כְּ	יִי	יְ	טִי	טְ	3.
li	li	ki	ki	yi	yi	ti	ti	
עִי	עְ	סִי	סְ	נִי	נְ	מִי	מְ	4.
'i	'i	si	si	ni	ni	mi	mi	
רִי	רְ	קִי	קְ	צִי	צְ	פִּי	פְּ	5.
ri	ri	qi	qi	tsi	tsi	pi	pi	
		תִי	תְּ	שִׁי	שְׁ	6.		
		ti	ti	shi	shi			

"Closed" Syllable Sounds

A syllable is called "closed" when it ends with a "stopping" sound:

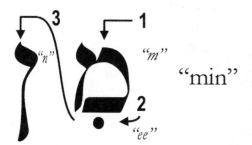

"min"

This syllable ends with a stopping "n" sound (i.e., Nun Sofit), so it is a "closed syllable." Remember that the "i" transliteration stands for an "ee" sound, so pronounce this as "meen."

The following syllables are called "closed" because they end with a "stopping" sound. Read each syllable aloud.

רֵם	בִּיל	כַּז	קַס	צִית	אֶשׁ	מִין	מָן	**1.**
rim	bil	kiz	qis	tsit	'ish	min	min	

שֶׁל	צִיץ	צֵים	יֵץ	סִיס	שִׁין	מִיד	פִּד	**2.**
shil	tsits	tsim	yits	sis	shin	mid	pid	

גֵּר	רֵשׁ	תִּף	הֶם	מַךְ	וֶשׁ	עֵם	בִּס	**3.**
gir	rish	tif	him	mikh	vish	'im	bis	

Wisdom

The Scriptures refer to wisdom as "a tree of life" (*'etz chayim*) to all who lay hold of it, and promises happiness to all who retain it (Prov. 3:18).

'Etz chayim is also the name for one of the two wooden shafts attached to the ends of a Torah scroll. Each shaft extends beyond the top and bottom of the scroll and is used both as a handle to hold the Sefer Torah and as a means to scroll from portion to portion when reading.

I-Type Writing Practice

Practice: Write the Hebrew Sounds

Write the Hebrew vowel marks for each letter of the Aleph-Bet. Use both possibilities for the "I-Type" vowels you have studied (for example, Aleph can take a Chiriq and a Chiriq Yod, so there are two possibilities). Use cursive for your answers.

1.

| hi | hi | di | di | gi | gi | bi | bi | 'i | 'i |

2.

| yi | yi | ti | ti | chi | chi | zi | zi | vi | vi |

3.

| si | si | ni | ni | mi | mi | li | li | ki | ki |

4.

| ri | ri | qi | qi | tsi | tsi | pi | pi | 'i | 'i |

5.

| ti | ti | shi | shi |

Did you know?

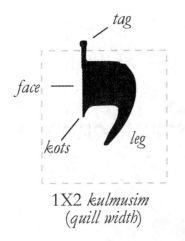

tag

face

kots *leg*

1X2 *kulmusim*
(*quill width*)

Although some Jews think that the square Hebrew script used in Torah scrolls was actually used when Moses received the Ten Commandments, it is most likely that Ezra the Scribe instituted using the Aramaic script for the Scriptures sometime around 450 B.C. This script has come to be known as *Ketav Ashuri* (or *Ketav Meruba*, square script).

Evidence of earlier forms of Hebrew (sometimes called *paleo-Hebrew*) can be seen in portions of the Dead Sea Scrolls and in other early inscriptions. The Samaritan Torah also uses an earlier form of Hebrew script—and Ezra the Scribe might have wanted to distance the returning Jewish community from the Samaritan transplants by using the Aramaic alphabet for the Hebrew scriptures (*see* Nehemiah 8:8).

It should be noted, however, that an article of orthodox Jewish faith is that God originally revealed the Torah to Moses using Ketav Ashurit, not ketav Ivri, since the earlier script was considered profane and riddled with paganism. After Moses broke the first set of tablets, however, God wrote the second set using the profane script.

I-Type Reading Practice

One syllable:

רִיב	אִישׁ	פִּי	אִם	מִן	מִי	לִי	כִּי	1.
riv	'ish	fi	'im	min	mi	li	ki	

הֵא	עִיר	בִּב	פִּד	קִת	אִד	זִר	עִם	2.
hi	'ir	viv	pid	kit	'id	zir	'im	

Two syllables:

וִיהִי	בָּתִי	עִמִּי	שִׁשִׁי	לִבִּי	אִמִּי	אִתִּי	3.
vi·hi	bi·ti	'i·mi	shi·shi	lib·bi	'i·mi	'it·ti	

תִּקַּח	מִגֵּן	נִסִּי	קִצִּי	מִמִּי	חִכִּי	מִבִּן	4.
ti·qach	mi·gan	ni·si	ki·tsi	mi·mi	chik·ki	mib·bin	

הִנֵּה	יִרֶב	תִּתֵּן	שִׁלַח	יִחַד	כִּכַּר	מִיַּד	5.
hi·neh	yi·rev	ti·ten	shi·lach	yi·chad	kik·kar	mi·yad	

מִכֶּם	מִזֶּה	פִּיהָ	מִקֵּץ	מִשָּׁם	עִמָּהּ	אִשָּׁה	6.
mi·khem	mi·zeh	pi·ha	mi·qets	mi·sham	'i·mah	'i·shah	

Three or more syllables:

צִוִּיתִי	חֲמִשָּׁה	אֵימְנָה	וַיִּצֶר	וַיִּפַּח	וַיִּתֵּן	7.
tsi·vi·ti	cha·mi·shah	'ei·mi·nah	va·yi·tser	va·yip·pach	va·yi·ten	

חֲבֵאתִיהָ	מִמְּרֶם	מֵרֵאשִׁית	יִלָבֵת	מִמָּוֶת	רִמִּתִי	8.
cha·ve·ti·ha	mi·me·rem	me·re'·shit	yi·la·vet	mi·ma·vet	ri·mi·ti	

Adonai Nissi

The LORD is my banner

I-Type Transliteration Practice

Hebrew to English

Transliterate each row of Hebrew words into English. Read the Hebrew words from right to left, but write the English transliterations from left to right. Pronounce each word out loud when finished. The first word is done for you.

אִיר	אַחִים	שְׁנִי	אִגֶּרֶת	אָבִיב	.1
				'a·viv	
גָּלִיל	בִּינָה	בָּתִּים	אֲנִי	אִמָּה	.2
חֶדֶר	חָבִיד	הִנֵּה	הַלֵּל	דִּין	.3
כִּפָּה	כִּסֵּא	יָחִיד	טַלִּית	חָסִיד	.4
נָגִיד	נָבִיא	חַיִל	דָּוִד	מַגִּיד	.5
סֵדֶר	נֶפֶשׁ	נָפִיל	נִסִּים	נִיסָן	.6
סִיוָן	עַיִן	עֲזָאזֵל	עֲדִים	עֲבֵרָה	.7
רֵאשִׁית	פָּנִים	צָדִי	צִיצִית	קָרָאִי	.8

Lesson Nine Summary

In this lesson you learned the main I-type vowels:

Simple Vowel

Vowel Mark	Vowel Name	Sound	Hebrew	Trans.	Class
אִ	Chireq	"ee" as in green	חִירֶק	i	Short

Full Vowel (Variant)

The following vowel is a variation on the simple vowel shown above:

אִי	Chireq Yod	"ee" as in green	חִירֶק יוֹד	i	Long

Notes:

- Although these vowel marks look different, they all represent an "ee" **sound**.
- Note which vowel is **long** (Chireq Yod) and which is **short** (Chireq).

Quick Summary:

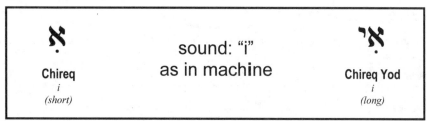

אִ	sound: "i" as in machine	**אִי**
Chireq *i* *(short)*		**Chireq Yod** *i* *(long)*

Lesson Nine Quiz

1. Write the Vowel Marks

In this lesson you learned two vowel marks. Write the mark, its sound, and its transliteration in the columns next to its name.

Name	Mark	Sound	Transliteration
Chireq			
Chireq Yod			

2. Write the Vowel Names

Write the name for the vowel in the column next to its mark.

Mark	Name	Sound	Transliteration
אִ			
אִי			

3. Identify the Vowel Class

For each vowel, indicate if it is long or short in the column next to the vowel mark:

Mark	Name	Sound	Class
אִי			
אִ			

4. Completely fill in the vowel table you have studied this lesson:

I-Type:

Mark	Name	Sound	Hebrew	Trans.	Class
אִ					
אִי					

5. **Transliterate the following Hebrew words**

Remember there is one syllable per Hebrew vowel. The first word is done for you.

Word		Transliteration	Word		Transliteration
אֲנִי	(I)	'a·ni	הִיא	(she)	
נִסִּי	(my banner)		עִיר	(city)	
חִטָּה	(wheat)		דָּוִד	(David)	
הִשָּׁמֶר	(you watch)		שִׁיר	(song)	

6. **Review the A-Type Vowels**

Complete the following table for the A-Type vowels you learned in Lesson Seven. For extra credit, try writing the Hebrew name for the vowel:

A-Type:

Mark	Name	Sound	Hebrew	Trans.	Class
אָ					
אַ					
אֲ					
אָה					

7. **Review the E-Type Vowels**

Complete the following table for the E-Type vowels you learned in Lesson Eight.

E-Type:

Mark	Name	Sound	Hebrew	Trans.	Class
אֵ					
אֶ					
אֱ					
אֵי					
אֶי					

8. **Completely fill in the vowel table:**

Note that the table includes the "A-Type," the "E-Type," and the "I-Type vowels."
For extra credit, try writing the Hebrew name for the vowel:

Vowel Table:

Mark	Name	Sound	Hebrew	Trans.	Class
אָ					
אַ					
אֲ					
אָה					
אֵ					
אֶ					
אֱ					
אֵי					
אֶי					
אִ					
אִי					

Adonai Nissi

The LORD *is my banner*

Quick Vowel Review

Here is a list of the Hebrew vowels you have studied so far. You may want to make flash cards for the new vowels you have learned.

A-Type:

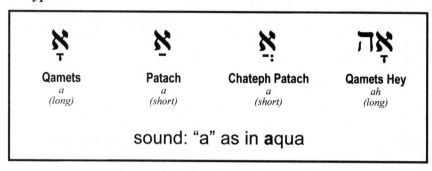

E-Type:

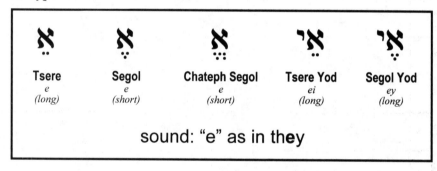

I-Type:

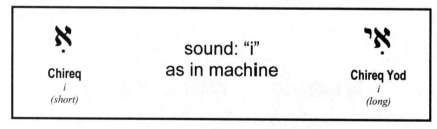

Lesson Ten

O - T Y P E   V O W E L S

שָׁעוּר עֲשִׂירִי

Lesson Introduction

In this lesson you will learn additional Hebrew vowels. In particular, you will learn:

- ✓ The vowel marks for the "O-type" vowels
- ✓ How to write the vowel marks with Hebrew letters
- ✓ How to pronounce Hebrew letters and words with vowel marks
- ✓ How to accurately transliterate the vowel sounds
- ✓ How to read Hebrew words using the vowel marks
- ✓ The names of the Hebrew vowels
- ✓ The classification for the vowels (long or short)

Lesson at a glance

After you have studied this lesson, the following information should be clear:

Basic Vowels

The basic vowel marks you will learn are as follows:

Vowel Mark	Vowel Name	Sound	Hebrew	Trans.	Class
אֹ	Cholem	"o" as in yellow	חוֹלֶם	o	Long
אֳ	Chateph Qamets	"o" as in yellow	חֲטֶף קָמֶץ	o	Reduced

Full Vowel (Variant)

The following vowel is a variation of the Cholem vowel:

אוֹ	Cholem Vav	"o" as in yellow	חוֹלֶם וָו	o	Long

Advanced Information

An "advanced" vowel mark of the O-Class is as follows (this is *not* Qamets):

אָ	Qamets Chatuph	"o" as in yellow	קָמֶץ חָטוּף	o	Short

O-Type Vowels

The next vowel group you will learn is sometimes called the "O-type" because it indicates an "**oh**" sound (as in "r**o**ll" or "yell**ow**") when combined with a letter. The following table shows the most common O-type vowels:

Vowel Mark	Vowel Name	Sound	Hebrew	Trans.	Class
אֹ	Cholem	"o" as in yell**ow**	חוֹלֶם	o	Long
אֳ	Chateph Qamets	"o" as in yell**ow**	חָטֵף קָמֶץ	o	Reduced
אוֹ	Cholem Vav	"o" as in yell**ow**	חוֹלֶם וָו	o	Long

Notes:

- Although these vowel marks look different, they all represent an "oh" **sound**. To simplify matters, we will transliterate these vowels using an "o" in English.

- Note that Cholem and Cholem Vav are **long**; Chateph Qamets is short (reduced).

- By far the **most common** of these vowels is Cholem and Cholem Vav.

"Simple" and "Mixed" Hebrew Vowels

Cholem and Chateph Qamets are simple vowels and the Cholem Vav is a "mixed" vowel:

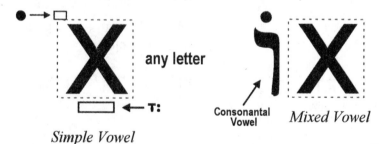

Simple Vowel   *Mixed Vowel*

Note that the "**X**" refers to any Hebrew letter (for example א, ב, ג, and so on) and the rectangular boxes below and to the upper left of the letter refer to a possible vowel mark location. When a Vav (with a **dot on top**) follows a letter, it does not function as a consonant but as a vowel. This is called a "consonantal vowel" and the result is called a "mixed" or "full" vowel.

Sounding Out the Vowels

To sound out the vowel, *first* pronounce the letter sound and *then* add the vowel sound. Thus you would read בוֹ as "bo" (not "ob").

דוֹ	דֹ	גוֹ	גֹ	בוֹ	בֹ	אֳ	אוֹ	אֹ	1.
do	do	go	go	bo	bo	'o	'o	'o	

O-Type Syllables

"Open" Syllable Sounds

A syllable is called "open" when it does not end with a "stopping" sound. Both of these syllables end with an "o" sound, so they are "open syllables":

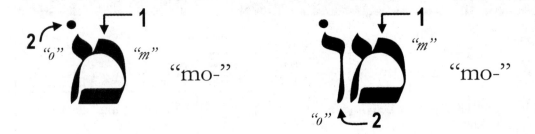

The following syllables are called "open" because they do not end with a "stopping" sound. Read each syllable aloud.

דֹ	גוֹ	גֹ	בוֹ	בֹ	אָֽ	אוֹ	אֹ	1.
do	go	go	bo	bo	'o	'o	'o	
זוֹ	זֹ	ווֹ	וֹ	הָֽ	הוֹ	הֹ	דוֹ	2.
zo	zo	vo	vo (*)	ho	ho	ho	do	
כֹ	יוֹ	יֹ	טוֹ	טֹ	חָֽ	חוֹ	חֹ	3.
ko	yo	yo	to	to	cho	cho	cho	
סֹ	נוֹ	נֹ	מוֹ	מֹ	לוֹ	לֹ	כוֹ	4.
so	no	no	mo	mo	lo	lo	ko	
צוֹ	צֹ	פוֹ	פֹ	עָֽ	עוֹ	עֹ	סוֹ	5.
tso	tso	po	po	'o	'o	'o	so	
תוֹ	תֹ	שוֹ	שֹ	רוֹ	רֹ	קוֹ	קֹ	6.
to	to	sho	sho	ro	ro	qo	qo	

"Closed" Syllable Sounds

A syllable is called "closed" when it ends with a "stopping" sound:

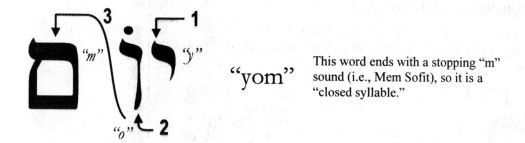

"yom"

This word ends with a stopping "m" sound (i.e., Mem Sofit), so it is a "closed syllable."

The following syllables are called "closed" because they end with a "stopping" sound. Read each syllable aloud.

1.

תֵּל	בּוֹל	יוֹד	יוֹם	עֹם	טוֹב	כֹּל	אוֹר
tol	bol	yod	yom	'om	tov	kol	'or

2.

זֹאת	לֹק	מֹץ	תּוֹכ	עֹד	תּוֹף	צֹן	רֹאשׁ
zot	loq	mots	tokh	'od	tof	tson	rosh

Note:

- The examples (זֹאת) and (רֹאשׁ) show a **"quiescent Aleph"** (i.e., the Aleph is "quiet" and not pronounced).

I am the light of the world.

אָנֹכִי אוֹר הָעוֹלָם

O-Type Writing Practice

Practice: Write the Hebrew Sounds

Write the Hebrew vowel marks for each letter of the alphabet. Use all the possibilities for the "O-Type" vowels you have studied (for example, Aleph can take a Cholem, a Cholem Vav, and a Chateph Qamets, so there are three possibilities). Use cursive for your answers.

												1.
	ho	do	do	go	go	bo	bo	'o	'o	'o		

											2.
to	cho	cho	cho	zo	zo	vo	vo	ho	ho		

											3.
no	mo	mo	lo	lo	ko	ko	yo	yo	to		

											4.
tso	tso	po	po	'o	'o	'o	so	so	no		

											5.
		to	to	sho	sho	ro	ro	qo	qo		

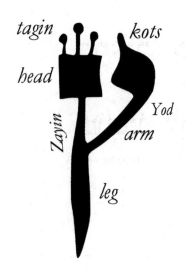

tagin ... *kots*
head
Zayin ... *Yod*
arm
leg

Did you know?

Many Hebrew scribal letters are actually composed of other Hebrew letters (e.g., the Tsade Sofit (shown left) is composed of a Yod and a Zayin), and the letter's proportions are defined in terms of a *kulmus*, or the width of the tip of the kosher quill.

A specific nomenclature has developed within the scribal traditions that name certain distinct parts of the Hebrew letters. For example, a *qots* is a small stick or point sticking out of the letter; a *tag* (plural *tagin*) is a single short line ascending from a letter's head (which usually has a "crown" at the top), and so on. There are also different schools of thought regarding letter formation: Bet Yosef (Ashkenaz), Bet Ari (Chassidic), and Sefardi (Veilish) are the major scribal traditions extant today.

O-Type Reading Practice

One syllable:

צֹאן	זֹאת	רֹאשׁ	עֹד	פֹּה	לֹא	כֹּל	בֹּא	1.
tson	zot	rosh	od	poh	lo'	kol	bo'	

אוֹת	שׁוֹב	קוֹל	מוֹת	עוֹף	יוֹם	טוֹב	אוֹר	2.
'ot	shov	kol	mot	'of	yom	tov	'or	

Two syllables:

כֹּחוֹ	קֹלוֹ	מוֹרָה	אוֹתָם	אִמּוֹ	יָדוֹ	שָׁלוֹם		3.
ko·cho	qo·lo	mo·rah	'o·tam	'i·mo	ya·do	sha·lom		

יוֹצֵר	לָמוֹ	יוֹשֵׁב	יִבּוֹל	הֲלוֹא	אוֹיֵב	דֹּדוֹ	4.
yo·tser	la·mo	yo·shev	yib·bol	ha·lo'	'o·yev	do·do	

סוֹדוֹ	עוֹרוֹ	שֹׂכוֹ	יוֹמוֹ	אוֹתוֹ	מוֹתוֹ	קוֹלִי	5.
so·do	'o·ro	so·kho	yo·mo	'o·to	mo·to	ko·li	

דֹּדִים	רֹאשִׁי	רוֹמֵשׂ	אֲנִי	חֵרֶם	חֳלִי	עֳנִי	6.
do·dim	ro·shi	ro·mes	'o·ni	cho·rem	cho·li	'o·ni	

Three syllables:

קוֹמָתוֹ	בַּהֲמוֹת	הַסּוֹבֵב	חָרְבוֹת	עֲמָלוֹ	הַמָּאוֹר	7.
qo·ma·to	ba·ha·mot	ho·so·vev	cho·ra·vot	'a·ma·lo	ham·ma·or	

הַקּוֹלֹת	מוֹצָאוֹ	תּוֹדֶךָ	אוֹדֶךָ	לַעֲשׂוֹת	מוֹשָׁבוֹ	8.
ha·qo·lot	mo·tsa·'o	to·de·kha	'o·de·kha	la·'a·sot	mo·sha·vo	

shalom

O-Type Transliteration Practice

Hebrew to English

Transliterate each row of Hebrew words into English. Read the Hebrew words from right to left, but write the English transliterations from left to right. Pronounce each word out loud when finished. The first word is done for you.

אַהֲרֹן	אֹהֶל	אָדוֹן	יַעֲקֹב	אָבוֹת	.1
				ʼa·vot	
הוֶה	בִּימָה	הַטוֹב	בָּנוֹת	אָנֹכִי	.2
עוֹלָם	חֹל	חָזוֹן	חוֹטֵא	זֹהַר	.3
כֹּל	יוֹסֵף	אָנָה	יוֹדִים	יוֹאֵל	.4
סוֹפִית	מַעֲרִיב	מִלִּים	מוֹסָד	מוֹהֵל	.5
צִידוֹן	תּוֹכָחָה	עָמוֹס	עוֹזֵר	סָמֶם	.6
קוֹף	קוֹלֵל	קֹהֶלֶת	צָמִית	צוֹם	.7
תּוֹדָה	שׁוֹפָר	שׁוֹמֵר	רִאשׁוֹן	קוֹץ	.8

Lesson Ten Summary

In this lesson you learned the main O-type vowels:

Simple Vowels

Vowel Mark	Vowel Name	Sound	Hebrew	Trans.	Class
אֹ	Cholem	"o" as in yell**o**w	חוֹלֶם	o	Long
אֳ	Chateph Qamets	"o" as in yell**o**w	חֲטָף קָמֶץ	o	Reduced

Full Vowel (Variant)

The following vowel is a variation of the Cholem vowel:

אוֹ	Cholem Vav	"o" as in yell**o**w	חוֹלֶם וָו	o	Long

Notes:

- Although these vowel marks look different, they all represent an **"oh" sound**. We will transliterate each of these with the English letter "o."
- The dot of the Cholem after a Shin (i.e., שׁ) can look like the left-sided dot of the Sin; and the dot of the Cholem after a Sin (i.e., שׂ) may overlap with the Sin's dot.
- By far the most common of these vowels is Cholem and Cholem Vav (i.e., Chateph Qamets appears only under the guttural letters).

Quick Summary:

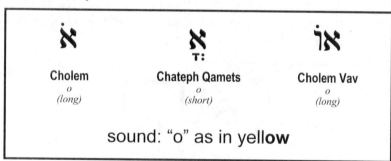

Cholem	Chateph Qamets	Cholem Vav
o	*o*	*o*
(long)	*(short)*	*(long)*

sound: "o" as in yell**o**w

Advanced Information: Qamets Chatuph

One vowel that might cause some trouble is the "Qamets Chatuph," an O-Type vowel that looks identical to the regular A-Type Qamets vowel:

Vowel Mark	Vowel Name	Sound	Hebrew	Trans.	Class
X̣	Qamets Chatuph	"o" as in yellow	קָמֶץ חָטוּף	o	Short

Note:

- Qamets Chatuph appears 630 times in the *Tanakh* (Hebrew Bible) and occurs only in closed, unaccented syllables (e.g., כָּל). We will study accents later.

Qamets or Qamets Chatuph?

When you see a *Qamets*, you must ask 1) is it in a closed syllable? (i.e., a syllable that ends in a stopping sound) *and* 2) is the syllable *un*accented? (most Hebrew words are accented on the last syllable). If *both* conditions are met, the Qamets is *Chatuph* and should be pronounced as an "o" sound. For example:

va·**ya**·qom

In the example above, the last syllable is closed (it ends in Mem) and is *un*accented, and thus the vowel is Qamets *Chatuph*: *qom*.

Generally speaking, whenever you see the Qamets vowel mark you should assume that it is pronounced "ah." In ambiguous cases, sometimes a small vertical mark (called a *Meteg* mark) appears just to the left of the Qamets to indicate that it is an open syllable and should be pronounced "ah" and *not* "o":

Meteg

ve·ra·chats·ta

Note:

- In order to avoid confusion, some modern printers display Qamets Chatuph with a somewhat elongated "stem" (𐤒).
- Do not be overly concerned about this information: you will learn more about accents and Qamets Chatuph later in this book.

Lesson Ten Complete Summary

Simple Vowels

Vowel Mark	Vowel Name	Sound	Hebrew	Trans.	Class
אֹ	Cholem	"o" as in yellow	חֹלֶם	o	Long
אֳ	Chateph Qamets	"o" as in yellow	חֲטֶף קָמֶץ	o	Reduced

Full Vowel (Variant)

The following vowel is a variation of the Cholem vowel:

אוֹ	Cholem Vav	"o" as in yellow	חֹלֶם וָו	o	Long

Qamets Chatuph

An "advanced" vowel mark of the O-Class is as follows:

אָ	Qamets Chatuph	"o" as in yellow	קָמֶץ חָטוּף	o	Short

Notes:

- Although these vowel marks look different, they all represent an "oh" **sound**. We transliterate each of these vowels using the English letter "o."

- By far the most common of these vowels is Cholem and Cholem Vav.

- Qamets Chatuph occurs *only* in closed, unaccented syllables (e.g., כָּל).

- A **Meteg** is a small vertical line that is sometimes placed to the left of a Qamets to indicate that the syllable is open (and therefore should be pronounced "ah").

Quick Summary:

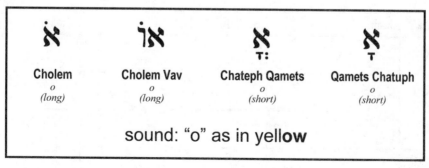

Cholem	Cholem Vav	Chateph Qamets	Qamets Chatuph
o	*o*	*o*	*o*
(long)	*(long)*	*(short)*	*(short)*

sound: "o" as in yellow

Lesson Ten Quiz

1. Write the Vowel Marks

In this lesson you learned four new vowel marks. Write the mark, its sound, and its transliteration in the columns next to its name.

Name	Mark	Sound	Transliteration
Cholem			
Cholem Vav			
Chateph Qamets			
Qamets Chatuph			

2. Write the Vowel Names

Write the name for the vowel in the column next to its mark.

Mark	Name	Sound	Transliteration
אֹ			
אוֹ			
אָ֖			
אָ			

3. Identify the Vowel Class

For each vowel, indicate if it is long or short in the column next to the vowel mark (reduced vowels are considered short):

Mark	Name	Sound	Class
אֹ			
אָ֖			
אָ			
אוֹ			

4. **Completely fill in the vowel table you have studied:**

Complete the following table. For extra credit, try writing the Hebrew name for each "O-Type" vowel:

O-Type:

Mark	Name	Sound	Hebrew	Trans.	Class
אֹ					
אָ					
אָ					
אוֹ					

5. **Transliterate the following Hebrew words**

Remember there is one syllable per Hebrew vowel. The first word is done for you.

Word		Transliteration	Word		Transliteration
שָׁלוֹם	(peace)	sha·lom	אוֹת	(sign)	
כָּל	(all)		אוֹר	(light)	
לֹא	(no)		אֳנִי	(ship)	
רֹאשׁ	(head)		אֳהֳלֹה	(his tent)	

6. **Review the A-Type Vowels**

Complete the following table for the A-Type vowels you learned in Lesson Seven. For extra credit, try writing the Hebrew name for the vowel:

A-Type:

Mark	Name	Sound	Hebrew	Trans.	Class
אָ					
אַ					
אֲ					
אָה					

7. Review the E-Type Vowels

Complete the following table for the E-Type *vowels you learned in Lesson Eight.*

E-Type:

Mark	Name	Sound	Hebrew	Trans.	Class
אֵ					
אֶ					
אֱ					
אֵי					
אֶי					

8. Review the I-Type Vowels

Complete the following table for the I-Type *vowels you learned in Lesson Nine.*

I-Type:

Mark	Name	Sound	Hebrew	Trans.	Class
אִ					
אִי					

9. True or False

Circle the correct answer:

1. Chateph Qamets can only appear under guttural letters.

    True
    False

2. Qamets Chatuph only can appear in closed, unaccented syllables.

    True
    False

3. There is one Hebrew vowel per syllable in a word.

    True
    False

10. Completely fill in the vowel table:

Note that the table includes the "A-Type," "E-Type," "I-Type vowels," and the "O-Type" vowels. For extra credit, try writing the Hebrew name for the vowel:

Vowel Table:

Mark	Name	Sound	Hebrew	Trans.	Class
אָ					
אַ					
אֲ					
אָה					
אֵ					
אֶ					
אֱ					
אֵי					
אֶי					
אִ					
אִי					
אֻ					
אָֽ					
אָ					
אוֹ					

Quick Vowel Review

Here is a list of the Hebrew vowels you have studied so far. You may want to make flash cards using this summary as a guide (write a vowel mark on one side of a card and its sound, transliteration, and class on the other side).

A-Type:

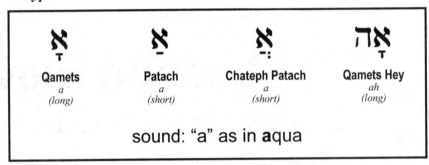

Qamets	Patach	Chateph Patach	Qamets Hey
a	*a*	*a*	*ah*
(long)	*(short)*	*(short)*	*(long)*

sound: "a" as in **a**qua

E-Type:

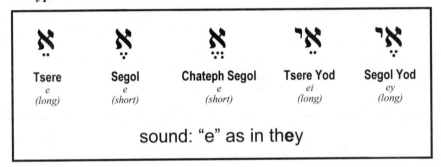

Tsere	Segol	Chateph Segol	Tsere Yod	Segol Yod
e	*e*	*e*	*ei*	*ey*
(long)	*(short)*	*(short)*	*(long)*	*(long)*

sound: "e" as in th**ey**

I-Type:

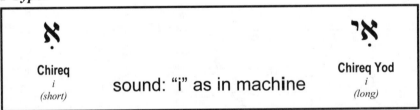

Chireq		Chireq Yod
i	sound: "i" as in mach**i**ne	*i*
(short)		*(long)*

O-Type:

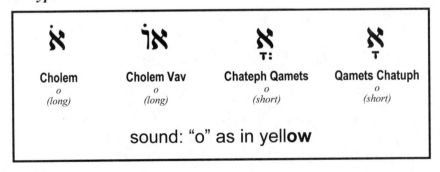

Cholem	Cholem Vav	Chateph Qamets	Qamets Chatuph
o	*o*	*o*	*o*
(long)	*(long)*	*(short)*	*(short)*

sound: "o" as in yell**ow**

Lesson Eleven

U-TYPE VOWELS AND REVIEW

Lesson Introduction

In this lesson you will learn additional Hebrew vowels. In particular, you will learn:

✓ The vowel marks for the "U-type" vowels

✓ How to write the vowel marks with Hebrew letters

✓ How to pronounce Hebrew letters and words with vowel marks

✓ How to accurately transliterate the vowel sounds

✓ How to read Hebrew words using the vowel marks

✓ The names of the Hebrew vowels

✓ The classification for the vowels (long or short)

✓ Review all of the Hebrew vowel marks you have studied so far

Lesson at a glance

After you have studied this lesson, the following information should be clear:

Basic Vowel

The basic vowel mark you will learn is as follows:

Vowel Mark	Vowel Name	Sound	Hebrew	Trans.	Class
אֻ	Qibbuts	"u" as in blue	קִבּוּץ	u	Short

Full Vowel (Variant)

The following vowel is a variation on the simple vowel shown above:

אוּ	Shureq	"u" as in blue	שׁוּרֶק	u	Long

U-Type Vowels

The last vowel group you will learn is sometimes called the "U-type" because it indicates an **"oo"** sound (as in "bl**ue**" or "cl**ue**") when combined with a letter. The following table shows the main U-type vowels:

Vowel Mark	Vowel Name	Sound	Hebrew	Trans.	Class
X	Qibbuts	"u" as in bl**ue**	קִבּוּץ	u	Short
X**וּ**	Shureq	"u" as in bl**ue**	שׁוּרֶק	u	Long

Notes:

- Although these vowel marks look different, they both represent an **"oo" sound**. To simplify matters, we transliterate each of these using the English letter "u."
- Note which vowel is **short** (Qibbuts) and which is **long** (Shureq).
- **Unlike** other vowels, Shureq is sometimes used to start a word.

"Simple" and "Mixed" Hebrew Vowels

The Qibbuts is a simple vowel and the Shureq is a "mixed" vowel:

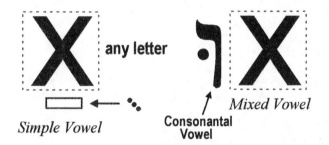

Note that the "**X**" refers to any Hebrew letter (for example א, בּ, ג, and so on) and the rectangular box below the letter refers to a vowel mark location. When a Vav (with a **dot in the middle**) follows a letter, it does not function as a consonant but as a vowel (consonantal vowel) and the result is called a "mixed" or "full" vowel.

Sounding Out the Vowels

To sound out the vowel, *first* pronounce the letter sound (represented by the "**X**") and then add the vowel sound. Thus you would read בּוּ as "bu" (not "ub").

1.   אֻ   אוּ   בֻּ   בּוּ   גֻ   גוּ   רֻ   רוּ

       u   u   bu   bu   gu   gu   du   du

U-Type Syllables

"Open" Syllable Sounds

Since both of these syllables end with an **"oo" sound** (i.e., "u"), they are "open syllables":

The following syllables are called "open" because they do not end with a "stopping" sound. Read each syllable aloud:

דוּ	דְּ	גוּ	גְּ	בוּ	בְּ	אוּ	אֲ	1.
du	du	gu	gu	bu	bu	'u	'u	
חוּ	חֲ	זוּ	זְ	ווּ	וְ	הוּ	הֲ	2.
chu	chu	zu	zu	vu	vu	hu	hu	
לוּ	לְ	כוּ	כְּ	יוּ	יְ	טוּ	טְ	3.
lu	lu	ku	ku	yu	yu	tu	tu	
עוּ	עֲ	סוּ	סְ	נוּ	נְ	מוּ	מְ	4.
'u	'u	su	su	nu	nu	mu	mu	
רוּ	רְ	קוּ	קְ	צוּ	צְ	פוּ	פְּ	5.
ru	ru	qu	qu	tsu	tsu	pu	pu	
		תוּ	תְּ	שׁוּ	שְׁ			6.
		tu	tu	shu	shu			

"Closed" Syllable Sounds

A syllable is called "closed" when it ends with a "stopping" sound:

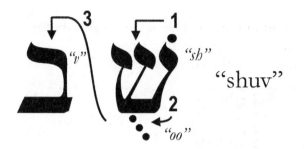

"shuv"

This word ends with a stopping "v" sound, so it is a "closed syllable."

The following syllables are called "closed" because they end with a "stopping" sound. Read each syllable aloud.

מֻשׁ	אוֹר	סוֹס	רוֹם	טוֹד	מוֹם	קֻם	יוֹד	.א
mush	'ur	sus	rum	tud	mum	qum	yud	

הוּא	גֶט	כֻּף	אוּו	צוֹם	נֶץ	יָד	קוֹם	.ב
hu'	gut	kuf	'uv	tsum	nuts	yud	qum	

Note:

- The word הוּא is another example of a **"quiescent Aleph."**

Did you know?

The Jewish prayer book is called a *Siddur* (סִדּוּר), a word that derives from a root that means "to set in order, arrange."

The Siddur arranges prayers and responsive readings according to the order of the Jewish calendar. Many *Siddurim* [pl.] are designed to be used for different festivals of the Jewish year.

The related word *Sidrah* (סִדְרָה) refers to the ordered Torah portion that is to be read every week in synagogues around the world.

Prayer Book

U-Type Writing Practice

Practice: Write the Hebrew Sounds

Write the Hebrew vowel marks for each letter of the alphabet. Use both possibilities for the "U-Type" vowels you have studied (for example, Aleph can take a Qibbuts and a Shureq, so there are two possibilities). Use cursive to write your answers.

1. אֻ

| hu | hu | du | du | gu | gu | bu | bu | u' | u' |

2.

| yu | yu | tu | tu | chu | chu | zu | zu | vu | vu |

3.

| su | su | nu | nu | mu | mu | lu | lu | ku | ku |

4.

| ru | ru | qu | qu | tsu | tsu | pu | pu | 'u | 'u |

5.

| | | | | | | tu | tu | shu | shu |

Did you know?

There are a number of scribal "oddities" in the *Sofer Torah* (Torah Scroll) that a scribe must faithfully reproduce.

For instance, there are extra-large letters, extra-small letters, stretched letters, letters with dots written on top of them, and even a broken letter (i.e., the Vav that appears in the word "shalom" in Numbers 25:12).

The sages have sometimes argued about these textual oddities, with one sage maintaining one thing and another maintaining something else; however it is believed that when Elijah the prophet comes he will resolve the various scribal disagreements that have sprung up and set the text in perfect order (Avot d'Rabbi Natan 30b).

↑ *Enlarged*   *The "Shema" (Deut. 6:4)*   ↑ *Enlarged*

U-Type Reading Practice

One syllable:

זוּ	לוּ	פֻּם	חֻר	שֻׁם	רֻץ	קֻם	שֻׁב	1.
zu	lu	pum	chur	shum	ruts	qum	shuv	

Two syllables:

עֻזוּ	חֻקוֹ	עֻצוּ	נֻכוּ	שֻׁבוּ	עֻלוֹ	כֻּלוֹ	2.
u·zo	chu·qo	ʻu·tsu	nu·ku	shu·vu	u·lo	ku·lo	

עֻזִּי	חֻשָׁם	עֻנּוֹת	יֻלַּד	יֻקַם	לֻקַּח	וּבוֹ	3.
ʻu·zi	chu·sham	ʻu·not	yu·lad	yu·qam	lu·qach	u·vo	

שֻׁבִי	יֻכַל	רֻחִי	הֻחַל	תֻּבַל	וּמִן	כֻּלָּם	4.
shu·vi	yu·khal	ru·chi	hu·chal	tu·val	u·min	ku·lam	

צוּרִים	מֻכִּים	הֻבָאת	שָׁאוּל	יָרוּם	צָרוּף	תֹהוּ	5.
tsu·rim	mu·kim	hu·vat	sha·ʼul	ya·rum	tsa·ruf	to·hu	

Three syllables:

מִמֶּנּוּ	כֻּלָּנוּ	וּשְׁמִי	אֱלֹהִים	יָחִילוּ	וָבֹהוּ	7.
mi·me·nu	ku·la·nu	u·shu·mi	ʼe·lo·him	ya·chi·lu	va·vo·hu	

יָשׁוּבוּ	טָמְנוּ	שָׁאֲלוּ	יֵבֹשׁוּ	עָלֵנוּ	יָקֻמוּ	8.
ya·shu·vu	ta·ma·nu	sha·ʼa·lu	ye·vo·shu	ʻa·**le**·nu	ya·qu·mu	

Four (or more) syllables:

בִּישׁוּעָתֶךָ	וַיַּנִחֵהוּ	נֶאֱלָחוּ	הָאֲדַוִלוּ	אֲדֹנֵינוּ	7.
bi·shu·ʻa·te·kha	va·ya·ni·che·hu	ne·ʼe·la·chu	ha·ʼa·da·vi·lu	ʼa·do·nei·nu	

E l o h i m

U-Type Transliteration Practice

Hebrew to English

Transliterate each row of Hebrew words into English. Read the Hebrew words from right to left, but write the English transliterations from left to right. Pronounce each word out loud when finished. The first word is done for you.

א.   שַׁאֲלוּ   רוּחִי   אֲבֵלוּת   אָבִינוּ   אַדִּירֵנוּ
     sha·'a·lu

ב.   אוּרִים   כֵּאלֹהֵינוּ   אֱלֹהֵינוּ   אֱלוּל   בִּטָּחוֹן

ג.   בָּרוּךְ   בַּת־קוֹל   גֹּלֶם   גִּבּוֹר   גָּלוּת

ד.   דּוּכָן   הַשִּׁילוּשׁ   חוּמָשׁ   חַנּוּן   חֲנֻכִּיָּה

ה.   אִמּוֹת   חֻפָּה   חֻצְפָּה   כָּתוּב   תּוֹרָה

ו.   מַבּוּל   מוּסָף   מוּסָר   רַבֵּנוּ   נוּן

ז.   סוּף   סֻכָּה   סֻכּוֹת   סִלּוּק   עֵדוּת

ח.   עָלֶיהָ   פּוּרִים   פֶּסַח   פָּרוּשׁ   צָדּוּק

Lesson Eleven Summary

In this lesson you learned the main U-Type vowels:

Simple Vowel

Vowel Mark	Vowel Name	Sound	Hebrew	Trans.	Class
אֻ	Qibbuts	"u" as in bl**u**e	קִבּוּץ	u	Short

Full Vowel (Variant)

The following vowel is a variation on the simple vowel shown above:

Vowel Mark	Vowel Name	Sound	Hebrew	Trans.	Class
אוּ	Shureq	"u" as in bl**u**e	שׁוּרֶק	u	Long

Notes:

- Although these vowel marks look different, they both represent an **"oo" sound**. Each of these vowels is transliterated using the English letter "u."
- Note which vowel is **short** (Qibbuts) and which is **long** (Shureq).
- Unlike other vowels, Shureq is sometimes used to start a word (this constitutes the only exception that a Hebrew word cannot begin with a vowel).
- Sometimes Qibbuts is pronounced "Qubbuts."

U-Type Quick Summary:

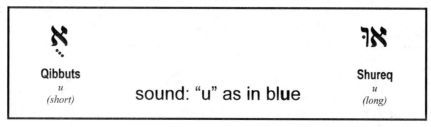

אֻ		אוּ
Qibbuts	sound: "u" as in bl**u**e	**Shureq**
u (short)		*u* (long)

Hebrew Vowels Review

A-Type:

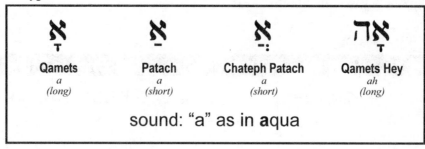

Qamets	**Patach**	**Chateph Patach**	**Qamets Hey**
a	*a*	*a*	*ah*
(long)	*(short)*	*(short)*	*(long)*

sound: "a" as in **a**qua

E-Type:

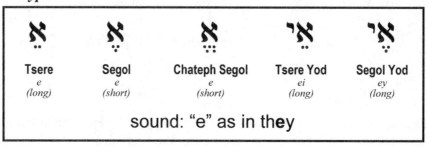

Tsere	**Segol**	**Chateph Segol**	**Tsere Yod**	**Segol Yod**
e	*e*	*e*	*ei*	*ey*
(long)	*(short)*	*(short)*	*(long)*	*(long)*

sound: "e" as in th**ey**

I-Type:

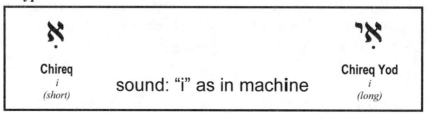

Chireq	**Chireq Yod**
i	*i*
(short)	*(long)*

sound: "i" as in mach**i**ne

O-Type:

Cholem	**Cholem Vav**	**Chateph Qamets**	**Qamets Chatuph**
o	*o*	*o*	*o*
(long)	*(long)*	*(short)*	*(short)*

sound: "o" as in yell**ow**

U-Type:

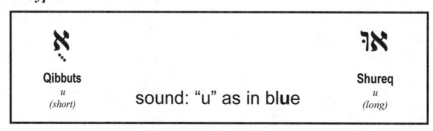

Qibbuts	**Shureq**
u	*u*
(short)	*(long)*

sound: "u" as in bl**u**e

Review Readings

A-Type sounds

1.   בְּ   רַב   שָׁ   שַׁשׁ   מָה   עֲ   עֲנ   אֲנִי

      ba   rav   sha   shash   ma   'a   'an   'a·ni

E-Type sounds

2.   בֵּן   רֵי   שֵׁשׁ   שֶׁ   מֵד   אֶ   חֵת   יֵשׁ

      ben   rey   shesh   she   med   'e   chet   yesh

I-Type sounds

3.   בְּ   תִי   שִׁ   מְ   מִשְׁי   כִי   יִשׁ   סִי

      bi   ti   shi   mi   mish·i   khi   yish   si

O-Type sounds

4.   בֹּ   תוֹ   שׁוֹ   מֹ   חָ   דֹשׁ   דוֹשׁ   סֹ

      bo   to   sho   mo   cho   dosh   dosh   so

U-Type sounds

5.   בֻּ   תוּ   שׁוּ   מֻ   מוּשׁ   דֻשׁ   דוּשׁ   יוּב

      bu   tu   shu   mu   mush   dush   dush   yuv

Combined Sounds

6.   שָׁלוֹם   טוֹבָה   חֶסֶד   רַחֲמִים   הָעוֹלָם   אֱלֹהֵנוּ   שֵׁמוֹת

      sha·lom   to·vah   che·sed   ra·cha·mim   ha·'o·lam   'e·lo·he·nu   she·mot

Review Readings

Read the following Hebrew words aloud until you can read them with ease. Remember that there is one syllable per Hebrew vowel (for more information, see Lesson Twelve).

1. מֶלֶךְ   חֵן   שַׁבָּת   שָׁלוֹם   לֶחֶם   כֵּן   חֹרֶף

2. אֶרֶז   קַו   הָיָה   שֶׁמֶשׁ   סוֹף   זַז   אָהַב

3. אֶלֶף   נָתַן   שָׁאַל   חוֹדֶשׁ   שָׂרִים   סוּר   מָגֵן

4. בָּנִים   יוֹם   טוֹבָה   אָקוּם   נוֹתֵן   עִם   זָכַר

5. בֶּגֶד   עָלָה   בּוֹא   דוֹרוֹת   חָזַק   נֵר   בִּימָה

6. יֶלֶד   כָּבַד   אֲנִי   לָרֶדֶת   אָנוּ   כֹּל   שָׁנָה

7. אֶרֶץ   עִם   אֵשׁ   בָּנוֹת   אֲשֶׁר   פֶּה   שׁוֹפָר

8. לֵבָב   רָעָה   אֶת   זֵיתִים   קוֹדֶשׁ   בָּם   בֹּקֶר

9. עָפָר   רוֹפֵא   מוֹדֶה   טַבַּעַת   קוֹל   תֵּן   מָקוֹם

10. עוֹלָם   שֶׁהוּא   נֶאֱמָן   אִירָה   אָדָם   רַב   רֹאשׁ

11. לָמָה   כֻּלָם   דֶּרֶךְ   מֵאִישׁ   עִיר   אַף   אַהֲבָה

12. אֱמֶת   אֶחָד   רוּחִי   חֲנֻכָּה   אֵלֶיךָ   הַשֵּׁם   עֵץ

Transliteration Practice

Transliterate the following words (all from Psalm 1) into English:

א. תֹּאבֵד אֲשֶׁר הָלַךְ בַּעֲצַת דֶּרֶךְ חַטָּאִים עָמָד

to'·ved

ב. לֵצִים יָשָׁב תּוֹרָה תּוֹרָתוֹ יוֹמָם הָיָה שָׁתוּל

ג. יִתֵּן יַעֲשֶׂה יִבּוֹל צַדִּיקִים כֵּן הָאִישׁ יָקֻמוּ

Transliterate the following words (all from Psalm 2) into English:

א. לָמָה רִיק אֶרֶץ יָחַד יוֹשֵׁב אֲדֹנָי לָמוֹ

ב. אָמַר אֶת כֹּל הַיּוֹם יֶאֱנַף נַחֲלָתֶךָ וַאֲנִי

נַחֲלָתֶךָ

na·cha·la·te·kha

(5)	(4)	(3)	(2)	(1)
ךָ	תֶֽ	לָ	חֲ	נַ
kha	te	la	cha	na

Scripture Readings

The following Scripture readings are from the Salkinson-Ginsburg edition of the Hebrew New Testament (Copyright © 1999 by The Society For Distributing Hebrew Scriptures).

אָנֹכִי אוֹר הָעוֹלָם

ha·'o·lam   'or   'a·no·khi

"I am the light of the world."
(John 8:12)

אָנֹכִי הוּא לֶחֶם הַחַיִּים

ha·**chai**·yim   le·chem   hu'   'a·no·khi

"I am the bread of life." (John 6:35)

אֲנִי הוּא הָרֹעֶה הַטּוֹב

ha·tov   ha·ro·'eh   hu'   'a·ni

"I am the Good Shepherd." (John 10:11)

אָמֵן אָמֵן אֲנִי אֹמֵר לָכֶם כָּל הַמַּאֲמִין בִּי יֶשׁ־לוֹ חַיֵּי־עוֹלָם

chai·yei-'o·lam   yesh·lo   bi   ham·ma·'a·min   kol   la·khem   'o·mer   'a·ni   'a·men   'a·men

"Truly truly I say to you, he that believes in me has life forever." (John 6:47)

כָּבוֹד לֵאלֹהִים בַּמָּרוֹם שָׁלוֹם עֲלֵי־אָרֶץ

'a·lei-'a·rets   sha·lom   ba·ma·rom   le·'lo·him   ka·vod

"Glory to God in the highest and peace on earth." (Luke 2:14)

Lesson Eleven Quiz

1. Write the Vowel Marks

In this lesson you learned two additional vowel marks. Write the mark, its sound, and its transliteration in the columns next to the name:

Name	Mark	Sound	Transliteration
Qibbuts			
Shureq			

2. Write the Vowel Names

Write the name for the vowel in the column next to its mark.

Mark	Name	Sound	Transliteration
אֻ			
אוּ			

3. Identify the Vowel Class

For each vowel, indicate if it is long or short in the column next to the vowel mark:

Mark	Name	Sound	Class
אֻ			
אוּ			

4. Completely fill in the vowel table you have studied this lesson:

U-Type:

Mark	Name	Sound	Hebrew	Trans.	Class
אֻ					
אוּ					

5. Review the A-Type Vowels

Complete the following table for the A-Type vowels you learned in Lesson Seven.
For extra credit, try writing the Hebrew name for the vowel:

A-Type:

Mark	Name	Sound	Hebrew	Trans.	Class
אָ					
אַ					
אֲ					
אָה					

6. Review the E-Type Vowels

Complete the following table for the E-Type vowels you learned in Lesson Eight.

E-Type:

Mark	Name	Sound	Hebrew	Trans.	Class
אֶ					
אֵ					
אֱ					
אֵי					
אֶי					

7. Review the I-Type Vowels

Complete the following table for the I-Type vowels you learned in Lesson Nine.

I-Type:

Mark	Name	Sound	Hebrew	Trans.	Class
אִ					
אִי					

8. **Review the O-Type Vowels**

Complete the following table for the O-Type vowels you learned in Lesson Ten.

O-Type:

Mark	Name	Sound	Hebrew	Trans.	Class
אָ					
אֳ					
אָ					
אוֹ					

9. **Review the U-Type Vowels**

Complete the following table for the U-Type vowels you learned in this Lesson.

U-Type:

Mark	Name	Sound	Hebrew	Trans.	Class
אֻ					
אוּ					

10. **Transliterate the following Hebrew names**

The first word is done for you.

English	Hebrew	Transliteration	English	Hebrew	Transliteration
Joseph	יוֹסֵף	yo·seph	Job	אִיּוֹב	
Sarah	שָׂרָה		Saul	שָׁאוּל	
Jonah	יוֹנָה		Cain	קַיִן	
Nathan	נָתָן		Daniel	דָּנִיֵּאל	
Aaron	אַהֲרוֹן		Elijah	אֵלִיָּה	
Abel	הֶבֶל		Moses	מֹשֶׁה	
Eli	עֵלִי		Eden	עֵדֶן	

11. Completely fill in the vowel table:

Note that the table includes places for all the vowels you have studied so far.

Vowel Table:

Mark	Name	Sound	Hebrew	Class	Type
אָ					
אַ					
אֲ					A-Type
אָה					
אֵ					
אֶ					
אֱ					E-Type
אֵי					
אֶי					
אִ					I-Type
אִי					
אׂ					
אָֽ					
אָ					O-Type
אוֹ					
אֻ					U-Type
אוּ					

12. Review the Hebrew letter names

At this point you should be able to read the Hebrew names of the letters you so carefully studied in your previous lessons. *Write the English transliteration for the Hebrew letter name in the column. The first letter name is transliterated for you.*

Hebrew	Transliteration	Book	Print	Cursive	Transliteration
אָלֶף	a·leph	א	X	ℂ	'
בֵּית		ב			
גִּמֶל		ג			
דָּלֶת		ד			
הֵא		ה			
וָו		ו			
זַיִן		ז			
חֵית		ח			
טֵית		ט			
יוֹד		י			
כָּף		כ			
לָמֶד		ל			
מֵם		מ			
נוּן		נ			
סָמֶךְ		ס			
עַיִן		ע			
פֵּא		פ			
צָדִי		צ			
קוֹף		ק			
רֵישׁ		ר			
שִׁין		שׁ			
תָּו		ת			

The Complete Hebrew Vowel List

Mark	Name	Sound	Hebrew	Trans.	Class	Type
אָ	Qamets	"a" as in aqua	קָמֵץ	a	Long	A-Type
אַ	Patach	"a" as in aqua	פַּתַח	a	Short	
אֲ	Chateph Patach	"a" as in aqua	חָטֵף פַּתַח	a	Reduced	
אָה	Qamets Hey	"a" as in aqua	קָמֵץ הֵא	ah	Long	
אֵ	Tsere	"e" as in they	צֵרֵי	e	Long	E-Type
אֶ	Segol	"e" as in they	סֶגּוֹל	e	Short	
אֱ	Chateph Segol	"e" as in they	חָטֵף סֶגּוֹל	e	Reduced	
אֵי	Tsere Yod	"ei" as in eight	צֵרֵי יוֹד	ei	Long	
אֶי	Segol Yod	"ey" as in obey	סֶגּוֹל יוֹד	ey	Long	
אִ	Chireq	"i" as in machine	חִירֶק	i	Short	I-Type
אִי	Chireq Yod	"i" as in machine	חִירֶק יוֹד	i	Long	
אֹ	Cholem	"o" as in yellow	חוֹלֵם	o	Long	O-Type
אֳ	Chateph Qamets	"o" as in yellow	חָטֵף קָמֵץ	o	Reduced	
אָ	Qamets Chatuph	"o" as in yellow	קָמֵץ חָטוּף	o	Short	
אוֹ	Cholem Vav	"o" as in yellow	חוֹלֵם וָו	o	Long	
אֻ	Qibbuts	"u" as in blue	קֻבּוּץ	u	Short	U-Type
אוּ	Shureq	"u" as in blue	שׁוּרֶק	u	Long	

SIMPLE VOWELS: *Vowel points* placed underneath or to the upper left of a single Hebrew letter.

FULL VOWELS: The letters: ו, י, and ה first were used to indicate vowel sounds (called *matres lectiones* [Latin for mothers of reading]); later they were combined with *vowel points* to form the "full" vowels.

REDUCED VOWELS: Only under **gutturals**: א, ה, ח, ע. Reduced vowels are a form of Sheva (see Lesson Twelve) and are considered short vowels.

DIPTHONGS: A cluster of vowels acting as a unit and producing its own unique sound (see Lesson Twelve).

Lesson Twelve

THE SHEVA AND SYLLABLES

שָׁעוּר שְׁנֵים־עָשָׂר

Lesson Introduction

Mazal Tov! (congratulations) In this pivotal lesson you will begin to properly pronounce (and read) Hebrew words. In particular, you will study the following:

✓ Two basic rules for dividing a Hebrew word into syllables

✓ Two types of dotted letters and how they affect word division

✓ The sheva and how to know when it is vocal or silent

✓ The "furtive patach"

✓ Hebrew dipthongs and how to pronounce them

Lesson at a glance

After you have studied this lesson, the following information should be clear:

Dotted Letters

Any Hebrew letter (*except* the gutturals א, ה, ח, ע and ר) can have a dot inside of it called a "dagesh mark" (*dagesh* means "emphasis"). The presence or absence of a dagesh mark may affect the way in which a Hebrew word is divided into syllables and pronounced.

The Sheva

The "sheva" is a mark placed under a letter that does *not* have a vowel. The sheva directly affects how to divide a Hebrew word into syllables.

Vowel Mark	Name	Sound	Hebrew	Transliteration
אְ	Sheva	*Vocal*: short "e" *Silent*: no sound	שְׁוָא	vocal: e (*or* ') silent: none

Combined Sounds

A *dipthong* is a cluster or combination of vowels acting as a unit and producing a unique sound. From the point of view of word division, a dipthong represents a distinct syllable in Hebrew.

אַי	אָי	אֲי	אוֹי	אוּי	אָיו
'ai	'ai	'aiy	'oy	'uy	'av
(long)	*(long)*	*(long)*	*(long)*	*(long)*	*(long)*

Dividing Words into Syllables

In order to properly pronounce a Hebrew word, you will need to understand how the word is divided into syllables (i.e., units of distinct sound). There are **two basic rules** for dividing a Hebrew word into syllables, as explained below.

1. # Syllables = # Vowels

A syllable always begins with a consonant (except when a word begins with וּ, which is a form of conjunction) and may end with either a consonant or another vowel. Since there is one vowel per syllable, *the number of syllables in a word is the same as the number of vowels*. We will indicate word division by drawing a line between the syllables and then placing the numbers (1), (2), and so on, directly below (or sometimes above) each consecutive syllable:

One Vowel:	**Two Vowels:**	**Three Vowels:**	**Four Vowels:**
כִּי	דָּ לֶת	לָ רֶ דֶת	הָ רָ חָ מָה
(1)	(2) (1)	(3) (2) (1)	(4) (3) (2) (1)
ki	let da	det re la	mah cha ra ha
One Syllable	*Two Syllables*	*Three Syllables*	*Four Syllables*

2. Syllables can be "Open" or "Closed"

Open syllables end with a vowel sound and closed syllables end with a letter without a vowel. We will indicate open syllables with (**O**) and a closed syllable with (**C**):

One Syllable:	**Two Syllables:**	**Three Syllables:**	**Four Syllables:**
כִּי	דָּ לֶת	לָ רֶ דֶת	הָ רָ חָ מָה
(O)	(C) (O)	(C) (O) (O)	(O) (O) (O) (O)
ki	let da	det re la	mah cha ra ha
One Vowel	*Two Vowels*	*Three Vowels*	*Four Vowels*

שִׁעוּר שְׁנֵים־עָשָׂר

Dividing a Hebrew word (Analysis)

When first analyzing a Hebrew word, it is often helpful to count each letter with a vowel, draw a vertical line between the resulting syllables, and place the numbers (1), (2), and so on, directly above each consecutive syllable. Including additional details about each syllable (transliteration, vowel, vowel class, and syllable status) is also a useful exercise:

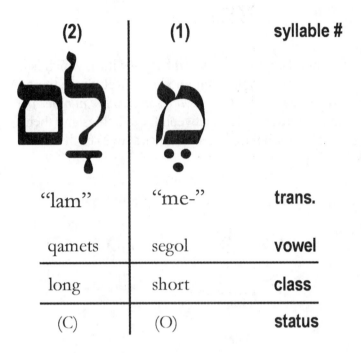

(2)	(1)	syllable #
"lam"	"me-"	trans.
qamets	segol	**vowel**
long	short	**class**
(C)	(O)	**status**

Sounding out the word (Synthesis)

When sounding out a Hebrew word, the syllables run together in a fluid way, with the accent (unless otherwise indicated) on the last syllable. The following diagram details the separate steps performed when sounding out a word:

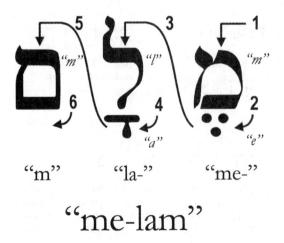

"m"   "la-"   "me-"

"me-lam"

Word division Examples

Here are some examples of dividing Hebrew words into their syllable sounds:

Example 1:

לֶחֶם Hebrew

(2)	(1)	Syll #
חֶם	לְ	
chem	le	Trans.
segol	segol	Vowel
short	short	Class
(C)	(O)	Status
lechem		English

Example 2:

נוֹתֵן Hebrew

(2)	(1)	Syll #
תֵן	נוֹ	
ten	no	Trans.
tsere	chol-vav	Vowel
long	long	Class
(C)	(O)	Status
noten		English

Example 3:

אֱלֹהִים Hebrew

(3)	(2)	(1)	Syll #
הִים	לֹ	אֱ	
him	lo	'e	Trans.
chir. yod	cholem	c-segol	Vowel
long	long	short	Class
(C)	(O)	(O)	Status
'elohim			English

Example 4:

עֵינֵיכֶם Hebrew

(3)	(2)	(1)	Syll #
כֶם	נֵי	עֵי	
chem	nei	ei	Trans.
segol	t-yod	t-yod	Vowel
short	long	long	Class
(C)	(O)	(O)	Status
'eineikhem			English

Example 5:

אֲדֹנֵינוּ Hebrew

(4)	(3)	(2)	(1)	Syll #
נוּ	נֵי	דֹ	אֲ	
nu	nei	do	'a	Trans.
shureq	t-yod	cholem	c-patach	Vowel
long	long	long	short	Class
(O)	(O)	(O)	(O)	Status
'adoneinu				English

Example 6:

נֶאֱלָחוּ Hebrew

(4)	(3)	(2)	(1)	Syll #
חוּ	לָ	אֱ	נֶ	
chu	la	'e	ne	Trans.
shureq	qamets	c-segol	segol	Vowel
long	long	short	short	Class
(O)	(O)	(O)	(O)	Status
ne'elachu				English

Divide and Conquer

Divide each Hebrew word into syllables. Include the details about each syllable (i.e., its transliteration, vowel, vowel class, and status). Write down your transliteration for the entire word. When finished, sound out the word. The first example is done for you.

מִמֶּרֶם **Hebrew**

(3)	(2)	(1)	Syll #
רֶם	מֶ	מִ	
rem	me	mi	Trans.
segol	segol	chireq	Vowel
short	short	short	Class
(C)	(O)	(O)	Status
mimerem			English

הֶעָרֵל **Hebrew**

	Syll #
	Trans.
	Vowel
	Class
	Status
	English

שׁוֹפָר **Hebrew**

	Syll #
	Trans.
	Vowel
	Class
	Status
	English

בַּהֲמוֹת **Hebrew**

	Syll #
	Trans.
	Vowel
	Class
	Status
	English

תּוֹדֶךָ **Hebrew**

	Syll #
	Trans.
	Vowel
	Class
	Status
	English

חֲדָשִׁים **Hebrew**

	Syll #
	Trans.
	Vowel
	Class
	Status
	English

Dotted Letters and Word Division

Any Hebrew letter (*except* the gutturals א, ה, ח, ע and ר) can have a dot inside of it called a "dagesh mark" (*dagesh* means "emphasis"). There are basically two kinds of *dageshim* that you need to learn about: the *Dagesh Lene* and the *Dagesh Forte*.

1. The Dagesh Lene

Six Hebrew letters you have studied, namely, Bet (ב), Gimmel (ג), Dalet (ד), Kaf (כ), Pey (פ), and Tav (ת) may appear with or without a dot placed within them. This dot is called a "*Dagesh Lene.*" If one of these six letters has a Dagesh Lene mark it will have a *hard* pronunciation, otherwise it has a softer pronunciation.

Collectively these letters are sometimes called "**Begedkephat** letters" as an acronym for the names of letters (ת פ כ ד ג ב). The Begedkephat letters are as follows:

kephat			beged		
תּ	פּ	כּ	דּ	גּ	בּ
Tav: "t" as in "**t**all"	Pey: "p" as in "**p**ark"	Kaf: "k" as in "**k**ite"	Dalet: "d" as in "**d**oor"	Gimmel: "g" as in "**g**irl"	Bet: "b" as in "**b**oy"

In **modern Hebrew**, only **three letters** change their sound when there is no dot inside: Bet, Kaf, and Pey (the other three letters are pronounced exactly the same as their non-dotted cousins). Consequently you only need to remember to pronounce these three letters differently when they do not have the Dagesh Lene mark:

פ / פּ	כ / כּ	ב / בּ
Fey / Pey "f" / "p"	Khaf / Kaf "kh" / "k"	Vet / Bet "v" / "b"

Notes:

- *You already know these letters!* The letter Vet, for example, is simply the letter Bet without the dot (i.e., Dagesh Lene) inside. The presence or the absence of the dot only affects the way you will pronounce the word.

- **Ashkenazi Jews** (those Jews of Eastern European descent) tend to pronounce the Aleph-Bet differently that **Sephardic Jews** (those Jews of Spain, Northern Africa, and Israel). For example, Ashkenazi pronunciation of Tav (ת)—without the Dagesh—is pronounced as a "s" sound. In this book we will use the Sephardic pronunciation since it is the one used in the land of Israel.

- **Remember:** Only **three letters** change their sound when there is a dot inside: the other three Begedkephat letters are pronounced exactly the same as their non-dotted cousins.

2. The Dagesh Forte

All of the Hebrew letters (except the gutturals)—*including the Begedkephat letters*—can take dot that looks exactly like the Dagesh Lene but is called a *Dagesh Forte.*

Unlike the Dagesh Lene, a Dagesh Forte does not affect the pronunciation of a letter, but rather affects a word's syllabification by **doubling the value of the consonant**.

A letter with a Dagesh Forte always causes the previous syllable (if any) to be closed and in effect "divides" the syllable at the letter:

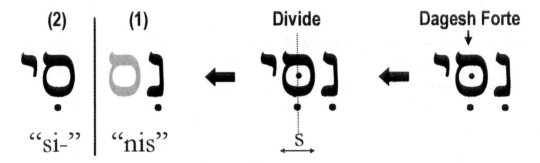

In the example above, we notice first that the word has a Dagesh Forte in the Samekh. The value of this letter is "doubled," and we thus count the first "s" as a closing sound of the previous syllable (i.e., **nis**) and the second "s" as the first sound of the following syllable (i.e., **si**). We would transliterate the word as nis·si.

Lene or Forte?

The Begedkephat letters can also take a Dagesh Forte, but, as we mentioned, the dots are identical. So how can you tell if a Begedkephat letter has a Lene or a Forte dot?

The rule goes like this: the dot in a Begedkephat letter is Forte only if it is *preceded* by a vowel (otherwise it is Lene).

In the example above, notice first that the word has a dagesh in the Bet. Now, is this a Dagesh Forte or a Dagesh Lene? Since it is preceded by a vowel (i.e., the Patach of the first syllable), the Bet must have a Dagesh Forte. Thus we divide the word into two closed syllables and transliterate as: shab·bat (note that if a Begedkephat letter has a Dagesh Forte, it is pronounced exactly the same as if it had a Dagesh Lene: the presence of a Forte only "doubles" the value of the letter).

(2) | (1)   Dagesh Lene

כָּר | כִּ ← כִּכָּר

"khar" | "ki-"

not preceded

In the example above, we notice first that the word has a dagesh in the Kaf. Is this a Dagesh Forte or a Dagesh Lene? Since it is *not* preceded by a vowel (i.e., there is no syllable with a vowel preceding it), the Kaf must have a Dagesh Lene. Thus we divide the word into one open syllable and one closed syllable and transliterate as: *ki·khar*.

The General Rule...

If there is a "dot" inside a letter, "double" its value; but if it is a Begedkephat letter, double the value *only if* it is preceded by a vowel.

Summary:

- Any letter (except a guttural) can have a dot called a Dagesh Forte.

- This dot "doubles" the value of the consonant and causes the previous syllable (if any) to be closed.

- A dot in a Begedkephat letter is Forte only if it is *preceded* by a vowel (otherwise it is Lene).

Dagesh Transliteration Examples

Each word has one or more dagesh mark. The type of dagesh mark is identified (Lene or Forte) and the transliteration is given.

עַמּוּד	צַדִּיק	צִוָּה	דִּבֶּר	דָּבָר	word	א.
forte	forte	forte	lene / forte	lene	dagesh type	
'am·mud	tsad·diq	tsiv·vah	dib·ber	da·var	transliteration	

הִגִּיד	בֶּגֶד	שִׁשָּׁה	אַתָּה	אָהַבְתָּ	word	ב.
forte	lene	forte	forte	lene	dagesh type	
hig·gid	**be**·ged	shish·shah	'at·tah	'a·hav·ta	transliteration	

Letters without Vowels

Earlier we said that every Hebrew *syllable* is composed of a letter with at least one vowel. However, this does *not* mean that every Hebrew *letter* must have a vowel. For example, a letter that closes a syllable does not have a vowel (if it *did* have a vowel, it would not "close" the syllable!).

For example, the word אֶחָת ends with a letter without a vowel:

(2)	(1)	syllable #
חָת ← *no vowel*	אֶ	
"chat"	"e-"	trans.
qamets	segol	**vowel**
long	short	**class**
(C)	(O)	**status**

In this example, we first determine that the word has two syllables, since it has two vowels. The first syllable is comprised of an Aleph with a Segol, and, since the next letter of the word has its own vowel, we decide that it is an open syllable. The second syllable is comprised of a Chet with a Qamets, but since the next letter of the word does not have a vowel, we decide that it is a closed syllable, that is, it ends with a "stopping" sound. We would transliterate the word as *'e·chat*.

A letter without a vowel at the end of a syllable

(2)		(1)	syllable #
כָה		מָל	
		no vowel	
"kah"		"mal"	**trans.**
qamets hey		qamets	**vowel**
long		long	**class**
(O)		(C)	**status**

In this example, we determine that the word has two syllables, since it has two vowels. The first syllable begins with a Mem and Qamets and continues to the closing Lamed. The second syllable begins with a Kaf and Qamets Hey but remains open, since there is no stopping sound following the vowel. We would transliterate the word as *mal·kah*.

The closing Sheva

In Hebrew, a letter that closes a syllable (in the middle of a word) is marked with a character called the **sheva**. Thus the way the word above would appear using a sheva is as follows:

(2)		(1)	syllable #
כָה		מָל	
		Sheva	
"kah"		"mal"	**trans.**
qamets hey		qamets	**vowel**
long		long	**class**
(O)		(C)	**status**

In this example, the sheva mark (:) indicates that the Lamed does not have a vowel and should be understood to **close** the first syllable. When a syllable ends with a letter without a vowel, the sheva mark indicates that the letter's sound should close off the syllable.

A letter without a vowel at the beginning of a syllable

(3)	(2)	(1)	syllable #
כִּים	לְ	מ	
		No vowel	
"khim"	"la-"	"m"	trans.
chireq yod	qamets	?	vowel
long	long	?	class
(C)	(O)	?	status

In this example, we are not sure what to do with the Mem that begins the word, since there is no vowel associated with it. How do you pronounce a letter without a vowel?

The Opening Sheva

In Hebrew, a letter that does not take a vowel but opens a syllable is also marked with the **sheva**. Thus the way the word above would appear using a sheva is as follows:

(3)	(2)	(1)	syllable #
כִּים	לְ	מְ	
		Sheva	
"khim"	"la-"	"m-"	trans.
chireq yod	qamets	none	vowel
long	long	short	class
(C)	(O)	(O)	status

Note that the Sheva is normally not placed under a letter that closes the sound of the last syllable in a Hebrew word. In the example given here, no Sheva is placed under the Mem sofit.

In this example, the sheva mark (:) indicates that the Mem does not have a vowel but should be understood to **open** the first syllable. When a syllable begins with a letter without a vowel, the sheva mark indicates that the letter sound should be very quickly *vocalized*—as if you were trying just to pronounce the letter by itself. We would transliterate this word as *me·la·khim*.

The Sheva

The sheva is a mark placed under a letter that does *not* have a vowel:

Vowel Mark	Name	Sound	Hebrew	Transliteration
X ְ	Sheva	*Vocal*: short "e" *Silent*: no sound	שְׁוָא	vocal: e (*or* ') silent: none

Notes:

- The vocal sheva represents the sound of a letter without a vowel. When it opens a syllable it sounds almost as if you were trying to pronounce the letter by itself (for example, the Nun in the word נְבִי is pronounced "nᵉ" (*nevi*)).

- Usually we will **transliterate** a sheva that opens a syllable with an "e" (or sometimes with an apostrophe); we will not transliterate the silent sheva at all.

- The Hebrew guttural letters (א, ה, ח, ע) *cannot* take a vocal sheva but use Chateph forms (i.e., Chateph Patach, Chateph Segol, and Chateph Qamets) instead (Chateph forms are really a combination of the sheva with one of the other vowel signs).

Silent or Vocal

The sheva can be either vocal or silent. If a sheva opens a syllable it is vocal, whereas if it closes a syllable, it is silent.

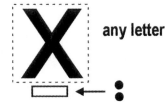 **any letter**　　**Opens syllable? Vocal**
　　　　　　　　　　　　　　　　Closes syllable? Silent

Note that the "**X**" refers to any Hebrew letter (for example א, ב, ג, and so on) and the rectangular box below the letter refers to the sheva mark location.

Sounding Out the Vocal Sheva

To sound out the vocal sheva, try just to pronounce the letter by itself (i.e., *first* pronounce the letter sound (represented by the "**X**") and then add a very hurried "e" sound. Thus you would read בְ as "bᵉ").

טְ	זְ	וְ	דְ	גְ	בְ	בְּ	א
te	ze	ve	de	ge	ve	be	

The Sheva and Syllables

When it opens (i.e., begins) a syllable, the sheva has a *very* short "e" sound; when it closes (i.e., ends) a syllable, it is silent.

The Vocal Sheva

There are four cases when the sheva is vocal (i.e., opens a syllable):

1. When it *begins* a word:

בְּרָכָה   Hebrew

כָה   רָ   בְּ
(3)   (2)   (1)
khah   ra   be

2. When the second of two in a row:

מִשְׁפְּטֵי   Hebrew

טֵי   פְּ   מִשְׁ
(3)   (2)   (1)
tei   pe   mish

3. When under a Dagesh Forte letter:

הַמְּלָנִים   Hebrew

נִים   לָ   מְּ   הַ
(4)   (3)   (2)   (1)
nim   la   me   ham

4. When following a long vowel:

כֹּתְבִים   Hebrew

בִים   תְ   כֹּ
(3)   (2)   (1)
vim   te   ko

צְדָקָה

tse·da·qah

love, charity

Did you know?

The word for charity, (tsedaqah) is related to the Hebrew word for righteousness (tsedeq), which indicates that it is a righteous thing to give charity to those who are in need.

The Silent Sheva

On the other hand, there are four cases when the sheva is silent (i.e., closes a syllable):

1. When it *ends* a word:

מֶלֶךְ   Hebrew

מֶ   לֶךְ
(2)   (1)
lekh   me

2. When the first of two in a row:

 Hebrew

מִשׁ   פְּ   טֵי
(3)   (2)   (1)
tei   pe   mish

3. When it closes a syllable:

מַלְכָּה   Hebrew

מַל   כָּה
(2)   (1)
kah   mal

4. When following a short vowel:

פַּרְעֹה   Hebrew

פַּר   עֹה
(2)   (1)
'oh   par

The Holy Language

le·shon   haq·qo·desh

Hebrew used for the sacred purposes of prayer and study is sometimes referred to as "*Leshon Haqqodesh*," or the holy language. During the Diaspora many Jewish communities that dispensed with the sacred language in liturgies often withered away, but those that continued to use it thrived.

Vocal Sheva Examples

1. At the *beginning* of a word:

א.

מְאֹד   שְׁמַע   כְּתָב   בְּרֵאשִׁית   בְּלִי   קְדוֹשׁ

me·'od   she·ma'   ke·tav   be·re·shit   be·li   qe·dosh

2. *Second* of two in a row:

ב.

יִכְתְּבוּ   שִׁבְתְּךָ   רַגְלְכֶם   יִשְׁמְרוּ   קָדְשְׁךָ

yikh·te·vu   shiv·te·kha   rag·le·khem   yish·me·ru   qad·she·kha

3. Under a Dagesh Forte letter:

ג.

הַמְלָנִים   עַמְּךָ   נְנַתְּקָה   יִתְיַצְּבוּ   בַּמְּלָאכָה

ham·me·la·nim   'am·me·kha   ne·nat·te·qah   yit·yats·tse·vu   bam·me·la·khah

4. Following a *long* vowel:

ד.

לְבָבְךָ   בְּעָנְיִי   וּבְנָיָהוּ   זוֹלְלִים   הָיְתָה

le·va·ve·kha   be·'a·ne·yi   u·ve·na·ya·hoo   zol·le·lim   ha·ye·tah

Advanced Note:

- There is another case wherein you will pronounce a sheva as vocal, and that is when it immediately precedes the *same Hebrew letter* (or similar sounding letter) in a word. For example:

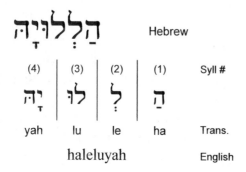

	(4)	(3)	(2)	(1)	Syll #
הַלְלוּיָהּ	יָהּ	לוּ	לְ	הַ	Hebrew
	yah	lu	le	ha	Trans.
		haleluyah			English

Silent Sheva Examples

1. At the *end* of a word:

אָ.   בָּךְ   לָךְ   חָרַתְּ   מַתְ   דֶּרֶךְ   אַךְ   מֶלֶךְ

bakh   lakh   cha·rat   mat   de·rekh   akh   me·lekh

2. *First* of two in a row:

בָּ.   קָדְשְׁךָ   יִשְׁמְרוּ   רַגְלְכֶם   שִׁבְתְּךָ   יִכְתְּבוּ

qad·she·kha   yish·me·ru   rag·le·khem   shiv·te·kha   yich·te·vu

3. Closing a syllable:

גַּ.   אָהַבְתָּ   נַפְשְׁךָ   יִשְׂרָאֵל   שִׁמְךָ   מִלְחָמָה

’a·hav·ta   naf·she·kha   yis·ra·’el   shim·kha   mil·cha·mah

4. Following a *short* vowel:

דַּ.   מַרְפֵּא   אָסַפְתִּי   מַלְכָּה   פַּרְעֹה   מִרְמוֹת

mar·pe’   ’a·saf·ti   mal·kah   par·‘oh   mir·mot

A friend of the Jewish People

אוֹהֵב יִשְׂרָאֵל

ohev yisrael

A friend of the Jewish people is sometimes called "*ohev Yisrael*" (while love for Israel is referred to as "*ahavat Yisrael*"). The ohev Yisrael recognizes the Jewish people as the object of Adonai's special concern as His chosen people. Many ohev Yisrael helped rescue more than a million Jewish people from the Nazis during the worst years of the Holocaust. Not surprisingly, most of these friends of Israel were devout Christians.

Sheva Transliteration Examples

Each word has one or more sheva. The type of sheva is identified (vocal or silent) and the transliteration is given.

בַּמִּדְבָּר	חֶרְפָּה	פְּלִשְׁתִּים	תְּפִלָּה	**word**	**א.**
silent	silent	vocal / silent	vocal	**sheva type**	
bam·mid·bar	cher·pah	pe·lish·tim	te·fil·lah	**transliteration**	

וְכִבְשֻׁהָ	לְמֶמְשֶׁלֶת	לְהַבְדִּיל	לְבִלְתִּי	**word**	**ב.**
vocal / silent	vocal / silent	vocal / silent	vocal / silent	**sheva type**	
ve·khiv·shu·ha	le·mem·she·let	le·hav·dil	le·vil·ti	**transliteration**	

וְנִשְׂאוּ	מַרְחֶשֶׁת	שָׁרְצוּ	הָיְתָה	**word**	**ג.**
vocal / silent	silent	vocal	vocal	**sheva type**	
ve·nas·'u	mar·che·shet	sha·re·tsu	ha·ye·tah	**transliteration**	

מִשְׁפְּחֹת	מַשְׁבֹת	וְנִפְקְחוּ	יִשְׁרְצוּ	**word**	**ד.**
silent / vocal	vocal	vocal / silent / vocal	silent / vocal	**sheva type**	
mish·pe·chot	mash·she·vot	ve·nif·ke·chu	yish·re·tsu	**transliteration**	

וְנִשְׂמְחָה	עַבְדְּךָ	יִלְמְדוּ	בִּטְנְךָ	**word**	**ה.**
vocal /silent/ vocal	silent / vocal	silent / vocal	silent / vocal	**sheva type**	
ve·nis·me·chah	'av·de·kha	yil·me·du	bit·ne·kha	**transliteration**	

שָׁוְא	פְּנֵי	יְעוֹפֵף	הַמְּלָנִים	**word**	**ו.**
vocal	vocal	vocal	vocal	**sheva type**	
she·va'	pe·nei	ye·'o·fef	ham·me·la·nim	**transliteration**	

Sheva Transliteration Practice

Hebrew to English

Transliterate each row of Hebrew words into English. Read the Hebrew words from right to left, but write the English transliterations from left to right. Pronounce each word out loud when finished. The first word is done for you.

א. מַלְכֵּנוּ יִשְׂרָאֵל אַבְרָהָם אֲנַחְנוּ אַרְבַּע
    mal·ke·nu

ב. אַרְבָּעִים אֶשְׁכְּנַז אֶתְרוֹג בְּבַקָּשָׁה בְּדִיקָה

ג. בִּלְהָה בְּמִדְבַּר בְּנֵי מִצְוָה בָּרוּךְ

ד. בְּרִית בִּרְכוֹת בְּשׂוֹרָה גְּבוּרָה גָּדְלָה

ה. גְּלִילָה גְּמָרָה דְּבִיר דְּבָרִים דָּנִיֵּאל

ו. דְּרָשָׁה הִנְנִי הַשְׁגָּחָה הִתְגַּלּוּת וַיִּקְרָא

ז. זְכַרְיָה זִלְפָּה טֻמְאָה טְרֵפָה יְהוּדָה

ח. יִצְחָק יְשֻׁרוּן כַּשְׁרוּת כְּתוּבִים מְלָכִים

The "Furtive Patach" and Syllables

Normally, to sound out a syllable you *first* pronounce the letter sound and then add the vowel sound. Thus דַ is pronounced "da" and not "ad." There an exception to this rule, however: when a word *ends* in a Chet (ח), an 'Ayin (ע) or a dotted Hey (הּ *mappiq*) and has a Patach vowel mark (i.e., חַ, עַ, or הַּ), you *first* pronounce the vowel sound and then add the letter sound.

Thus the following word is pronounced "ru-ach," *not* "ru-cha":

(2)	(1)	syllable #
חַ	רוּ	
Furtive Patach		
"ach"	"ru-"	**trans.**
patach	shureq	**vowel**
short	long	**class**
(C)	(O)	**status**

And the following word (the name for Jesus) is pronounced "ye-shu-a":

(3)	(2)	(1)	syllable #
עַ	שׁוּ	יֵ	
Furtive Patach			
"a"	"shu-"	"ye-"	**trans.**
patach	shureq	tsere	**vowel**
short	long	long	**class**
(O)	(O)	(O)	**status**

Note: Normally the accent is on the syllable just before the furtive Patach (ye-**shu**-a').

Furtive Patach Transliteration Examples

The following words each have a furtive patach. Transliterations are provided.

בֹּרֵחַ	לָשׂוּחַ	מָנוֹחַ	רוּחַ	נֹחַ	א.
bo·re·ach	la·su·ach	ma·no·ach	ru·ach	no·ach	
יוֹדֵעַ	שָׂרוּעַ	מַדּוּעַ	פֹּשֵׁעַ	יֵשׁוּעַ	ב.
yo·de·a'	sa·ru·a'	mad·du·a'	po·she·a'	ye·shu·a'	
מוֹשִׁיעַ	מָשִׁיחַ	שָׂמֵחַ	שָׁלִיחַ	שַׁבֵּחַ	ג.
mo·shi·a'	ma·shi·ach	sa·me·ach	sha·li·ach	shab·be·ach	
לָנוּחַ	בֹּטֵחַ	צָבוּעַ	כִּשְׁמֹעַ	הַמָּשִׁיחַ	ד.
la·nu·ach	bo·te·ach	tsa·vu·a'	kish·mo·a'	ham·ma·shi·ach	
מַזְרִיעַ	יַגִּיהַּ	מִתְמַהְמֵהַּ	מַגְבִּיהַּ	גָּבֹהַּ	ה.
maz·ri·a'	yag·gi·ah	mit·mah·me·ah	mag·bi·ah	ga·vo·ah	
יְהוֹשֻׁעַ	וְנֹסוֹעַ	רָבוּעַ	וְרוּחַ	זֹרֵעַ	ו.
ye·ho·shu·a'	ve·no·so·a'	ra·vu·a'	ve·ru·ach	zo·re·a'	

יֵשׁוּעַ הַמָּשִׁיחַ

Jesus the Messiah

Furtive Patach Transliteration Practice

Hebrew to English

Transliterate each row of Hebrew words into English. Read the Hebrew words from right to left, but write the English transliterations from left to right. Pronounce each word out loud when finished. The first word is done for you.

א.   יֵשׁוּעַ   הַמָּשִׁיחַ   מוֹשִׁיעַ   יוֹדֵעַ   מָנוֹחַ

       ye·shu·aʻ

ב.   הָרוּחַ   יָרֵחַ   מַפְתֵּחַ   יְשׁוּעָה   יְהוֹשֻׁעַ

ג.   לוּחַ   שִׂיחַ   רֵיחַ   פִּיחַ   וּמֹחַ

Hebrew to English

Transliterate the verse of Scripture, below:

אַתָּה הוּא הַמָּשִׁיחַ בֶּן־אֱלֹהִים חַיִּים

You are the Messiah, Son of the Living God.

Matt. 16:16

Hebrew Dipthongs

A *dipthong* is a cluster or combination of vowels acting as a unit and producing a unique sound. From the point of view of word division, a dipthong represents a distinct syllable in Hebrew.

The dipthongs you will see in Hebrew are as follows:

Dipthong	Sound	Transliteration	Class
אַֽי	"ai" as in **ai**sle	ai	Long
אָֽי	"ai" as in **ai**sle	ai	Long
אֲִֽי	"a-yee" ("ai" as in **ai**sle and "yee")	aiy	Long
אֹוֽי	"oi-yee" ("oi" as in **oi**l and "yee")	oy	Long
אֽוּֽי	"oo-ee" ("oo" as in g**oo** and "ee")	uy	Long
אָֽיו	"av" as in la**va**	av	Long

Dipthong Transliteration Examples

	שַׁדַּי	אֵלַי	חַי	מִצְוֺתַי	אֱלֹהַי	א.
	shad·dai	'e·lai	chai	mits·vo·tai (note that Vav takes cholem here)	'e·lo·hai	

	שָׂרַי	אֲדֹנָי	סִינַי	בְּרַגְלַי	חַיַּי	ב.
	sa·rai	'a·do·nai	si·nai	ve·rag·lai	chaiy·yai	

	בַּיִת	מָאתַיִם	עֵינַיִם	מַיִם	חַיִּים	ג.
	bayit	ma·tai·yim	'ei·nai·yim	mayim	chaiy·yim	

	גּוֹי	אוֹיְבַי	הוּי	פָּנָיו	אֵלָיו	ד.
	goy	'o·ye·vai	huy	pa·nav	'e·lav	

Lesson Twelve Summary

1. Dividing Words into Syllables

There are two main rules for dividing Hebrew words into syllables:

- The number of syllables in a word is the same as the number of vowels.
- Syllables can be open or closed (open syllables end with a vowel sound and closed syllables end with a letter without a vowel).

When analyzing a Hebrew word, we count each letter with a vowel, draw a vertical line between the resulting syllables, and place the numbers (1), (2), and so on, directly above each consecutive syllable. We also include additional details about each syllable (transliteration, vowel, vowel class, and syllable status):

אֱלֹהִים			Hebrew
(3)	(2)	(1)	Syll #
הִים	לֹ	אֱ	
him	lo	'e	Trans.
chir. yod	cholem	c-segol	Vowel
long	long	short	Class
(C)	(O)	(O)	Status
	'elohim		English

2. Dagesh Lene and Dagesh Forte

Any Hebrew letter (*except* the gutturals א, ה, ח, ע and ר) can have a dot inside of it called a "dagesh mark" (*dagesh* means "emphasis").

The "**Begedkephat** letters (ב ג ד כ פ ת) may appear with or without a dot placed within them. This dot is called a *"Dagesh Lene."* If one of these six letters has a dot it will have a *hard* pronunciation, otherwise it has a softer pronunciation. In modern Hebrew, only ב כ פ change their sound when there is a dot inside.

All of the Hebrew letters—*including the Begedkephat letters*—can take a dot that looks exactly like the Dagesh Lene but is called a *Dagesh Forte*. Unlike the Dagesh Lene, a Dagesh Forte does not affect the pronunciation of a letter, but rather affects a word's syllabification by 1) doubling the value of the consonant and 2) causing the previous syllable (if any) to be closed.

The general rule for determining whether a letter has a Dagesh Lene or Dagesh Forte goes like this: If there is a "dot" inside a letter, "double" its value; but if it is a Begedkephat letter, double the value *only if* it is preceded by a vowel.

3. The Sheva

The sheva is a mark placed under a letter that does *not* have a vowel:

Vowel Mark	Name	Sound	Hebrew	Transliteration
X֔	Sheva	*Vocal*: short "e" *Silent*: no sound	שְׁוָא	vocal: e (*or* ') silent: none

The sheva can be either vocal or silent. If a sheva opens a syllable it is vocal; otherwise, if it closes a syllable, it is silent.

The sheva is vocal under four circumstances:

1. When it appears under the first letter of a word.
2. When it is the second of two in a row.
3. When it appears under a Dagesh Forte letter.
4. When it follows a long vowel.

In all other cases the sheva is silent.

4. Furtive Patach

When a word *ends* in a Chet (ח), an Ayin (ע) or a dotted Hey (הּ *mappiq*) and has a Patach vowel mark (i.e., חַ, עַ, or הַּ), *first* pronounce the vowel sound and then add the letter sound.

5. Hebrew Dipthongs

A *dipthong* is a cluster or combination of vowels acting as a unit and producing a unique sound. All dipthongs make their own syllable and are considered *long vowels*.

אַי	אָי	אֵי	אוֹי	אוּי	אָיו
'ai *(long)*	'ai *(long)*	'aiy *(long)*	'oy *(long)*	'uy *(long)*	'av *(long)*

Hebrew Dipthongs

Review Readings

Read the following Biblical Hebrew words aloud until you can read them with ease.

שִׁבְתְּךָ	שָׁמַע	כְּתָב	בֶּגֶד	צַדִּיק	א.
נַפְשֶׁךָ	יִשְׁמְרוּ	לְבָבְךָ	פְּנֵי	הָיְתָה	ב.
יֵשׁוּעַ	אֱלֹהֵי	רוּחַ	אֲדֹנָי	עַמְּךָ	ג.
חַיִּים	מִלְחָמָה	שָׂמֵחַ	פָּנָיו	חֶרְפָּה	ד.
מַשְׁבֵּת	בַּמִּדְבָּר	הַשָּׁמַיִם	שַׁבֵּחַ	כְּשָׁמְעַ	ה.
יוֹשֵׁב	בֹּטֵחַ	דֶּרֶךְ	כָּבוֹד	אָקוּם	ו.
יִשְׂרָאֵל	אֵל שַׁדַּי	מְרֻשָׁעִים	כּוֹרְעִים	יִכְתּוֹב	ז.
כִּי־טוֹב	הַגּוֹאֵל	חַסְדְּךָ	וְדֹרְשֵׁי	שְׂכָרוֹ	ח.

Note:

- The last example uses a dash called a *Maqqef* (מַקֵּף) which means "binder." The Maqqef is common in the scriptures and functions much like a hyphen in English.

מַיִם חַיִּים

Transliteration Practice

Practice reading Genesis 1:1-4. The transliteration is provided, but you may want to cover it up with a piece of paper and check yourself as you read:

א. בְּרֵאשִׁית בָּרָא אֱלֹהִים אֵת הַשָּׁמַיִם וְאֵת הָאָרֶץ:

ha·ʾa·rets	ve·ʾet	hash·sha·**may**im	ʾet	ʾe·lo·him	ba·ra	be·re·shit
the earth	*and*	*the heavens*	*( )*	*God*	*he created*	*in beginning*

ב. וְהָאָרֶץ הָיְתָה תֹהוּ וָבֹהוּ וְחֹשֶׁךְ עַל־פְּנֵי תְהוֹם

te·hom	ʾal·pe·nei	ve·**cho**·shekh	va·**vo**·hu	**to**·hu	ha·ye·tah	ve·ha·ʾa·rets
deep	*over the surface*	*and darkness*	*and void*	*formless*	*was*	*and the earth*

וְרוּחַ אֱלֹהִים מְרַחֶפֶת עַל־פְּנֵי הַמָּיִם:

ham·**may**im	ʾal·pe·nei	me·ra·**che**·fet	ʾe·lo·him	ve·**ru**·ach
the waters	*over the surface*	*brooding*	*God*	*and spirit of*

ג. וַיֹּאמֶר אֱלֹהִים יְהִי אוֹר וַיְהִי־אוֹר:

vai·hi·ʾor	ʾor	ye·hi	ʾe·lo·him	vai·**yo**·mer
and there was light	*light*	*let be*	*God*	*and he said*

ד. וַיַּרְא אֱלֹהִים אֶת־הָאוֹר כִּי־טוֹב וַיַּבְדֵּל אֱלֹהִים

ʾe·lo·him	vai·yavd·del	ki·tov	et·ha·ʾor	ʾe·lo·him	vai·**yar**
God	*and separated*	*that good*	*the light*	*God*	*and saw*

בֵּין הָאוֹר וּבֵין הַחֹשֶׁךְ:

ha·**cho**·shekh	u·vein	ha·ʾor	bein
the darkness	*and between*	*the light*	*between*

Note:

- A verse of scripture is called a *pasuq* (plural: *pesuqim*), and the mark at the end of the verse (**:**) is called a *sof pasuq*.

- Notice that words like וַיֹּאמֶר have a dipthong as their first syllable, since the Yod has a dagesh mark and is therefore a Dagesh Forte. We transliterate **vai**-yo-mer.

Transliteration Practice

Practice reading John 5:24 from the New Testament (*B'rit Chadashah*) in Hebrew. The transliteration is provided, but you may want to cover it up with a piece of paper and check yourself as you read.

לִדְבָרַי	וּמַאֲמִין	הַמַּקְשִׁיב	לָכֶם	אֹמֵר	אֲנִי	אָמֵן	אָמֵן
lid·va·rai	u·ma·'a·min	ham·mak·shiv	la·khem	'o·mer	'a·ni	'a·men	'a·men
my word	*and believing*	*the one hearing*	*to you*	*say*	*I*	*truly*	*truly*

בִּשְׁלֹחִי	יֶשׁ־לוֹ	חַיֵּי	עוֹלָם	וְלֹא	יָבֹא	לְהִשָּׁפֵט
be·**shol**·chi	yesh-lo	chai·yei	'o·lam	ve·lo'	ya·vo'	le·hish·sha·pet
in the one who sent me	*there is to him*	*life*	*eternal*	*and not*	*will come*	*to judgment*

כִּי־עָבַר	מִמָּוֶת	לַחַיִּים:
ki-'a·var	mim·ma·vet	la·**chai**·yim
but has passed	*from death*	*to life*

- Notice that לַחַיִּים has a dipthong for its second syllable, since the Yod has a dagesh mark and is therefore a Dagesh Forte. We transliterate la-chai-yim.

"Verily, verily, I say unto you,
he that heareth my word,
and believeth on him
that sent me,
hath everlasting life,
and shall not come into condemnation;
but is passed from death unto life."

The Master

Lesson Twelve Quiz

1. Divide the Words

For the following words, count each letter with a vowel, draw a vertical line between the resulting syllables, and place the numbers (1), (2), and so on, directly above each consecutive syllable. Transliterate the syllable and identify the syllable's vowel, vowel class, and syllable status. The first exercise is done for you.

מִשְׁפְּטֵי	Hebrew		תְּמוּנָה	Hebrew	
(3) (2) (1)	Syll #			Syll #	
טֵי פְּ מִשׁ	Trans.			Trans.	
tei pe mish	Vowel			Vowel	
t-yod sheva chireq	Class			Class	
long short short	Status			Status	
(O) (O) (C)				English	
mishpetei	English				

בְּרִית	Hebrew		לַעֲשׂוֹת	Hebrew
	Syll #			Syll #
	Trans.			Trans.
	Vowel			Vowel
	Class			Class
	Status			Status
	English			English

הַמִּדְבָּר	Hebrew		הַשְּׁבִיעִי	Hebrew
	Syll #			Syll #
	Trans.			Trans.
	Vowel			Vowel
	Class			Class
	Status			Status
	English			English

שִׁעוּר שְׁנַיִם־עָשָׂר

2. Identify the Dagesh

In the following words, indicate whether the dagesh mark is lene or forte. Provide a transliteration for the word (remember that if it is in a Begedkephat letter, double the value only if it is preceded by a vowel). The first exercise is done for you:

א.

	word				
כִּסֵּה	דִּבֵּר	אַתָּה	שִׁבַּר	word	
			forte	dagesh type	
			shib·bar	transliteration	

ב.

שִׁשִּׁי	הִנֵּה	תְּמוּנָה	תְּפִלָּה	word
				dagesh type
				transliteration

ג.

בָּתִּים	אִשָּׁה	בְּרָכָה	חַיָּה	word
				dagesh type
				transliteration

ד.

הִגִּיד	אַתֶּנָּה	מַלְכָּה	חֻקָּה	word
				dagesh type
				transliteration

ה.

יַרְדֵּן	דְּבָרִים	מִתּוֹךְ	תּוֹרוֹת	word
				dagesh type
				transliteration

3. Begedkephat letters

Write the six Begedkephat letters in the boxes below.

kephat			beged		

4. Furtive Patach

What three letters may a "furtive patach" appear under? Where does it occur?

5. List the Vocal Sheva Rules

There are four cases when a sheva is vocal. Write them down in the spaces below.

1. _____
2. _____
3. _____
4. _____

6. Identify the Sheva Type

The following words have one or more shevas. Determine whether the sheva is vocal or silent and provide the transliteration. The first word is done for you.

בִּימָיו	אֶפְדָּם	מִשְׁזָר	נַפְשִׁי	word	א.
			silent	sheva type	
			naf·shi	transliteration	
לְשִׁפְחָה	וְכִבְשֻׁהָ	בְּצַלְמוֹ	פְּלִשְׁתִּים	word	ב.
				sheva type	
				transliteration	
וְיִרְשׁוּ	בְּכַפְּךָ	וְאָכְלוּ	שְׂכַרְתִּיךָ	word	ג.
				sheva type	
				transliteration	
בְּדַלְתוֹת	לְתִתְּךָ	בְּהֶמְתֶּךָ	מְצַוֶּךָ	word	ד.
				sheva type	
				transliteration	
וְיִשְׂמְחוּ	לְבַבְכֶם	וְיֹנְקִים	וְאַנְשֵׁי	word	ה.
				sheva type	
				transliteration	

7. **Completely fill in the vowel table:**

Mark	Name	Sound	Hebrew	Class	Type
אָ					
אַ					A-Type
אֲ					
אָה					
אֵ					
אֶ					
אֱ					E-Type
אֵי					
אֶי					
אִ					I-Type
אִי					
אֹ					
אֳ					O-Type
אָ					
אוֹ					
אֻ					U-Type
אוּ					
אְ					Sheva

8. **Write the dipthong sounds**

Write the transliteration for each Hebrew dipthong:

אַי	אָי	אַי	אוֹי	אוּי	אָיו

The Complete Hebrew Alphabet

Book Print	Name	Block	Cursive	Pronounced	Transliteration
א	Aleph	X	IC	silent letter	' (or none)
בּ	Bet	בּ	ב	**b** as in **b**oy	b
ב	Vet	ב	ב	*no dot:* **v** as in **v**ine	v
ג	Gimmel	λ	ح	**g** as in **g**irl	g
ד	Dalet	ד	3	**d** as in **d**oor	d
ה	Hey	ה	ה	**h** as in **h**ay	h
ו	Vav	ו	I	**v** as in **v**ine; "consonantal vowel"	v
ז	Zayin	ז	ڵ	**z** as in **z**ebra	z
ח	Chet	ח	n	**ch** as in Ba**ch**	ch (or ḥ)
ט	Tet	ט	G	**t** as in **t**ime	t (or ṭ)
י	Yod	י	י	**y** as in **y**es; "consonantal vowel"	y
כ	Kaf	כּ	כ	**k** as in **k**ite	k
כ	Khaf	כ	כ	*no dot:* **ch** as in ba**ch**	kh
ך		ך	ך	*sofit form*	
ל	Lamed	7	ℓ	**l** as in **l**ook	l
מ	Mem	Δ	N	**m** as in **m**om	m
ם		ם	◫	*sofit form*	
נ	Nun	נ	J	**n** as in **n**ow	n
ן		ן	I	*sofit form*	
ס	Samekh	▽	O	**s** as in **s**on	s
ע	'Ayin	ע	୪	silent letter	' (or none)
פּ	Pey	פּ	∂	**p** as in **p**ark	p
פ	Fey	פ	∂	**ph** as in **ph**one	ph / f
ף		ף	ℓ	*sofit form*	
צ	Tsade	צ	3	**ts** as in nu**ts**	ts / tz (or ṣ)
ץ		ץ	ℓ	*sofit form*	
ק	Qof	ק	ק	**q** as in **q**ueen	q (or k)
ר	Resh	ר	ר	**r** as in **r**ain	r
שׁ	Shin	שׁ	ℯ	**sh** as in **sh**y	sh (or š)
שׂ	Sin	שׂ	ℯ	**s** as in **s**un	s (or ś)
ת	Tav	ת	ת	**t** as in **t**all	t

שִׁעוּר שְׁנֵים־עָשָׂר

The Complete Hebrew Vowel List

Mark	Name	Sound	Hebrew	Trans.	Class	Type
אָ	Qamets	"a" as in aqua	קָמֵץ	a	Long	A-Type
אַ	Patach	"a" as in aqua	פַּתַח	a	Short	
אֲ	Chateph Patach	"a" as in aqua	חֲטֵף פַּתַח	a	Reduced	
אָה	Qamets Hey	"a" as in aqua	קָמֵץ הֵא	ah	Long	
אֵ	Tsere	"e" as in they	צֵרִי	e	Long	E-Type
אֶ	Segol	"e" as in they	סֶגּוֹל	e	Short	
אֱ	Chateph Segol	"e" as in they	חֲטֵף סֶגּוֹל	e	Reduced	
אֵי	Tsere Yod	"ei" as in eight	צֵרִי יוֹד	ei	Long	
אֶי	Segol Yod	"ey" as in obey	סֶגּוֹל יוֹד	ey	Long	
אִ	Chireq	"i" as in machine	חִירֶק	i	Short	I-Type
אִי	Chireq Yod	"i" as in machine	חִירֶק יוֹד	i	Long	
אֹ	Cholem	"o" as in yellow	חוֹלֶם	o	Long	O-Type
אֳ	Chateph Qamets	"o" as in yellow	חֲטֵף קָמֵץ	o	Reduced	
אָ	Qamets Chatuph	"o" as in yellow	קָמֵץ חָטוּף	o	Short	
אוֹ	Cholem Vav	"o" as in yellow	חוֹלֶם וָו	o	Long	
אֻ	Qibbuts	"u" as in blue	קִבּוּץ	u	Short	U-Type
אוּ	Shureq	"u" as in blue	שׁוּרֶק	u	Long	
אְ	Sheva'	*Vocal*: short "e" *Silent*: no sound	שְׁוָא	e	(vocal) Short	Sheva

Combined Sounds

אַי	אָי	אַי	אוֹי	אוּי	אָיו
'ai	'ai	'aiy	'oy	'uy	'av
(long)	*(long)*	*(long)*	*(long)*	*(long)*	*(long)*

Lesson Thirteen

SHEMA YISRAEL / ASERET HADIBEROT

Lesson Introduction

In this lesson you will reinforce what you have studied by reading the famous *Shema*, considered by most Jews to be the quintessential Jewish prayer. Learning to read the Shema will not only help you sound out Hebrew words, but will directly acquaint you with the Hebraic mindset that underlies the rest of the Hebrew Bible.

After reading the Shema, we will read the *Aseret Hadiberot* or Ten Commandments.

Lesson Tip

Read the following pages as best as you can (use a piece of paper to cover the transliterations and then check your pronunciation after finishing a given word or line). Do not be discouraged if you find yourself faltering over the syllables! Learning to read Hebrew fluently takes a lot of practice and *repetition*. May the Lord God of Israel, the One true God, bless you as you study to know His word more fully.

Introduction to the Shema

The Shema is the central prayer in the Jewish prayerbook (*Siddur*) and is often the first verse of Scripture that a Jewish child learns. During its recitation in the synagogue, Orthodox Jews pronounce each word very carefully and cover their eyes with their right hand. Many Jews recite the Shema at least twice daily: once in the morning and once in the evening. It is also sometimes said as a bedtime prayer ("the bedtime Shema").

The complete Shema is actually composed of three parts linked together into a unity.

1. **Deuteronomy 6:4-9 (*Shema*):** The core Hebrew prayer. Special emphasis is given to the first six Hebrew words of this passage (*Shema Yisrael, 'Adonai 'eloheinu, Adonai 'echad*) and a six-word response is said in an undertone (*Barukh shem kevod malkhuto le'olam va'ed*). After a pause, Deuteronomy 6:5-9 is then recited, which stresses the commandment to love the Lord your God with all of your heart, soul, and might.

2. **Deuteronomy 11:13-21 (*Vehayah*):** This moving passage stresses the blessings that come through obedience to the Lord and the consequences that come through disobedience.

3. **Numbers 15:37-41 (*Vaiyomer*):** This passage concerns the use of the *Tallit*, a rectangular prayer shawl with four fringes (called *tsitsit*). One tsitsit is attached to each corner of the Tallit. The reason for wearing the tsitsit is to remind oneself to observe all of the commandments of the Lord.

The Shema marks the declaration that God is One. Interestingly, the word *'echad* in Hebrew can imply a unity in diversity (the word for one and only one, i.e., unique, is more often rendered as *yachid*). For example, in Exodus 26:6 the parts of the Tabernacle (*mishkan*) are to be constructed so that "it shall be one (*echad*) tabernacle," and Ezekiel spoke of two "sticks" (representing fragmented Israel) as being reunited into one: "and they shall be one (*echad*) stick in My hand" (Ezekiel 37:19).

The Shema: First Part
שְׁמַע

When recited apart from a minyan:

When the Shema is recited without a minyan (i.e., a group of ten males who are *bar mitzvah*), the following phrase is first said:

אֵל מֶׁלֶךְ נֶאֱמָן.

ne·'e·man   **me·**lekh   'el

faithful   King   God (is)

God is a faithful King.

(Some sages have taught that the word "Amen" is an acronym derived from this phrase.)

Here is the first affirmation of the Shema:

שְׁמַע יִשְׂרָאֵל יְיָ אֱלֹהֵינוּ יְיָ אֶחָד.

'e·chad   Adonai   'e·lo·hey·nu   Adonai   yis·ra·'el   she·ma'

Hear O Israel, the Lord our God the Lord is one.

In an undertone, the following is said in response:

בָּרוּךְ שֵׁם כְּבוֹד מַלְכוּתוֹ לְעוֹלָם וָעֶד.

va·'ed   le·'o·lam   mal·khu·to   ke·vod   shem   ba·rukh

forever and ever   his kingdom   glorious   name   Blessed

Blessed is the Name of His glorious kingdom forever.

- **Note:** The Siddur often uses (יְיָ) in place of the sacred Name (יְהֹוָה).

Enlarged Letters

- In the Torah, the two letters (ע) and (ד) are enlarged in the first sentence of the *Shema*. Together, these letters form the word (עֵד), which means "witness," suggesting that the Shema is a testimony of the sovereignty of God.

שְׁמַע יִשְׂרָאֵל יהוה אֱלֹהֵינוּ יהוה אֶחָד

Hear O Israel, the Lord our God, the Lord is one

The Shema: First Part (continued)

וְאָהַבְתָּ

The next portion of the *Shema* (called the *Ve'ahavta*) comes from Deuteronomy 6:5-9:

וְאָהַבְתָּ אֵת יְהוָה אֱלֹהֶיךָ בְּכָל־לְבָבְךָ וּבְכָל־נַפְשְׁךָ

u·ve·khol-**naf**·she·kha	be·**khol**-le·**vav**·kha	'e·lo·**hei**·kha	'Adonai	'et	ve·'a·**hav**·ta
and with all your soul	*with all your heart*	*your God*	*the Lord*		*you shall love*

וּבְכָל־מְאֹדֶךָ וְהָיוּ הַדְּבָרִים הָאֵלֶּה אֲשֶׁר אָנֹכִי מְצַוְּךָ

me·**tsav**·ve·kha	'a·no·khi	'a·sher	ha·'el·leh	had·de·va·rim	ve·ha·yu	u·ve·khol-me·'o·de·kha
I command you		*that*	*these words*		*They should be*	*and with all your strength*

הַיּוֹם עַל־לְבָבֶךָ וְשִׁנַּנְתָּם לְבָנֶיךָ וְדִבַּרְתָּ בָּם בְּשִׁבְתְּךָ

be·**shiv**·te·kha	bam	ve·di·**bar**·ta	le·va·**ne**·kha	ve·shi·**nan**·tam	'al-le·va·**ve**·kha	hai·yom
when you sit		*and speak of them*	*teach them diligently to your children*		*upon your heart*	*today*

בְּבֵיתֶךָ וּבְלֶכְתְּךָ בַדֶּרֶךְ וּבְשָׁכְבְּךָ וּבְקוּמֶךָ וּקְשַׁרְתָּם

uq·**shar**·tam	uv·ku·**me**·kha	uv·shokh·be·kha	vad·**der**·rekh	uv·**lekh**·te·kha	be·vey·**te**·kha
And bind them	*when you rise up*	*when you lie down*	*in the way*	*while you walk*	*in your home*

לְאוֹת עַל־יָדֶךָ וְהָיוּ לְטֹטָפֹת בֵּין עֵינֶיךָ וּכְתַבְתָּם

ukh·**tav**·tam	'ei·**ney**·kha	bein	le·to·ta·fot	ve·ha·yu	'al-ya·**de**·kha	le·'ot
And write them	*your eyes*	*between*	*they should be tefillin*		*on your hand*	*for a sign*

עַל־מְזוּזֹת בֵּיתֶךָ וּבִשְׁעָרֶיךָ

u·vish·'a·**rey**·kha	bey·**te**·kha	'al·me·zu·zot
and on your gates	*your house*	*on the doorposts of*

The Shema: Second Part
וְהָיָה

The next portion of the traditional *Shema* (called the *vehayah*) is Deuteronomy 11:13-21.

מְצַוֶּה	אָנֹכִי	אֲשֶׁר	אֶל־מִצְוֺתַי	תִּשְׁמְעוּ	אִם־שָׁמֹעַ	וְהָיָה
me·tsav·veh	'a·no·khi	'a·sher	'el-mits·vo·tai	tish·me·'u	'im-sha·**mo**·a'	ve·ha·yah
command	*I*	*which*	*to My commandments*	*you will hearken*	*that if you hearken*	*And it will be*

וּלְעָבְדוֹ	אֱלֹהֵיכֶם	אֶת־יְהֹוָה	לְאַהֲבָה	הַיּוֹם	אֶתְכֶם
u·le·'av·do	'e·lo·hei·khem	'et-'Adonai	le·'a·ha·vah	hai·yom	'et·khem
and to serve Him	*your God*	*the LORD*	*to love*	*today*	*you*

מְטַר־אַרְצְכֶם	וְנָתַתִּי	וּבְכָל־נַפְשְׁכֶם	בְּכָל־לְבַבְכֶם
me·tar-'ar·tse·khem	ve·nat·ta·ti	u·ve·khol **naf**·she·khem	be·khol-le·**vav**·khem
rain to your land	*(then) I will give*	*and with all your soul*	*with all your heart*

וְיִצְהָרֶךָ	וְתִירֹשְׁךָ	דְגָנֶךָ	וְאָסַפְתָּ	וּמַלְקוֹשׁ	יוֹרֶה	בְּעִתּוֹ
ve·yits·ha·**re**·kha	ve·ti·**rosh**·kha	de·ga·**ne**·kha	ve·'a·**saf**·tah	u·mal·qosh	yo·reh	be·'it·to
and your oil.	*and your wine*	*your grain*	*so you may gather*	*and late rain*	*early rain*	*in its time*

וְשָׂבָעְתָּ	וְאָכַלְתָּ	לִבְהֶמְתֶּךָ	בְּשָׂדְךָ	עֵשֶׂב	וְנָתַתִּי
ve·sa·va·'ta	ve·'a·**khal**·ta	liv·hem·**te**·kha	be·sa·de·kha	'e·sev	ve·nat·tat·ti
and be content.	*and you will eat*	*for your cattle*	*in your field*	*grass*	*I will give*

וַעֲבַדְתֶּם	וְסַרְתֶּם	לְבַבְכֶם	יִפְתֶּה	פֶּן	לָכֶם	הִשָּׁמְרוּ
va·'a·vad·tem	ve·sart·tem	le·vav·khem	yift·teh	pen	la·khem	hish·sham·ru
and you serve	*and you turn aside*	*your hearts*	*seduced*	*lest*	*to yourselves*	*Beware*

אַף־יְהֹוָה	וְחָרָה	לָהֶם	וְהִשְׁתַּחֲוִיתֶם	אֲחֵרִים	אֱלֹהִים
'af-'Adonai	ve·cha·rah	la·hem	ve·hish·ta·cha·vi·tem	'a·che·rim	'e·lo·him
the anger of Adonai	*and burns*	*to them*	*and you bow down*	*of others*	*gods*

וְהָאֲדָמָה	מָטָר	וְלֹא־יִהְיֶה	אֶת־הַשָּׁמַיִם	וְעָצַר	בָּכֶם
ve·ha·'a·da·mah	ma·tar	ve·lo-yi·yeh	'et-hash·sha·mayim	ve·'a·tsar	ba·chem
and the ground	*rain*	*and not there will be*	*the heavens*	*He will restrain*	*against you*

The Shema: Second Part (continued)
וְהָיָה

לֹא תִתֵּן אֶת־יְבוּלָהּ וַאֲבַדְתֶּם מְהֵרָה מֵעַל הָאָרֶץ

ha·’a·rets	me·’al	me·he·rah	va·’a·vad·tem	’et-ye·vu·lah	tit·ten	lo
from the land		and you will be quickly removed		its produce	will give	not

הַטֹּבָה אֲשֶׁר יְהוָה נֹתֵן לָכֶם: וְשַׂמְתֶּם אֶת־דְּבָרַי אֵלֶּה

’el·leh	’et-de·va·rai	ve·sam·tem	la·khem	no·ten	’Adonai	’a·sher	hat·to·vah
these	words of mine	Put	to you.	gives	the LORD	which	the good

עַל־לְבַבְכֶם וְעַל־נַפְשְׁכֶם וּקְשַׁרְתֶּם אֹתָם לְאוֹת

le·’ot	’o·tam	uq·shart·tem	ve·’al·naf·she·chem	’al-le·vav·khem
for a sign	them	and bind	and upon your soul	upon your heart

עַל־יֶדְכֶם וְהָיוּ לְטוֹטָפֹת בֵּין עֵינֵיכֶם: וְלִמַּדְתֶּם אֹתָם

’o·tam	ve·lim·mad·tem	’ei·nei·khem	bein	le·to·ta·fot	ve·ha·yu	‘al-yed·khem
them	And teach	your eyes.	between	and they will be Tefillin		upon your hands

אֶת־בְּנֵיכֶם לְדַבֵּר בָּם בְּשִׁבְתְּךָ בְּבֵיתֶךָ וּבְלֶכְתְּךָ בַּדֶּרֶךְ

ba·de·rekh	uv·lekh·te·kha	be·vey·te·kha	be·shiv·te·kha	bam	le·dab·ber	’et-be·nei·khem
on the way	and when you walk	in your home	when you sit	them	to speak	to your children

וּבְשָׁכְבְּךָ וּבְקוּמֶךָ: וּכְתַבְתָּם עַל־מְזוּזוֹת בֵּיתֶךָ וּבִשְׁעָרֶיךָ:

u·vish·‘a·rey·kha	bei·te·kha	‘al-me·zu·zot	ukh·tavt·tam	uv·qu·me·kha	uv·shokh·be·kha
and on your gates.	your house	on the doorposts of	And write them	and when you rise.	and when you sit

לְמַעַן יִרְבּוּ יְמֵיכֶם וִימֵי בְנֵיכֶם עַל הָאֲדָמָה אֲשֶׁר נִשְׁבַּע

nish·ba‘	’a·sher	ha·’a·da·mah	‘al	ve·nei·chem	vi·mei	ye·mei·khem	yir·bu	le·ma·‘an
He swore	which	the land	upon	and days of your children		your days are prolonged		So that

יְהוָה לַאֲבֹתֵיכֶם לָתֵת לָהֶם כִּימֵי הַשָּׁמַיִם עַל־הָאָרֶץ:

‘al- ha·’a·rets	hash·sha·mayim	ki·mey	la·hem	la·tet	la·’a·vo·tei·chem	’Adonai
on the earth.	as the days of heaven		to them	to give	to your descendants	the LORD

The Shema: Third Part
וַיֹּאמֶר

The last part of the complete *Shema* (called the *vaiyomer*) is Numbers 15:37-41.

וַיֹּאמֶר יְהוָה אֶל־מֹשֶׁה לֵּאמֹר: דַּבֵּר אֶל־בְּנֵי יִשְׂרָאֵל

vai·**yo**·mer	'Adonai	'el·mo·she	le·mor	da·ber	'el·be·nei	yis·ra·'el
The LORD said		*to Moses*	*saying:*	*Speak*		*to the children of Israel*

וְאָמַרְתָּ אֲלֵהֶם וְעָשׂוּ לָהֶם צִיצִת עַל־כַּנְפֵי בִגְדֵיהֶם

ve·'a·mar·ta	'a·le·hem	ve·'a·su	la·hem	tsi·tsit	'al·kan·fei	vig·dey·hem
and say	*to them*	*make to themselves*		*tsitsit*	*on the corners*	*of their garments*

לְדֹרֹתָם וְנָתְנוּ עַל־צִיצִת הַכָּנָף פְּתִיל תְּכֵלֶת וְהָיָה

ve·ha·yah	te·khe·let	pe·til	ha·ka·naf	'al·tsi·tsit	ve·nat·nu	le·do·ro·tam
and it will be	*violet*	*a fringe*	*the corner*	*and put on the tsitsit*		*for generations*

לָכֶם לְצִיצִת וּרְאִיתֶם אֹתוֹ וּזְכַרְתֶּם אֶת־כָּל־מִצְוֹת

'et·kol·mits·vot	uz·khar·tem	'o·to	ur·i·tem	le·tsi·tsit	la·khem
all the commandments of	*and remember*	*it*	*so you may see*	*tsitsits*	*to them*

יְהוָה וַעֲשִׂיתֶם אֹתָם וְלֹא־תָתֻרוּ לְבַבְכֶם אַחֲרֵי וְאַחֲרֵי

ve·'a·cha·rei	le·vav·khem	'a·cha·rei	ve·lo·ta·tu·ru	'o·tam	va·'a·si·tem	'Adonai
and after	*your heart*	*after*	*and not seek out*	*them*	*and do*	*the LORD*

עֵינֵיכֶם אֲשֶׁר־אַתֶּם זֹנִים אַחֲרֵיהֶם: לְמַעַן תִּזְכְּרוּ

tiz·ke·ru	le·ma·'an	'a·cha·rei·hem	zo·nim	'a·sher·'a·tem	'ei·nei·khem
you remember	*so that*	*after them*	*lust*	*which you*	*your eyes*

וַעֲשִׂיתֶם אֶת־כָּל־מִצְוֹתָי וִהְיִיתֶם קְדֹשִׁים לֵאלֹהֵיכֶם:

le·lo·hei·khem	qe·do·shim	vih·yi·tem	'et·kol·mits·vo·tai	va·'a·si·tem
to your God	*holy*	*and be*	*all my commandments*	*and do*

The Shema: Third Part (continued)

וַיֹּאמֶר

אֲנִי יְהוָה אֱלֹהֵיכֶם אֲשֶׁר הוֹצֵאתִי אֶתְכֶם מֵאֶרֶץ

me·'e·rets	'et·khem	ho·tse·ti	'a·sher	'e·lo·hei·khem	'Adonai	'a·ni
from the land	*you*	*has brought out*	*Who*	*your God*	*Adonai*	*I am*

מִצְרַיִם לִהְיוֹת לָכֶם לֵאלֹהִים אֲנִי יְהוָה אֱלֹהֵיכֶם:

'e·lo·hei·cham	'Adonai	'a·ni	le·lo·him	la·khem	lih·yot	mits·rai·yim
your God	*Adonai*	*I am*	*God*	*for you*	*to be*	*of Egypt*

The cantor (or chazzan) then says:

יְהוָה אֱלֹהֵיכֶם אֱמֶת.

'e·met	'e·lo·hei·chem	Adonai
is true	*your God*	*The LORD*

Yeshua the Messiah and the Shema

Jesus (*Yeshua*) the Messiah (*hamashiach*) understood the importance of the Shema, as we read in the *B'rit Chadashah* (New Covenant):

Matthew 22:37-39

וַיֹּאמֶר יֵשׁוּעַ אֵלָיו וְאָהַבְתָּ אֵת יְהוָה אֱלֹהֶיךָ

בְּכָל־לְבָבְךָ וּבְכָל־נַפְשְׁךָ וּבְכָל־מְאֹדֶךָ: זוֹ הִיא

הַמִּצְוָה הַגְּדֹלָה וְהָרִאשֹׁנָה: וְהַשְּׁנִיָּה דְּמְתָה לָה

וְאָהַבְתָּ לְרֵעֲךָ כָּמוֹךָ:

"Yeshua said unto him, 'You shall love Adonai your God with all your heart (*lev*), and with all your soul (*nephesh*), and with all your might (*me'od*). This is the first and great commandment (*mitzvah*). And the second is like unto it, You shall love your neighbor (*re'ah*) as yourself.'"

The Ten Commandments
עֲשֶׂרֶת הַדִּבְּרוֹת

The Ten Commandments, called *aseret hadiberot* (or sometimes *aseret hadevarim* – "the Ten Words"), represent the minimal moral requirements for mankind. In the early Temple period, the commandments were recited immediately before the *Shema* as part of the *seder* (order) of worship. For each commandment, I provide a short *drash* (interpretation) of the text.

First: "I am Adonai Your God."

א. אָנֹכִי יְהוָה אֱלֹהֶיךָ

’e·lo·**hey**·kha   Adonai   ’a·no·khi

your God   *Adonai*   *I am*

Drash: Many of the Jewish sages taught that the greatest of all the *mitzvot* (commandments) is the very first commandment, "I am the LORD your God" (Ex. 20:2a). Why is that? Well, until we are really willing to accept Adonai as *our* God, the rest of the commandments are not likely to be obeyed. The God of Israel is calling us to obey the glorious truth that He is our God. Are we willing to obey?

Second: "Thou shalt have no other gods before Me."

ב. לֹא יִהְיֶה־לְךָ אֱלֹהִים אֲחֵרִים עַל־פָּנָי:

‘al-pa·nai   ’a·che·rim   ’e·lo·him   yih·yeh-le·kha   lo’

before me   *other*   *gods*   *you shall have*   *Not*

Drash: The second of the ten *mitzvot* (commandments) is, "Thou shalt have no other gods before Me." Why does Adonai command us not to have other gods before Him? Well, first because He is a "jealous God" (see Ex. 34:14; Deut. 4:24), which suggests that He watches us lovingly and closely, like a faithful and passionate bridegroom watches over his betrothed. He loves us and has given Himself to us passionately; He is entirely committed to our relationship with Him. Are we putting other desires, affections, or interests ahead of God's love?

עֲשֶׂרֶת הַדִּבְּרוֹת

aseret hadiberot

The Ten Commandments (continued)
עֲשֶׂרֶת הַדִּבְּרוֹת

Third: "You shall not take the Name of Adonai Your God in vain."

ג. לֹא תִשָּׂא אֶת־שֵׁם־יְהוָה אֱלֹהֶיךָ לַשָּׁוְא:

lash·shav	'el·lo·hey·kha	'et-shem-Adonai	tis·sa	lo'
to vanity	*Your God*	*the Name of Adonai*	*you shall take*	*Not*

Drash: Many of the Jewish sages taught that the word translated "Name" (*shem*) powerfully refers to the character or reputation of the one who bears it. The revealed name of the LORD (י-ה-ו-ה) thus can be understood as the invocation for the very presence of God Himself. The word translated "in vain" probably comes from another word that pictures a rushing and destructive storm (*shoah*). One way to understand this mitzvah, then, is that we should never invoke Adonai's name in a thoughtless, careless, or "stormy" manner (for this reason, Orthodox Jews never pronounce the literal name, but substitute the word "Adonai" or "HaShem" instead).

When we call upon the LORD, we are actually invoking the one true God of the universe to manifest Himself to us. Since God is faithful and will be true to His name, He will really be present whenever He is called. This is serious business. We should never take it lightly.

Fourth: "Remember the Sabbath day, to keep it separate."

ד. זָכוֹר אֶת־יוֹם הַשַּׁבָּת לְקַדְּשׁוֹ:

le·qad·de·sho	hash·shab·bat	'et-yom	za·khor
for holiness	*the Sabbath day*		*Remember*

Drash: The word translated "remember" (*zakhor*) means more than merely recalling something past, but suggests *actively focusing* the mind upon something in the present. But what are we to "remember"?

In Genesis 2:3 we are told that Adonai rested from His creative activity and set apart the seventh day as the memorial of the work of His hands. Adonai called the seventh day "holy" (*qadosh*), which means set apart as sacred, as exalted, as honored.

Just as Adonai set apart a time to focus on and honor the marvelous works of His hands, so we are commanded to regularly set apart a time to focus on and honor our own creative life in God. Notice that both Adonai and man are to set apart the Sabbath and share in the glory of this shared creative life. Are we regularly setting apart a time to remember the sacred work of God in our lives?

The Ten Commandments (continued)
עֲשֶׂרֶת הַדִּבְּרוֹת

Fifth: "Honor your father and your mother."

ה. כַּבֵּד אֶת־אָבִיךָ וְאֶת־אִמֶּךָ

ve·'et-i·**me**·kha   '*et-'a·**vi**·kha   kab·bed

and your mother   *your father*   *Honor!*

Drash: The fifth *mitzvah* marks a transition from the first four (which have to do with our vertical relationship with Adonai) to the following five (which have to do with our horizontal relationship with others). In this pivotal commandment, the word translated "honor" (*kabed*) derives from a root word meaning "weighty," in terms of impressiveness or importance. The same word is also used to refer to our heartfelt attitude toward Adonai.

Adonai intended that the *mishpakhah* (family) would picture His relationship with us. Just as Adonai created both man and woman in His image (Gen. 1:27), so children are to regard their parents as divinely ordained and truly significant.

The first four *mitzvot* tell us about God; and it is only through obedience to these commandments that we are able to really understand our own identity—as well as the identity of others in our family, our community, and our world.

Sixth: "You shall not murder."

ו. לֹא תִּרְצָח:

tir·tsach   lo'

you shall murder   *Not*

Drash: The Jewish sages note that the word *retsach* applies only to illegal killing (e.g., premeditated murder or manslaughter)—and is never used in the administration of justice or for killing in war. Hence the KJV translation as "thou shalt not kill" is too broad.

Since man is made in the image of God, his life is infinitely precious—only God Himself has the right to give and take life. In the *Mishnah* it is written, "Why was only one man (i.e., Adam) created by God?—to teach that whoever takes a single life destroys thereby a whole world."

But murder can be figurative as well as literal. The *Talmud* notes that shaming another publicly is like murder, since the shame causes the blood to leave the face. Moreover, gossip or slander are considered murderous to the dignity of man. The *Pirkei Avot* (*Ethics of the Fathers*) states, "The evil tongue slays three persons: the utterer of the evil, the listener, and the one spoken about…" The Lord Jesus also linked the ideas of our words and attitudes with murder (*see* Matt. 15:19).

The Ten Commandments (continued)

עֲשֶׂרֶת הַדִּבְּרוֹת

Seventh: "You shall not commit adultery."

ז. לֹא תִנְאָף:

tin·**'af**   lo'

you shall   *Not*
commit adultery

Drash: Adultery refers to sexual union between a married person and someone other than his or her spouse. The penalty for adultery was severe (*see* Deut. 22:22, Lev. 20:10).

From the verse, "The … adulterer waits for twilight saying, No eye shall see me" (Job 24:15), the *Talmud* identifies the adulterer as a practical atheist, since he does not say, No *man* shall see me, but no *eye*—neither the eye of one below nor the eye of Him above.

The Lord Jesus identified the root condition of adultery as a problem with the heart: "For out of the *heart* proceed…adulteries." The heart's true affections are evidenced by the use of one's *eyes* (*see* Matt. 5:27–28).

Adultery is a grave sacrilege, since it not only violates the sworn promise of parties to a sacred covenant, but perverts the picture of our union with God Himself. As Paul wrote to the *qehillah* (assembly or "church") at Ephesus, "We are members of his body, of his flesh, and of his bones. For this cause shall a man leave his father and mother, and shall be joined unto his wife, and they two shall be one flesh. This is a great mystery: but I speak concerning messiah and the church" (Eph. 5:30–32).

Seventh: "You shall not steal."

ח. לֹא תִגְנֹב:

tig·nov   lo'

you shall steal   *Not*

Drash: Stealing, in the sense of the Hebrew word *ganav*, refers to both the act of carrying off by stealth that which is not one's own (i.e., theft), but also to the deceptive inner disposition that accompanies the action. And ultimately that deceptive inner disposition is a form of self-deception.

None of us really "owns" anything at all, since God alone is the Creator and Giver of all of life. Stealing arrogantly (and vainly) attempts to seize some "thing" and to claim it for oneself – blindly disregarding the fact that "in Him we live and move and have our being" (Acts 17:28). At bottom, stealing is an act based on fear, since the attitude behind the action evidences a lack of trust that God will meet all our needs.

The Ten Commandments (continued)
עֲשֶׂרֶת הַדִּבְּרוֹת

Ninth: "You shall not bear false witness against your neighbor."

ט. לֹא־תַעֲנֶה בְרֵעֲךָ עֵד שָׁקֶר:

sha·qer	'ed	ve·re·'a·kha	lo-ta·'a·neh
false	*witness*	*against your neighbor*	*not you shall bear*

Drash: The ninth commandment prohibits swearing falsely against your neighbor in matters of law and civil proceedings, but, on a deeper level, it implicitly indicates the responsibility to be a witness of the truth at all times. Note that the Hebrew word for "truth" ('emet) is composed from the first, the middle, and the last letters of the Hebrew alphabet, thus indicating that it encompasses the first things, the last things, and everything in between. Thus, in relation to our neighbor (who is really everyone), we are to be truthful and bear witness to the truth in all our moments of life. By lying, by bearing false testimony, we effectively deny the relationship to the One who said, "I am the Way and the Truth and the Life."

Tenth: "You shall not covet."

י. לֹא תַחְמֹד

tach·mod	lo'
you shall covet	*Not*

Drash: The word translated covet usually refers to selfish desire or lust (e.g., "Lust not after her beauty in thine heart..." Prov. 6:25), and thus speaks directly to the heart's innermost intention, which, even if unacknowledged by ourselves, is always revealed before God: "Your Father who *sees in secret*" (Mt. 6:6). On the other hand, selfish desire can—if we are willing to be honest with ourselves—reveal to ourselves the condition of our hearts and thus mark our need for deliverance from the power of sin. As *Sha'ul* (Paul) wrote to the *qehillah* (congregation) in Rome: "I had not known sin ...except the law had said, 'Thou shalt not covet'" (Rom. 7:7).

Now here is a paradox: How can we refrain from desiring that which we, in fact, do desire? How can we be made free from the endless cycle of desire-sin/desire-sin? By walking in the power of the *Ruach Haqqodesh* (Holy Spirit) by the grace of God through Yeshua the Messiah: "Walk in the Spirit, and ye shall not fulfil the lust of the flesh" (Gal. 5:24, KJV). May God help you walk in His Ruach always.

Lesson Fourteen

SHABBAT BLESSINGS AND HAVDALAH

Shabbat
שַׁבָּת

In Genesis 2:3 we are told that God rested (שָׁבַת) from His creative activity and set apart the seventh day as the memorial of the work of His hands. God called the seventh day "**holy**" (קֹדֶשׁ), which means set apart as sacred, exalted, and honored.

The fourth of the ten *mitzvot* (commandments) is, "Remember the Sabbath day, to keep it holy" (KJV):

זָכוֹר אֶת־יוֹם הַשַּׁבָּת לְקַדְּשׁוֹ:

le·qa·de·sho	hash·shab·bat	ʾet-yom	za·khor
to keep it holy	*the Sabbath*	*the day (of)*	*Remember*

Remember the sabbath day, to keep it holy (Exodus 20:8)

The word translated "**remember**" (*zakhor*) means to recall or recollect past events and experiences and renew them in the present. In a sense, then, such remembering is a form of re-creation, where we reinterpret our lives and our identities in new ways.

Interestingly, the fourth commandment is repeated in Deuteronomy 5:12:

שָׁמוֹר אֶת־יוֹם הַשַּׁבָּת לְקַדְּשׁוֹ:

le·qa·de·sho	hash·shab·bat	ʾet-yom	sha·mor
to keep it holy	*the Sabbath*	*the day (of)*	*Keep*

Keep the sabbath day to sanctify it... (Deuteronomy 5:12)

The word translated "**keep**" (*shamor*) means to guard something held in trust, to protect and to watch closely. Not only are we to remember the Sabbath, but we are to guard and protect its sanctity as something of great value.

Just as God set apart a time to focus on and honor the marvelous works of His hands, so we are commanded to regularly set apart a time to focus and honor our own creative life in God. Notice that both God and man set apart the Sabbath day and share in the glory of creative life.

Some Jewish sages have said that the Sabbath is a picture of the *ʿOlam Ha Bah*, or world to come. In the rhythm of the *ʿOlam Ha Zeh*, or present world, however, the Sabbath is a sacred time to become spiritually re-connected with our true identities as God's very children. Are we regularly setting apart a time to remember the sacred work of God in our lives? The Sabbath is our God-given opportunity and privilege.

Shabbat Blessings

The Jewish Sabbath (Shabbat) begins at sunset on Friday evening and ends Saturday night when three stars are visible in the sky. On Shabbat Jews remember that God created the world and then rested from His labors.

Shabbat is considered the most important of the Jewish holidays—even more important than Yom Kippur or the other High Holidays. This is a special day to be marked by three qualities: rest (*menuchah*), holiness (*qedushah*), and joy (*'oneg*).

There are three main rituals regarding Shabbat observance:

1) Lighting the candles

2) Saying *Qiddush* (often spelled *Kiddush* in English)

3) Reciting *ha-motsi* over challah

The Shabbat meal is a time when friends and families share highlights from the week and sing table songs, called *zemirot*.

At the synagogue, a Friday night service, called *Qabbalat Shabbat* (a special *Ma'ariv* or evening service to welcome the Sabbath) is offered in addition to regular Saturday services (this service is held between the candle-lighting ceremony and the Shabbat meal). This service includes the recital of six nature Psalms (95-99, 24), corresponding in number to the six days of the creation, and the special psalm of the Sabbath (Psalm 92). The song *Lekhah Dodi* is often sung to welcome the in the Sabbath as a groom welcomes his bride. Shabbat is concluded with a *Havdalah* observance Saturday night.

The Shabbat Table

Since it is a special day of rest, preparations for Shabbat normally occur throughout the week, and especially early on Friday (or sometimes on Thursday, if the household's schedule is tight). The house is cleaned, the food is cooked, and other chores are finished up so that everyone can relax and enjoy the sanctity of time apart from their normal routines.

The Shabbat table should be set with at least two candles (representing the dual commandments to *remember* (*zakhor*) and to *observe* (*shamor*) the Sabbath), a glass of wine or grape juice (in a *Qiddush* [or *Kiddush*] cup), and at least two loaves of braided bread called *challah* (the two loaves represent the double portion of manna the ancient Israelites received each Friday during their wilderness wandering). Challah loaves are baked whole and usually covered with a decorative bread cover or napkin.

Lighting the Candles

Shabbat candles are lit by the (eldest) woman of the house no later than 18 minutes *before* sundown on Friday evening (i.e., before the Sabbath begins). After kindling the candles, she waives her hands over the flames three times (as if welcoming in the Sabbath), and covering her eyes with her hands (so as not to see the candles burning) says:

בָּרוּךְ אַתָּה יְיָ אֱלֹהֵינוּ מֶלֶךְ הָעוֹלָם, אֲשֶׁר קִדְּשָׁנוּ

qid·de·**sha**·nu ’a·sher ha·’o·**lam** **me**·lekh ‘e·lo·hey·nu ’Adonai ’at·**tah** ba·**rukh**

בְּמִצְוֹתָיו, לְהַדְלִיק נֵר שֶׁל שַׁבָּת.

shab·bat shel ner le·had·liq be·mits·vo·tav

"Blessed are You, Lord our God, King of the universe, who sanctified us with His commandments and commanded us to kindle the Shabbat light."

She then removes her hands from her eyes and looks at the light shining from the candles.

Blessing the Children

It is customary for the father of the household to bless his children on Shabbat:

For Boys:

יְשִׂמְךָ אֱלֹהִים כְּאֶפְרַיִם וְכִמְנַשֶּׁה.

ve·khi·me·na·sheh ke·’ef·rayim ’e·lo·him ye·sim·kha

"May God make you like Ephraim and Manasseh."

For Girls:

יְשִׂמֵךְ אֱלֹהִים כְּשָׂרָה רִבְקָה רָחֵל וְלֵאָה.

ve·le·’ah ra·chel riv·qah ke·sa·rah ’e·lo·him ye·si·mekh

"May God make you like Sarah, Rebecca, Rachel, and Leah."

For Both:

יְבָרֶכְךָ יְיָ וְיִשְׁמְרֶךָ. יָאֵר יְיָ פָּנָיו אֵלֶיךָ וִיחֻנֶּךָּ. יִשָּׂא יְיָ פָּנָיו

אֵלֶיךָ, וְיָשֵׂם לְךָ שָׁלוֹם.

"The Lord bless thee, and keep thee: The Lord make his face shine upon thee, and be gracious unto thee: The Lord lift up his countenance upon thee, and give thee peace."

Friday Night Qiddush (Kiddush)

Qiddush [Kiddush] is recited while holding a cup of wine, usually by the father of the household. It starts with Genesis 1:31-2:3 and ends with thanks God for the gift of the holy Sabbath:

וְהָאָ֖רֶץ הַשָּׁמַ֖יִם וַיְכֻלּ֛וּ הַשִּׁשִּׁ֑י י֖וֹם [וַיְהִי־עֶ֥רֶב וַיְהִי־בֹ֖קֶר]

ve·ha·'a·rets — ha·sha·mayim — vai·khu·lu — ha·shi·shi — yom — vai·hi·vo·qer — vai·hi·'e·rev

and the earth — the heavens — were finished — the sixth day. — and there was evening and morning

עָשָׂ֑ה אֲשֶׁ֣ר מְלַאכְתּ֖וֹ הַשְּׁבִיעִ֔י בַּיּ֤וֹם אֱלֹהִים֙ וַיְכַ֤ל צְבָאָֽם׃ וְכָל־

'a·sah — 'a·sher — me·lakh·to — hash·she·vi·'i — bai·yom — 'e·lo·him — vai·khal — tse·va·'am — vekhol

He did — that — His work — on the seventh day — and God finished — their host — and all

וַיְבָ֖רֶךְ עָשָׂ֑ה אֲשֶׁ֣ר מְלַאכְתּ֖וֹ מִכָּל־ הַשְּׁבִיעִ֔י בַּיּ֤וֹם וַיִּשְׁבֹּת֙

vai·va·rekh — 'a·sah — 'a·sher — me·lakh·to — mik·kol — hash·she·vi·'i — bai·yom — vai·yish·bot

and He blessed — He did — which — His works — from all — on the seventh day — and He rested

אֱלֹהִים֙ אֶת־י֣וֹם הַשְּׁבִיעִ֔י וַיְקַדֵּ֖שׁ אֹת֑וֹ כִּ֣י ב֤וֹ שָׁבַת֙ מִכָּל־

mik·kol — sha·vat — vo — ki — 'o·to — vai·qa·desh — hash·she·vi·'i — 'et-yom — 'e·lo·him

from all — He rested — on it — for — it — and sanctified — the seventh day — God

מְלַאכְתּ֕וֹ אֲשֶׁר־בָּרָ֥א אֱלֹהִ֖ים לַעֲשֽׂוֹת׃

la·'a·sot — 'e·lo·him — ba·ra — 'a·sher — me·lakh·to

to make. — God created — which — His works

הַגָּֽפֶן. פְּרִי בּוֹרֵא הָעוֹלָם, מֶלֶךְ אֱלֹהֵינוּ יְיָ אַתָּה בָּרוּךְ

hag·ga·fen — pe·ri — bo·re — ha·'o·lam — me·lekh — 'e·lo·hey·nu — 'Adonai — 'at·tah — ba·rukh

the vine. — fruit of — Who creates — the universe — King of — our God — Lord — are You — Blessed

קִדְּשָׁנוּ אֲשֶׁר הָעוֹלָם, מֶלֶךְ אֱלֹהֵינוּ יְיָ אַתָּה בָּרוּךְ

qid·de·sha·nu — 'a·sher — ha·'o·lam — me·lekh — 'e·lo·hey·nu — 'Adonai — 'at·tah — ba·rukh

sanctified us — Who — the universe — King of — our God — Lord — are You — Blessed

הִנְחִילָֽנוּ, וּבְרָצוֹן בְּאַהֲבָה קָדְשׁוֹ וְשַׁבַּת בָ֫נוּ וְרָצָא בְּמִצְוֹתָיו

hin·chi·la·nu — uv·ra·tson — be·a·ha·vah — qa·de·sho — ve·shab·bat — va·nu — ve·ra·tsa — be·mits·vo·tav

He guided us — and in favor — in love — and His holy Sabbath — and was pleased with us — with His mitzvot

זִכָּרוֹן	לְמַעֲשֵׂה	בְרֵאשִׁית.	כִּי	הוּא	יוֹם	תְּחִלָּה	לְמִקְרָאֵי	קֹדֶשׁ,
zik·ka·ron	le·ma·'a·seh	ve·re·shit	ki	hu	yom	te·chil·lah	le·miq·ra·ei	qo·desh
a memorial	of the work	of creation.	for	it is	the day	opening	to convocations	holy

זֵכֶר	לִיצִיאַת	מִצְרָיִם.	כִּי	בָנוּ	בָחַרְתָּ,	וְאוֹתָנוּ	קִדַּשְׁתָּ,
ze·kher	liy·tsi·at	mits·rai·yim	ki	va·nu	va·char·ta	ve·'o·ta·nu	qi·dash·ta
a memorial	of the Exodus	from Egypt.	For	us	did You choose	and us	did You sanctify

מִכָּל	הָעַמִּים.	וְשַׁבַּת	קָדְשְׁךָ	בְּאַהֲבָה	וּבְרָצוֹן	הִנְחַלְתָּנוּ.
mik·kol	ha·'a·mim	ve·shab·bat	qad·she·kha	be·'a·ha·vah	uv·ra·tson	hin·chal·ta·nu
from all	the nations.	and Your holy Sabbath		with love	and favor	You guided us

בָּרוּךְ	אַתָּה	יְיָ	מְקַדֵּשׁ	הַשַּׁבָּת.	[אָמֵן.]
ba·rukh	'at·tah	'Adonai	me·qa·desh	hash·shab·bat	'a·men
Blessed	are You	Lord	Who sanctifies	the Sabbath.	Amen.

After the blessing is recited, it is customary to give each person present some wine from the Qiddush cup.

Washing of the hands

נְטִילַת יָדַיִם

After the Qiddush is recited but before the Shabbat meal is eaten, each person in the household washes their hands by filling a cup with water and pouring it over the top and bottom of the right hand and then the left hand. Before wiping the hands dry on a towel, the following blessing is recited:

בָּרוּךְ	אַתָּה	יְהוָה	אֱלֹהֵינוּ	מֶלֶךְ	הָעוֹלָם,	אֲשֶׁר	קִדְּשָׁנוּ
ba·rukh	'at·tah	'Adonai	'e·lo·hey·nu	me·lekh	ha·'o·lam	'a·sher	qid·de·sha·nu
Blessed	are you	Lord	our God	king (of)	the universe	who	sanctified us

בְּמִצְוֹתָיו,	וְצִוָּנוּ	עַל	נְטִילַת	יָדָיִם.
be·mits·vo·tav	ve·tsi·va·nu	'al	ne·ti·lat	ya·dai·yim
with his mitzvot	and commanded us about		washing	hands

Note: The ritual of *Netilat Yadayim* is actually a "ceremonial" cleansing. In fact, before engaging in this ritual, your hands should *already* be clean! The Lord Jesus our Mashiach opposed this traditional ritual of cleansing as essentially being meaningless (Matthew 15:1-14, Mark 7:3-16). It is included here for educational purposes only.

The Blessing of the Bread

Immediately after washing hands and before eating, the head of the household removes the covering from the two challah loaves. He then lifts them up while reciting the following blessing:

בָּרוּךְ אַתָּה יְהוָה אֱלֹהֵינוּ מֶלֶךְ הָעוֹלָם,

ha·'o·lam	me·lekh	'e·lo·hey·nu	'Adonai	'at·tah	ba·rukh
the universe	*king (of)*	*our God*	*Lord*	*are you*	*Blessed*

הַמּוֹצִיא לֶחֶם מִן הָאָרֶץ.

ha·'a·rets	min	le·chem	ham·mo·tsi
the earth	*from*	*bread*	*Who brings forth*

The challah is then ripped into pieces or sliced and passed around the table, so that each person may have a piece. The family meal may then begin.

Grace after meals

The full grace said after meals, called *Birchat Hamazon*, is a rather long prayer that involves several blessings (see a good Siddur for the recitation). An alternative, shorter version (often used among Reform Jews and written in Aramaic) reads like this:

בְּרִיךְ רַחֲמָנָא מַלְכָּא דְעָלְמָא מָרֵיהּ דְהַאי פִּתָּא. [אָמֵן.]

'a·men	pit·ta	de·hai	ma·reh	de·al·ma	mal·ka	ra·kha·ma·na	be·rikh

"Blessed are You, Merciful One, the One Who is everywhere, always, Creator of this bread. Amen.

Havdalah Blessings
הַבְדָּלָה

The *Havdalah* (literally, "separation") ceremony is recited at the end of the Sabbath (on Saturday night when three stars are visible in the sky) to mark the distinction between the departing sacred day and the ordinary weekday (*yom khol*) that is beginning. One way to begin your Havdalah ceremony is to go outside and look at the stars to behold the wonder of God's creation.

The ceremony is usually celebrated at home with family or friends and includes three blessings—over wine, spices, and light—as well as the *hamavdil*, a blessing thanking God for separating the days and making the Shabbat sacred. Three components are required for the home ceremony: a tall, braided candle with several wicks, a Qiddush cup of wine, and a box filled with fragrant spices (*besamim*).

Opening Scripture

The Havdalah ceremony usually begins with the recitation of a number of biblical verses commemorating God's salvation. For example, Isaiah 12:2-3 is often recited:

הַנֵּה	אֵל	יְשׁוּעָתִי	אֶבְטַח	וְלֹא	אֶפְחָד	כִּי־עָזִי	וְזִמְרָת	יָהּ	יְהוָה
hin·neh	'el	ye·shu·'a·ti	'ev·tach	ve·lo	'ef·chad	ki·'o·zi	ve·zim·rat	yah	'Adonai
behold	God is	my salvation	I will trust	and not	be afraid	for my strength	and my song		is Lord God

וַיְהִי־לִי	לִישׁוּעָה:	וּשְׁאַבְתֶּם־מַיִם	בְּשָׂשׂוֹן	מִמַּעַיְנֵי	הַיְשׁוּעָה:
vai·hi·li	liy·shu·'ah	ush·'av·tem·mayim	be·sa·son	mim·ma·'ai·nei	hai·shu·'ah
and He is to me	my salvation	you will draw water	with joy	from the wellsof	salvation

Behold, God is my salvation; I will trust, and not be afraid: for the LORD Adonai is my strength and my song; he also is become my salvation. Therefore with joy shall ye draw water out of the wells of salvation. (Isaiah 12:2-3)

And Psalm 116:13 is also often recited:

כּוֹס	יְשׁוּעוֹת	אֶשָּׂא	וּבְשֵׁם	יְהוָה	אֶקְרָא:
kos	ye·shu·'ot	'es·sa	u·ve·shem	'Adonai	'ek·ra
Cup	of salvation	I lift	on the name	Lord	I call

I will take the cup of salvation, and call upon the name of the LORD
(Psalm 116:13)

Blessing over the wine

Just as Sabbath is welcomed with wine, so it is concluded with wine as well. We lift the Qiddush cup of wine and say the blessing, but do not drink from the cup at this time:

בָּרוּךְ	אַתָּה	יְיָ	אֱלֹהֵינוּ	מֶלֶךְ	הָעוֹלָם,	בּוֹרֵא	פְּרִי	הַגָּפֶן.
ba·rukh	ʾat·tah	ʾAdonai	ʾe·lo·hey·nu	me·lekh	ha·ʿo·lam	bo·rei	pe·ri	hag·**ga**·fen
Blessed	are You	Lord	our God	King of	the universe	Who creates	fruit of	the vine.

Blessed are You, Lord our God, King of the universe,
Who creates the fruit of the vine.

Blessing over the spices

A special spice box filled with fragrant herbs (*besamim*) is used to represent the redolence of Shabbat (the spices commonly used are cloves, cinnamon, or bay leaves). Since smelling spices helps distinguish special fragrance from the more ordinary, part of the reason for the *besamim box* is to illustrate another separation of the sacred from the profane. The following blessing is said upon smelling the spice box:

בָּרוּךְ	אַתָּה	יְיָ	אֱלֹהֵינוּ	מֶלֶךְ	הָעוֹלָם,	בּוֹרֵא	מִינֵי	בְשָׂמִים.
ba·rukh	ʾat·tah	ʾAdonai	ʾe·lo·hey·nu	me·lekh	ha·ʿo·**lam**	bo·**re**	mi·nei	ve·sa·mim
Blessed	are You	Lord	our God	King of	the universe	Creator	of all	spices.

Blessed are You, Lord our God, King of the universe, Creator of all spices.

Blessing over the fire

The Havdalah candle represents light, the first element created by God at the beginning of the first week. Lighting this candle is the first act of work permitted on the *yom khol*. After lighting, hold your hands close to the flame in order to see the reflection of the flame on our fingernails or the shadow on your palm. This light represents the light by which we can now work with our hands in the world around us. The following blessing is said upon considering the light:

בָּרוּךְ	אַתָּה	יְיָ	אֱלֹהֵינוּ	מֶלֶךְ	הָעוֹלָם,	בּוֹרֵא	מְאוֹרֵי	הָאֵשׁ.
ba·rukh	ʾat·tah	ʾAdonai	ʾe·lo·hey·nu	me·lekh	ha·ʿo·**lam**	bo·rei	me·ʾo·rei	ha·**ʾesh**
Blessed	are You	Lord	our God	King of	the universe	Creator	of the light	of the fire.

Blessed are You, Lord our God, King of the universe,
Creator of the light of fire.

Havdalah Blessing

The last blessing of the ceremony is the *hamavdil*, the blessing over the separation of different things. This blessing is recited over the Qiddush cup of wine. After the blessing is complete, the wine is drunk. A few drops of wine are used to extinguish the flame from the candle (some people extinguish the candle by dipping it into the wine cup and listening to it sizzle).

קֹדֶשׁ	בֵּין	הַמַּבְדִּיל,	הָעוֹלָם,	מֶלֶךְ	אֱלֹהֵינוּ	יְיָ	אַתָּה	בָּרוּךְ
qo·desh	bein	ham·**mav**·dil	ha·'o·**lam**	**me**·lekh	'e·lo·hey·nu	'Adonai	'at·tah	ba·rukh
the holy	between	Who separates	the universe	King of	our God	Lord	are You	Blessed

	בֵּין	יִשְׂרָאֵל	לָעַמִּים,	בֵּין	לְחֹשֶׁךְ,	אוֹר	בֵּין	לְחוֹל,
	bein	yis·ra·'el	la·'am·mim	bein	le·cho·shekh	'or	bein	le·chol
	between	Israel	and the nations	between	and darkness	light	between	the profane

הַמַּבְדִּיל	יְיָ	אַתָּה	בָּרוּךְ	הַמַּעֲשֶׂה.	יְמֵי	לְשֵׁשֶׁת	הַשְּׁבִיעִי	יוֹם
ham·**mav**·dil	'Adonai	'at·tah	ba·rukh	ham·ma·'a·seh	ye·mei	le·she·shet	ha·shev·i·'i	yom
Who separates	Lord	are You	Blessed	and the six days of work			the seventh day	

[אָמֵן.]	לְחוֹל.	קֹדֶשׁ	בֵּין
'a·men	le·chol	**qo**·desh	bein
Amen.	the profane	the holy	between

Blessed are You, Lord our God, King of the universe,
Who separates the holy from the profane, light from darkness, Israel from the nations,
the seventh day from the six days of labor. Blessed are You, Lord our God,
Who separates between the holy from the profane.

At the end of the ceremony, the song *Eliyahu Hanavi* ("The Prophet Elijah") is often sung and everyone present is wished "*Shavu'a Tov*" – a good week ahead!

Shavu'a   Tov!

Lesson Fifteen

SIDDUR BLESSINGS AND PRAYERS I

Lesson Introduction

Hebrew Blessings

Many Hebrew blessings found in the prayer book (or *Siddur*) include the opening invocation:

בָּרוּךְ אַתָּה יְיָ אֱלֹהֵינוּ מֶלֶךְ הָעוֹלָם,

ba·rukh   ’at·tah   ’Adonai   ‘e·lo·**hei**·nu   **me**·lekh   ha·‘o·lam

"Blessed are You, Lord our God, King of the universe,"

This phrase is sometimes called the *Shem umalkhut* (the name and the sovereignty) and constitutes the affirmation that God is King over the entire universe.

Jewish tradition requires that we personally bless the LORD for each detail of our daily experience. Such a requirement, if not practiced legalistically, surely points to a deep inward appreciation for the good things God personally provides for us throughout each day. As the Lord Jesus said, our heavenly Father knows the very number of the hairs on our head (Matt 10:30), and, if our eyes are open to His grace, we too will notice His provision even in the smallest details of our lives. And we will thank Him for His care.

It is interesting to note that the word translated "blessed" בָּרוּךְ (*barukh*) is related to the Hebrew word for "knee" בֶּרֶךְ (*berekh*), as is the word for "blessing" בְּרָכָה (*berakha*), thus implying an association between humbling ourselves (i.e., kneeling before Him in recognition of His blessedness) and receiving personal blessing from Him. Yes, "Blessed be the God and Father of our Lord Jesus Christ, who hath blessed us with all spiritual blessings in heavenly places in Messiah Jesus" (Eph.1:3).

Hebrew Prayers

The English word *pray* derives from a root word meaning "to beg or entreat," whereas the Hebrew word (*hitpallel*) comes from a verb meaning "to judge oneself." When we pray, we first inwardly examine ourselves and then sincerely call upon the Lord with reverent singleness of heart.

In Jewish thinking, devotion from the heart, called *kavanat ha lev*, is considered essential to true prayer. *Kavanah* implies concentration, worship, and single-mindedness: you simply cannot reach the Lord without earnestness and passion of the whole heart (*see* Jer. 29:13, Heb 11:6). One of the Jewish sages wrote, "Prayer without *kavanah* is like a body without a soul," suggesting that merely mouthing the "right words" of a prayer is empty hypocrisy if the inmost heart is not also profoundly involved. And will God, who is Spirit, listen to such insincerity from our lips? (*see* Isa. 29:13)

The goal of this lesson is to enhance your reading skills and to familiarize yourself with some common Hebrew prayers and blessings. For detailed study of Hebrew prayers, there is no substitute for purchasing and studying your own Siddur.

The Siddur and Prayer Cycles

Jewish prayer is connected with times and seasons: the time of the day, the day of the week, the ordinary day (*yom khol*) and the sacred day (*yom tov*), the ordinary seasons and the festival seasons (*mo'adim*), special events (such as a *berit milah* (circumcision and naming of a child), a *bar* or *bat mitzvah*, a Jewish marriage, a Jewish death), and so on.

The Hebrew word for prayerbook is *Siddur*, which comes from a Hebrew root (סדר) meaning "order." The Siddur, then, is a book that sets forth certain Hebrew prayers in a very specific (time-based) order. There are many types of Siddurim available, but they all share a similar underlying structure.

Observant Jews pray in formal worship services three times a day, every day (corresponding to the sacrifices once offered at the Temple). Accordingly, most (weekday) Siddurim include *Tefillat Shacharit* (morning prayers), *Tefillat Minchah* (afternoon prayers), and *Tefillat Ma'ariv* (evening prayers). In each case, one prayer—the *Shemoneh 'Esreh* (also known as the *'Amidah*)—is recited. The last prayer to be said each day is the *Qeri'at Shema 'al hamitah* (the bedtime Shema). Shabbat Siddurim are ordered in accordance with the routine of Shabbat. Since it begins in the evening, the first set of prayers concern candle lighting and welcoming the Shabbat.

עֶרֶב וָבֹקֶר וְצָהֳרַיִם אָשִׂיחָה וְאֶהֱמֶה וַיִּשְׁמַע קוֹלִי:

Evening, and morning, and at noon, will I pray, and cry aloud: and he shall hear my voice.

Psalm 55:17

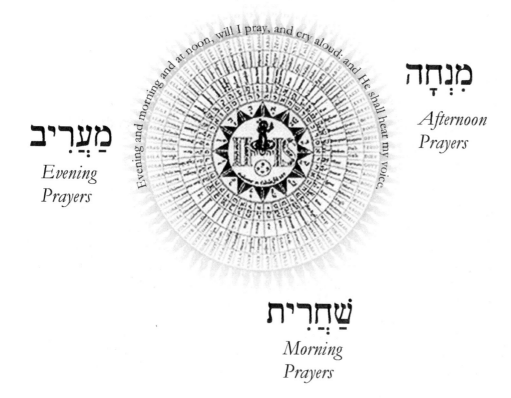

מַעֲרִיב
Evening Prayers

מִנְחָה
Afternoon Prayers

שַׁחֲרִית
Morning Prayers

Upon Arising

הַשְׁכָּמַת הַבּוֹקֶר

When we wake in the morning, God graciously restores our soul (*neshamah* or *nefesh*) within us in order to experience another day of life. This awakening is an analog of the resurrection from the dead: just as God revives us from the depths of our sleep and enables our eyes to once again receive light, so will He ultimately revive the dead from their state and bring them into the glorious presence of His Light.

The *Modeh 'Ani*, one of the first prayers a Jewish child is taught, expresses gratitude to God for the gift of a new day of life (note that women say "modah" instead of "modeh"):

מוֹדֶה	אֲנִי	לְפָנֶיךָ,	מֶלֶךְ	חַי	וְקַיָּם,
mo·deh	'a·ni	le·fa·**ney**·kha	**me**·lekh	chai	ve·qai·yam
thank	*I*	*before you*	*king*	*living*	*and eternal*

שֶׁהֶחֱזַרְתָּ	בִּי	נִשְׁמָתִי	בְּחֶמְלָה,	רַבָּה	אֱמוּנָתֶךָ.
she·he·che·**zar**·ta	bi	nish·ma·ti	be·chem·lah	rab·bah	'e·mu·na·**te**·kha
for you returned	*in me*	*my soul*	*in compassion*	*great (is)*	*your faithfulness.*

I thank you, living and eternal King,
for returning my soul within me in compassion,
great is your faithfulness.

M o d e h   A n i

"In the service of the Almighty, the point of departure is Modeh Ani."
—*Rabbi Sholom Dov Ber of Lubavitch*

The Fear of Adonai
יִרְאַת יְהֹוָה

The "fear of the Lord" (*Yir'at 'Adonai*) does not denote a cringing terror of God but a reverential awe at the glory of His Presence as He daily condescends to be involved in our lives. *Yir'ah* is really a form of devotion, a consciousness of the sacredness and mystery of receiving life itself from the Living God (*El Chai*), and essentially draws upon gratitude to God for this great gift.

Such an attitude of devotion yields wisdom (*chokhmah*) and is a result of "practicing the presence" of the Lord in our daily lives. As James tells us, this wisdom is "first pure, then full of peace, gentleness, mercy, good fruits, and sincerity" (*see* James 3:17).

Since we are created by God to worship and know Him, Psalm 110:10 is often recited in the morning to remind us that the fear of the Lord is the beginning of wisdom:

'o·sei·hem	le·khol	tov	se·khel	'Adonai	yir·'at	choch·mah	re·shit
who do	*to all*	*good*	*insight*	*LORD*	*the fear of*	*the beginning of wisdom*	

la·'ad	'o·me·det	te·hil·la·to
forever	*endures*	*his praise*

va·'ed	le·'o·lam	mal·khu·to	ke·vod	shem	ba·rukh
forever and ever		*his glorious kingdom*		*Blessed is the name of*	

The fear of the LORD is the beginning of wisdom:
a good understanding have all they that do his commandments:
his praise endureth for ever.
Blessed be the name of his glorious kingdom forever.

Yirat Adonai
The fear of the Lord

While Washing Oneself

נְטִילַת יָדַיִם

Some of the Jewish sages have said that, immediately after arising, you should wash your hands from a vessel like the laver a priest used before performing his service in the Holy Temple. The morning ritual of washing oneself is sanctified by the *netilat yadayim*:

בָּרוּךְ אַתָּה יְהוָה אֱלֹהֵינוּ מֶלֶךְ הָעוֹלָם,

ha·ʻo·lam	me·lekh	ʼe·lo·**hey**·nu	ʼAdonai	ʼat·tah	ba·rukh
the universe	*king (of)*	*our God*	*Lord*	*are you*	*Blessed*

אֲשֶׁר קִדְּשָׁנוּ בְּמִצְוֹתָיו, וְצִוָּנוּ עַל נְטִילַת יָדָיִם.

ya·**dai**·yim	ne·ti·lat	ʻal	ve·tsi·**va**·nu	be·mits·vo·tav	qid·de·**sha**·nu	ʼa·sher
hands	*washing*	*and commanded us about*		*with his commandments*	*sanctified us*	*who*

Putting On the Tallit
עֲטִיפַת טַלִּית

Traditionally worn at weekday morning synagogue services, a *Tallit* is a rectangular prayer shawl with four fringes—*tsitsit*—one attached at each corner. A Tallit is worn to remind oneself to observe all of the commandments of the Lord (*see* Numbers 15:38-9). The following prayer is recited when putting on a Tallit and observing the tsitsit.

בָּרְכִי נַפְשִׁי אֶת יְהוָה, יְהוָה אֱלֹהַי גָּדַלְתָּ מְּאֹד

me·'od	ga·**dal**·ta	'e·lo·hai	'Adonai	'Adonai	'et	naf·shi	ba·re·**khi**
very	*you are great*	*my God*	*Adonai*	*Adonai*	*( )*	*O my soul*	*Bless*

הוֹד וְהָדָר לָבָשְׁתָּ. עֹשֶׂה אוֹר כַּשַּׂלְמָה,

ka·**sal**·mah	'or	'**o**·seh	la·**vash**·ta	ve·ha·dar	hod
as a garment	*light*	*donning*	*you wore*	*and majesty*	*glory*

נוֹטֶה שָׁמַיִם כַּיְרִיעָה.

kai·ri·'ah	sha·**mai**·yim	no·teh
as a curtain	*heavens*	*stretching*

טַלִּית

טַלִּית

Numbers 15:38-9

צִיצִית ←

Mah Tovu
מַה טֹבוּ

The *Mah Tovu* is a mixture of verses from different places in the Hebrew Bible. The first is from Numbers 24:5, and the others are from different places in the Psalms. The custom is to recite Mah Tovu as one enters the synagogue or shortly thereafter.

מַה טֹבוּ אֹהָלֶיךָ יַעֲקֹב, מִשְׁכְּנֹתֶיךָ יִשְׂרָאֵל. וַאֲנִי בְּרֹב

mah	to·vu	'o·ha·**ley**·kha	ya·'a·kov	mish·ke·no·**tey**·kha	yis·ra·'el	va·'a·ni	be·rov
How	goodly	your tents	O Jacob	your dwellings	O Israel	As for me	in the multitude

חַסְדְּךָ אָבוֹא בֵיתֶךָ, אֶשְׁתַּחֲוֶה אֶל הֵיכַל קָדְשְׁךָ בְּיִרְאָתֶךָ.

chas·de·kha	'a·vo	vey·te·kha	esh·ta·cha·veh	'el	hei·chal	qad·she·kha	be·yir·'a·**te**·kha
your favor	I will come	into your house	I will prostrate myself	unto	the sanctuary of Your holiness	in awe of You

יְהוָה, אָהַבְתִּי מְעוֹן בֵּיתֶךָ, וּמְקוֹם מִשְׁכַּן כְּבוֹדֶךָ. וַאֲנִי

'Adonai	'a·**hav**·ti	me·'on	bey·**te**·kha	um·qom	mish·kan	ke·vo·**de**·kha	va·'a·ni
Lord	I love	shelter	Your house	and place	tabernacle	of Your glory	and I

אֶשְׁתַּחֲוֶה וְאֶכְרָעָה, אֶבְרְכָה לִפְנֵי יְהוָה עֹשִׂי. וַאֲנִי,

'esh·ta·cha·veh	ve·'ech·**ra**·'ah	'ev·re·khah	lif·nei	'Adonai	'o·si	va·'a·ni
will prostrate myself	and bow	I will kneel	before	the Lord	my Maker	and I

תְפִלָּתִי לְךָ יהוה, עֵת רָצוֹן, אֱלֹהִים בְּרֹב חַסְדֶּךָ,

te·fil·**la**·ti	le·kha	'Adonai	'et	ra·tson	'e·lo·him	be·rov	chas·**de**·kha
may my prayer	to You	Lord	a time	favorable	O God	in the multitude	of your favor

עֲנֵנִי בֶּאֱמֶת יִשְׁעֶךָ.

'a·**ne**·ni	be·'e·met	yish·'e·kha
answer me	in the truth	of Your salvation

Before Reading the Torah
בִּרְכוֹת הַתּוֹרָה

Torah reading is considered a part of an everyday experience for the observant Jew. This prayer is often said as part of morning services in the synagogue:

בָּרוּךְ אַתָּה יהוה אֱלֹהֵינוּ מֶלֶךְ הָעוֹלָם, אֲשֶׁר

'a·sher	ha·'o·lam	me·lekh	'e·lo·hey·nu	'Adonai	'at·tah	ba·rukh
who	the universe	king (of)	our God	Lord	are you	Blessed

קִדְּשָׁנוּ בְּמִצְוֹתָיו, וְצִוָּנוּ לַעֲסוֹק בְּדִבְרֵי תוֹרָה.

to·rah	be·div·rei	la·'a·sok	ve·tsi·va·nu	be·mits·vo·tav	qi·de·sha·nu
of Torah	in the words	to engross ourselves	and commanded us	in His commandments	has sanctified us

וְהַעֲרֶב נָא יהוה אֱלֹהֵינוּ אֶת דִּבְרֵי תוֹרָתְךָ בְּפִינוּ

be·fi·nu	to·ra·te·kha	div·rei	'et	'e·lo·hey·nu	'Adonai	na	ve·ha·'a·rev
in our mouth	of Your Torah	the words	( )	our God	Lord	please	sweeten

וּבְפִי עַמְּךָ בֵּית יִשְׂרָאֵל. וְנִהְיֶה אֲנַחְנוּ וְצֶאֱצָאֵינוּ

ve·tse·'e·tse·'ei·nu	a·nach·nu	ve·nih·yeh	yis·ra·'el	beit	'am·me·kha	uv·fi
and our offspring	we	that we may be	of Israel	the house	in the mouth of your people

וְצֶאֱצָאֵי עַמְּךָ בֵּית יִשְׂרָאֵל כֻּלָּנוּ יוֹדְעֵי שְׁמֶךָ

she·me·kha	yo·de·'ey	kul·la·nu	yis·ra·'el	beit	'am·me·kha	ve·tse·'e·tsa·'ei
your Name	who know	all of us	of Israel	house	of your people	and the offspring

וְלוֹמְדֵי תוֹרָתְךָ לִשְׁמָהּ. בָּרוּךְ אַתָּה יהוה הַמְלַמֵּד

ha·me·lam·med	'Adonai	'at·tah	ba·rukh	lish·mah	to·ra·te·kha	ve·lo·me·dei
who teaches	Lord	are you	Blessed	for its own sake	your Torah	and study

תּוֹרָה לְעַמּוֹ יִשְׂרָאֵל.

yis·ra·'el	le·'a·mo	to·rah
Israel	to his people	Torah

Before Reading the Torah (continued)
בִּרְכוֹת הַתּוֹרָה

אֲשֶׁר הָעוֹלָם מֶלֶךְ אֱלֹהֵינוּ יְהוָה אַתָּה בָּרוּךְ

'a·sher — ha·'**o**·lam — **me**·lekh — 'e·lo·**hey**·nu — 'Adonai — 'at·tah — ba·rukh

who — the universe — king (of) — our God — Lord — are you — Blessed

תּוֹרָתוֹ. אֶת לָנוּ וְנָתַן הָעַמִּים מִכָּל בָּנוּ בָּחַר

to·ra·to — et — **la**·nu — ve·na·tan — ha·'am·mim — mik·kol — **ba**·nu — **ba**·char

his Torah — ( ) — to us — and gave — the peoples — from all — us — chose

בָּרוּךְ אַתָּה יְהוָה, נוֹתֵן הַתּוֹרָה.

hat·to·rah — no·ten — 'Adonai — 'at·tah — ba·rukh

(of) the Torah — giver — Lord — are you — Blessed

יְבָרֶכְךָ יְהוָה וְיִשְׁמְרֶךָ.

ve·yish·me·**re**·kha — 'Adonai — ye·va·re·khe·kha

and protect you — May the Lord bless you

יָאֵר יְהוָה פָּנָיו אֵלֶיךָ וִיחֻנֶּךָ.

vi·chun·**ne**·ka — 'e·**ley**·kha — pa·nav — 'Adonai — ya·'er

and be gracious to you — to you — his face — May the Lord shine

יִשָּׂא יְהוָה פָּנָיו אֵלֶיךָ, וְיָשֵׂם לְךָ שָׁלוֹם.

sha·lom — le·kha — ve·ya·sem — 'e·**ley**·kha — pa·nav — 'Adonai — yi·sa

peace — to you — and give — to you — his face — May the Lord turn his face

Additional Morning Blessings
בִּרְכוֹת הַשַּׁחַר

A variety of blessings are often recited in the morning service to remind us of the Lord's daily provisions and care for us (for a complete list, consult a good Siddur).

For giving the heart understanding:

בָּרוּךְ אַתָּה יְהֹוָה אֱלֹהֵינוּ מֶלֶךְ הָעוֹלָם,

ha·ʻo·lam	me·lekh	ʼe·lo·hey·nu	ʼAdonai	ʼat·tah	ba·rukh
the universe	king (of)	our God	Lord	are you	Blessed

אֲשֶׁר נָתַן לַשֶּׂכְוִי בִינָה לְהַבְחִין בֵּין יוֹם וּבֵין לָיְלָה.

lai·lah	u·vein	yom	bein	le·hav·chin	vi·na	la·sekh·vi	na·tan	ʼa·sher
night	and between	day	between	to distinguish	understanding	the heart	gave	who

For meeting all my needs:

בָּרוּךְ אַתָּה יְהֹוָה אֱלֹהֵינוּ מֶלֶךְ הָעוֹלָם,

ha·ʻo·lam	me·lekh	ʼe·lo·hey·nu	ʼAdonai	ʼat·tah	ba·rukh
the universe	king (of)	our God	Lord	are you	Blessed

שֶׁעָשָׂה לִי כָּל צָרְכִּי.

tsor·ki	kol	li	she·ʻa·sah
my needs	all	for me	who provides

For giving strength to the weary:

בָּרוּךְ אַתָּה יְהֹוָה אֱלֹהֵינוּ מֶלֶךְ הָעוֹלָם,

ha·ʻo·lam	me·lekh	ʼe·lo·hey·nu	ʼAdonai	ʼat·tah	ba·rukh
the universe	king (of)	our God	Lord	are you	Blessed

הַנּוֹתֵן לַיָּעֵף כֹּחַ.

ko·ach	lai·ya·ʻef	ha·no·ten
strength	to the weary	who gives

Yetser Hara / Yetser Hatov
יֵצֶר הָרָע / יֵצֶר הַטּוֹב

The *yetser hara'* represents the inner impulse or tendency within the human heart to gravitate toward selfish gratification (the word *yetser* first appears in Genesis 6:5 where the wickedness of man is described as "every *imagination* of the thoughts of his heart was only evil continually"). The *yetser hatov*, on the other hand, represents the inner impulse to do good.

Yetser is also used in Scripture to refer to something formed or shaped, like pottery fashioned by the hand of a potter. Just as a potter *purposes* a shape in his or her mind before forming an object, so that which is *intended* within the mind will shape or form our character and disposition, especially with regard to our relationship with God.

בָּרוּךְ אַתָּה יְהוָה אֱלֹהֵינוּ מֶלֶךְ הָעוֹלָם,

ha·ʻo·lam	me·lekh	ʼe·lo·hey·nu	ʼAdonai	ʼat·tah	ba·rukh
the universe	king (of)	our God	Lord	are you	Blessed

הַמַּעֲבִיר שֵׁנָה מֵעֵינַי וּתְנוּמָה מֵעַפְעַפָּי. וִיהִי רָצוֹן

ra·tson	vi·hi	me·af·ʻa·pai	ut·nu·mah	me·ʻey·nai	she·nah	ham·ma·ʻa·vir
the will	may it be	from my eyelids	and slumber	from my eyes	sleep	who removes

מִלְּפָנֶיךָ, יְהוָה אֱלֹהֵינוּ וֵאלֹהֵי אֲבוֹתֵינוּ, שֶׁתַּרְגִּילֵנוּ

shet·tar·gi·lei·nu	ʼa·vo·tei·nu	ve·lo·hei	ʼe·lo·hey·nu	ʼAdonai	mil·fa·ne·kha
that you accustom us	our fathers	and God of	our God	Lord	before You

בְּתוֹרָתֶךָ וְדַבְּקֵנוּ בְּמִצְוֹתֶיךָ, וְאַל תְּבִיאֵנוּ לֹא לִידֵי

li·dei	lo'	te·vi·ʼe·nu	ve·ʼal	be·mits·vo·tey·kha	ve·da·be·ke·nu	be·to·ra·te·kha
to the hands	not	lead us	and don't	to your mitzvot	and attach us	in your Torah

חֵטְא וְלֹא לִידֵי עֲבֵרָה וְעָוֹן, וְלֹא לִידֵי נִסָּיוֹן,

nis·sa·yon	li·dei	ve·lo'	ve·ʻa·von	ʻa·ve·rah	li·dei	ve·lo	chet
of temptation	into hands	nor	and perversity	of pride	into hands	nor	of sin

וְלֹא לִידֵי בִזָּיוֹן, וְאַל תַּשְׁלֶט בָּנוּ יֵצֶר הָרָע.

ha·ra'	ye·tser	ba·nu	tash·let	ve·ʼal	vi·ze·yon	li·dei	ve·lo'
of evil	inclination	over us	let rule	and don't	of scorn	into hands	nor

The Aqedah
עֲקֵדָה

The 'Aqedah (sometimes called the 'Aqedat Yitschak) is the story of how Abraham was tested by God to bind his beloved son Isaac and offer him as a sacrifice on Mount Moriah. At the last moment, God stopped Abraham from going through with the sacrifice and provided a substitute (*see* Genesis 22). (Aqedah means "binding".)

As Messianic believers, we understand the *Aqedah* as a foreshadowing of the ultimate sacrifice the heavenly Father would give on our behalf: unlike Abraham, God the Father actually offered His only Son in order to make salvation available to all who believe (*see* John 3:16). As Abraham said, "God Himself will provide a lamb" (Genesis 22:8).

אֱלֹהֵינוּ	וֵאלֹהֵי	אֲבוֹתֵינוּ	זָכְרֵנוּ	בְּזִכָּרוֹן	טוֹב	לְפָנֶיךָ
'e·lo·**hey**·nu	ve·lo·hei	'a·vo·**tei**·nu	zokh·**re**·nu	be·zik·ka·ron	tov	le·fa·**ney**·kha
Our God	and God of	our fathers	remember us	with memory	good	before you

וּפָקְדֵנוּ	בִּפְקֻדַּת	יְשׁוּעָה	וְרַחֲמִים	מִשְּׁמֵי	שְׁמֵי	קֶדֶם.
u·faq·**de**·nu	bif·qud·dat	ye·shu·'ah	ve·ra·cha·mim	mi·she·mei	she·mei	**qe**·dem
and recall	in recollection	salvation	and mercy	from heaven	of heavens	of old

וּזְכֹר	לָנוּ	יהוה	אֱלֹהֵינוּ	אַהֲבַת	הַקַּדְמוֹנִים	אַבְרָהָם
uz·khor	la·nu	'Adonai	'e·lo·**hey**·nu	'a·ha·vat	haq·qad·mo·nim	'av·ra·ham
remember	for us	Lord	our God	the love of	the ancients	Abraham

יִצְחָק	וְיִשְׂרָאֵל	עֲבָדֶיךָ	אֶת	הַבְּרִית	וְאֶת	הַחֶסֶד	וְאֶת
yits·chak	ve·yis·ra·'el	'a·va·**dey**·kha	'et	hab·be·rit	ve·'et	ha·**che**·sed	ve·'et
Isaac	and Israel	your servants	( )	the covenant	and ( )	the mercy	and ( )

הַשְּׁבוּעָה	שֶׁנִּשְׁבַּעְתָּ	לְאַבְרָהָם	אָבִינוּ	בְּהַר	הַמּוֹרִיָּה
ha·she·**vu**·'ah	shen·nish·**ba**·ta	le·'av·ra·ham	'a·**vi**·nu	be·har	ham·mo·riy·yah
the oath	that you swore	to Abraham	our father	on mount	Moriah

וְאֶת	הָעֲקֵדָה	שֶׁעָקַד	אֶת	יִצְחָק	בְּנוֹ	עַל	גַּבֵּי	הַמִּזְבֵּחַ
ve·'et	ha·'a·ke·dah	she·'a·qad	'et	yits·chak	be·no	'al	gab·bei	ha·miz·**be**·ach
and ( )	the Akedah	when he bound	( )	Isaac	his son	on	top of	the altar

L'olam
לְעוֹלָם

The *L'olam* portion of the *Shacharit* prepares the heart for the recitation of the Shema, the most significant declaration of the unity of God in the Jewish liturgy. A portion of this prayer is included for you to practice your reading:

לְעוֹלָם יְהֵא אָדָם יְרֵא שָׁמַיִם בְּסֵתֶר וּבַגָּלוּי, וּמוֹדֶה

le·'o·lam	ye·he	'a·dam	ye·re	sha·**mai**·yim	be·**se**·ter	u·va·**ga**·luy	u·mo·**deh**
Forever	should	a man	fear	heaven	privately	and publicly	and attest

עַל הָאֱמֶת וְדוֹבֵר אֱמֶת בִּלְבָבוֹ וְיַשְׁכֵּם וְיֹאמַר:

'al	ha·'e·met	ve·do·ver	'e·met	bil·va·vo	ve·yash·kem	ve·yo·mar
to	the truth	and speak	truth	in the heart	and rise early	and say

רִבּוֹן כָּל הָעוֹלָמִים, לֹא עַל צִדְקוֹתֵינוּ אֲנַחְנוּ מַפִּילִים

rib·bon	kol	ha·'o·la·mim	lo'	'al	tsid·qo·**tei**·nu	'a·**nach**·nu	ma·pi·lim
Master	of all	the worlds	not	of	our righteousness	we	cast

תַּחֲנוּנֵינוּ לְפָנֶיךָ, כִּי עַל רַחֲמֶיךָ הָרַבִּים. מַה אֲנַחְנוּ,

ta·cha·nu·**nei**·nu	le·fa·**nei**·kha	ki	'al	ra·cha·**mey**·kha	ha·rab·bim	mah	'a·**nach**·nu
our supplications	before you	but because	your mercy	that is great	what	(are) we?	

מֶה חַיֵּינוּ, מַה חַסְדֵּנוּ, מַה צִדְקוֹתֵינוּ, מַה יְשׁוּעָתֵנוּ,

meh	chai·**yei**·nu	mah	chas·**de**·nu	mah	tsid·qo·**tei**·nu	mah	ye·shu·'a·**tei**·nu
what	our life?	what	our kindness?	what	our righteousness?	what	our salvation?

מַה כֹּחֵנוּ, מַה גְבוּרָתֵנוּ. מַה נֹּאמַר לְפָנֶיךָ, יְהוָה

mah	ko·**che**·nu	mah	ge·vu·ra·**te**·nu	mah	no·mar	le·fa·**nei**·kha	'Adonai
what	our strength?	what	our might?	what	can we say	before you	Lord

אֱלֹהֵינוּ וֵאלֹהֵי אֲבוֹתֵינוּ.

'e·lo·**hey**·nu	ve·lo·hei	'a·vo·**tei**·nu
our God	and God of	our fathers?

Mourner's Qaddish (Kaddish)
קַדִּישׁ יָתוֹם

The *Qaddish* is an (Aramaic) anthem of praise to God recited daily in the synagogue. There are several types of *Qaddish*, such as the *Rabbi's Qaddish* and the *Learner's Qaddish*. The most well-known is the *Mourner's Qaddish*, recited during the *shiv'ah* (mourning) period. In the following, text in brackets is said in response to the mourner's recitation:

יִתְגַּדַּל וְיִתְקַדַּשׁ שְׁמֵהּ רַבָּא. [אָמֵן.] בְּעָלְמָא דִּי בְרָא

yit·ga·dal	ve·yit·qa·dash	she·meh	rab·ba'	'a·men	be·'al·mah	di	ve·ra'
Be exalted	*and sanctified*	*his name*	*great*	*Amen*	*in the world*		*that he created*

כִרְעוּתֵה, וְיַמְלִיךְ מַלְכוּתֵה, בְּחַיֵּיכוֹן וּבְיוֹמֵיכוֹן וּבְחַיֵּי

khir·'u·teh	ve·yam·likh	mal·chu·teh	be·chai·ye·chon	uv·yo·mei·khon	uv·chai·yei
according to his will	*and may he reign*	*his kingship*	*in your lifetimes*	*and in your days*	*and in the lifetimes of*

דְכָל בֵּית יִשְׂרָאֵל, בַּעֲגָלָא וּבִזְמַן קָרִיב. וְאִמְרוּ אָמֵן.

de·khol	beit	yis·ra·'el	ba·'a·ga·la	u·viz·man	qa·riv	ve·'im·ru	'a·men
of all	*the house of Israel*		*speedily and in a near time*			*and say ye*	*amen*

[אָמֵן. יְהֵא שְׁמֵהּ רַבָּא מְבָרַךְ לְעָלַם וּלְעָלְמֵי עָלְמַיָּא.]

'a·men	ye·he	she·meh	rab·ba'	me·va·rakh	le·'a·lam	ul·'a·le·mei	'a·le·mai·ya
Amen	*may*	*his name*	*great*	*be blessed*	*forever*		*and for all eternity*

יְהֵא שְׁמֵהּ רַבָּא מְבָרַךְ לְעָלַם וּלְעָלְמֵי עָלְמַיָּא. יִתְבָּרַךְ

ye·he	she·meh	rab·ba'	me·va·rakh	le·'a·lam	ul·'a·le·mei	'a·le·mai·ya	yit·ba·rakh
may	*his name*	*great*	*be blessed*	*forever*		*and for all eternity*	*Blessed*

וְיִשְׁתַּבַּח וְיִתְפָּאַר וְיִתְרוֹמַם וְיִתְנַשֵּׂא וְיִתְהַדָּר וְיִתְעַלֶּה

ve·yish·ta·bakh	ve·yit·pa·'ar	ve·yit·ro·mam	ve·yit·na·se	ve·yit·had·dar	ve·yit·'al·leh
and praised	*and glorified*	*and exalted*	*and uplifted*	*and honored*	*and elevated*

וְיִתְהַלָּל שְׁמֵהּ דְּקֻדְשָׁא בְּרִיךְ הוּא [בְּרִיךְ הוּא]

ve·yit·hal·lal	she·meh	de·qud·sha	ba·rikh	hu	bar·ikh	hu
and lauded	*the name*	*the holy one*	*blessed be*	*he*	*blessed be*	*he*

Mourner's Qaddish (continued)
קַדִּישׁ יָתוֹם

לְעֵׄלָא מִן כָּל בִּרְכָתָא וְשִׁירָתָא תֻּשְׁבְּחָתָא וְנֶחֱמָתָא,

le·'e·la	min	kol	bir·kha·ta	ve·shi·ra·ta	tush·be·cha·ta	ve·ne·che·ma·ta
beyond	from	all	blessing	and song	praise	and consolation

דַּאֲמִירָן בְּעָלְמָא. וְאִמְרוּ אָמֵן. [אָמֵן.] יְהֵא שְׁלָמָא רַבָּא

da·'a·mi·ran	be·'a·le·ma	ve·im·ru	'a·men	'a·men	ye·he	she·la·ma	rab·ba
that are uttered in the world		and say ye	Amen	[Amen]	May there be great peace		

מִן שְׁמַיָּא, וְחַיִּים עָלֵינוּ וְעַל כָּל יִשְׂרָאֵל. וְאִמְרוּ אָמֵן.

min	she·mai·ya	ve·chai·yim	'a·**lei**·nu	ve·'al	kol	yis·ra·'el	ve·im·ru	'a·men
from heaven		and life	upon us	and on	all	Israel	and say ye	Amen

[אָמֵן.] עֹשֶׂה שָׁלוֹם בִּמְרוֹמָיו, הוּא יַעֲשֶׂה שָׁלוֹם עָלֵינוּ,

'a·men	'o·seh	sha·lom	bim·ro·mav	hu	ya·'a·seh	sha·lom	'a·lei·nu
[Amen]	he makes	peace	in high places	may he	make	peace	upon us

וְעַל כָּל יִשְׂרָאֵל. וְאִמְרוּ אָמֵן. [אָמֵן.]

ve·'al	kol	yis·ra·'el	ve·im·ru	'a·men	'a·men
and on	all	Israel	and say ye	Amen	[Amen]

Note:

- The Qaddish (often spelled *Kaddish* in English) is written in Aramaic, a language closely related to Hebrew, and commonly spoken by Jews in the time of Jesus. Pronunciation and transliteration are the same as in Hebrew. As you read the Qaddish, try to identify cognate Hebrew words you may already know.

Barukh She'amar
בָּרוּךְ שֶׁאָמַר

The *Barukh She'amar* is normally included as part of the core service in the synagogue. In Orthodox synagogues, this prayer is said while standing. This prayer is the start of the *Pesuqei Dezimrah* and is considered the proper prelude to the recitation of the *Shema* and *Shemoneh 'Esreh*. It concludes with the *Yishtabach*, another blessing of praise to God.

בָּרוּךְ שֶׁאָמַר וְהָיָה הָעוֹלָם, בָּרוּךְ הוּא.

ba·rukh	she·'a·mar	ve·ha·ya	ha·'o·lam	ba·rukh	hu
Blessed is	He who spoke	and the world came into being		Blessed is He	

בָּרוּךְ אוֹמֵר וְעֹשֶׂה, בָּרוּךְ גּוֹזֵר וּמְקַיֵּם, בָּרוּךְ מְרַחֵם

ba·rukh	'o·mer	ve·'o·seh	ba·rukh	go·zer	u·me·qai·yem	ba·rukh	me·ra·chem
Blessed is He Who speaks		and Who does	blessed is	He Who decrees and finishes		Blessed is He who has mercy	

עַל הָאָרֶץ, בָּרוּךְ מְרַחֵם עַל הַבְּרִיּוֹת, בָּרוּךְ מְשַׁלֵּם

'al	ha·'a·rets	ba·rukh	me·ra·chem	'al	hab·be·ri·yot	ba·rukh	me·shal·lem
on	the earth	blessed is	He Who has mercy on creation			Blessed is	He who gives

שָׂכָר טוֹב לִירֵאָיו, בָּרוּךְ חַי לָעַד וְקַיָּם לָנֶצַח,

sa·khar	tov	li·re·'av	ba·rukh	chai	la·'ad	ve·qai·yam	la·ne·tsach
a good reward		to those who fear Him	Blessed is He who lives forever			and endures	to perpetuity

בָּרוּךְ פּוֹדֶה וּמַצִּיל, בָּרוּךְ שְׁמוֹ. בָּרוּךְ אַתָּה יהוה

ba·rukh	po·deh	u·mats·tsil	ba·rukh	she·mo	ba·rukh	'at·tah	'Adonai
Blessed is He who rescues and redeems			Blessed is His Name		Blessed are You, Lord		

אֱלֹהֵינוּ מֶלֶךְ הָעוֹלָם, הָאֵל הָאָב הָרַחֲמָן הַמְהֻלָּל

'e·lo·hey·nu	me·lekh	ha·'o·lam	ha·'el	ha·'av	ha·ra·cha·man	ham·hul·lal
our God	king (of)	the universe	the merciful heavenly Father			who is praised

בְּפֶה עַמּוֹ, מְשֻׁבָּח וּמְפֹאָר בִּלְשׁוֹן חֲסִידָיו וַעֲבָדָיו.

be·feh	'am·mo	me·shu·bach	um·fo·ar	bil·shon	cha·si·dav	va·'a·va·dav
in the mouth	of His people	praised	and glorified	by the tongue	of his pious	and servants

Barukh She'amar (continued)
בָּרוּךְ שָׁאָמַר

וּבְשִׁירֵי דָוִד עַבְדְּךָ נְהַלֶּלְךָ יְהוָה אֱלֹהֵינוּ, בִּשְׁבָחוֹת

uv·shi·rei	da·vid	'av·de·kha	ne·hal·lel·kha	'Adonai	'e·lo·hey·nu	bish·va·chot
and through songs of David		*Your servant*	*we praise You*	*O Lord*	*our God*	*with praises*

וּבְזְמִרוֹת נְגַדֶּלְךָ וּנְשַׁבֵּחֲךָ וּנְפָאֶרְךָ וְנַזְכִּיר שִׁמְךָ

u·viz·mi·rot	ne·gad·del·kha	un·sha·be·cha·kha	un·fa·'er·kha	ve·naz·kir	shim·kha
and songs	*we exalt You*	*and praise You*	*and glorify You*	*and declare*	*Your Name*

וְנַמְלִיכְךָ, מַלְכֵּנוּ אֱלֹהֵינוּ, יָחִיד חֵי הָעוֹלָמִים מֶלֶךְ

ve·nam·lich·kha	mal·kei·nu	'e·lo·hey·nu	ya·chid	chei	ha·'o·la·mim	me·lekh
and proclaim Your rule	*our King*	*our God*	*Unique Life-Giver*		*of the worlds*	*King*

מְשֻׁבָּח וּמְפֹאָר עֲדֵי עַד שְׁמוֹ הַגָּדוֹל. בָּרוּךְ אַתָּה יְהוָה

me·shu·bach	um·fo·'ar	'a·dei	'ad	she·mo	hag·ga·dol	ba·rukh	'at·tah	'Adonai
praised	*and glorified*	*forever*		*His great Name*		*Blessed are You, Lord*		

מֶלֶךְ מְהֻלָּל בַּתִּשְׁבָּחוֹת. [אָמֵן.]

me·lekh	me·hul·lal	ba·tish·ba·chot	'a·men
King	*who is praised*	*in praises*	*[Amen]*

Blessed is Adonai, Who spoke and the universe came into being. Blessed is Adonai, Who keeps the whole world going. Blessed is Adonai, Who does what He says. Blessed is Adonai, Who decrees and finishes. Blessed is He Who has mercy upon the earth; Blessed is He Who has mercy upon creation. Blessed is Adonai Who gives a good reward to those who fear Him. Blessed is Adonai, Who lives and endures forever. Blessed is He Who rescues and redeems us, blessed is His Name. Blessed are You, Lord our God, King of the universe and our merciful Heavenly Father, Who is praised by His people and glorified by the tongue of his pious servants. We praise You through the songs of David, Your servant, O Lord our God, with praises and songs. We glorify You and declare Your Name and Your rule, O God and our King. You are the Life-Giver to the worlds; You are the King to be praised and Your great Name glorified forever and ever. Blessed are You, Lord, the King Who is to be praised. Amen.

Yishtabach

יִשְׁתַּבַּח

The *Pesuqei Dezimrah* concludes with this standing prayer of praise to God:

יִשְׁתַּבַּח שִׁמְךָ לָעַד מַלְכֵּנוּ, הָאֵל הַמֶּֽלֶךְ הַגָּדוֹל

hag·ga·dol   ham·**me**·lekh   ha·'el   mal·**ke**·nu   la·'ad   shim·kha   yish·tab·bach

O God the great King   *Praised is Your Name forever, our King,*

וְהַקָּדוֹשׁ, בַּשָּׁמַֽיִם וּבָאָֽרֶץ. כִּי לְךָ נָאֶה, יהוה אֱלֹהֵֽינוּ

'e·lo·**hey**·nu   'Adonai   na·'eh   le·kha   ki   u·va·'a·rets   ba·sha·mayim   ve·haq·qa·dosh

our God   *O Lord*   *For to you it is fitting*   *and on earth.*   *in heaven*   *and the Holy One*

וֵאלֹהֵי אֲבוֹתֵֽינוּ, שִׁיר וּשְׁבָחָה, הַלֵּל וְזִמְרָה, עֹז

'oz   ve·zim·rah   hal·lel   ush·va·chah   shir   'a·vo·**tei**·nu   vei·lo·hei

strength   *song and praise, acclaim and praise*   *our fathers*   *and God of*

וּמֶמְשָׁלָה, נֶֽצַח גְּדֻלָּה וּגְבוּרָה, תְּהִלָּה וְתִפְאֶֽרֶת, קְדֻשָּׁה

qe·du·shah   v·tif·**e**·ret   te·hil·lah   ug·vu·rah   ge·dul·lah   **ne**·tsach   u·mem·sha·lah

holiness   *and glory*   *praise*   *and might*   *greatness*   *eminence*   *and dominion*

וּמַלְכוּת, בְּרָכוֹת וְהוֹדָאוֹת מֵעַתָּה וְעַד עוֹלָם.

'o·lam   ve·'ad   me·'at·tah   ve·ho·da·'ot   be·ra·khot   u·mal·chut

eternity.   *until*   *from now*   *and thanks*   *blessings*   *and reign*

בָּרוּךְ אַתָּה יְיָ אֵל מֶֽלֶךְ גָּדוֹל בַּתִּשְׁבָּחוֹת, אֵל

'el   bat·tish·ba·chot   ga·dol   **me**·lekh   'el   'Adonai   'at·tah   ba·rukh

God   *through praises*   *O God the great King*   *Blessed are You, Lord*

הַהוֹדָאוֹת, אֲדוֹן הַנִּפְלָאוֹת, הַבּוֹחֵר בְּשִׁירֵי זִמְרָה,

zim·rah   be·shi·rei   ha·bo·cher   han·nif·la·'ot   'a·don   ha·ho·da·'ot

sweetness   *songs of*   *Who chooses*   *of wonders,*   *Master*   *thanksgivings*

מֶֽלֶךְ, אֵל, חֵי הָעוֹלָמִים. [אָמֵן.]

'a·men   ha·'o·la·mim   chai   'el   me·lekh

[Amen]   *Life-Giver of the world.*   *God,*   *King,*

The Barekhu
בָּרְכוּ

The *Barekhu* is the call to worship in the synagogue, and traditionally is recited by the cantor (or *chazzan*) in the presence of a *minyan*, a group of ten males who are bar mitzvah (the requirement for ten males comes from the account of Abraham's intercession for Sodom, wherein the Lord agreed that if there were ten righteous people in the city, He would spare it from destruction). The *Barekhu* is also said by a person called up to the public reading of the Torah.

The cantor will chant the following:

בָּרְכוּ אֶת־יְיָ הַמְבֹרָךְ.

ha·me·vo·rakh   'et-'Adonai   ba·re·khu

"Praise Adonai, who is to be praised."

And the minyan responds with:

בָּרוּךְ יְיָ הַמְבֹרָךְ לְעוֹלָם וָעֶד.

va·'ed   le·'o·lam   ha·me·vo·rakh   'Adonai   ba·rukh

"Praised is Adonai, who is to praised forever and ever."

Note about the Name of God:

- Some Jews refuse to pronounce the sacred Name of God (יהוה) to avoid the risk of breaking the third commandment (i.e., "Thou shalt not take the name of the LORD your God in vain" Ex. 20:7) and therefore substitute (יי) (read "Adonai" or "Hashem") instead. See Lesson Eighteen, "The Names of God" for more information.

Did you know?

Bar Mitzvah means "son of the commandment," and refers to a Jewish boy who is considered accountable to fulfill the *mitzvot* (commandments) of the Torah (usually by age 13). A Bar Mitzvah may participate in a *minyan*, read from the *Torah*, wear a *tallit*, and fast on Yom Kippur.

בַּר־מִצְוָה

A Bar Mitzvah ceremony usually occurs during a Shabbat morning service where the young man is called to his first *aliyah*, or public Torah reading. The ceremony is normally followed with a special *qiddush-meal* to commemorate the event.

Lesson Sixteen

SIDDUR BLESSINGS AND PRAYERS II

Lesson Introduction

Daily Services

There are three daily services prescribed by Jewish tradition: *Ma'ariv* (evening service), *Shacharit* (morning service), and *Minchah* (afternoon service). *Musaf* is an additional service for Shabbat and holidays, after the Torah reading.

SERVICE	WHEN	MAJOR ELEMENTS
Ma'ariv	Evening after sundown	Includes preliminary prayers, the Shema and its blessings, the 'Amidah and concluding prayers.
Shacharit	Morning	Includes preliminary prayers, the Shema and its blessings, the 'Amidah and concluding prayers. Includes Torah reading on Shabbat, on holidays, and on Monday and Thursday.
Musaf	Additional service	The 'Amidah and concluding prayers.
Minchah	Afternoon	Preliminary prayers and the 'Amidah (includes Torah reading only on Shabbat, fast days, and Yom Kippur).

Special Services

In addition to the regular daily services, there are additional services that occur in connection with the Jewish holidays and festivals.

SERVICE	WHEN	MAJOR ELEMENTS
Qabbalat Shabbat	Friday evening at sundown	Welcome the Shabbat with a series of psalms and songs.
Kol Nidre	Yom Kippur eve	Includes Kol Nidre prayer and special inclusions for Yom Kippur.
'Avodah	Yom Kippur day	Recounts the service of the High Priest in the sanctuary on Yom Kippur when the Temple stood.
Yizkor	Yom Kippur, Sukkot, Pesach, and Shavuot	Memorial service for those who have died.
Megillah Reading	Purim	The Book of Esther is read from a scroll to the exuberant efforts of the congregation to drown out the name of Haman.

Shemoneh Esreh (Amidah)
שְׁמוֹנֶה עֶשְׂרֵה

The *Shemoneh 'Esreh* is the central prayer of all four Jewish services: *Shacharit* (morning), *Mincha* (afternoon), *Ma'ariv* (evening), and *Musaf* (additional). Sometimes called the *'Amidah* ("standing"), the prayer is *recited silently* while facing the Aron Qodesh (the ark that houses the Torah scroll). Jews stand with their feet together during the prayer, sometimes bowing or taking steps forward or backward.

Shemoneh 'Esreh means "eighteen," and originally there were 18 blessings divided into three general types: 1) praise (the first three), 2) petitions (the next 13), and 3) thanks (the last three). (The careful reader will note that this adds up to 19, not 18. The reason for this was that an additional "blessing" (now number 12) was added later.)

Blessing One: אָבוֹת (fathers)

אַבְרָהָם	אֱלֹהֵי	אֲבוֹתֵנוּ	וֵאלֹהֵי	אֱלֹהֵינוּ	יְהוָה	אַתָּה	בָּרוּךְ
'av·ra·ham	'e·lo·hei	'a·vo·**te**·nu	vei·lo·hei	'e·lo·**hey**·nu	'Adonai	'at·tah	ba·rukh
Abraham	God of	our fathers	and God of	our God	Lord	are you	Blessed

וְהַנּוֹרָא	הַגִּבּוֹר	הַגָּדוֹל	הָאֵל	יַעֲקֹב	וֵאלֹהֵי	יִצְחָק	אֱלֹהֵי
ve·han·no·ra	hag·gi·bor	hag·ga·dol	ha·'el	ya·'a·kov	vei·lo·hei	yits·chak	'e·lo·hei
and awesome	the mighty	the great	God	Jacob	and God of	Isaac	God of

וְזוֹכֵר	הַכֹּל	וְקוֹנֵה	טוֹבִים	חֲסָדִים	גּוֹמֵל	עֶלְיוֹן	אֵל
ve·zo·kher	ha·kol	ve·qo·neh	to·vim	cha·sa·dim	go·mel	'el·yon	'el
who recalls	everything	and creates	plentiful	kindnesses	who gives	Most High	God

שְׁמוֹ	לְמַעַן	בְּנֵיהֶם	לִבְנֵי	גּוֹאֵל	וּמֵבִיא	אָבוֹת	חַסְדֵי
she·mo	le·ma·'an	ve·**nei**·hem	liv·nei	go·'el	u·me·vim	'a·vot	chas·dei
for the sake of His name		to children's children		a Redeemer	and brings	the fathers	kindnesses of

בְּאַהֲבָה.	מֶלֶךְ	עוֹזֵר	וּמוֹשִׁיעַ	וּמָגֵן.	בָּרוּךְ	אַתָּה	יְהוָה
be·'a·ha·vah	**me**·lekh	'o·zer	u·mo·**shi**·a'	u·ma·gein	ba·rukh	'at·tah	'Adonai
with love	O King	helper	Savior	and shield	Blessed	are you	Lord

אַבְרָהָם.	מָגֵן
'av·ra·ham	ma·gen
of Abraham	sheild

Blessing Two: גְּבוּרוֹת

(God's Might)

אַתָּה גִּבּוֹר לְעוֹלָם אֲדֹנָי, מְחַיֵּה מֵתִים אַתָּה, רַב
| rav | 'at·tah | me·tim | me·chai·yeh | 'a·do·nai | le·'o·lam | gib·bor | 'at·tah |
| greatly | You are | of the dead | restorer | O Lord | forever | mighty | You are |

לְהוֹשִׁיעַ. מְכַלְכֵּל חַיִּים בְּחֶסֶד, מְחַיֵּה מֵתִים בְּרַחֲמִים
| be·ra·cha·mim | me·tim | me·chai·yeh | be·**che**·sed | chai·yim | me·khal·kel | le·ho·**shi**·a‘ |
| with mercy | the dead | who revives | in kindness | the living | Who sustains | able to save |

רַבִּים, סוֹמֵךְ נוֹפְלִים, וְרוֹפֵא חוֹלִים, וּמַתִּיר אֲסוּרִים,
| 'a·su·rim | u·mat·tir | cho·lim | ve·ro·fei | no·fe·lim | so·mekh | rab·bim |
| the captives | and releases | the sick | and heals | the fallen | who supports | abundant |

וּמְקַיֵּם אֱמוּנָתוֹ לִישֵׁנֵי עָפָר. מִי כָמוֹךָ בַּעַל גְּבוּרוֹת
| ge·vu·rot | **ba**·‘al | kha·mo·kha | mi | ‘a·far | lish·nei | 'e·mu·na·to | um·qai·yem |
| of mighty deeds | O Master | is like you | who | to those asleep in the dust | his faith | who maintains |

וּמִי דוֹמֶה לָּךְ, מֶלֶךְ מֵמִית וּמְחַיֶּה וּמַצְמִיחַ יְשׁוּעָה.
| ye·shu·‘ah | u·mats·**mi**·ach | um·chai·yeh | me·mit | **me**·lekh | lakh | **do**·meh | u·mi |
| salvation | and brings forth | who makes life and death | O King | to you | compares | and who |

וְנֶאֱמָן אַתָּה לְהַחֲיוֹת מֵתִים. בָּרוּךְ אַתָּה יְהֹוָה,
| 'Adonai | 'at·tah | ba·rukh | me·tim | le·ha·cha·yot | 'at·tah | ve·ne·'e·man |
| Lord | are you | Blessed | the dead | to revive | are you | and faithful |

מְחַיֵּה הַמֵּתִים.
| ham·me·tim | me·chai·yeh |
| the dead | who revives |

I am the resurrection and the life

John 11:25

אָנֹכִי הַתְּקוּמָה וְהַחַיִּים

Blessing Three: קְדֻשַּׁת הַשֵּׁם

(Holiness of God's Name)

יְהַלְלוּךָ	יוֹם	בְּכָל	וּקְדוֹשִׁים,	קָדוֹשׁ	וְשִׁמְךָ	קָדוֹשׁ	אַתָּה
ye·ha·le·lu·kha	yom	be·khol	u·qe·du·shim	qa·dosh	ve·shim·kha	qa·dosh	'at·tah
praise you	*day*	*every*	*and your holy ones*	*is holy*	*and your name*	*holy*	*You are*

סֶלָה.	בָּרוּךְ	אַתָּה	יְהוָה,	הָאֵל	הַקָּדוֹשׁ.
se·lah	ba·rukh	'at·tah	'Adonai	ha·'el	haq·qa·dosh
forever	*Blessed*	*are you*	*Lord*	*the God*	*who is holy*

You are holy and your name is holy, and your
holy ones praise You every day. Blessed are You, Adonai,
the God Who is holy.

Blessing Four: דַּעַת

(wisdom)

בִּינָה:	לֶאֱנוֹשׁ	וּמְלַמֵּד	דַּעַת	לְאָדָם	חוֹנֵן	אַתָּה
bi·nah	le·'e·nosh	u·me·lam·med	da·'at	le·'a·dam	cho·nen	'at·tah
understanding	*to a mortal*	*and teach*	*of wisdom*	*to a man*	*show favor*	*You*

אַתָּה	בָּרוּךְ	וְהַשְׂכֵּל.	בִּינָה	דֵּעַת	מֵאִתְּךָ	חָנֵּנוּ
'at·tah	ba·rukh	ve·has·kel	bi·nah	de·'at	me·'it·te·kha	cho·ne·nu
are You	*Blessed*	*and intellect*	*of understanding*	*a mind*	*from You*	*be gracious to us*

יְהוָה	חוֹנֵן	הַדָּעַת.
'Adonai	cho·nen	had·da·'at
Lord	*who favors*	*wisdom*

You show favor to a man of wisdom, and You teach
understanding to a mortal man. Be gracious to us; a
mind of understanding and intellect is from You.
Blessed are You, Adonai, Who favors us with
wisdom.

Blessing Five: תְּשׁוּבָה

(repentance)

הֲשִׁיבֵנוּ אָבִינוּ לְתוֹרָתֶךָ וְקָרְבֵנוּ מַלְכֵּנוּ לְעֲבוֹדָתֶךָ

le·'a·vo·da·**te**·kha	mal·**ke**·nu	ve·qa·re·**ve**·nu	le·to·ra·**te**·kha	'a·**vi**·nu	cha·shi·**ve**·nu
to serve you	*our King*	*draw us near*	*to Your Torah*	*our Father*	*Return us*

וְהַחֲזִירֵנוּ בִּתְשׁוּבָה שְׁלֵמָה לְפָנֶיךָ. בָּרוּךְ אַתָּה יְהוָה

'Adonai	'at·tah	ba·rukh	le·fa·**ney**·kha	she·le·mah	bit·shu·vah	ve·ha·cha·zi·**re**·nu
Lord	*are You*	*Blessed*	*to your presence*	*complete*	*in repentance*	*restore us*

הָרוֹצֶה בִּתְשׁוּבָה.

bit·shu·vah	ha·ro·tse
in repentance	*who desires*

Return us, our Father, to Your Torah; draw us near our King to serve You. Restore us to Your presence in complete repentance. Blessed are You, O Lord, Who desires repentance.

Blessing Six: סְלִיחָה

(forgiveness)

סְלַח לָנוּ אָבִינוּ כִּי חָטָאנוּ, מְחַל לָנוּ מַלְכֵּנוּ, כִּי

ki	mal·**ke**·nu	**la**·nu	me·chal	cha·tanu	ki	'a·**vi**·nu	**la**·nu	se·lach
for	*our King*	*us*	*pardon*	*we have sinned*	*for*	*our Father*	*us*	*Forgive*

פָּשָׁעְנוּ, כִּי מוֹחֵל וְסוֹלֵחַ אָתָּה. בָּרוּךְ אַתָּה יְהוָה

'Adonai	'at·tah	ba·rukh	'at·tah	ve·so·le·ach	mo·chel	ki	pa·sha·'nu
Lord	*are You*	*Blessed*	*are You*	*and forgiver*	*a pardoner*	*for*	*we have rebelled*

חַנּוּן הַמַּרְבֶּה לִסְלוֹחַ.

lis·**lo**·ach	ham·mar·beh	chan·nun
forgives	*who abundantly*	*the gracious*

Forgive us, our Father, for we have sinned; pardon us, our King, for we have rebelled; for You are a pardoner and a forgiver. Blessed are you, Lord, the gracious One who abundantly forgives.

Blessing Seven: גְּאוּלָה

(redemption)

שְׁמֶךָ,	לְמַּעַן	מְהֵרָה	וּגְאָלֵנוּ	רִיבֵנוּ,	וְרִיבָה	וְעָנְיֵנוּ,	רְאֵה
she·me·kha	le·ma·'an	me·he·rah	u·ge·'a·le·nu	ri·ve·nu	ve·ri·vah	ve·'o·nei·nu	re·'eh
Your name	*for the sake of*	*speedily*	*and redeem us*	*our cause*	*champion*	*our affliction*	*behold*

יִשְׂרָאֵל.	גּוֹאֵל	יְהוָה	אַתָּה	בָּרוּךְ	אַתָּה.	חָזָק	גּוֹאֵל	כִּי
yis·ra·'el	go·'el	'Adonai	'at·tah	ba·rukh	'at·tah	cha·zaq	go·'el	ki
of Israel	*Redeemer*	*Lord*	*are You*	*Blessed*	*You are*	*strong*	*Redeemer*	*for*

Behold our affliction and champion our cause,
and redeem us speedily for the sake of Your Name.
Blessed are You, Lord, Redeemer of Israel.

Blessing Eight: רְפוּאָה

(healing)

תְּהִלָּתֵנוּ	כִּי	וְנִוָּשֵׁעָה,	הוֹשִׁיעֵנוּ	וְנֵרָפֵא,	יְהוָה	רְפָאֵנוּ
te·hil·la·te·nu	ki	ve·niv·va·she·'ah	ho·shi·'e·nu	ve·ne·ra·fe'	'Adonai	re·fa·'e·nu
the one we praise	*for*	*and we will be saved*	*save us*	*and we will be healed*	*Lord*	*Heal us*

אֵל	כִּי	מַכּוֹתֵינוּ,	לְכָל	שְׁלֵמָה	רְפוּאָה	וְהַעֲלֵה	אָתָּה,
'el	ki	ma·ko·tei·nu	le·khol	she·le·mah	re·fu·'ah	ve·ha·'a·leh	'at·tah
O God	*for*	*our sicknesses*	*for all*	*complete*	*healing*	*Bring*	*is You*

יְהוָה	אַתָּה	בָּרוּךְ	אָתָּה.	וְרַחֲמָן	נֶאֱמָן	רוֹפֵא	מֶלֶךְ
'Adonai	'at·tah	ba·rukh	'at·tah	ve·ra·cha·man	ne·'e·man	ro·fei	me·lekh
Lord	*are You*	*Blessed*	*are You*	*faithful and compassionate*	*faithful*	*Healer*	*King*

יִשְׂרָאֵל.	עַמּוֹ	חוֹלֵי	רוֹפֵא
yis·ra·'el	'a·mo	cho·lei	ro·fe'
Israel	*his people*	*the sick*	*Healer*

Heal us, Lord, and we shall be healed;
save us, and we will be saved, for the one
we praise is You. Bring complete healing
for all our sicknesses, for O God, for You
are our faithful and compassionate Healer
and King. Blessed are you, Lord, the
Healer of the sick of Israel.

Blessing Nine: בִּרְכַּת הַשָּׁנִים

(year of plenty)

כָּל	וְאֶת	הַזֹּאת	הַשָּׁנָה	אֶת	אֱלֹהֵינוּ	יְהוָה	עָלֵינוּ	בָּרֵךְ
kol	ve·'et	ha·zot	hash·sha·nah	'et	'e·lo·hey·nu	'Adonai	'a·**lei**·nu	ba·rekh
all	and	this	the year	( )	our God	Lord	on our behalf	Bless

הָאֲדָמָה,	פְּנֵי	עַל	בְּרָכָה	וְתֵן	לְטוֹבָה	תְּבוּאָתָהּ	מִינֵי
ha·'a·da·mah	pe·nei	'al	be·ra·khah	ve·ten	le·to·vah	te·vu·a·**tah**	mi·nei
the earth	face of	on	blessing	and give	for goodness	crops	kinds of

הַטּוֹבוֹת.	כַּשָּׁנִים	שְׁנָתֵנוּ	וּבָרֵךְ	מִטּוּבֶךָ,	וְשַׂבְּעֵנוּ
hat·to·vot	kash·sha·nim	she·na·**te**·nu	u·va·rekh	mit·tu·**ve**·kha	ve·sab·**'ei**·nu
that were good	like the years	our year	and bless	from your bounty	and satisfy us

הַשָּׁנִים.	מְבָרֵךְ	יְהוָה,	אַתָּה	בָּרוּךְ
hash·sha·nim	me·va·rekh	'Adonai	'at·tah	ba·rukh
the years	Who blesses	Lord	are You	Blessed

Bless for us, Adonai our God, this year and its crops. Grant us a blessing on the earth. Satisfy us from Thy bounty and bless our year like other good years. Blessed are You, O Lord, Who blesses the years.

Blessing Ten: קִבּוּץ גָּלֻיּוֹת

(Ingathering of exiles)

גָּלֻיּוֹתֵינוּ,	לְקַבֵּץ	נֵס	וְשָׂא	לְחֵרוּתֵנוּ	גָּדוֹל	בְּשׁוֹפָר	תְּקַע
ga·luy·yo·**tei**·nu	le·qab·bets	nes	ve·sam	le·che·ru·**te**·nu	ga·dol	be·sho·far	te·qa'
our exiles	to gather	banner	and put	for our freedom	great	the shofar	Sound

יְהוָה,	אַתָּה	בָּרוּךְ	הָאָרֶץ.	כַּנְפוֹת	מֵאַרְבַּע	יַחַד	וְקַבְּצֵנוּ
'Adonai	'at·tah	ba·rukh	ha·'a·rets	kan·fot	me·'ar·ba'	**ya**·chad	ve·qab·e·**tse**·nu
Lord	are You	Blessed	of the earth	corners	from the four	together	and gather us

יִשְׂרָאֵל.	עַמּוֹ	נִדְחֵי	מְקַבֵּץ
yis·ra·'el	'a·mo	nid·chei	me·qa·bets
Israel	of His people	the scattered	Who regathers

Blessing Eleven: דִּין

(Restoration of Justice)

וְהָסֵר	כְּבַתְּחִלָּה	וְיוֹעֲצֵינוּ	כְּבָרִאשׁוֹנָה	שׁוֹפְטֵינוּ	הָשִׁיבָה
ve·ha·ser	ke·vat·te·chal·lah	ve·yo'a·tsei·nu	ke·va·ri·sho·nah	sho·fe·**tei**·nu	ha·**shi**·vah
remove	as at the beginning	and our counselors	as at the early times	our judges	Restore

בְּחֶסֶד	לְבַדְּךָ	יְהֹוָה אַתָּה	עָלֵינוּ	וּמְלֹוך	וְאַנְחָה,	יָגוֹן	מִמֶּנּוּ
be·che·sed	le·vad·de·kha	'Adonai 'at·tah	'a·lei·nu	um·loch	ve·a·na·cha	ya·gon	mi·me·nu
with kindness	alone	Lord You	over us	and rule	and pain	sorrow	from us

אוֹהֵב	מֶלֶךְ	יְהֹוָה,	אַתָּה	בָּרוּךְ	בַּמִּשְׁפָּט.	וְצַדְּקֵנוּ	וּבְרַחֲמִים
'o·hev	me·lekh	'Adonai	'at·tah	ba·rukh	bam·mish·pat	ve·tsa·de·ke·nu	uv·rach·a·mim
who loves	king	Lord	are You	Blessed	in judgment	and justify us	and compassion

Restore our judges as at the early times, and advisors as there once were. Remove our sorrows and troubles: we want You, Adonai, to rule over us with kindness and compassion and to justify us in justice. Blessed are You, Lord, the King Who loves righteousness and justice.

וּמִשְׁפָּט.	צְדָקָה
u·mish·pat	tse·da·qah
and justice	righteousness

Blessing Twelve: בִּרְכַּת הַמִּינִים

(Against Heretics)

This "blessing," originally the nineteenth of the Shemoneh Esreh, was instituted at the council of Yavneh sometime after the destruction of the second Temple, and was composed in response to the Essenes and early Christians. Only part of this blessing is reproduced here.

זֵדִים.	וּמַכְנִיעַ	אֹיְבִים	שׁוֹבֵר	יְהֹוָה,	אַתָּה	בָּרוּךְ
ze·dim	u·mach·ni·a'	'oy·vim	sho·ver	'Adonai	'at·tah	ba·rukh
sinners	and humbles	enemies	who breaks	Lord	are You	Blessed

Blessed are You, Lord, who destroys enemies and humbles sinners.

Blessing Thirteen: צַדִּיקִים

(The Righteous)

עַל הַצַּדִּיקִים וְעַל הַחֲסִידִים, וְעַל זִקְנֵי עַמְּךָ בֵּית

beit — 'am·me·kha — ziq·nei — ve·'al — ha·cha·si·dim — ve·'al — hats·tsad·di·qim — 'al

house of — your people — the elders — and on — the devout — and on — the righteous — on

יִשְׂרָאֵל, וְעַל פְּלֵיטַת סוֹפְרֵיהֶם, וְעַל גֵּרֵי הַצֶּדֶק וְעָלֵינוּ,

ve·'a·lei·nu — hats·tse·deq — ge·rei — ve·'al — sof·rei·hem — pe·lei·tat — ve·'al — yis·ra·'el

the righteous — the righteous — converts — and on — of their scholars — the remnant — and on — Israel

יֶהֱמוּ רַחֲמֶיךָ יְהוָה אֱלֹהֵינוּ, וְתֵן שָׂכָר טוֹב לְכָל

le·khol — tov — sha·khar — ve·ten — 'e·lo·hey·nu — 'Adonai — ra·cha·me·kha — ye·he·mu

to all — good — reward — and give — our God — Lord — your compassion — may it rise

הַבּוֹטְחִים בְּשִׁמְךָ בֶּאֱמֶת, וְשִׂים חֶלְקֵנוּ עִמָּהֶם לְעוֹלָם,

le·'o·lam — 'im·ma·hem — hel·qe·nu — ve·sim — be·'e·met — be·shim·kha — hab·bo·te·chim

forever — with them — our lot — and put — in truth — in your name — who trust

וְלֹא נֵבוֹשׁ כִּי בְךָ בָּטָחְנוּ. בָּרוּךְ אַתָּה יְהוָה, מִשְׁעָן

mish·'an — 'Adonai — 'at·tah — ba·rukh — ba·tach·nu — ve·kha — ki — ne·vosh — ve·lo

stronghold — Lord — are You — Blessed — we trust — in you — for — ashamed — and not

וּמִבְטָח לַצַּדִּיקִים.

lats·tsad·di·qim — u·miv·tach

of the righteous — and assurance

Upon the righteous, upon the pious, upon the elders of your people of the house of Israel, upon the remnant of their scholars, upon the righteous converts, and upon ourselves, may Your compassion arise, O Lord our God, and give good reward to all who sincerely believe in your name. Include us with them forever, and let us not be ashamed, for we put our trust in You. Blessed are You, Lord, the stronghold and assurance of the righteous.

Blessing Fourteen: בִּנְיַן יְרוּשָׁלַיִם

(Rebuilding Jerusalem)

כַּאֲשֶׁר בְּתוֹכָהּ וְתִשְׁכּוֹן תָּשׁוּב בְּרַחֲמִים עִירְךָ וְלִירוּשָׁלַיִם
ka·'a·sher / be·to·khah / ve·tish·kon / ta·shuv / be·ra·cha·mim / 'ir·kha / ve·li·ru·sha·lai·yim
as / within it / and rest / return / in compassion / Your city / and to Jerusalem

דָּוִד וְכִסֵּא עוֹלָם בִּנְיַן בְּיָמֵינוּ בְּקָרוֹב אוֹתָהּ וּבְנֵה דִּבַּרְתָּ
da·vid / ve·khi·se / 'o·lam / bin·yan / be·ya·**mey**·nu / be·qa·rov / 'o·tah / uv·neh / dib·**bar**·ta
David / and throne / forever / a structure / and in our days / soon / it / Rebuild / You said

יְרוּשָׁלַיִם. בּוֹנֵה יְהֹוָה, אַתָּה בָּרוּךְ תָּכִין לְתוֹכָהּ מְהֵרָה
yi·ru·sha·lai·yim / bo·neh / 'Adonai / 'at·tah / ba·rukh / ta·khin / le·to·chah / me·he·rah
of Jerusalem / builder / Lord / are You / Blessed / establish / within it / speedily

Return in compassion to Your city, Jerusalem, and rest within it as
You have said. Rebuild it speedily, and in our days, a structure forever.
And may You establish the throne of David within Jerusalem speedily.
Blessed are You, Lord, the Builder of Jerusalem.

Blessing Fifteen: מַלְכוּת בֵּית דָּוִד

(Kingdom of David)

בִּישׁוּעָתֶךָ, תָּרוּם וְקַרְנוֹ תַּצְמִיחַ מְהֵרָה עַבְדְּךָ דָּוִד צֶמַח אֶת
bi·shu·'a·**te**·kha / ta·rum / ve·qar·no / tats·**mi**·ach / me·he·rah / 'av·de·kha / da·vid / tse·mach / 'et
may You prosper and exalt in your salvation / flourish / speedily / David Your servant / seed of / The

קֶרֶן מַצְמִיחַ יְהֹוָה, אַתָּה בָּרוּךְ הַיּוֹם. כָּל קִוִּינוּ לִישׁוּעָתְךָ כִּי
qe·ren / mats·mi·ach / 'Adonai / 'at·tah / ba·rukh / hai·yom / kol / qi·vi·nu / li·shu·'at·kha / ki
horn of / grower of / Lord / are You / Blessed / the day / all / we hope / your salvation / for

יְשׁוּעָה.
ye·shu·'ah
of salvation.

May the offspring of David Thy servant flourish speedily and may You exalt
in Your salvation. For in your salvation do we hope all the day. Blessed are
You, Lord, Who makes the seeds of our salvation grow.

Blessing Sixteen: קַבָּלַת תְּפִלָּה

(Acceptance of Prayer)

שְׁמַע	קוֹלֵנוּ	יְהוָה	אֱלֹהֵינוּ,	חוּס	וְרַחֵם	עָלֵינוּ	וְקַבֵּל	בְּרַחֲמִים
she·ma‘	qo·le·nu	'Adonai	'e·lo·hey·nu	chus	ve·ra·chem	'a·lei·nu	ve·qa·bel	be·rach·a·mim
Hear	our voice	Lord	our God	have pity	and mercy	on us	and accept	in mercy

וּבְרָצוֹן	אֶת	תְּפִלָּתֵנוּ,	כִּי	אֵל	שׁוֹמֵעַ	תְּפִלּוֹת	וְתַחֲנוּנִים	אָתָּה.
u·ve·ra·tson	'et	te·fi·la·tei·nu	ki	'el	sho·me·a‘	te·fi·lot	ve·tach·nu·nim	'at·tah
and in favor	--	our prayer	for	God	who hears	prayers	and supplications	are You

וּמִלְּפָנֶיךָ	מַלְכֵּנוּ	רֵיקָם	אַל	תְּשִׁיבֵנוּ,	כִּי	אַתָּה	שׁוֹמֵעַ	תְּפִלַּת
u·mil·le·fa·ne·kha	mal·ke·nu	rei·qam	'al	te·shi·ve·nu	ki	'at·tah	sho·me·a‘	te·fil·lat
from before You	our King	empty	do not	turn us away	for	You	hear	the prayer of

עַמְּךָ	יִשְׂרָאֵל	בְּרַחֲמִים.	בָּרוּךְ	אַתָּה	יְהוָה,	שׁוֹמֵעַ	תְּפִלָּה.
‘am·me·kha	yis·ra·'el	be·ra·cha·mim	ba·rukh	'at·tah	'Adonai	sho·me·a‘	te·fil·lah
Your people	Israel	in mercy	Blessed	are You	Lord	who hears	prayer

*Hear our voice, O Lord our God, and have pity and mercy upon us
and accept in mercy and in favor our prayer, for You are a God
Who hears prayers and supplications. Do not turn us away from before You
empty, for in mercy You hear the prayer of Your people Israel.
Blessed are You, Lord, Who hears prayer.*

Blessing Seventeen: עֲבוֹדָה

(Temple Service)

וְהָשֵׁב, וּבִתְפִלָּתָם, יִשְׂרָאֵל בְּעַמְּךָ אֱלֹהֵינוּ יְהוָה רְצֵה
ve·ha·shev   u·vit·fil·la·tam   yis·ra·'el   be·'am·me·kha   'e·lo·hey·nu   'Adonai   re·tseh
and restore   *and to their prayer*   *Israel*   *Your people*   *our God*   *Lord*   *Accept*

הָעֲבוֹדָה לִדְבִיר בֵּיתֶךָ. וְאִשֵּׁי יִשְׂרָאֵל וּתְפִלָּתָם בְּאַהֲבָה
be·a·ha·vah   ut·fil·la·tam   yis·ra·'el   ve·'ish·shei   bei·te·kha   lid·vir   ha·'av·o·dah
in love   *and their prayer*   *of Israel*   *and the fires*   *of Your house*   *most holy*   *the service*

תְקַבֵּל בְּרָצוֹן וּתְהִי לְרָצוֹן תָּמִיד עֲבוֹדַת יִשְׂרָאֵל עַמֶּךָ.
'am·me·kha   yis·ra·'el   'a·vo·dat   ta·mid   le·ra·tson   ut·hi   be·ra·tson   te·ka·bel
Your people   *of Israel*   *the service*   *always*   *and may it please You*   *in favor*   *accept*

וְתֶחֱזֶינָה עֵינֵינוּ בְּשׁוּבְךָ לְצִיּוֹן בְּרַחֲמִים. בָּרוּךְ אַתָּה
'at·tah   ba·rukh   be·ra·cha·mim   le·tsiy·yon   be·shu·ve·kha   'ei·nei·nu   ve·te·che·zey·nah
are You   *Blessed*   *in compassion*   *You return to Zion*   *may our eyes*   *behold*

יְהוָה, הַמַּחֲזִיר שְׁכִינָתוֹ לְצִיּוֹן.
le·tsi·yon   she·khi·na·to   ham·ma·cha·zir   'Adonai
to Zion   *His Presence*   *Who restores*   *Lord*

Accept Your people, O Lord our God, and receive their prayer. Restore the most holy service of Your house and accept in love the offerings and prayers of Israel. May it please You always to want to accept the service of Your people Israel. May our eyes see You return to Zion in mercy. Blessed are You, O Lord, Who restores His Presence to Zion.

Blessing Eighteen: הוֹדָאָה

(Thanksgiving)

Traditional Jews bow at the word "*modim*" and straighten up when the name "*Adonai*" is said:

אֲבוֹתֵינוּ	וֵאלֹהֵי	אֱלֹהֵינוּ	יְהוָה	הוּא	שָׁאַתָּה	לָךְ	אֲנַחְנוּ	מוֹדִים
'a·vo·tei·nu	vei·lo·hei	'e·lo·hey·nu	'Adonai	hu	sha·'at·tah	lakh	'a·nach·nu	mo·dim
our fathers	*and God of*	*our God*	*for You are Adonai*			*You*	*we*	*we thank*

וָדוֹר.	לְדוֹר	הוּא	אַתָּה	יִשְׁעֵנוּ	מָגֵן	חַיֵּינוּ,	צוּר	וָעֶד.	לְעוֹלָם
ve·dor	le·dor	hu	'at·tah	yish·'ei·nu	ma·gen	chai·yey·nu	tsur	va·'ed	le·'o·lam
You are from generation to generation				*our salvation*	*Sheild of*	*of our lives*	*Rock*	*and ever*	*forever*

בְּיָדֶךָ,	הַמְּסוּרִים	חַיֵּינוּ	עַל	תְּהִלָּתֶךָ	וּנְסַפֵּר	לְךָ	נוֹדֶה
be·ya·de·kha	ham·me·su·rim	chai·yei·nu	'al	te·hil·la·te·kha	u·ne·sap·per	le·kha	no·deh
into Your hands	*are entrusted*	*our lives*	*for*	*Your praise*	*and tell*	*You*	*We will thank*

עִמָּנוּ,	יוֹם	שֶׁבְּכָל	נִסֶּיךָ	וְעַל	לָךְ,	הַפְּקוּדוֹת	נִשְׁמוֹתֵינוּ	וְעַל
'im·ma·nu	yom	sheb·be·khol	nis·sey·kha	ve·'al	lach	hap·pe·qo·dot	nish·mo·tei·nu	ve·'al
with us	*that every day are*		*Your miracles*	*and for*	*to You*	*entrusted*	*our souls*	*and for*

וְצָהֳרָיִם.	וָבֹקֶר	עֶרֶב,	עֵת,	שֶׁבְּכָל	וְטוֹבוֹתֶיךָ	נִפְלְאוֹתֶיךָ	וְעַל
ve·tsa·ho·rayim	va·vo·qer	'e·rev	'eit	sheb·be·khol	ve·to·vo·tey·kha	nif·le·'o·tey·kha	ve·'al
and afternoon	*and morning*	*evening*	*that are at all times*		*and favors*	*Your wonders*	*and for*

חֲסָדֶיךָ,	תַמּוּ	לֹא	כִּי	וְהַמְרַחֵם,	רַחֲמֶיךָ	כָלוּ	לֹא	כִּי	הַטּוֹב
kha·sa·dey·cha	tam·mu	lo	ki	ve·ham·ra·chem	ra·cha·me·kha	kha·lu	lo	ki	hat·tov
Your kindness	*ended*	*not*	*for*	*and compassions*	*your mercies*	*exhausted*	*not*	*for*	*O Good*

לָךְ.	קִוִּינוּ	מֵעוֹלָם
lach	qiv·vi·nu	me·'o·lam
in You	*we hope*	*forever*

We thank You, for it is You alone Who is Adonai our God and the God of our fathers, forever and ever. You are the Rock and Shield of our salvation, You alone, from generation to generation. We thank You and tell of Your praise, for our lives are in Your hands and our souls are trusting in You. Every day Your miracles are with us: Your wonders and favors are at all times, evening, morning, and afternoon. O Good One, Your compassions are never exhausted and Your kindnesses are continual.
We put our hope in You.

Blessing Eighteen: הוֹדָאָה

(Conclusion)

In the closing portion of the blessing, traditional Jews bend the knees at "*barukh*", bow at "*attah*," and straighten up when "*Adonai*" is said:

וְעַל	כֻּלָּם	יִתְבָּרַךְ	וְיִתְרוֹמַם	שִׁמְךָ	מַלְכֵּנוּ	תָּמִיד	לְעוֹלָם
ve·'al	kul·lam	yit·ba·rakh	ve·yit·ro·mam	shim·kha	mal·ke·nu	ta·mid	le·'o·lam
and for	*all this*	*blessed*	*and exalted*	*is Your Name*	*our King*	*always*	*forever*

וָעֶד.	וְכֹל	הַחַיִּים	יוֹדֽוּךָ	סֶּלָה,	וִיהַלְלוּ	אֶת	שִׁמְךָ	בֶּאֱמֶת,
va·'ed	ve·chol	ha·chai·yim	yo·du·kha	se·lah	vi·hal·le·lu	'et	shim·kha	be·'e·met
and ever	*and all*	*the living*	*will praise You*	*forever*	*and praise*	*( )*	*Your Name in truth*	

הָאֵל	יְשׁוּעָתֵֽנוּ	וְעֶזְרָתֵֽנוּ	סֶּלָה.	בָּרוּךְ	אַתָּה	יְהֹוָה,	הַטּוֹב	שִׁמְךָ
ha·'el	ye·shu·'a·te·nu	ve·'ez·ra·te·nu	se·lah	ba·rukh	'at·tah	'Adonai	hat·tov	shim·kha
O God of our salvation		*and our help*	*forever*	*Blessed*	*are You*	*Lord*	*The Good*	*Your Name*

וּלְךָ	נָאֶה	לְהוֹדוֹת.
u·le·kha	na·'eh	le·ho·dot
and to You	*it is right*	*to give thanks*

For all these things we bless and exalt Your Name our King forever and evermore. And all the living shall confess You forever and praise Your Name in truth, O God of our salvation and our help forever! Blessed are You, Adonai, "The Good One" is Your Name, and to You it is right to give thanks.

Blessing Nineteen: שִׂים שָׁלוֹם
(Establish Peace)

וְעַל	עָלֵינוּ	וְרַחֲמִים	וָחֶסֶד	חֵן,	וּבְרָכָה,	טוֹבָה,	שָׁלוֹם	שִׂים
ve·'al	'a·lei·nu	ve·ra·cha·mim	va·che·sed	chen	uv·ra·kha	to·vah	sha·lom	sim
and upon	upon us	and compassion	and kindness	grace	and blessing	goodness	peace	Grant

פָּנֶיךָ,	בְּאוֹר	כְּאֶחָד	כֻּלָּנוּ	אָבִינוּ,	בָּרְכֵנוּ	עַמֶּךָ.	יִשְׂרָאֵל	כָּל
pa·ney·kha	be·'or	ke·'e·chad	kul·la·nu	'a·vi·nu	ba·re·khe·nu	'am·me·kha	yis·ra·'el	kol
of Your face	with light	as one	all of us	our Father	bless us	Your people	Israel	all

חַיִּים	תּוֹרַת	אֱלֹהֵינוּ,	יְהוָה,	לָנוּ	נָתַתָּ	פָּנֶיךָ	בְאוֹר	כִּי
chai·yim	to·rat	'e·lo·hey·nu	'Adonai	la·nu	na·ta·ta	pa·ney·kha	ve·'or	ki
of life	the Torah	our God	Lord	to us	You gave	of Your face	with light	for

וְטוֹב	וְשָׁלוֹם.	וְחַיִּים,	וְרַחֲמִים,	וּצְדָקָה,	חֶסֶד	וְאַהֲבַת
ve·tov	ve·sha·lom	ve·chai·yim	ve·ra·cha·mim	uts·da·kah	che·sed	ve·'a·ha·vat
may it be good	and peace	and life	and compassion	and righteousness	of kindness	and love

שָׁעָה	וּבְכָל	עֵת	בְּכָל	יִשְׂרָאֵל,	עַמְּךָ	אֶת	לְבָרֵךְ	בְּעֵינֶיךָ
sha·'ah	u·ve·khol	'et	be·khol	yis·ra·'el	'am·me·kha	'et	le·va·rekh	be·'ey·ney·kha
hour	and at every	time	at every	Israel	Your people	()	to bless	in Your eyes

בַּשָּׁלוֹם.	יִשְׂרָאֵל	עַמּוֹ	אֶת	הַמְבָרֵךְ	יְהוָה,	אַתָּה	בָּרוּךְ	בִּשְׁלוֹמֶךָ.
ba·sha·lom	yis·ra·'el	'amo	'et	ham·va·rekh	'Adonai	'at·tah	ba·rukh	bish·lo·me·kha
with peace	his people Israel	()	()	Who blesses	Lord	are You	Blessed	with Your peace

Grant peace, goodness, blessing, grace, kindness, and compassion upon us and upon all of Your people Israel. Bless us, our Father, all of us as one, with the light of Your face, for with the light of Your face You gave to us, Adonai our God, the Torah of life and love of kindness, righteousness, blessing, compassion, life, and peace. And may it be good in Your eyes to bless Your people Israel at every time and at every hour with Your peace. Blessed art You, Lord, Who blesses His people Israel with peace.

This blessing ends with the following ritual: Bow to the left for the phrase "oseh shalom bimromav," bow forward for during "hu ya'aseh shalom 'aleinu," and straighten up for "ve'al kol yisrael. Veimru amen":

אָמֵן.	וְאִמְרוּ	יִשְׂרָאֵל.	כָּל	וְעַל	עָלֵינוּ,	שָׁלוֹם	יַעֲשֶׂה	הוּא	בִּמְרוֹמָיו,	שָׁלוֹם	עֹשֶׂה
'a·men	ve·'im·ru	yis·ra·'el	kol	ve·'al	'a·lei·nu	sha·lom	ya·'a·seh	hu	bim·ro·mav	sha·lom	'o·seh
Amen	and say ye	Israel	all	and on	upon us	peace	make	may he	in His heights		He Who makes peace

Aleinu
עָלֵינוּ

The *Aleinu* is a prayer of praise to God recited at the conclusion of every regular prayer service: *Shacharit, Minchah, Ma'ariv*. According to some sources, this declaration of faith was composed by Joshua after he led the children of Israel into the promised land.

עָלֵינוּ לְשַׁבֵּחַ לַאֲדוֹן הַכֹּל, לָתֵת גְּדֻלָּה לְיוֹצֵר בְּרֵאשִׁית,
'a·lei·nu le·sha·**be**·ach la·'a·don ha·kol, la·tet ge·du·lah le·yo·tser be·rei·shit
It is our duty to praise — the Lord of all things, — to ascribe — greatness — to the Molder of creation

שֶׁלֹּא עָשָׂנוּ כְּגוֹיֵי הָאֲרָצוֹת, וְלֹא שָׂמָנוּ כְּמִשְׁפְּחוֹת הָאֲדָמָה.
shel·lo 'a·**sa**·nu ke·goyei ha·'a·ra·tsot, ve·lo' sa·ma·nu ke·mish·pe·chot ha·'a·da·mah.
for not — He made us — like the nations of the lands — nor — placed us — like the families of the earth.

שֶׁלֹּא שָׂם חֶלְקֵנוּ כָּהֶם, וְגוֹרָלֵנוּ כְּכָל הֲמוֹנָם. שֶׁהֵם מִשְׁתַּחֲוִים
she·lo sam chel·qe·nu ka·hem, ve·go·ra·le·nu ke·khol ha·mo·nam. she·hem mish·ta·cha·vim
for not — he put — our portion — like theirs — and our lot — as all — their crowd. — For they — bow down

לְהֶבֶל וָרִיק, וּמִתְפַּלְלִים אֶל אֵל לֹא מוֹשִׁיעַ.
le·he·vel va·riq, u·mit·pal·le·lim 'el 'el lo' mo·shei·'a.
to vanity and emptiness — and pray — to — a god — who does not save.

וַאֲנַחְנוּ כּוֹרְעִים וּמִשְׁתַּחֲוִים וּמוֹדִים, לִפְנֵי מֶלֶךְ מַלְכֵי הַמְּלָכִים
va·'a·nach·nu ko·re·'im u·mish·ta·cha·vim u·mo·dim, lif·nei **me**·lekh mal·khei ham·me·la·khim
but we — bend our knees — and bow — and thank — before — King — the King of king of kings

הַקָּדוֹשׁ בָּרוּךְ הוּא. שֶׁהוּא נוֹטֶה שָׁמַיִם וְיֹסֵר אָרֶץ, וּמוֹשַׁב
haq·qa·dosh ba·rukh hu. she·hu no·teh sha·mayim ve·yo·ser 'a·rets, u·mo·shav
The Holy One — bend our knees — and bow — He — stretches — heaven — and fixes — earth — the seat

יְקָרוֹ בַּשָּׁמַיִם מִמַּעַל, וּשְׁכִינַת עֻזּוֹ בְּגָבְהֵי מְרוֹמִים. הוּא אֱלֹהֵינוּ
ye·qa·ro ba·sha·mayim mim·ma·'al, ush·chi·nat 'uz·zo be·ga·vehei me·ro·mim. hu 'e·lo·hey·nu
His glory is in the heavens above — His power and presence — in the loftiest heights — He is our God

אֵין עוֹד. אֱמֶת מַלְכֵּנוּ, אֶפֶס זוּלָתוֹ כַּכָּתוּב בְּתוֹרָתוֹ:
'ein 'od. 'e·met mal·ke·nu, 'e·fes zu·la·to ka·ka·tuv be·to·ra·to:
there is none other — True is — our King — nothing — beside Him — as it is written in His Torah:

Aleinu (continued)

עָלֵינוּ

וְיָדַעְתָּ הַיּוֹם וַהֲשֵׁבֹתָ אֶל־לְבָבֶךָ כִּי יְהוָה הוּא הָאֱלֹהִים
ha·'e·lo·him   hu   'Adonai   ki   'el·le·va·ve·kha   va·ha·she·vo·ta   hai·yom   ve·ya·da'·ta
the God   *He is*   *Lord*   *that*   *to your heart*   *and take*   *this day*   *Know!*

בַּשָּׁמַיִם מִמַּעַל וְעַל הָאָרֶץ מִתָּחַת אֵין עוֹד: ...
'od   'ein   mi·ta·chat   ha·'a·rets   ve·'al   mi·ma·'al   bash·sha·mayim
there is no other.   *below*   *the earth*   *and on*   *above*   *in heaven*

כִּי הַמַּלְכוּת שֶׁלְּךָ הִיא וּלְעוֹלְמֵי עַד תִּמְלֹךְ בְּכָבוֹד,
be·kha·vod   tim·lokh   'ad   ul·'o·le·mey   hi   shel·kha   ham·mal·khut   ki
in glory   *You will reign*   *and forever and ever*   *is Yours*   *the Kingdom*   *For*

כַּכָּתוּב בְּתוֹרָתֶךָ: יְהוָה יִמְלֹךְ לְעֹלָם וָעֶד.
va·'ed   le·'o·lam   yim·lokh   'Adonai   be·to·ra·te·kha   kak·ka·tuv
and ever   *forever*   *will rule*   *Lord*   *As it is written in Your Torah*

וְנֶאֱמַר: וְהָיָה יְהוָה לְמֶלֶךְ עַל כָּל הָאָרֶץ בַּיּוֹם הַהוּא
ha·hu   bai·yom   ha·'a·rets   kol   'al   le·me·lekh   'Adonai   ve·ha·yah   ve·ne·'e·mar
on that day   *the earth*   *all*   *over*   *be King*   *Lord*   *He will*   *and it is said:*

יִהְיֶה יְהוָה אֶחָד וּשְׁמוֹ אֶחָד:
'e·chad   ush·mo   'e·chad   'Adonai   yi·yeh
one   *and his Name*   *one*   *Lord*   *will be*

And the LORD shall be king over all the earth:
in that day shall there be one LORD, and his name one.
Zechariah 14:9 KJV

Priestly Blessing
בִּרְכַּת כֹּהֲנִים

The priestly blessing is found in Numbers 6:23-27. Traditionally, the priests blessed the people every morning after the sacrifice (and today many synagogues end their service with this blessing as a benediction). When recited, the priest raises his hands with the palms facing outward and the thumbs of his outspread hands touching. The four fingers on each hand are split into two sets of two fingers each (thus forming the letter Shin, an emblem for *Shaddai*). In the following, the text in brackets is said in response to the cantor's recitation:

יְבָרֶכְךָ יְהוָה וְיִשְׁמְרֶךָ.

ve·yish·me·**re**·kha   'Adonai   ye·va·re·khe·kha

and protect you   *May the Lord bless you*

[כֵּן יְהִי רָצוֹן.]

ra·tson   ye·hi   ken

Yes, may it be His will.

יָאֵר יְהוָה פָּנָיו אֵלֶיךָ וִיחֻנֶּךָּ.

vi·chun·**ne**·kha   'e·**ley**·kha   pa·nav   'Adonai   ya·'er

and be gracious to you   *to you*   *his face*   *May the Lord shine*

[כֵּן יְהִי רָצוֹן.]

ra·tson   ye·hi   ken

Yes, may it be His will.

יִשָּׂא יְהוָה פָּנָיו אֵלֶיךָ, וְיָשֵׂם לְךָ שָׁלוֹם.

sha·lom   le·kha   ve·ya·sem   'e·**ley**·kha   pa·nav   'Adonai   yi·sa

peace   *to you*   *and give*   *to you*   *his face*   *May the Lord turn his face*

[כֵּן יְהִי רָצוֹן.]

ra·tson   ye·hi   ken

Yes, may it be His will.

Speak unto Aaron and unto his sons, saying, On this wise ye shall bless the children of Israel, saying unto them, The Lord bless thee, and keep thee: The Lord make his face shine upon thee, and be gracious unto thee: The Lord lift up his countenance upon thee, and give thee peace. And they shall put my name upon the children of Israel; and I will bless them. (Numbers 6:23-27, KJV)

Ein Keloheinu
אֵין כֵּאלֹהֵינוּ

The *'Ein Keloheinu* is a well-known synagogue song that exalts the Lord. It is noteworthy on account of its memorable melody and the easy Hebrew phrasing. One charming custom in Orthodox synagogues is to appoint a child to be the *chazzan* (or cantor) for this song at the end of a *Musaf* (additional) service.

אֵין כֵּאלֹהֵינוּ,	אֵין כַּאדוֹנֵינוּ,	אֵין כְּמַלְכֵּנוּ,	אֵין כְּמוֹשִׁיעֵנוּ,
'ein ke·lo·**hei**·nu	'ein ka·do·**nei**·nu	'ein ke·mal·**ke**·nu	'ein ke·mo·shi·'**e**·nu
There is none like our God,	*There is none like our Lord,*	*There is none like our King,*	*There is none like our Savior,*
מִי כֵּאלֹהֵינוּ,	מִי כַּאדוֹנֵינוּ,	מִי כְּמַלְכֵּנוּ,	מִי כְּמוֹשִׁיעֵנוּ,
mi khei·lo·**hei**·nu	mi ka·do·**nei**·nu	mi khe·mal·**ke**·nu	mi khe·mo·shi·'**e**·nu
Who is like our God?	*Who is like our Lord?*	*Who is like our King?*	*Who is like our Savior?*
נוֹדֶה לֵאלֹהֵינוּ,	נוֹדֶה לַאדוֹנֵינוּ,	נוֹדֶה לְמַלְכֵּנוּ,	נוֹדֶה לְמוֹשִׁיעֵנוּ,
no·deh lei·lo·**hei**·nu	no·deh la·do·**nei**·nu	no·deh le·mal·**ke**·nu	no·deh le·mo·shi·'**e**·nu
Give thanks to our God,	*Give thanks to our Lord,*	*Give thanks to our King,*	*Give thanks to our Savior,*
בָּרוּךְ אֱלֹהֵינוּ,	בָּרוּךְ אֲדוֹנֵינוּ,	בָּרוּךְ מַלְכֵּנוּ,	בָּרוּךְ מוֹשִׁיעֵנוּ.
ba·rukh 'e·lo·**hey**·nu	ba·rukh 'a·do·**nei**·nu	ba·rukh mal·**ke**·nu	ba·rukh mo·shi·'**e**·nu
Blessed is our God,	*Blessed is our Lord,*	*Blessed is our King,*	*Blessed is our Savior.*

אַתָּה הוּא אֱלֹהֵינוּ,	אַתָּה הוּא אֲדוֹנֵינוּ,
'at·tah hu 'e·lo·**hey**·nu	'at·tah hu 'a·do·**nei**·nu
It is You who are our God,	*It is You who are our Lord,*
אַתָּה הוּא מַלְכֵּנוּ,	אַתָּה הוּא מוֹשִׁיעֵנוּ.
'at·tah hu mal·**ke**·nu	'at·tah hu mo·shi·'**e**·nu
It is You who are our King,	*It is You who are our Savior.*

אַתָּה הוּא שֶׁהִקְטִירוּ אֲבוֹתֵינוּ לְפָנֶיךָ אֶת קְטֹרֶת הַסַּמִּים.
'at·tah hu she·hiq·**ti**·ru 'a·vo·**tei**·nu le·fa·**ney**·kha 'et qe·to·ret has·sam·mim
It is to You that our fathers burned sweet incense before

Additional Blessings

The Siddur offers a wealth of blessings for virtually every aspect of the Jew's life. We have included a few of the more common blessings at the end of this lesson.

Blessing When Affixing a Mezuzah

A mezuzah is a kosher parchment scroll (inscribed with the Shema on one side and the word *Shaddai* on the other side) that is rolled up and inserted into a decorative case. The case is then affixed to the upper third of a doorway (on an angle pointing upward, toward the inside of the home, and to the right side as you enter), in fulfillment of the commandment given in Deuteronomy 11:20, "And thou shalt write them upon the doorposts (*mezuzot*) of thine house, and upon thy gates."

The word *mezuzah* is used as a noun 18 times in the Scriptures. The Israelites applied blood to the two *mezuzot* of their homes at the time of their liberation from Egypt, and the word is used to describe the gateposts of the Temple, both those built by Solomon and those envisioned by Ezekiel. As believers in the Messiah Jesus, the mezuzah can remind us that we too are bought with a price, and that our homes our dedicated to God.

Many *mezuzot* are beautiful pieces of artwork and are often given as housewarming gifts. The letter Shin often appears on the outside of the mezuzah case and stands for the Name of God: *Shaddai* (the Mighty). The three letters of the word שַׁדַּי are said to be the initials of שׁוֹמֵר דַּלְתוֹת יִשְׂרָאֵל "Guardian of the doors of Israel."

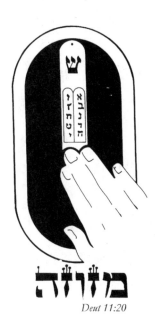

מְזוּזָה
Deut 11:20

בָּרוּךְ אַתָּה יְיָ אֱלֹהֵינוּ מֶלֶךְ הָעוֹלָם,
ha·'o·**lam**   me·lekh   'e·lo·hey·nu   'Adonai   'at·**tah**   ba·**rukh**

"Blessed are You, Lord our God, King of the universe,"

אֲשֶׁר קִדְּשָׁנוּ בְּמִצְוֹתָיו,
be·mits·vo·tav   qid·de·**sha**·nu   'a·sher

"who sanctified us with His commandments"

וְצִוָּנוּ עַל לִקְבֹּעַ מְזוּזָה.
me·zu·zah   liq·**bo**·'a   'al   v'·tsi·**va**·nu

"and commanded us to attach a mezuzah."

Blessing over foods

The *Ha-motsi* is the blessing said before eating bread:

בָּרוּךְ אַתָּה יְיָ אֱלֹהֵינוּ מֶּלֶךְ הָעוֹלָם,

ha·‘o·**lam**   **me**·lekh   ‘e·lo·hey·nu   ’Adonai   ’at·**tah**   ba·**rukh**

"Blessed are You, Lord our God, King of the universe,"

הַמּוֹצִיא לֶחֶם מִן הָאָרֶץ.

ha·’a·rets   min   le·khem   ham·**mo**·tsi

"who brings forth bread from the earth."

The following blessing, the *Borei Peri*, is said before drinking wine or grape juice:

בָּרוּךְ אַתָּה יְיָ אֱלֹהֵינוּ מֶּלֶךְ הָעוֹלָם,

ha·‘o·**lam**   **me**·lekh   ‘e·lo·hey·nu   ’Adonai   ’at·**tah**   ba·**rukh**

"Blessed are You, Lord our God, King of the universe,"

בּוֹרֵא פְּרִי הַגָּפֶן.

hag·**ga**·fen   pe·ri   bo·**rei**

"who created the fruit of the vine."

The following is said before eating grains, such as wheat products, barley, ryes, etc.

בָּרוּךְ אַתָּה יְיָ אֱלֹהֵינוּ מֶּלֶךְ הָעוֹלָם,

ha·‘o·**lam**   **me**·lekh   ‘e·lo·hey·nu   ’Adonai   ’at·**tah**   ba·**rukh**

"Blessed are You, Lord our God, King of the universe,"

בּוֹרֵא מִינֵי מְזוֹנוֹת.

me·zo·not   mi·nei   bo·rei

"who creates different types of nourishment."

Blessing over foods

The following is said before eating fruit that grows from a tree:

בָּרוּךְ אַתָּה יְיָ אֱלֹהֵינוּ מֶלֶךְ הָעוֹלָם,

ha·ʻo·**lam** me·lekh ʻe·lo·hey·nu ʼAdonai ʼat·**tah** ba·**rukh**

"Blessed are You, Lord our God, King of the universe,"

בּוֹרֵא פְּרִי הָעֵץ.

ha·ʻets pe·ri bo·rei

"who creates the fruit of the tree."

The following blessing may be said before eating any other food:

בָּרוּךְ אַתָּה יְיָ אֱלֹהֵינוּ מֶלֶךְ הָעוֹלָם,

ha·ʻo·**lam** me·lekh ʻe·lo·hey·nu ʼAdonai ʼat·**tah** ba·**rukh**

"Blessed are You, Lord our God, King of the universe,"

שֶׁהַכֹּל נִהְיֶה בִּדְבָרוֹ.

bid·va·ro nih·yeh she·hak·kol

"through whose word everything is created."

The Shehecheyanu
שֶׁהֶחֱיָּנוּ

The *Shehecheyanu* blessing is said to offer thanks for new and unusual experiences (such as seeing a baby's first steps, beginning a new year at school, reaping the first produce from a garden, etc.). This blessing is also often recited at the beginning of holidays (e.g., on the first night of Chanukah) or to celebrate any long-awaited special occasion.

בָּרוּךְ אַתָּה יְיָ אֱלֹהֵינוּ מֶלֶךְ הָעוֹלָם,

ba·**rukh** ’at·**tah** ’Adonai ‘e·lo·hey·nu **me**·lekh ha·‘o·**lam**

"Blessed are You, Lord our God, King of the universe,"

שֶׁהֶחֱיָּנוּ וְקִיְּמָנוּ וְהִגִּיעָנוּ לַזְּמַן הַזֶּה.

she·he·che·**ya**·nu ve·qi·ye·**ma**·nu ve·hi·gi·‘**a**·nu laz·ze·man haz·zeh

"for keeping us alive, taking care of us, and bringing us to this time."

Lesson Seventeen

THE TANAKH AND B'RIT CHADASHAH

Lesson Introduction

The Tanakh

The Hebrew Bible is called the *Tanakh* (sometimes transliterated as *Tanak* or *Tanach* in English), an acronym for *Torah*, *Nevi'im*, and *Ketuvim*. The *Tanakh* is divided into three main sections, as follows:

DIVISION	HEBREW	MAJOR ELEMENTS
Torah	תּוֹרָה	The first five books of Moses. The actual Torah itself is referred to as the *Sefer Torah*, or sacred Torah scroll. The *Chumash* is a book form of the *Torah*, usually subdivided into 54 smaller literary units called *parashiot* (the name of each *parashah* comes from a key word of the section). The word *Torah* is better understood as "teaching" or "understanding" rather than "law."
Prophets (*Nevi'im*)	נְבִיאִים	The prophetical books are subdivided into two parts: Four books of the "Former" prophets and 15 books of the "Latter" prophets. Weekly readings are called *haftarah portions*.
Writings (*Ketuvim*)	כְּתוּבִים	Assorted sacred writings, including Psalms, Proverbs, and some historical books. There are 12 books in this division of the *Tanakh*.

Notes:

- Some Jews refer to the entire Hebrew Bible (i.e., the *Tanakh*) simply as the *Torah*—without making the distinction of the divisions shown above.
- Though the Christian *Old Testament* is the result of the canonization of the Jewish scriptures, the order of the books in the *Tanakh* is not identical to the Christian Old Testament (though content is the same).
- Chapter and verse references are not always identical between the Old Testament and the *Tanakh*.

Testament or Covenant?

Most Messianic Jewish believers do not refer to the *Tanakh* as the "Old Testament" but prefer to use the phrase "Earlier Covenant." The reason for this is that the word (mis)translated as "testament" is the Hebrew word *Berit*, meaning "covenant" or "contract." The idea of a testament, in the sense of a will, is alien to the Hebraic mindset.

First Part of the Tanakh: The Torah

The word *Torah* comes from the root word *yarah* meaning "to shoot an arrow" or "to hit the mark." Properly used, the word means "teaching" or "instruction." Teaching is associated with the Holy Spirit, and God Himself is described as a Teacher: He taught Moses what to do and say (*see* Ex. 4:15). And it is clear that the Lord Jesus assumed the title of Rabbi and performed much of his ministry as a Teacher (*see* John 1:38).

The Torah is divided into five main sections, as follows:

BOOK	HEBREW	MAJOR ELEMENTS
Genesis (*Bereshit*)	בְּרֵאשִׁית	The story of the creation of the universe by the God of Israel, and how He chose the Jewish people to be His own covenant people. *Bereshit* means "in the beginning."
Exodus (*Shemot*)	שְׁמוֹת	The story of the liberation of the Jewish people from their bondage in Egypt. The giving of the Mosaic covenant to Israel. *Shemot* means "names."
Leviticus (*Vaiyiqra*)	וַיִּקְרָא	Detailed instructions for the ancient priesthood regarding how Israel might approach God by means of the rituals in the *mishkan* (tabernacle). *Vaiyiqra* means "And He called."
Numbers (*Bemidbar*)	בְּמִדְבַּר	The story of how Moses led the wandering Jewish people through the wastelands of Sinai. *Bemidbar* means "In the wilderness."
Deuteronomy (*Devarim*)	דְּבָרִים	Renewal of the Mosaic covenant with blessings for obedience and consequences for disobedience. *Devarim* means "words" and is referred by Jews as the "repetition" of the Torah.

אֲרוֹן קֹדֶשׁ

Aron Qodesh

Did you know?

The written *Torah* of Moses is called the *Sefer Torah*, or Torah Scroll, and is the most sacred object of Jewish life. The *Sefer Torah* is meticulously hand-written in Hebrew calligraphy with *tagin* ("crowns") on kosher parchment (this style of writing is known as STA"M). You are not supposed to directly touch a *Sefer Torah*, but use a *yad* (pointer) instead. Torah scrolls are kept covered with fabric and are often ornamented with silver crowns on the handles of the scrolls and a silver breastplate on the front – adorned, in fact, like the high priest described in *Vaiyiqra*. Torah scrolls are kept in a special cabinet in the synagogue called an "ark" (an acronym of "aron qodesh," meaning "holy cabinet").

Second Part of the Tanakh: The Prophets

The word *Nevi'im* is the plural form of *Navi*, or prophet. The *Nevi'im*, or Hebrew prophetical books, are subdivided into two major parts: four books of the "Former" prophets and 14 books of the "Latter" prophets. Together these books trace Jewish history from the time of Moses' death until the destruction of the First Temple and the subsequent exile of the southern kingdom to Babylonia.

The Former Prophets (נְבִיאָם רִאשׁוֹנִין)

BOOK	HEBREW	MAJOR ELEMENTS
Joshua (Yehoshua')	יְהוֹשֻׁעַ	The story of the commission of Joshua to lead the children of Israel into the promised land. The name *Yehoshua'* means "the Lord saves." *Yeshua'* (Jesus) is a shortened form of this name.
Judges (Shofetim)	שׁוֹפְטִים	The story of how Adonai raised up twelve remarkable individuals (called judges or *shofetim*) to deliver Israel from her enemies. The book ranges over the first 350 years in the Promised Land, from the time of Joshua to Saul.
Samuel (Shemu'el)	שְׁמוּאֵל	The rise and rule of Samuel, Israel's greatest judge, and the story of the transition to the Israeli monarchy. The great Davidic covenant is established in this book. In the *Tanakh*, *Samuel* is one book, whereas in the Christian Bible, it is divided into 1 and 2 Samuel. *Shemu'el* means "heard of God."
Kings (Melakhim)	מְלָכִים	The history of the undivided kingdom under David and Solomon, the divided kingdom, the fall of Israel in 722 B.C. and Judah's captivity in 586 B.C. In the *Tanakh*, *Melakhim* is one book, whereas in the Christian Bible, it is divided into 1 and 2 Kings. *Melakhim* means "kings."

"Thy kingdom shall be established for ever before thee"
2 Samuel 7:16

The Davidic Covenant

When King David sought to build the First Temple unto the LORD, the LORD told him that instead He would build David a house and grant him a kingdom that would never end (*see* 2 Samuel 7).

The Messiah Yeshua, as a descendant of David, fulfilled the promise of Adonai. Concerning His birth it is written: "He shall be great, and shall be called the Son of the Highest: and the Lord God shall give unto him the throne of his father David: And he shall reign over the house of Jacob for ever; and of his kingdom there shall be no end" (Luke 1:31-3, KJV).

The Latter Prophets

The books of the "Latter" prophets contain oracles, admonitions, and fiery revelations from Israel's greatest visionaries. Ranging over 400 years (from 800-400 B.C.), Israel's prophets constantly sought to call both Israel (in the north) and Judah (in the south) back to Adonai -- before inevitable judgment would take place.

The Three Major Latter Prophets

The Latter Prophets may also be divided into the three major prophets (Isaiah, Jeremiah, and Ezekiel) and "The Twelve" so-called minor prophets.

BOOK	HEBREW	MAJOR ELEMENTS
Isaiah (*Yesh'ayahu*)	יְשַׁעְיָהוּ	Adonai's messenger to Judah during her declining years regarding the coming Messiah and Israel's true King. *Yesh'ayahu* means "Adonai is Salvation."
Jeremiah (*Yirmeyahu*)	יִרְמְיָהוּ	Adonai's messenger to Judah during her final years before falling to the Babylonians, Jeremiah's message centers on the impending judgment on Jerusalem but holds out hope for the city's ultimate glory. *Yirmeyahu* means "Adonai will Lift Up."
Ezekiel (*Yechezqi'el*)	יְחֶזְקֵאל	The son of a priest who was deported to Babylon, Ezekiel prophesied to the exiles about the judgment on Jerusalem, the nations, and the final restoration of Israel in the last days. *Yechezqi'el* means "God Strengthens."

ירושׁלים

"The Twelve" Prophetical Books (תְּרֵי עָשָׂר) (traditionally one scroll)

BOOK	HEBREW	MAJOR ELEMENTS
Hosea (Hoshea‘)	הוֹשֵׁעַ	Adonai's messenger to the northern kingdom during her declining years regarding the love of God despite Israel's failures. *Hoshea‘* means "Adonai is Deliverer."
Joel (Yo'el)	יוֹאֵל	Adonai's messenger to Judah during her declining years regarding the great Day of the Lord and the judgment of the nations. *Yo'el* means "Adonai is God."
Amos ('Amos)	עָמוֹס	Messenger to the northern kingdom during her declining years regarding impending judgment. *'Amos* means "burden."
Obadiah ('Ovadyah)	עֹבַדְיָה	The shortest book of the *Tanakh*, Obadiah is a pronouncement against Edom and a foretelling of the coming Day of the Lord. *'Ovadyah* means "servant of Adonai."
Jonah (Yonah)	יוֹנָה	A messenger to the northern Kingdom, Jonah tells the story of God's love for the goyim -- and Israel's mission to be a light unto the nations. *Yonah* means "dove."
Micah (Mikhah)	מִיכָה	A messenger to Judah during her declining years, Micah warns of judgment and foretells the messianic kingdom. *Michah* means "Who is like Adonai?"
Nahum (Nachum)	נַחוּם	A messenger to Judah during her declining years, Nahum foretells the doom of the Assyrian empire. *Nachum* means "Consolation," or "Comforter."
Habakuk (Chavaquq)	חֲבַקּוּק	A messenger to Judah regarding her judgment by the Chaldeans. *Chavaquq* means "Embracer."
Zephaniah (Tsefanyah)	צְפַנְיָה	Zephaniah spoke of restoring the remnant and the coming Day of the Lord. *Tsefanyah* means "Adonai has hidden."
Haggai (Chagai)	חַגַּי	Haggai ministered to the exiles and spoke of the rebuilding of the Temple and the coming kingdom of Messiah Yeshua. *Chagai* means "Festive."
Zechariah (Zekharyah)	זְכַרְיָה	Zechariah, a prophet to the restored remnant, speaks of the Messiah's two comings and God's faithfulness to Israel. *Zekharyah* means "God has remembered."
Malachi (Malakhi)	מַלְאָכִי	Malachi, a prophet to the restored remnant, speaks of the Lord's love for His erring people and warns of judgment. *Malakhi* means "Messenger of Adonai."

Third Part of the Tanakh: The Writings

The word *Ketuvim* is the plural form of *Ketav*, or writing. The *Ketuvim*, or Hebrew literary books, are subdivided into three major parts: Wisdom Literature, Megillot (scrolls), and Histories (which, somewhat strangely, includes Daniel, an apocalyptic book).

Wisdom Literature

BOOK	HEBREW	MAJOR ELEMENTS
Psalms (Tehillim)	תְּהִלִּים	Sacred prayerbook and hymnal. Divided into five separate "books" (Psalms 1-41, 42-72, 73-89, 90-106, and 107-150, respectively). Messianic Psalms include 2, 8, 16, 22, 45, 69, 72, 89, 100, 118, 132. *Tehillim* means "praises."
Proverbs (Mishlei)	מִשְׁלֵי	Manual for moral and spiritual instruction. A proverb is a concise regulatory maxim or rule for behavior. *Mishlei* means "proverbs" or "parables."
Job ('Iyov)	אִיּוֹב	The question of why the righteous suffer as told through the narrative and poetry of Job and his "comforters." *'Iyov* means "persecuted" or "hated."

Megillot (Scrolls) חָמֵשׁ מְגִלּוֹת

The *Chamesh Megillot* (five scrolls) are read during major Jewish festivals:

BOOK	HEBREW	MAJOR ELEMENTS
Song of Songs (Shir Hashirim)	שִׁיר הַשִּׁירִים	Written by King Solomon and considered an allegory of the relations between Adonai and Israel (and Messiah's love for the Church). Read during *Pesach* (Passover). *Shir Hashirim* means "Song of (all) songs."
Ruth (Rut)	רוּת	A wonderful love story of redemption that prefigures the Messiah as our kinsman Redeemer. Read during *Shavuot* (Pentecost). *Rut* means "satiated."
Lamentations ('Eikha)	אֵיכָה	Jeremiah's acrostic lament over Jerusalem's destruction by the Babylonians. Read during *Tish'ah b'Av*. *'Eikha* means "How!," or "Alas!"
Ecclesiastes (Qohelet)	קֹהֶלֶת	Solomon's study of the futility and meaninglessness inherent in natural reasoning "under the sun." Read during *Sukkot* (Tabernacles). *Qohelet* means "one who assembles."
Esther (Ester)	אֶסְתֵּר	The story of God's providence in the affairs of the Jews during the time of Xerxes (486-465 B.C.), ruler of Persia. Ester is read during *Purim*.

Histories

BOOK	HEBREW	MAJOR ELEMENTS
Daniel (Dani'el)	דָּנִיֵּאל	Daniel was a messenger to the exiles who received portentous visions for the future. His writings, some of which are written in Aramaic, provide the key for understanding New Testament prophecy. *Dani'el* means "God is Judge."
Ezra ('Ezra)	עֶזְרָא	The story of the return of the remnant from Babylon under Zerubbabel, the rebuilding of the Temple, and the revival of true worship of Adonai under the leadership of Ezra the priest. *'Ezra* means "help" or "aid." (Originally Ezra and Nehemiah were one book in the Jewish tradition).
Nehemiah (Nechemyah)	נְחֶמְיָה	The rebuilding of the walls of Jerusalem and reestablishment of civil authority under Nehemiah. *Nechemyah* means "consolation of God."
Chronicles (Divrei Hayyamim)	דִּבְרֵי הַיָּמִים	The history of Judah (i.e., the southern kingdom) and the role of King David as the establisher of Temple worship. In the *Tanakh*, Chronicles is one book, whereas in the Christian Bible, it is divided into two. *Divrei Hayyamim* means the "things or words of the days."

The Bible the Lord Jesus Used

Did the Messiah use the Greek Septuagint (otherwise known as the LXX [meaning 70] and from which the Christian Old Testament was initially translated into Latin) or the Hebrew *Tanakh*, as outlined in this lesson?

In the *B'rit Chadashah* (New Testament) the Lord says: "From the blood of Abel unto the blood of Zacharias, which perished between the altar and the temple: verily I say unto you, It shall be required of this generation" (Luke 11:51 KJV).

Why did the Lord Jesus make this statement? Well, as you now know, the Hebrew *Tanakh* runs from Genesis to Chronicles (with the 12 minor prophets in the middle and not the end as in the Christian Old Testament). Now Abel was killed by his brother according to Genesis 4:8 and Zacharias was killed in 2 Chronicles 24:20-22. Thus Jesus was naming the first and last martyrs according to the order of the books found in the *Tanakh* – and He assumed His listeners would understand the reference through their familiarity with the Hebrew scriptures.

Moreover, in Matthew 5:18 Jesus refers to a "jot" and a "tittle" of the Scriptures. Jot refers to the smallest letter in Hebrew (the Yod) and tittle probably refers to the serifs in the Hebrew letterforms (not necessarily the *tagin*). This statement would be strange if Jesus were reading from the Greek Septuagint!

Tanakh
The Scriptures Jesus Used

1. Torah
תּוֹרָה

Genesis	בְּרֵאשִׁית
Exodus	שְׁמוֹת
Leviticus	וַיִּקְרָא
Numbers	בְּמִדְבַּר
Deuteronomy	דְּבָרִים

2. Prophets
נְבִיאִים

Former

Joshua	יְהוֹשֻׁעַ
Judges	שׁוֹפְטִים
Samuel	שְׁמוּאֵל
Kings	מְלָכִים

Latter

Major

Isaiah	יְשַׁעְיָהוּ
Jeremiah	יִרְמְיָהוּ
Ezekiel	יְחֶזְקֵאל

Minor

Hosea	הוֹשֵׁעַ
Joel	יוֹאֵל
Amos	עָמוֹס
Obadiah	עֹבַדְיָה
Jonah	יוֹנָה
Micah	מִיכָה
Nahum	נַחוּם
Habakuk	חֲבַקּוּק
Zephaniah	צְפַנְיָה
Haggai	חַגַּי
Zachariah	זְכַרְיָה
Malachi	מַלְאָכִי

3. Writings
כְּתוּבִים

Wisdom

Psalms	תְּהִלִּים
Proverbs	מִשְׁלֵי
Job	אִיוֹב

Megillot

Song of Songs	שִׁיר הַשִּׁירִים
Ruth	רוּת
Lamentations	אֵיכָה
Ecclesiastes	קֹהֶלֶת
Ester	אֶסְתֵּר

Histories

Daniel	דָּנִיֵּאל
Ezra	עֶזְרָא
Nehemiah	נְחֶמְיָה
Chronicles	דִּבְרֵי הַיָּמִים

Introducing the Masoretic Text

The Soferim

Within the earliest Jewish traditions, groups of Jewish scholars counted the number of times each letter appeared in the Scriptures (as well as the number of words, verses, paragraphs, etc.). These textual specialists were called *Soferim* (counters). The Soferim ensured that every Torah scroll (and the other books of the *Tanakh*) were identical, noting any unusual words and spellings and replicating them exactly through their scribal arts. Many Jews believe that Ezra the Scribe instituted many of the practices of the Soferim.

The Masoretes and the Masoretic Text

A group of Soferim called the *Masoretes* flourished in Tiberias (in Israel) between the 7th and 9th centuries A.D. In addition to counting the letters, words, and so on found in the Scriptures, the Masoretes added vowel signs (*niqqudot*), cantillation symbols (*ta'amim*), and accent marks to the text (their process was called the *Masorah*). The marked text was called the *Masoretic Text* and became the standard text for the Jews around the world (a particular Masoretic family, named ben-Asher, was instrumental in standardizing this text, and thus the Masoretic text is sometimes called the *ben-Asher* text). The Leningrad Codex (1010 C. E.) is the oldest complete Masoretic *Tanakh* preserved.

The Masoretic Text is the traditional Hebrew text of both Judaism and Western Christianity (the Catholic Church, historically, used the Latin translation of Jerome based on pre-Masoretic Hebrew sources). In 1524-25, Daniel Bomberg published an edition of the Masoretic Text called the *Miqra'ot Gedolot* which is considered the definitive edition of the *Tanakh* (this edition was used by the translators of the King James Bible for their work in the Old Testament). Today, the standard critical biblical text is called *Biblia Hebraica Stuttgartensia* (abbreviated BHS), and was published as a complete work in 1977.

Until the discovery of the Dead Sea Scrolls (DSS) in 1947, there was little evidence for pre-Masoretic Hebrew text of the *Tanakh*. But with the discovery of the DSS, scholars generally agree that we now have Hebrew manuscripts of the *Tanakh* dating from the time of Messiah that remarkably agree with the Masoretic Text.

The Septuagint (LXX) and the Apocrypha

The most important ancient translation of the *Tanakh* is the Greek Septuagint, originally produced for Greek-speaking Jews in Egypt. Parts of it date from as early as the third and second centuries B.C. Although the LXX is useful for doing certain types of biblical research, it is a *translation* of a Hebrew text (called *Targum Hashiv'im*), which differs from the Masoretic Text, and should not be considered an authoritative text over the original Hebrew. Jews have never accepted the LXX as authoritative Scripture (though it is still in use in Eastern Orthodox, Greek Orthodox, Russian, Coptic, etc., churches).

The Apocrypha (*Sefarim Chitsoniyim* in Hebrew) is a collection of 14 books written sometime before the Jewish canon was established (in the second century B.C.). These books were never recognized by the Jews as part of their sacred scriptures.

Accents of the Masoretic Text

Every word in the *Tanakh* (except those joined by a hyphen or *maqqef*) carries an accent mark on its **"tone" syllable** (i.e., the syllable that receives the stress). In the *Biblia Hebraica Stuttgartensia* there are 27 prose and 21 poetic accent marks used in the text. These marks (like the vowel marks) may appear above or below the word.

Here is an example of what Genesis 1:1-3a looks like in a typical *Tanakh* using the Masoretic accent marks:

פרשת בראשית

א־ב בְּרֵאשִׁית בָּרָא אֱלֹהִים אֵת הַשָּׁמַיִם וְאֵת הָאָרֶץ: וְהָאָרֶץ הָיְתָה תֹהוּ
וָבֹהוּ וְחֹשֶׁךְ עַל־פְּנֵי תְהוֹם וְרוּחַ אֱלֹהִים מְרַחֶפֶת עַל־פְּנֵי הַמָּיִם:
ג־ד וַיֹּאמֶר אֱלֹהִים יְהִי אוֹר וַיְהִי־אוֹר: וַיַּרְא אֱלֹהִים אֶת־הָאוֹר כִּי־טוֹב

Notes:

- The phrase at the top is read "*Parashat Bereshit*" and indicates the start of a weekly Torah portion (the Torah is divided into 54 weekly readings, called *parashiot*, and each week a specific portion is read at the synagogue).
- The letters to the right (e.g., א־ב) of each line indicate the verses (*pesuqim*) of the current chapter. The symbol that looks like a colon (e.g., ׃) is called a *Sof Pasuq* and indicates the end of the verse.
- The additional markings in the text (besides the vowel marks you have studied) are the accent and cantillation marks.
- In addition to showing syllable stress, accent marks are used to specify how to *chant* the text, and provide punctuation information to the chanter/reader. There are actually different chanting traditions within world Jewry, with the Ashkenazi chanting one way and the Sephardim chanting another, but the marks created by the Masoretes are common to both.

Did you know?

When the Torah is chanted from a *Sefer Torah* (Torah Scroll) in a synagogue, no vowel or accent marks appear in the text. Instead, the cantor will study the pronunciation of the text from another book, called a *Tiqun* (pl. *Tiqunim*) which has all of the cantillation marks, vowels, and accent marks on the right side of the page, and the text as it appears in the Sefer Torah on the left side (many preparing for their Bar or Bat Mitzvah make use of a Tiqun).

Three Main Accent Marks

Most accent marks can be classified according to whether they are *disjunctive* (pausal) or *conjunctive* (connecting).

Disjunctive Accents

Disjunctive accents mark a pause or break in the reading of the text, and function something like commas, semicolons, and colons in English. There are 18 disjunctive accent marks you might see in the Masoretic text, but the two most important are:

1. *'Atnach* (ˏ)—Placed under the last word of the first half of a verse.
2. *Silluq* (ˏ)—Placed under the last word of the second half of a verse.

Note that the major divisions of a verse are determined by the sense of the verse, not necessarily by the length.

Conjunctive Accents

Conjunctive accents connect two words in the text. There are 9 conjunctive accent marks you might see in the Masoretic text, but the most important is:

1. *Munach* (ˌ)—Placed under a word that is connected with a following word.

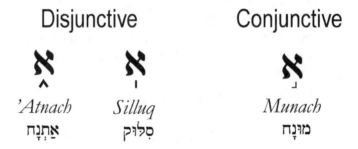

Disjunctive		Conjunctive
אָ	אִ	אֻ
'Atnach	*Silluq*	*Munach*
אַתְנָח	סִלּוּק	מוּנַח

The following shows Genesis 1:1 as you might see it in a typical Masoretic text:

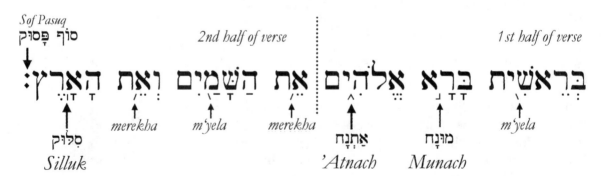

Important Note: For the purposes of this book, you do **not** need to memorize these accent marks, since they do not affect the way Hebrew is read (only how it is chanted). However, now you know what these marks are used for when you see them in the *Tanakh*.

Chapters and Verses

The Masoretic text divides the text into books, chapters (*pereqim*) and verses (*pesuqim*). For example, in a printed *Tanakh*, you might see something like the following on a page:

Pesuqim Pereq Book

בראשית א:א־ד

פרשת בראשית ⸺ *Parashat Hashavua'*

Pesuqim

א־ב בְּרֵאשִׁית בָּרָא אֱלֹהִים אֵת הַשָּׁמַיִם וְאֵת הָאָרֶץ: וְהָאָרֶץ הָיְתָה תֹהוּ
וָבֹהוּ וְחֹשֶׁךְ עַל־פְּנֵי תְהוֹם וְרוּחַ אֱלֹהִים מְרַחֶפֶת עַל־פְּנֵי הַמָּיִם:
ג־ד וַיֹּאמֶר אֱלֹהִים יְהִי אוֹר וַיְהִי־אוֹר: וַיַּרְא אֱלֹהִים אֶת־הָאוֹר כִּי־טוֹב
וַיַּבְדֵּל אֱלֹהִים בֵּין הָאוֹר וּבֵין הַחֹשֶׁךְ:

The page header indicates that *Bereshit* chapter 1 (*pereq* א) verses 1-4 (*pesuqim* א־ד) are displayed on this page. In addition, the weekly Torah portion (*parashat hashavua'*) is listed as a header above the running text. The right margin indicates the pesuq(im) for each line of the text (for example, the first line shows pesuqim (א־ב), or verses 1-2). Each verse ends with a *sof pasuq* (:) mark. Many *Tanakhs* include a running commentary at the bottom of the page that include comments from various Jewish sages such as Rashi and Ramban.

In order to recognize chapters and verses you will need to recall how Hebrew letters can be used as numbers and compute the values accordingly:

The B'rit Chadashah

The New Testament is called the *B'rit Chadashah* in Hebrew, meaning "New Covenant" (the word *Berit* means "covenant" and *Chadashah* means "new"). Like the *Tanakh*, it can be divided into three main parts: *Gospels/Acts* (corresponding to *Torah*), Letters (corresponding to *Ketuvim*), and Revelation (corresponding to *Nevi'im*):

DIVISION	HEBREW	MAJOR ELEMENTS
Good News of Redemption (Besorat HaGe'ulah)	בְּשׂוֹרַת הַגְּאֻלָּה	The four portraits of the Messiah of Israel as given by His messengers (Luke/Acts may be considered as a unit). *Besorah* means "good news" and *Ge'ulah* means "redemption."
Letters (Iggerot)	אִגְּרוֹת	Eight "general" letters to Messianic Jewish communities and thirteen letters from Paul, the emissary to the Gentiles. The word *Iggeret* (pl. *Iggerot*) means "letter."
Revelation (Hitggalut)	הִתְגַּלּוּת	The revelation of Yeshua the Messiah as given to His emissary *Yochanan* (John). The word *Hitgalut* means "revelation" or "unveiling" (sometimes the word *Chazon* ("vision") is used instead).

Notes:

- Just as there were 400 of years of silence before Adonai sent Moses to deliver Israel from her bondage to Pharaoh, so there were 400 of years of silence before Adonai sent His own Son, Yeshua the Messiah, to utterly deliver Israel from her ultimate bondage to sin and death. Moses himself foretold of the coming of the Messiah (see *Devarim* 18:18).

- Some Messianic believers think that the order of the *B'rit Chadashah* books should be reworked so that the "Hebrew epistles" (i.e., the eight letters to the Messianic communities) appear *before* the Pauline letters. Why? Because the message of the Good News of Redemption is "to the Jew first, and also to the Greek," as Paul himself notes in the letter to the Romans (Rom. 1:16, 2:10).

- The New Testament was originally written in (Koine) Greek, not Hebrew. There are several Hebrew New Testaments that have been translated from Greek. This book relies upon the *Hebrew New Testament* (The Society For Distributing Hebrew Scriptures, 1886/1999) and *The Hebrew New Testament* (Trinitarian Bible Society, 1966/1998).

The New Covenant

First Part of the B'rit Chadashah: The Gospels

The Hebrew phrase *Besorat HaGeulah* means "Tidings of Redemption" (*Besorah* means "tidings" and *Ge'ulah* means "redemption").

There are five books that compose the *Besurat Hage'ulah* portion of the *B'rit Chadashah*. The four gospels all begin with the phrase *Habesorah 'al-pi,* which means "The tidings according to," followed by the author's name:

BOOK	HEBREW	MAJOR ELEMENTS
Matthew (*Habesorah 'al-pi Mattai*)	הַבְּשׂוֹרָה עַל־פִּי מַתַּי [מַתִּתְיָהוּ]	Yeshua as Israel's Messiah and the Son of King David. The author of this gospel is anonymous, though it is traditionally thought to be the tax collector mentioned in Matthew 10:3. *Mattai* (also rendered as *Mattityahu*) means "gift of God."
Mark (*Habesorah 'al-pi Markos*)	הַבְּשׂוֹרָה עַל־פִּי מַרְקוֹס	The portrait of Yeshua as the powerful Servant of God. Mark may have been authored by John Mark (Acts 12:12) and is directed primarily to the Roman world.
Luke (*Habesorah 'al-pi Lukas*)	הַבְּשׂוֹרָה עַל־פִּי לוּקָס	Yeshua as the second *Ben Adam*, the Son of Man, exemplifying perfect manhood. The author is traditionally thought to be "Luke, the doctor" (Col 4:14, 2 Tim 4:11).
John (*Habesorah 'al-pi Yochanan*)	הַבְּשׂוֹרָה עַל־פִּי יוֹחָנָן	Yeshua as *Ben Elohim*, the mighty Son of God. This gospel is traditionally thought to be from John, the "beloved disciple."
Acts (*Ma'asei HaShelichim*)	מַעֲשֵׂי הַשְּׁלִיחִים	The works of the *Ruach Haqodesh* (Holy Spirit) in the early church as reported by Luke (Luke 1:3. Acts 1:1). This book bridges the period from the ascension of Yeshua to the formation of the early church and shows the spread of the message of redemption from "Jerusalem, to all Judea, Samaria, and to the ends of the earth" (Acts 1:8). *Ma'asei Hashelichim* means "deeds of the sent ones" (i.e., apostles) in Hebrew.

Second Part of the B'rit Chadashah: The Letters

Letters of Paul

There are thirteen letters from *Sha'ul* (Paul) the *shaliach* (messenger) to the Gentiles. Collectively these may be called *Igerot Polos Hashaliach*, meaning "Letters of the messenger Paul":

אִגְּרוֹת פּוֹלוֹס הַשָּׁלִיחַ

BOOK	HEBREW	MAJOR ELEMENTS
Romans (*'El-HaRomiyim*)	אֶל־הָרוֹמִיִּים	Paul's letter to the *qehillah* (קְהִלָּה) (congregation) in Rome. This letter is perhaps Paul's greatest doctrinal work, expounding all of the key doctrines of the gospel of God (*besorat ha'elohim*) in a masterfully written summary.
1st Corinthians (*Harishonah 'el HaQorintiyim*)	הָרִאשׁוֹנָה אֶל־הָקוֹרִנְתִּיִּים	Paul's first letter to the *qehillah* in Corinth regarding worldly versus spiritual living.
2nd Corinthians (*Hasheniyyah 'el HaQorintiyim*)	הַשְּׁנִיָּה אֶל־הָקוֹרִנְתִּיִּים	Paul's second letter to the *qehillah* in Corinth, defending his authority as a *shaliach* of the Messiah.
Galatians (*'El-HaGalatiyim*)	אֶל־הַגָּלָטִיִּים	Paul's letter to the *qehillah* in the Roman province of Galatia regarding the errors of legalism and the justification of the believer through faith in the Messiah alone.
Ephesians (*'El-Ha'Efmiyim*)	אֶל־הָאָפְמִיִּים	Paul's letter to the *qehillah* in Ephesus regarding the believer's union with Messiah by faith and its implications.
Philippians (*'El-HaPhilipiyim*)	אֶל־הַפִילִפִּיִּים	Paul's letter to the *qehillah* in Philippi regarding the joy of knowing Messiah, despite hardship and suffering.
Colossians (*'El-HaQolamim*)	אֶל־הַקוֹלַמִּים	Paul's letter to the *qehillah* in Colosse regarding the supremacy of Messiah.
1st Thessalonians (*Harishonah 'el-HaThasloniqim*)	הָרִאשׁוֹנָה אֶל־הַתַסְלוֹנִיקִים	Perhaps Paul's earliest letter. Written to the young *qehillah* in Thessalonica regarding basic congregational order.
2nd Thessalonians (*Hasheniyyah 'el-HaTaslonikim*)	הַשְּׁנִיָּה אֶל־הַתַסְלוֹנִיקִים	Paul's second letter to the *qehillah* in Thessalonica clearing up misconceptions about the coming Day of the Lord.

Letters of Paul (continued)

BOOK	HEBREW	MAJOR ELEMENTS
1st Timothy (*Harishonah 'el-Timothiyos*)	הָרִאשׁוֹנָה אֶל־טִימוֹתִיּוֹס	Paul's letter to Timothy, the leader of the *qehillah* in Ephesus, urging him to expound sound doctrine and oppose errors.
2nd Timothy (*Hasheniyyah 'el-Timothiyos*)	הַשְּׁנִיָּה אֶל־טִימוֹתִיּוֹס	Paul's second letter to Timothy encouraging him to persevere despite the apostasy and opposition of many.
Titus (*'El-Titos*)	אֶל־טִיטוֹס	Paul's letter to Titus, the leader of *qehilliyot* in Crete, regarding the role of elders and deacons in the new assemblies being formed.
Philemon (*El-Phileimon*)	אֶל־פִילֵימוֹן	Paul's personal letter to Philemon on behalf of a runaway slave named Onesimus.

Letters to the Messianic Jewish Communities

There are eight "general" letters written by various *shalachim* (messengers) primarily intended for Messianic Jewish communities. These may be referred to as *Iggerot Meshichiyot* (Messianic Letters):

$$אִגְּרוֹת\ מְשִׁיחִיּוֹת$$

BOOK	HEBREW	MAJOR ELEMENTS
Hebrews (*Iggeret el ha'Ivrim*)	אִגֶּרֶת אֶל־הָעִבְרִים	This anonymous letter (most likely written before the destruction of the Jewish Temple in 70 A.D.) encourages Messianic Jews to hold fast to their faith in the Messiah and retain the blessings of the *B'rit Chadashah*. Yeshua the Messiah is presented as the *Kohen HaGadol* (the High Priest) of a new and better covenant (Heb 8:6, 12:24).
James (*Iggeret Ya'aqov*)	אִגֶּרֶת יַעֲקֹב	This letter, the *Mishlei* of the *B'rit Chadashah*, stresses that faith is inextricably bound to the practice of one's life. *Ya'aqov* is traditionally thought to be the half-brother of the Messiah Yeshua.

Letters to the Messianic Jewish Communities (continued)

BOOK	HEBREW	MAJOR ELEMENTS
1st Peter (Ha'Igeret Harishonah lePetros Hashaliach)	הָאִגֶּרֶת הָרִאשׁוֹנָה לְפֶטְרוֹס הַשָּׁלִיחַ	Peter's letter to the Jews of the early Diaspora encouraging them to persevere despite present troubles.
2nd Peter (Ha'Igeret Hasheniyah lePetros Hashaliach)	הָאִגֶּרֶת הַשְּׁנִיָּה לְפֶטְרוֹס הַשָּׁלִיחַ	Peter's second letter to the Jews of the early Diaspora encouraging them to grow in grace as they await the Lord's coming.
1st John (Ha'Igeret Harishonah leYochanan Hashaliach)	הָאִגֶּרֶת הָרִאשׁוֹנָה לְיוֹחָנָן הַשָּׁלִיחַ	Yochanan's first letter regarding the life of true fellowship with the Father by the grace of the Messiah Yeshua. Yochanan is traditionally thought to be the same author of the gospel of John.
2nd John ('Igeret Yochanan Hasheinit)	אִגֶּרֶת יוֹחָנָן הַשֵּׁנִית	Yochanan's personal note of warning against false teaching in the qeillah.
3rd John ('Igeret Yochanan Hashelishit)	אִגֶּרֶת יוֹחָנָן הַשְּׁלִישִׁית	Yochanan's letter regarding the importance of living in the truth.
Jude ('Igeret Yehudah)	אִגֶּרֶת יְהוּדָה	Yehudah's call to contend for the faith against the errors of false teaching.

Third Part of the B'rit Chadashah: The Hitgalut (or Chazon)

The great prophetic book of the B'rit Chadashah is called *Hitgalut*, traditionally thought to be written by the shaliach Yochanan while he was in exile on the Greek island of Patmos, probably around 90 A.D. All the themes of prophetic truth intimated in the *Tanakh* converge in this amazing book, including the Great Tribulation, the judgment of the nations, the restoration of Temple worship, the fulfillment of the messianic kingdom in the restoration of the glory of Israel, the final judgment of Satan, and so on.

BOOK	HEBREW	MAJOR ELEMENTS
Revelation (Hitgalut)	הִתְגַּלּוּת	The revelation of Yeshua the Messiah as given to His emissary *Yochanan* (John). The word *Hitgalut* means "revelation" or "unveiling" (sometimes the word *Chazon*, "vision," is used instead).

B'rit Chadasha
The New Covenant

1. *Gospels*
בְּשׂוֹרַת הַגְּאֻלָּה

Matthew	מַתַּי
Mark	מַרְקוֹס
Luke	לוּקַס
John	יוֹחָנָן
Acts	מַעֲשֵׂי הַשְּׁלִיחִים

2. *Letters*
אִגְּרוֹת

	Romans	אֶל־הָרוֹמִיִּים
	1 Corinthians	הָרִאשׁוֹנָה אֶל־הַקּוֹרִנְתִּיִּים
	2 Corinthians	הַשֵּׁנִים אֶל־הַקּוֹרִנְתִּיִּים
	Galatians	אֶל־הַגָּלָטִיִּים
	Ephesians	אֶל־הָאֶפְסִיִּים
	Philippians	אֶל־הַפִילִפִּיִּים
Sha'ul	Colossians	אֶל־הַקּוֹלַסִּים
	1 Thessalonians	הָרִאשׁוֹנָה אֶל־הַתַּסְלוֹנִיקִים
	2 Thessalonians	הַשֵּׁנִים אֶל־הַתַּסְלוֹנִיקִים
	1 Timothy	הָרִאשׁוֹנָה אֶל־טִימוֹתִיּוֹס
	2 Timothy	הַשֵּׁנִים אֶל־טִימוֹתִיּוֹס
	Titus	אֶל־טִיטוֹס
	Philemon	אֶל־פִּילֵימוֹן

	Hebrews	אֶל־הָעִבְרִים
	James	אִגֶּרֶת יַעֲקֹב
	1 Peter	הָרִאשׁוֹנָה לְפֶטְרוֹס הַשָּׁלִיחַ
	2 Peter	הַשֵּׁנִים לְפֶטְרוֹס הַשָּׁלִיחַ
Messianic	1 John	הָרִאשׁוֹנָה לְיוֹחָנָן הַשָּׁלִיחַ
	2 John	הַשֵּׁנִים לְיוֹחָנָן הַשָּׁלִיחַ
	3 John	שְׁלִישִׁית לְיוֹחָנָן הַשָּׁלִיחַ
	Jude	אִגֶּרֶת יְהוּדָה

3. *Revelation*
הִתְגַּלּוּת

Scripture Samples

Psalm 1 (Tehillim Aleph)

Mizmor   *Book*

תהלים - א

1 / א

Pasukim

א אַשְׁרֵי־הָאִישׁ אֲשֶׁר ׀ לֹא הָלַךְ בַּעֲצַת רְשָׁעִים וּבְדֶרֶךְ חַטָּאִים לֹא עָמָד

א־ב וּבְמוֹשַׁב לֵצִים לֹא יָשָׁב: כִּי אִם בְּתוֹרַת יְהֹוָה חֶפְצוֹ וּבְתוֹרָתוֹ

ב־ג יֶהְגֶּה יוֹמָם וָלָיְלָה: וְהָיָה כְּעֵץ שָׁתוּל עַל־פַּלְגֵי מָיִם אֲשֶׁר פִּרְיוֹ ׀

ג־ד יִתֵּן בְּעִתּוֹ וְעָלֵהוּ לֹא־יִבּוֹל וְכֹל אֲשֶׁר־יַעֲשֶׂה יַצְלִיחַ: לֹא־כֵן הָרְשָׁעִים

ד־ה כִּי אִם־כַּמֹּץ אֲשֶׁר־תִּדְּפֶנּוּ רוּחַ: עַל־כֵּן ׀ לֹא־יָקֻמוּ רְשָׁעִים בַּמִּשְׁפָּט

ה־ו וְחַטָּאִים בַּעֲדַת צַדִּיקִים: כִּי־יוֹדֵעַ יְהֹוָה דֶּרֶךְ צַדִּיקִים וְדֶרֶךְ רְשָׁעִים תֹּאבֵד:

[1] Blessed *is* the man that walketh not in the counsel of the ungodly, nor standeth in the way of sinners, nor sitteth in the seat of the scornful. [2] But his delight *is* in the law of the LORD; and in his law doth he meditate day and night. [3] And he shall be like a tree planted by the rivers of water, that bringeth forth his fruit in his season; his leaf also shall not wither; and whatsoever he doeth shall prosper. [4] The ungodly *are* not so: but *are* like the chaff which the wind driveth away. [5] Therefore the ungodly shall not stand in the judgment, nor sinners in the congregation of the righteous. [6] For the LORD knoweth the way of the righteous: but the way of the ungodly shall perish. (KJV)

Psalm 117 (Tehillim Qof-Yod-Zayin)

Mizmor   *Book*

תהלים - קיז

117 / קיז

Pasukim

א־ב הַלְלוּ אֶת־יְהֹוָה כָּל־גּוֹיִם שַׁבְּחוּהוּ כָּל־הָאֻמִּים: כִּי גָבַר עָלֵינוּ ׀ חַסְדּוֹ

ב וֶאֱמֶת־יְהֹוָה לְעוֹלָם הַלְלוּ־יָהּ:

[1] O praise the LORD, all ye nations: praise him, all ye people. [2] For his merciful kindness is great toward us: and the truth of the LORD *endureth* for ever. Praise ye the LORD. (KJV)

Scripture Samples

Matthew 5:3-12

Perek	Book
ה	מתי

Pasukim

ג אַשְׁרֵי עֲנִיֵּי הָרוּחַ כִּי לָהֶם מַלְכוּת הַשָּׁמָיִם׃

ד אַשְׁרֵי הַמִּתְאַבְּלִים כִּי־הֵם יִנָּחֵמוּ׃

ה אַשְׁרֵי הָעֲנָוִים כִּי־הֵמָּה יִירְשׁוּ־אָרֶץ׃

ו אַשְׁרֵי הָרְעֵבִים וְהַצְּמֵאִים לִצְדָקָה כִּי־הֵם יִרְוָיֻן׃

ז אַשְׁרֵי בַּעֲלֵי־רַחֲמִים כִּי־הֵם יְרֻחָמוּ׃

ח אַשְׁרֵי בָּרֵי לֵבָב כִּי־הֵם יֶחֱזוּ אֶת־אֱלֹהִים׃

ט אַשְׁרֵי עֹשֵׂי שָׁלוֹם כִּי־הֵם יִקָּרְאוּ בְּנֵי־אֱלֹהִים׃

י אַשְׁרֵי הַנִּרְדָּפִים עֵקֶב צִדְקָתָם כִּי לָהֶם מַלְכוּת הַשָּׁמָיִם׃

יא אַשְׁרֵיכֶם אִם־יְחָרְפוּ אִם־יִרְדְּפוּ אֶתְכֶם וּבְשֶׁקֶר יָבִיאוּ

דִּבַּתְכֶם רָעָה בַּעֲבוּר שְׁמִי׃

יב שִׂישׂוּ וְגִילוּ כִּי שְׂכַרְכֶם הַרְבֵּה מְאֹד בַּשָּׁמָיִם

כִּי־כֵן רָדְפוּ אֶת־הַנְּבִיאִים אֲשֶׁר הָיוּ לִפְנֵיכֶם׃

[3] Blessed *are* the poor in spirit: for theirs is the kingdom of heaven. [4] Blessed *are* they that mourn: for they shall be comforted. [5] Blessed *are* the meek: for they shall inherit the earth. [6] Blessed *are* they which do hunger and thirst after righteousness: for they shall be filled. [7] Blessed *are* the merciful: for they shall obtain mercy. [8] Blessed *are* the pure in heart: for they shall see God. [9] Blessed *are* the peacemakers: for they shall be called the children of God. [10] Blessed *are* they which are persecuted for righteousness' sake: for theirs is the kingdom of heaven. [11] Blessed are ye, when *men* shall revile you, and persecute *you*, and shall say all manner of evil against you falsely, for my sake. [12] Rejoice, and be exceeding glad: for great *is* your reward in heaven: for so persecuted they the prophets which were before you. (KJV)

מלכות השמים

The Kingdom of Heaven

Scripture Samples

John 3:16

כִּי־כֵן אָהֵב אֱלֹהִים אֶת־הָעוֹלָם עַד־אֲשֶׁר נָתַן בַּעֲדוֹ אֶת־בְּנוֹ אֶת־יְחִידוֹ
וְכָל־הַמַּאֲמִין בּוֹ לֹא־יֹאבַד כִּי בוֹ יִמְצָא חַיֵּי עוֹלָם:

For God (*'elohim*) so loved the world (*ha'olam*), that he gave his only begotten Son (*ben yachid*), that whosoever believeth in him should not perish, but have everlasting life (*chaiyei 'olam*). (KJV)

John 5:24

אָמֵן אָמֵן אֲנִי אֹמֵר לָכֶם הַמַּקְשִׁיב לִדְבָרַי וּמַאֲמִין בְּשֹׁלְחִי יֶשׁ־לוֹ
חַיֵּי עוֹלָם וְלֹא יָבֹא לְהִשָּׁפֵט כִּי־עָבַר מִמָּוֶת לַחַיִּים:

Verily, verily, I say unto you, He that heareth my word, and believeth on him that sent me, hath everlasting life (*chaiyei 'olam*), and shall not come into condemnation; but is passed from death unto life. (KJV)

John 10:28-30

צֹאנִי שֹׁמְעוֹת אֶת־קֹלִי וַאֲנִי יֹדֵעַ אֹתָן וְהֵנָּה הֹלְכוֹת אַחֲרָי:
וְחַיֵּי עוֹלָם אֶתֵּן לָהֶן לֹא תֹאבַדְנָה לָנֶצַח וְלֹא יַחְטֹף אֹתָן אִישׁ מִיָּדִי:
אָבִי אֲשֶׁר נְתָנָן לִי אַדִּיר הוּא מִכֹּל וְאֵין אִישׁ אֲשֶׁר־יוּכַל לַחֲטֹף אֶתְהֶן
מִיַּד הָאָב: וַאֲנִי וְהָאָב אֶחָד:

My sheep hear my voice, and I know them, and they follow me: And I give unto them eternal life; and they shall never perish, neither shall any man pluck them out of my hand. My Father, which gave them to me, is greater than all; and no man is able to pluck them out of my Father's hand. I and my Father are one. (KJV)

Matthew 5:17

אַל תַּחְשְׁבוּ כִּי בָאתִי לְהָפֵר הַתּוֹרָה אוֹ הַנְּבִיאִים לֹא לְהָפֵר בָּאתִי
כִּי אִם־לְמַלֹּאת:

Think not that I am come to destroy the law (*torah*), or the prophets (*nevi'im*): I am not come to destroy, but to fulfill. (KJV)

Scripture Samples

John 11:27

אָנֹכִי הֶאֱמַנְתִּי כִּי־אַתָּה הוּא הַמָּשִׁיחַ בֶּן־הָאֱלֹהִים הַבָּא אֶל־הָעוֹלָם:

I believe that You are the Messiah, the Son of God, who should come into the world.

John 17:3

וּמַה חַיֵּי עוֹלָם אֲשֶׁר יֵדְעוּ אֹתְךָ כִּי אַתָּה לְבַדְּךָ אֶל־אֱמֶת וְאֶת־יֵשׁוּעַ
הַמָּשִׁיחַ אֲשֶׁר שָׁלָחְתָּ:

And this is eternal life, that they might know You, the only true God, and Yeshua the Messiah, whom You sent.

John 1:1, 14

בְּרֵאשִׁית הָיָה הַדָּבָר וְהַדָּבָר הָיָה אֶת־הָאֱלֹהִים וְהוּא הַדָּבָר הָיָה
אֱלֹהִים: וְהַדָּבָר לָבַשׁ בָּשָׂר וַיִּשְׁכֹּן בְּתוֹכֵנוּ וְאֶת־כְּבוֹדוֹ רָאִינוּ
כִּכְבוֹד בֵּן יָחִיד לְאָבִיו מָלֵא חֶסֶד וֶאֱמֶת:

In the beginning (*Bereshit)* was the Word (*davar*), and the Word was with God, and the Word was God (*'elohim*). And the Word was made flesh (*basar*), and tabernacled among us, and we beheld his glory (*kavod*), the glory as of the only begotten (*ben yachid*) of the Father, full of mercy (*chesed*) and truth (*'emet*).

Matthew 22:37-39

וַיֹּאמֶר יֵשׁוּעַ אֵלָיו וְאָהַבְתָּ אֵת יְהֹוָה אֱלֹהֶיךָ בְּכָל־לְבָבְךָ
וּבְכָל־נַפְשְׁךָ וּבְכָל־מְאֹדֶךָ: זוֹ הִיא הַמִּצְוָה הַגְּדֹלָה וְהָרִאשֹׁנָה:
וְהַשְּׁנִיָּה דְּמְתָה לָהּ וְאָהַבְתָּ לְרֵעֲךָ כָּמוֹךָ:

Yeshua said unto him, You shall love Adonai your God with all your heart (*lev*), and with all your soul (*nephesh*), and with all your might (*me'od*). This is the first and great commandment (*mitzvah*). And the second is like unto it, You shall love your neighbor (*re'ah*) as yourself.

Scripture Samples

Matthew 6:9-13 (The Lord's Prayer)

אָבִינוּ שֶׁבַּשָּׁמַיִם יִתְקַדַּשׁ שְׁמֶךָ: תָּבֹא מַלְכוּתֶךָ יֵעָשֶׂה רְצוֹנְךָ בָּאָרֶץ

כַּאֲשֶׁר נַעֲשָׂה בַשָּׁמָיִם: תֶּן־לָנוּ הַיּוֹם לֶחֶם חֻקֵּנוּ:

וּסְלַח־לָנוּ אֶת־אַשְׁמָתֵנוּ כַּאֲשֶׁר סֹלְחִים אֲנַחְנוּ לַאֲשֶׁר אָשְׁמוּ לָנוּ:

וְאַל־תְּבִיאֵנוּ לִידֵי מַסָּה כִּי אִם־הַצִּילֵנוּ מִן־הָרָע

כִּי לְךָ הַמַּמְלָכָה וְהַגְּבוּרָה וְהַתִּפְאֶרֶת לְעוֹלְמֵי עוֹלָמִים אָמֵן:

Our Father (*avinu*), Who art in heaven (*shamayim*), hallowed by Thy Name (*shem*). Thy kingdom (*malkhut*) come; Thy will (*ratson*) be done, on earth (*erets*) as it is done in heaven (*shamayim*). Give us this day our daily bread (*lechem*), and forgive (*selichah*) us of our debts, as we forgive our debtors. And lead us not into temptation but deliver us from evil(*ra'*). For Thine is the kingdom (*mamlakhah*) and the might (*gevurah*) and the glory (*tif'eret*) forever and ever. Amen.

1 Chronicles 29:10b-13

בָּרוּךְ אַתָּה יְהוָה אֱלֹהֵי יִשְׂרָאֵל אָבִינוּ מֵעוֹלָם וְעַד־עוֹלָם:

לְךָ יְהוָה הַגְּדֻלָּה וְהַגְּבוּרָה וְהַתִּפְאֶרֶת וְהַנֵּצַח וְהַהוֹד כִּי־כֹל בַּשָּׁמַיִם

וּבָאָרֶץ לְךָ יְהוָה הַמַּמְלָכָה וְהַמִּתְנַשֵּׂא לְכֹל לְרֹאשׁ: וְהָעֹשֶׁר וְהַכָּבוֹד

מִלְּפָנֶיךָ וְאַתָּה מוֹשֵׁל בַּכֹּל וּבְיָדְךָ כֹּחַ וּגְבוּרָה וּבְיָדְךָ לְגַדֵּל וּלְחַזֵּק

לַכֹּל: וְעַתָּה אֱלֹהֵינוּ מוֹדִים אֲנַחְנוּ לָךְ וּמְהַלְלִים לְשֵׁם תִּפְאַרְתֶּךָ:

Blessed art Thou, Adonai God of Israel our father ('*avinu*), forever and ever. To You, Adonai, is the greatness (*gedulah*), and the power (*gevurah*), and the glory (*tif'arah*), and the victory (*netsach*), and the majesty (*hod*): for all that is in the heaven (*shamayim*) and in the earth ('*erets*) is Yours; Yours is the kingdom (*mamlakhah*), Adonai, and You are exalted as head (*rosh*) above all. Both riches ('*osher*) and honor (*kavod*) come of You, and You reign (*mashal*) over all; and in Your hand (*yad*) is power (*koach*) and might (*gevurah*); and in Your hand it is to make great (*gadal*), and to give strength (*chazaq*) unto all. Now therefore, our God, we thank You, and praise (*halal*) Your glorious Name (*shem*).

Lesson Eighteen

HEBREW NAMES OF GOD

Lesson Introduction

"for as his name is, so is he..." (1 Sam 25:25)

What's in a Name?

The relation between a name (*shem*) and a thing (*davar*) is of fundamental importance in the Scriptures. In the Hebraic mindset, naming and being are linked together to form a unity. The right use of a name denotes a right relationship with the thing named, as Adam established dominion over the creatures of the earth by giving them their names (see Genesis 2:19).

God created the universe *ex nihilo* (out of nothing) by means of His Word (Genesis 1:1). In the Scriptures, the first time God *speaks* we see that He *creates*:

$$\text{וַיֹּאמֶר אֱלֹהִים יְהִי אוֹר וַיְהִי־אוֹר׃}$$

"And God *said*, "*yehi 'or*" – let there be light – and there was light" (Genesis 1:3).

Moreover, God "spoke" Adam into being, as it is written:

$$\text{וַיֹּאמֶר אֱלֹהִים נַעֲשֶׂה אָדָם בְּצַלְמֵנוּ כִּדְמוּתֵנוּ}$$

"And God said 'Let us make man (*'adam*) in our image (*tselem*) and in our likeness (*demut*)...' (Genesis 1:26): and Adam became a "living soul" (*nefesh chaiyah*).

Since man was made in the image and likeness of God, we would expect a strong correlation between human language and reality. Unlike God, we do not literally *create* reality by means of our words, but we do *interpret* reality: we evaluate it, make decisions based on our assessments, and we shape the contours of our experience by means of the words we use. In short, each of us is responsible for how we describe reality and whether we will align our words with the truth of reality.

Shakespeare asked, "What's in a name? That which we call a rose by any other word would smell just as sweet" (Romeo and Juliet, II:2), but despite the mystery that may ultimately be implied in the relation between a name and a thing, the Hebraic mindset understands words to be of fundamental importance: since *davar* in Hebrew means not just "thing" but also "word," implying that knowing the thing is to know the word.

In modern American culture, we use names rather prosaically as identifiers for persons, places, and things. In ancient Hebrew, however, a name (*shem*) had symbolic and often prophetic significance, so much so that the name of a person literally was identified with that person's life, reputation, character, and even spiritual destiny. God Himself is strongly identified with His Name: in some passages *shem Adonai* is literally identified as an appearance of Adonai Himself (*see* Isa. 30:27); and Paul reminds us that the Pharaoh was raised up so that God could demonstrate the power of His deliverance, in order that "that my *Name* might be declared throughout all the earth" (Romans 9:17).

The Power of the Word

God graciously chose to reveal His Name (i.e., His character, His manifest Presence by means of His acts and deeds) to the world through the Jewish people. Through the ancient Hebrew Patriarchs, through the great deliverance God effected by means of His servant Moses, through the eloquent oracles and admonitions of the Hebrew prophets, and most especially through the manifestation of His Son *Yeshua'* (Jesus): in all these ways God has revealed His Name. In fact, the Scriptures make it clear that the name of God's Son Yeshua is so vital to our correct apprehension of reality that without it we are literally lost, since we are told explicitly that there is salvation in no other name, "for there is no other name by means of which it is necessary for us to be saved" (Acts 4:12).

Interestingly, we are told that Yeshua, being God's unique Son and therefore equal to God, "humbled Himself" by taking on the form of a servant and was made in the likeness (*demut*) of man (*'adam*)—going so far as to become the *kapparah* (Sin-Bearer) of the world by offering Himself up on the execution stake. "Therefore God has also highly exalted him, and given him a name that is above every name: That at the name of Jesus every knee should bow, of things in heaven, and things in earth, and things under the earth; and that every tongue should confess that Jesus Christ is Lord (*'Adonai*), to the glory of God the Father" (Phil. 2:6-11).

Man is made in the "image and likeness" of God, but instead of being able to create *ex nihilo* by means of his words, he is given the responsibility to properly confess and to believe the truth. As Paul put it: "If you confess [*homologeis*, from *logeo*, "say" and *homo*, "same"] with your mouth that Jesus is Lord (*'Adonai*) and believe in your heart that God has raised Him from the dead, you shall be saved. For with the heart man believes unto righteousness; and with the mouth confession is made unto salvation." (Romans 10:9-10).

The choice is ultimately yours: Just as God said, "*yehi 'or*"—let there be light—and there was light, so we are given the responsibility to speak forth the truth of God's salvation (*yeshu'ah*) and to believe it in our hearts.

The Revealed Names of God

When God personally reveals His Names to us, He is showing us something of what He is like—His character, His purposes, His will. Personally knowing and trusting in the Name of the Lord thus can be understood as a sort of response to the very presence of God Himself: we are given the great privilege and responsibility of speaking forth the truth of God's gracious disclosure by confessing and believing the truth. The right use of the name of God—with genuine *kavannah* and reverence—puts us in right relationship with God Himself.

מִגְדַּל־עֹז שֵׁם יְהוָה בּוֹ־יָרוּץ צַדִּיק וְנִשְׂגָּב

"The name of Adonai is a strong tower: the righteous one runs to it, and is safe." (Prov. 18:10)

Names of God in the Tanakh

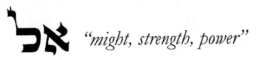 *"might, strength, power"*

The word *El* comes from a root word meaning "might, strength, power" and probably derives from the Ugaritic term for god. In Scripture, the primary meanings of this root are "god" (pagan or false gods), "God" (the true God of Israel), and sometimes "the mighty" (referring to men or angels). When used of the true God of Israel, *El* is almost always qualified by additional words that further define the meaning that distinguish Him from false gods. These other names or titles for God are sometimes called "construct forms."

Hebrew	Transliteration	Definition
אֵל	'el	Name for God meaning "strength, might, or power." Used over 250 times in the *Tanakh*.

Construct Forms (Compound Names)

As mentioned above, *El* is almost always qualified by additional words that further define the meaning. The most common construct forms are provided here:

Hebrew	Transliteration	Definition
אֵל אֶחָד	'el 'e·**chad**	The one God (Mal. 2:10). *'Echad* means one in Hebrew and hearkens to the *Shema*.
אֵל הַנֶּאֱמָן	'el han·ne·'e·**man**	The Faithful God (Deut. 7:9).
אֵל אֱמֶת	'el 'e·**met**	The God of Truth (Ps. 31:5).
אֵל־צַדִּיק	'el-tsad·**diq**	The Righteous God (Isa. 45:21).
אֵל שַׁדַּי	'el shad·**dai**	*El Shaddai*. The all sufficient God; *Shad* means "breast" in Hebrew (Gen. 17:1; 28:3; 35:11; Ex. 6:31; Ps. 91:1; etc. Occurs 48 times in the *Tanakh*).
אֵל עֶלְיוֹן	'el 'el·**yon**	*El Elyon*. The Most High God. This title stresses God's strength, sovereignty, and supremacy (Gen. 14:20; Ps. 9:2). Sometimes referred to in Scripture simply as *Elyon* (e.g., Num. 24:16).
אֵל עוֹלָם	'el 'o·**lam**	*El Olam*. God Everlasting; (Gen. 21:33, Ps. 90:1-3, 93:2; Isa. 26:4).
אֵל רָאִי	'el ro·**'i**	*El Roi*. God who sees me; Hagar's name for God when He saw her affliction (Gen. 16:13).
אֵל יְשֻׁרוּן	'el ye·shu·**run**	God of Yeshurun; *Yeshurun* means "the righteous (*yashar*) people": Israel's ideal character and high calling (Deut. 32:15; 33:5,26; Isa. 44:2).
אֵל גִּבּוֹר	'el gib·**bor**	*El Gibbor*. The Mighty God. Picture of God as a Warrior and Champion (Isa. 9:6).

Hebrew	Transliteration	Definition
אֵל דֵּעוֹת	'el de·'ot	The God of Knowledge (1 Sam. 2:3).
אֵל הַגָּדֹל	'el hag·ga·dol	The Great God (Deut. 10:17).
אֵל־הַכָּבוֹד	'el hak·ka·vod	The God of Glory (Ps. 29:3).
אֵל הַקָּדוֹשׁ	'el haq·qa·dosh	*El Haqqadosh.* The Holy God (Isa. 5:16).
אֵל הַשָּׁמַיִם	'el hash·sha·mayim	The God of the Heavens (Ps. 136:26).
אֵל חַיָּי	'el chai·yai	The God of my life (Ps. 42:8).
אֵל־חַנּוּן	'el chan·nun	The Gracious God (Jonah 4:2).
אֵל יִשְׂרָאֵל	'el yis·ra·'el	The God of Israel (Ps. 68:36).
אֵל סַלְעִי	'el sal·'i	God of my Strength (Ps. 42:9).
אֵל רַחוּם	'el ra·chum	The God of Compassion; Compassionate God (Deut. 4:31).
אֵל שִׂמְחַת גִּילִי	'el sim·chat gi·li	God, the Joy of my Exaltation (Ps. 43:4).
אֵל יְשׁוּעָתִי	'el ye·shu·'a·ti	*El Yeshuati.* The God of my Salvation (Isa. 12:2).
אֵל יִשׁוּעָתֵנוּ	'el ye·shu·'a·te·nu	The God of our Salvation (Psalm 68:19).
אֵל־קַנּוֹא	'el qan·no'	The Jealous God (Josh. 24:19).
עִמָּנוּ אֵל	'im·ma·nu 'el	*Immanuel.* God is with us (Isa. 7:14).

"*I m m a n u e l*"

*"Therefore the Lord himself shall give you a sign;
Behold, a virgin shall conceive, and bear a son,
and shall call his name Immanuel."* (Isa 7:14 KJV)

אֱלֹהִים *"mighty, powerful One"*

The word *Elohim* is the plural of *'El* and is the first name for God given in the *Tanakh*: *"In the beginning, God* (Elohim) *created the heavens and the earth"* (*Gen. 1:1*). The plural ending does not mean "gods" when referring to the true God of Israel, since the name is mainly used with singular verb forms and with adjectives and pronouns in the singular (e.g., see *Gen. 1:26*). However, the plural form allows for the plurality within the Godhead. The form *Elohim* occurs only in Hebrew and in no other Semitic language.

Hebrew	Transliteration	Definition
אֱלֹהִים	'e·lo·**him**	God; gods. The plural form of *'El*, meaning "Strong One." Occurs 2,570 times in the *Tanakh*. Isa. 54:5; Jer. 32:27; Gen. 1:1; Isa. 45:18; Deut. 5:23; etc.

Construct Forms

Elohim is combined with other words to provide additional description about God. These other names or titles for God are sometimes called "construct forms," indicating that they are "constructed" from the base name (e.g., Elohim) with other designators.

Hebrew	Transliteration	Definition
אֱלֹהֵי	'e·lo·**hei**	God of -; a "construct form."
אֱלֹהִים אֱלֹהַי	'e·lo·**him** 'e·lo·**hai**	God; my God (Ps. 43:4).
אֱלֹהֵי אַבְרָהָם	'e·lo·**hei** 'av·ra·**ham**	The God of Abraham (Ex. 3:15).
אֱלֹהֵי אַבְרָהָם אֱלֹהֵי יִצְחָק וֵאלֹהֵי יַעֲקֹב	'e·lo·**hei** 'av·ra·ham 'e·lo·**hei** yits·**chak** vei·lo·**hei** ya·a·qov	The God of Abraham, Isaac, and Jacob (Ex. 3:15).
אֱלֹהֵי חַסְדִּי	'e·lo·**hei** chas·**di**	God of my Kindness (Ps. 59:17).
אֱלֹהֵי יִשְׁעִי	'e·lo·**hei** yish·**'i**	God of my Salvation (Ps. 25:5).
אֱלֹהֵי הָאֱלֹהִים	'e·lo·**hei** ha·'e·lo·**him**	The God of gods (Deut. 10:17).
אֱלֹהֵי הָרוּחֹת לְכָל-בָּשָׂר	'e·lo·**hei** ha·ru·**chot** le·khol-ba·**sar**	God of the spirits of all flesh (Num. 16:22).
אֱלֹהֵי מָעוּזִּי	'e·lo·**hei** ma·'uz·**zi**	God of my Strength (Ps. 43:2).
אֱלֹהֵי מִקָּרֹב	'e·lo·**hei** miq·qa·**rov**	God who is near (Jer. 23:23).
אֱלֹהֵי מֵרָחֹק	'e·lo·**hei** me·ra·**choq**	God who is far (Jer. 23:23).

Hebrew	Transliteration	Definition
אֱלֹהֵי מָרוֹם	ʼe·lo·**hei** ma·**rom**	God of Heights (Micah 6:6).
אֱלֹהֵי מִשְׁפָּט	ʼe·lo·**hei** mish·**pat**	God of Justice (Isa. 30:18).
אֱלֹהֵי צְבָאוֹת	ʼe·lo·**hei** tse·va·ʼ**ot**	God of hosts or God of armies (2 Sam. 5:10).
אֱלֹהֵי צוּר	ʼe·lo·**hei** tsur	God of rock (2 Sam. 22:47).
אֱלֹהֵי קֶדֶם	ʼe·lo·**hei** qe·dem	God of the beginning; Eternal God (Deut. 33:27).
אֱלֹהֵי תְהִלָּתִי	ʼe·lo·**hei** te·hil·**la**·ti	God of my Praise (Ps. 109:1).
אֱלֹהֵינוּ	ʼe·lo·**hey**·nu	Our God (Ex. 3:18).
אֱלֹהֵי אֲבֹתֵינוּ	ʼe·lo·**hei** ʼa·vo·**tei**·nu	God of our fathers (Deut 26:7; 1 Chron. 12:17).
אֱלֹהִים אָבִינוּ	ʼe·lo·**him** ʼa·**vi**·nu	God our Father.
אֵל הַנּוֹרָא	ʼel han·no·**ra**ʼ	The Awesome God (Neh. 9:32).
אֱלֹהִים בַּשָּׁמַיִם	ʼe·lo·**him** bash·sha·**mai**·yim	God in Heaven (2 Chron. 20:6).
אֱלֹהִים אֱמֶת	e·lo·**him** e·**met**	The True God (Jer. 10:10).
אֱלֹהֵי נָחוֹר	ʼe·lo·**hei** na·**chor**	The God of Nahor (Abraham's father) (Gen. 31:53).
אֱלֹהִים הָאָב	ʼe·lo·**him** ha·ʼ**av**	God the Father.
אֱלֹהִים חַיִּים	ʼe·lo·**him** **chai**·yim	The Living God (Jer. 10:10).
אֱלֹהֵי הַחַיִּים	ʼe·lo·**hei** ha·**chai**·yim	God of the Living.

"The Living God"

אֱלוֹהַ *"mighty, powerful One"*

The word *Eloah* is the singular of *Elohim* and appears more than 70 times in the *Tanakh*, primarily in more poetic passages.

Hebrew	Transliteration	Definition
אֱלוֹהַ	ʼe·lo·ah	God (a singular form of *elohim*). (Deut. 32:15, 17; Job 3:4; Psalm 18:31; Psalm 50:22, etc.).

Like *El* and *Elohim*, *Eloah* is combined with other words to provide additional description about God:

Hebrew	Transliteration	Definition
אֱלוֹהַ יַעֲקֹב	ʼe·lo·ah ya·ʻa·qov	God of Jacob (Ps. 114:7).
אֱלוֹהַ סְלִיחוֹת	ʼe·lo·ah se·li·chot	God of Forgiveness (Neh. 9:17).

אֱלָה *"awesome, fearful One"*

The origin of the Aramaic word *Elah* is somewhat uncertain, though it might be related to a root meaning "fear" or "reverence." It is found only in the books of Ezra and Daniel.

Hebrew	Transliteration	Definition
אֱלָה	ʼe·lah	*Aramaic.* Name for God as Awesome One. Used in Ezra and Daniel in the *Tanakh.*

Like other construct forms, *Elah* is combined with other words to provide additional descriptions of God:

Hebrew	Transliteration	Definition
אֱלָה אֲבָהָתִי	ʼe·lah ʼa·va·ha·ti	*Aramaic.* God of my fathers (Dan. 2:23).
אֱלָה אֱלָהִין	ʼe·lah ʼe·la·hin	*Aramaic.* God of gods (Dan. 2:47).
אֱלָה יְרוּשְׁלֶם	ʼe·lah ye·rush·lem	*Aramaic.* God of Jerusalem (Ezra 7:19).
אֱלָה יִשְׂרָאֵל	ʼe·lah yis·ra·ʼel	*Aramaic.* God of Israel (Ez. 5:1).
אֱלָה שְׁמַיָּא	ʼe·lah she·mai·ya'	*Aramaic.* God of Heaven (Ezra 7:23).

יהוה *"The Unutterable Name"*

In the *Tanakh*, YHVH is the personal name of God and his most frequent designation, occurring more than 5,600 times. This is the Ineffable Name or Unutterable Name of the God of Israel. Because it is composed from the four Hebrew letters י-ה-ו-ה, it is also referred to as the "Tetragrammaton," which simply means "The Four Letters."

When God commissioned Moses to be Israel's liberator from the bondage of Pharaoh's Egypt, he asked for God's Name in order to validate his God-given role to the children of Israel (*see* Exodus 3:13). God simply answered Moses, "*Ehyeh-Asher-Ehyeh*":

$$\text{וַיֹּאמֶר אֱלֹהִים אֶל־מֹשֶׁה אֶהְיֶה אֲשֶׁר אֶהְיֶה}$$

The phrase *Ehyeh Asher Ehyeh* (rendered as "I am who I am" in the KJV) derives from the Hebrew verb "to be" (ה י ה), and indicates a connection between the Name YHVH and being itself. YHVH is the Source of all being and has being inherent in Himself (i.e., He is *necessary* Being). Everything else is *contingent* being that derives existence from Him. The name י-ה-ו-ה also bespeaks the utter transcendence of God. In Himself, God is beyond all "predications" or attributes of language: He is the Source and Foundation of all possibility of utterance and thus is beyond all definite descriptions.

This special Name of God (YHVH) was moreover combined with "The God of your fathers, the God of Abraham, the God of Isaac, and the God of Jacob" to be God's Name forever, "my memorial unto all generations" (*see* Exodus 3:14-15):

$$\text{יְהוָה אֱלֹהֵי אֲבֹתֵיכֶם אֱלֹהֵי אַבְרָהָם}$$
$$\text{אֱלֹהֵי יִצְחָק וֵאלֹהֵי יַעֲקֹב}$$

Revering the Name

In Exodus 20:7 it is written, "Thou shalt not take the name of the LORD thy God in vain; for the LORD will not hold him guiltless that taketh his name in vain." In Hebrew:

$$\text{לֹא תִשָּׂא אֶת־שֵׁם־יְהוָה אֱלֹהֶיךָ לַשָּׁוְא}$$
$$\text{כִּי לֹא יְנַקֶּה יְהוָה אֵת אֲשֶׁר־יִשָּׂא אֶת־שְׁמוֹ לַשָּׁוְא}$$

Jehovah?

On account of this, the Masoretes ensured that the Name of the LORD would not be taken in vain by substituting the vowel marks for Adonai and putting them under the letters י-ה-ו-ה in the running text (this is called *Qere* [what is to be read] as opposed to *Ketiv* [what is required to be written by the scribe]). The Hebrew text, then, contains the *Ketiv* but uses the vowels of the *Qere* for אדני, and this has led to obviously incorrect pronunciation of the Name as "Jehovah" (in older English, "J" had a "y" sound).

Yahweh?

It was later speculated that perhaps the Masoretes reversed the vowels for Adonai when applied to the letters י-ה-ו-ה in the running text, so some have attempted to "correct" the pronunciation by pronouncing the Name as "Yahoveh" or "Yahveh." This, too, is incorrect (though the construct form "Yah" might be part of the original pronunciation (e.g., see Psalm 68:4; Isaiah 26:4)).

Hashem: The Name

Since ancient Hebrew did not use any vowel markings, the actual pronunciation of the sacred Name is simply not known. In ancient Temple times, only the *Kohen Gadol* (high priest) would utter the Name during Yom Kippur [Yoma 39b].

The Jewish tradition is to not pronounce the sacred Name at all, but to substitute the word *Adonai* ("my Lord") in its place. Thus, when reading Torah, you do not attempt to vocalize the Name, but say *Adonai* instead. When not reading Torah or the Siddur, most observant Jews refer to the sacred Name simply as *Ha Shem* or "the Name" (Lev. 24:16).

In Hebrew the sacred Name is called *Shem HaMeforash*, "the ineffable Name." Attempts to provide an exposition of the Name have come to be known as *Shelosh 'Esreh Middot*, or the Thirteen Attributes of God and are usually based on exegesis of Exodus 34:6-7. Mystical speculation about the Name is found in the *Qabbalah*.

Note: Jewish custom does not prohibit writing the name of God; it prohibits only erasing or defacing a name of God. Therefore, observant Jews avoid writing any name of God casually because of the risk that the written name might later be accidentally defaced, obliterated, or destroyed.

YHVH

Though we do not know how to pronounce the sacred Name, we can be fairly confident that the letters י-ה-ו-ה probably derive from the Hebrew verb "to be" (ה י ה) and indicate God's utter transcendence as the Source and Ground of all being.

Hebrew	Transliteration	Definition
יְהוָה	'a·do·**nai** (*or* hashem)	The personal Name of Adonai, the transcendent Source and Ground of all being whatsoever. This Name appears more than 5,600 times in the *Tanakh* (rendered in the KJV as the LORD).
הַשֵּׁם	hash·**shem**	The Name (Lev. 24:16).

"*Shem Hameforash*"

Did you know?

The sacred Name for God was spoken only 10 times once per year (during *Yom Kippur*) by the Kohen Gadol. When the people heard the Name, they prostrated themselves in deep reverence (Yoma 39b).

Construct Forms

There are many forms of the Name used as "construct forms" in the *Tanakh*:

Hebrew	Transliteration	Definition
יְהוָה אֱלֹהִים	'a·do·**nai** 'e·lo·**him**	The LORD God (Gen. 2:4). This Name shows that the Source and Ground of all being is also the personal God and Creator of the entire universe.
יְהוָה אֱלֹהַי	'a·do·**nai** 'e·lo·**hai**	The LORD my God (Psalm 13:3).
יְהוָה אָבִינוּ	'a·do·**nai** 'a·**vi**·nu	The LORD our Father (Isa. 64:8).
יְהוָה אֵל עֶלְיוֹן	'a·do·**nai** 'el 'el·**yon**	The LORD Most High God (Gen. 14:22; Psalm 7:17; Psalm 47:2).
יְהוָה אֱלֹהֵי יִשְׂרָאֵל	'a·do·**nai** 'e·lo·**hei** yis·ra·'**el**	The LORD God of Israel. Identifies YHVH as the God of Israel in contrast to the false gods of the nations (Isa. 17:6).
יְהוָה יִרְאָה	'a·do·**nai** yir·'**eh**	The LORD who sees; Gen. 22:14; Adonai sees all and knows our needs intimately (rendered in the KJV as the *Jehovahjireh*).
יְהוָה מְקַדִּשְׁכֶם	'a·do·**nai** me·qad·dish·**khem**	"The Lord your Sanctifier." Portrays the Lord as our means of sanctification or as the one who sets believers apart for His purposes (Ex. 31:13).
יְהוָה נִסִּי	'a·do·**nai** **nis**·si	The LORD my Miracle, or The LORD my Banner; (Ex. 17:15) (rendered in the KJV as the *Jehovahnissi*).
יְהוָה עֹשֵׂנוּ	'a·do·**nai** '**o**·se·nu	The LORD our Maker (Ps. 95:6).
יְהוָה צִדְקֵנוּ	'a·do·**nai** tsid·**qe**·nu	The LORD our Righteousness (Jer. 33:16).
יְהוָה צְבָאוֹת	'a·do·**nai** tse·va·'**ot**	The LORD of armies (or hosts) (1 Sam. 1:11).
יְהוָה רֹעִי	'a·do·**nai** ro·'**i**	The LORD my Shepherd (Ps. 23:1).
יְהוָה רֹפְאֶךָ	'a·do·**nai** rof·'e·**kha**	The LORD who heals you (Ex. 15:26).
יְהוָה שָׁלוֹם	'a·do·**nai** sha·**lom**	The LORD of Peace (Judges 6:24) (rendered in the KJV as the *Jehovahshalom*).
יְהוָה אֱלֹהֵיכֶם	'a·do·**nai** 'e·lo·**hei**·khem	"The LORD your [pl.] God" (Lev. 19:3).
יְהוָה צוּרִי וְגֹאֲלִי	'a·do·**nai** tsu·**ri** ve·go·'a·**li**	"The LORD my Rock and my Redeemer" (Psalm 19:4).
יְהוָה אֱלֹהֵי דָוִד	'a·do·**nai** 'e·lo·**hei** da·**vid**	"The LORD God of David" (Isaiah 38:5).
יְהוָה סַלְעִי	'a·do·**nai** sal·'**i**	The LORD my Rock (or Hiding Place, as in the crag of a cliff) (Psalm 18:2).

יָהּ "The Unutterable Name"

It is generally thought that YAH is a shortened form of YHVH. This Name of God occurs about 50 times in the *Tanakh*. In Psalm 68:4 this Name is particularly stressed. The Name YAH is also found in the construct word "hallelu-YAH," which means "you [pl.] praise the LORD," as well as in many Biblical proper names (e.g., *Eliyahu*).

Hebrew	Transliteration	Definition
יָהּ	yah	An abbreviated, an often poetic form of the Name YHVH. This Name appears over 50 times in the *Tanakh*, and is first used in Exodus 15:2 (see Ex. 15:2; 17:16; Psalm 68:5, 19; 77:12; 89:9; 94:7, 12; 102:19; 105:45; 106:1, Isa. 12:2; 26:4; 38:11, etc.).
הַלְלוּ יָהּ	hal·le·lu **yah**	Plural imperative to praise Adonai (see Psalm 111; 112; 113; 117; 135; 146, 147, 148, 149, 150).
הַלְלוּיָהּ	hal·le·lu·**yah**	Plural imperative to praise Adonai (Psalm 106; 112; 113; 117; 135; 146, 147, 148, 149, 150).
אֵלִיָּהוּ	'e·li·**ya**·hu	"YHVH is my God"; the name for Elijah the Tishbite (1 Kings 17:1).

אֲדֹנָי "Master, Lord, LORD"

Adonai is the plural of *Adon*, meaning "Lord, Lord, LORD, master, or owner" (the word *Adon* derives from a Ugaritic word meaning "lord" or "father"). In the *Tanakh*, the word *Adon* can refer to men and angels as well as to the LORD God of Israel (e.g., Exodus 34:23). God is called the "Lord of lords"(Deuteronomy 10:17) and Psalm 8:1 mentions God as "YHVH our Lord."

The plural form *Adonai*, like the plural form *Elohim*, is regularly used with singular verbs and modifiers, so it is best to construe the Name as an "emphatic plural" or "plural of majesty." When the plural is formed using a singular possessive ending ("my Lords"), it always refers to God, and occurs over 300 times in the *Tanakh* in this form.

As previously mentioned, the Masoretes ensured that the sacred Name of the LORD (י-ה-ו-ה) would not be taken in vain by putting the vowel marks for Adonai under the letters י-ה-ו-ה in the running text. They did this to remind the reader to pronounce *Adonai* regardless of the consonants in the text. However, *Adon* and *Adonai* also appear as Names of God in the Hebrew Masoretic text, and some of these will be listed here.

Hebrew	Transliteration	Definition
אָדוֹן	'a·**don**	A title variously used to refer to men, angels, and to the true God of Israel, meaning "lord, master, owner" (Gen. 18:2; Isa. 10:33).
אֲדֹנָי	'a·do·**nai**	Lord; God; name used as a substitute for the sacred Tetragrammaton; emphatic form of *'Adon* (Isa. 6:1). Occurs 300 times in the *Tanakh*. The first use appears in Gen. 15:2.

Construct Forms

There are many forms of *Adonai* used as "construct forms" in the *Tanakh*:

Hebrew	Transliteration	Definition
אֲדֹנֵי הָאֲדֹנִים	'a·do·**nei** ha·'a·do·**nim**	Lord of lords (Deut. 10:17; Psalm 136:3).
אֲדֹנָי יְהוִה	'a·do·**nai** 'a·do·**nai**	Lord GOD (Gen 15:2; Isa. 30:15).
אֲדוֹן יְהוִה צְבָאוֹת	'a·**don** 'a·do·**nai** tse·va·'**ot**	The Lord GOD of hosts (Isaiah 10:33).
אֲדֹנִי	'a·do·**ni**	My Lord (Psalm 110:1).
הָאָדֹן יְהוִה	ha·'a·**don** 'a·do·**nai**	The Lord God (Ex. 34:23).
אֲדֹנֵנוּ	'a·do·**ne**·nu	Our Lord (1 Sam. 16:16; Psalm 8:1; 135:5; 147:5).
אֲדוֹן כָּל־הָאָרֶץ	'a·**don** kol-ha·'**a**·rets	Lord of all the earth (Psalm 97:5; Micah 4:13).

הַקָּדוֹשׁ *"The Holy One"*

Hebrew	Transliteration	Definition
הַקָּדוֹשׁ	haq·qa·**dosh**	The Savior or Deliverer; derived from a root word *yesha'* which means salvation (Isa. 57:15).
הַקָּדוֹשׁ בָּרוּךְ הוּא	haq·qa·**dosh** ba·rukh **hu**	The Holy One, blessed be He; another Name for God (used especially among Orthodox Jews).
יְהוָה הָאֱלֹהִים הַקָּדוֹשׁ	'a·do·**nai** ha·'e·lo·**him** haq·qa·**dosh**	Adonai the Holy God (1 Sam. 6:20).
קְדוֹשׁ יִשְׂרָאֵל	qe·**dosh** yis·ra·'**el**	The Holy One of Israel (2 Kings 19:22; Isa. 1:4).
קָדוֹשׁ	qa·dosh	The Holy (One) (Isa. 40:25).
יְהוָה אֱלֹהַי קְדֹשִׁי	'a·do·**nai** 'e·lo·hai qe·do·shi	The Lord my Holy God (Hab. 1:12).
אֵל הַקָּדוֹשׁ	'el haq·qa·**dosh**	*El Haqqadosh.* The Holy God (Isa. 5:16).

הַגֹּאֵל "The Redeemer"

Hebrew	Transliteration	Definition
הַגֹּאֵל	hag·go·'el	The Redeemer (Job 19:25; Ps. 19:14; 78:35; Prov. 23:11; Isa. 41:14; 43:14; 44:6, 24; 47:4; 48:17; 49:7, 26; 54:5, 8; 59:20; 60:16; 63:16; Jer. 50:34).
גֹּאֵל יִשְׂרָאֵל	go·'el yis·ra·'el	The Redeemer of Israel (Isa. 49:7).
יְהוָה צוּרִי וְגֹאֲלִי	'a·do·nai tsu·ri ve·go·'a·li	Lord, my Rock and my Redeemer (Psalm 19:14).

מוֹשִׁיעַ "Savior"

Hebrew	Transliteration	Definition
מוֹשִׁיעַ	mo·shi·a'	Savior (Isa. 43:11; 45:15).
הַמוֹשִׁיעַ	ha·mo·shi·a'	The Savior. Derived from a root word *yesha* which means "salvation."
יְשׁוּעָה	ye·shu·'ah	Salvation (Psalm 3:8, etc.).
אֱלֹהֵי יִשְׂרָאֵל מוֹשִׁיעַ	'e·lo·hei yis·ra·'el mo·shi·a'	God of Israel the Savior (Isa. 45:15).

מָשִׁיחַ "Messiah"

Hebrew	Transliteration	Definition
מָשִׁיחַ	ma·shi·ach	Messiah; Anointed (2 Sam. 1:21; Dan. 9:26).
מָשִׁיחַ נָגִיד	ma·shi·ach na·gid	Messiah the Prince (Dan. 9:25).
מְשִׁיחַ יְהוָה	me·shi·ach 'a·do·nai	The LORD's Annointed (Ps. 2:2).

שַׂר שָׁלוֹם "Captain of Peace"

Hebrew	Transliteration	Definition
שַׂר־שָׁלוֹם	sar-sha·lom	Prince of Peace (Isa. 9:6).

רוּחַ אֱלֹהִים   *"Spirit of God"*

Hebrew	Transliteration	Definition
רוּחַ אֱלֹהִים	ru·ach ʼe·lo·**him**	Spirit of God (Gen. 1:2).

וְרוּחַ אֱלֹהִים מְרַחֶפֶת עַל־פְּנֵי הַמָּיִם

And the Spirit of God moved upon the face of the waters (Gen. 1:2b)

רוּחַ הַקֹּדֶשׁ   *"The Holy Spirit"*

Hebrew	Transliteration	Definition
רוּחַ הַקֹּדֶשׁ	ru·ach haq·qo·**desh**	The Holy Spirit (Psalm 51:11).

רוּחַ יהוה   *"Spirit of Adonai"*

Hebrew	Transliteration	Definition
רוּחַ יְהוָה	ru·ach ʼa·do·**nai**	Spirit of the Lord GOD (Isaiah 11:2).
רוּחַ אֲדֹנָי יְהוִה	ru·ach ʼa·do·**nai** ʼa·do·**nai**	The Spirit of the LORD God (Isaiah 61:1).

וְנָחָה עָלָיו רוּחַ יְהוָה רוּחַ חָכְמָה וּבִינָה רוּחַ
עֵצָה וּגְבוּרָה רוּחַ דַּעַת וְיִרְאַת יְהוָה

And the spirit of the LORD shall rest upon him,
the spirit of wisdom and understanding, the spirit of counsel and might,
the spirit of knowledge and of the fear of the LORD (Isa. 11:2)

פֶּלֶא יוֹעֵץ   *"Wonderful Counselor"*

Hebrew	Transliteration	Definition
פֶּלֶא יוֹעֵץ	pe·leh yo··**ets**	Wonderful, Counselor (Isa. 9:6).

Other Names and Titles of God

Hebrew	Transliteration	Definition
אָבִינוּ	'a·vi·nu	Our Father (Isa. 63:16).
אֲבִיעַד	'a·vi·'ad	*Avi Ad.* Eternal Father; Father of Eternity; from *Av* and *Ad* (Isa. 9:6).
אֲבִיר יַעֲקֹב	'a·vir ya·'a·qov	The Mighty One of Jacob (Isa. 60:16).
אֶבֶן יִשְׂרָאֵל	'e·ven yis·ra·'el	Stone of Israel (Gen. 49:24).
אוֹר גּוֹיִם	'or go·yim	The Light of the nations (Isaiah 42:6).
אוֹר־יִשְׂרָאֵל	'or-yis·ra·'el	The Light of Israel (Isa. 10:17; Psalm 27:1).
בּוֹרֵא יִשְׂרָאֵל	bo·re yis·ra·'el	Creator of Israel (Isa. 43:15; see also Eccl. 12:1).
הַמַּלְאָךְ הַגֹּאֵל	ham·mal·'akh ha·go·'el	The Redeeming Angel (Gen. 48:16).
יָשָׁר	ya·shar	The Just One (Isaiah 26:7).
כּוֹכָב מִיַּעֲקֹב	ko·khav mi·ya·'a·qov	Star from Jacob (Num. 24:17).
מַלְאַךְ יְהוָה	mal·'akh 'a·do·nai	The Angel of the LORD (Gen 16:7; Judges 6:22, etc.)
מֶלֶךְ יִשְׂרָאֵל	me·lekh yis·ra·'el	The King of Israel (Zeph. 3:15; Isa. 6:5).
מֶלֶךְ הַכָּבוֹד	me·lekh hak·ka·vod	The King of Glory (Psalm 24:7).
מַחְסֶה	mach·seh	Fortress; Refuge; Shelter (Psalm 91:1).
מָעוֹן	ma·'on	Refuge; Dwelling place (Psalm 90:1).
צוּר	tsur	Rock; Strength (Psalm 18:2).
צוּר יִשְׂרָאֵל	tsur yis·ra·'el	Rock of Israel (2 Sam. 23:2).
צוּר יְשֻׁעָתוֹ	tsur ye·shu·'a·to	The Rock of His Salvation (Deut. 32:15).
צֶמַח	tse·mach	The Branch (Zech. 6:12).
רֹעֶה	ro·'eh	Shepherd (Gen. 49:24; Psalm 23:1; Psalm 80:1).
שִׁילֹה	shi·lo	Shiloh (Gen. 49:10). Another term for the Messiah.
שֹׁפֵט	sho·fet	Judge (Psalm 50:6).
אֵשׁ אֹכְלָה	'esh 'okh·lah	Consuming Fire (Deut. 4:24).

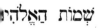

Names of God in the B'rit Chadashah

 *"Yeshua"*

Yeshua (Jesus) is Adonai in the flesh

Before listing the various Names of God as revealed in the *B'rit Chadashah*, it is crucial to understand that *Yeshua* (Jesus) is the Name for Adonai (LORD) in the *Tanakh*. In the table below, the Name (or title) of the LORD given from the *Tanakh* is cross-referenced with the Name (or title) of Yeshua given in the *B'rit Chadashah*:

Name or Title	LORD (Tanakh)	Yeshua (B'rit Chadashah)
God	Gen. 1:1; Psa. 45:6, 7; Isa. 9:6, 7; Zech. 13:7; 7:16; Ex. 3:4, 15; Num. 22:22; Dt. 4:34; 5:24; etc.	1 Tim. 3:16; John 1:1-14; 9:38; Titus 2:13; Heb. 1:8,9, 5:6; John 5:18; Rom. 9:5; Phil 2:5-11.
Creator	Gen. 1:1, 2:7; Isa. 64:8; 44:24; 1 Kings 8:23; Prov. 16:4.	Col. 1:15-17; Heb. 1:3; John 1:1; 14; Rev. 4:11; Heb. 1:8,10-12.
Savior	Isa. 43:11; 45:15, 21; Isa. 9:6-7.	Luke 2:11; Acts 5:31.
Redeemer	Isa. 41:14; 49:26; 60:16; Hos. 13:4; Job 19:25; Psa. 49:8.	Luke 1:68; Rom. 3:24; Eph. 1:7; Col. 1:14; Heb. 9:12.
Almighty	Gen. 17:1	Rev. 1:7-8; Phil. 2:5-11.
Lord of Lords	Deut. 10:17	Rev. 17:17; 19:16; 1 Tim. 6:15.
King of Kings	Dan. 2:47	Rev. 19:16
Judge of All	Mic. 5:1; Isa. 33:22; I Sam. 2:10.	John 5:22,7; Acts 10:42.
LORD of All	Gen. 2:4; Gen. 14:2; Deut. 4:29.	Acts 10:36
Lord of Glory	Psa. 24:8; Isa. 40:5.	John 1:1-3, 14; 1 Cor. 2:8.
Rock	Psa. 18:31; Deut. 32:3,4.	1 Cor. 10:4
Husband	Jer. 31:32	2 Cor. 11:2
King of Israel	Isa. 44:6; Zech. 9:9.	John 1:49; Mt. 2:2.
Prince of Salvation	Isa. 9:6	Heb. 2:10
The Holy One of Israel	Isa. 41:14; Isa. 43:15.	Acts 3:14; Mark 1:24.
Eternal One	Micah 5:2; Psa. 90:2.	Matt. 2:6
Self-Existent One	Ex. 3:14	John 5:26
Pre-Existent One	Ex. 3:14	John 8:56-9
Omnipresent One	1 Kings 8:27	Matt. 28:20
God Alone	1 Chron. 29:11	Rev. 4:11
Shepherd	Psa. 23:1	John 10:11,16
Salvation through His name alone	Isa. 12:2; Jer 3:23; Jon. 2:9; Zech 9:9; Psa. 68:19; Psa. 79:9.	John 1:12; Acts 4:12.
The First and the Last	Isa. 41:4; 44:6; 48:12.	Rev. 1:8, 11; 21:6; 22:13.
Every Knee Shall Bow to	Isa. 45:23	Rom. 14:11; Phil. 2:10.
Confession Saves	Joel 2:32	Rom. 10:9-13
Faith in Him Saves	Hab. 2:4	Rom. 1:17; Gal. 3:11.
Son of God	Psa. 2:2-9; 45:6; 110; Prov. 30:4.	Heb. 1:8-9; Mt. 22:44.
The Searcher of Hearts	Jer. 17:10; 1 Chron. 28:9.	Rev. 2:23
The Virgin Born	Isa. 7:14	Matt. 1:23
I AM HE	Isa. 43:10	John 8:24
Lion of Judah	Gen 49:9; Hos. 5:14.	Rev. 5:5
Light	Psa. 27:1	John 1:9; 8:12
Honored / Extolled	Psa. 30:1	John 5:23-4
The Pierced One	Zech. 12:10	John 19:34-37
Stone of Stumbling	Isa. 8:13-4	1 Pet. 2:7,8

רוּחַ הַקֹּדֶשׁ   *"The Holy Spirit"*

Ruach Haqodesh (the Holy Spirit) is Adonai

The *Ruach Haqodesh* (Holy Spirit) is likewise the Name for Adonai (LORD) in the *Tanakh*. Most of the revelation of the full deity of the *Ruach Haqodesh* is given in the *B'rit Chadashah*, although there are strong intimations found in the *Tanakh*.

Name or Title	LORD (Tanakh)	Holy Spirit (B'rit Chadashah)
God	Gen. 1:2; Gen. 6:3; Job 33:4.	Acts 5:3-4; John 4:24; Luke 12:10; 2 Cor 3:17; cp. 1 Cor. 3:16 and 6:19; Acts 13:2; Heb. 3:7-11.
Creator	Job 33:4; Psalm 33:6; 104:29-30	
Omnipresent	Psa. 139:7-10	1 Cor. 2:10-11
Omniscient	Isa. 40:13	John 14:16; 1 Cor. 2:10-11.
Omnipotent	Micah 2:7; Psalm 18:5	Matt. 12:28; Rom. 15:18-19.
Eternal	Isa. 48:16*; Isa. 61:1	John 14:16; Heb. 9:14.
Searcher of Hearts	Jer. 17:10; 1 Chron. 28:9.	1 Cor. 2:10
Knower of the Future	Ez. 11:24	
Sanctifier	Zech. 12:10	Heb. 10:29; Rom. 8:26; Eph. 6:18.

The Jewishness of the "Trinity"

Although the word "Trinity" (*Hashilush Haqadosh*) does not directly appear in the Scriptures, it is an entirely Jewish concept, derived from both the *Tanakh* and the *B'rit Chadashah*. Scripturally, God is revealed as "triune" in some of the following ways:

- **Plural Names**—*Elohim*, the third word in the *Tanakh*, is a plural form. This Name is often associated with singular verbs, though interestingly sometimes appears with plural forms (as in Genesis 35:7, Psalm 58:11).

- **Plural Pronouns**—The LORD God, speaking in Genesis 1:26, says "Let *us* make man in *our* image and in *our* likeness" (see also Gen. 3:22, 11:7, Isa. 6:8).

- **"Creators"**—In Ecclesiastes 12:1 it is written, "Remember your *Creators* in the days of your youth," and in Psalm 149:2 Israel is commanded to rejoice in his *Makers*. In Genesis 1:1-3, God (Elohim), the Spirit of God (Ruach Elohim), and the Word of God (and God said...), are all involved in the creation of the universe.

- **Plurality within the Godhead**—King David writes: "The LORD (YHVH) says to my Lord (Adonai): sit at my right hand until I make Your enemies a footstool for Your feet (Psalm 110:1), and Psalm 45:6-7 says "Your throne, O God (Elohim), is forever and ever....therefore God, Your God (Elohim), has anointed You with the oil of joy more than Your fellows."

- **Isaiah 48:12-16**—In this passage, the "First and the Last," declares that "the Lord God has sent Me and His Spirit. The Creator who is speaking claims to have been sent by the Lord God (YHVH) and His Spirit (Ruach).

The Jewishness of the "Trinity" (continued)

- **The Angel of the LORD**—This mysterious Angel was treated as God Himself, exercising divine prerogatives and receiving worship (see Gen. 16:7, 9, 11; Exodus 3:2-6; Judges 13:21-22).

- **Oneness (Achdut)**—In the Shema we read, *"Shema Yisra'el* (Hear, 0 Israel): *'Adonai 'Eloheinu (the Lord our Gods), 'Adonai 'Echad* (the Lord is one). Interestingly, the word *'echad* in Hebrew can imply a unity in diversity (the word for one and only one, i.e., unique, is more often rendered as *yachid*). For example, in Exodus 26:6 the parts of the Tabernacle (*mishkan*) are to be constructed so that "it shall be one (*'echad*) tabernacle," and Ezekiel spoke of two "sticks" (representing fragmented Israel) as being reunited into one: "and they shall be one (*'echad*) stick in My hand" (Ezekiel 37:19). Moses also uses *'echad* in Genesis 2:24 when he says: "And they (husband and wife) will become one flesh *(basar 'echad)."*

- **The *Tevilah* (Baptism) of Yeshua**—At the baptism of Yeshua we see the Holy Spirit descending as a Dove and the Father proclaim, "You are my well-beloved Son; in You I am well pleased" (Luke 3:21).

- **Yeshua Revealed the Trinity**—The Lord Jesus plainly spoke of the Trinity by commanding His disciples to baptize others in the Name (singular) of the Father, the Son, and the Holy Spirit (Matt. 28:19). He also equated Himself with the Father (John 8:58; 10:30; 14:8-9).

- **The Father is God**—Isaiah 64:8; Malachi 2:10; John 8:54; etc.

- **Yeshua is God**—1 Tim. 3:16; John 1:1-14; 9:38; Titus 2:13; Heb. 1:8,9, 5:6; John 5:18; Rom.9:5; Phil 2:5-11; etc.

- **The Holy Spirit is God**—Acts 5:3-4; John 4:24; Luke 12:10; 2 Cor. 3:17; cp. 1 Cor. 3:16 and 6:19; Acts 13:2; Heb. 3:7-11; etc.

- **Yeshua's Followers Taught the Trinity**—Jesus' followers ascribed to Him divine status as co-equal with the Father. Many "triadic" formulas also appear in the *B'rit Chadashah*, such as 1 Cor. 12:4-6, 2 Cor. 13:14, 1 Peter 1:2, Eph 4:4-6, and Matt. 28:19.

"The Holy Trinity"

B'rit Chadashah Names for the Father

Hebrew	Transliteration	Definition
אַבָּא	'ab·ba	*Aramaic.* Abba. "Daddy" or "dear Father"; term of endearment (Mark 14:26; Rom. 8:15; Gal. 4:6).
אַבָּא אָבִינוּ	'ab·ba 'a·vi·nu	*Aramaic.* Abba our Father (Rom. 8:15).
אָבִינוּ שֶׁבַּשָּׁמַיִם	'a·vi·nu she·bash·sha·**mai**·yim	"Our Father Who art in Heaven" (Matt. 6:9; Luke 11:2).
אֱלֹהִים אָבִינוּ	'e·lo·**him** 'a·**vi**·nu	God the Father (2 Tim. 1:2).
אֲבִיעַד	'a·vi·'ad	Everlasting Father (1 Cor. 8:6).
אֲבִי יֵשׁוּעַ הַמָּשִׁיחַ אֲדֹנֵינוּ	'a·vi ye·**shu**·'ah ham·ma·**shi**·ach 'a·do·**nei**·nu	Father of our Lord Jesus the Messiah (Col. 1:3; Rom. 15:6; 2 Cor. 1:3; 1 Pet. 1:3).
אֲבִי הַמְּאֹרֹת	'a·vi ham·mo'·**rot**	Father of Lights (James 1:17).
אֲבִי הַכָּבוֹד	'a·vi hak·ka·**vod**	Father of Glory (Eph. 1:17).
אֲבִי הָרוּחֹת	'a·vi ha·ru·**chot**	Father of spirits (Heb. 12:9).
אֲבִי הָרַחֲמִים	'a·vi ha·ra·cha·**mim**	Father of mercies (2 Cor. 1:3).
הָאָב לְיֵשׁוּעַ הַמָּשִׁיחַ	ha·'av le·ye·**shu**·a' ham·ma·**shi**·ach	The Father of Jesus the Messiah (2 Cor. 11:31).
אֱלֹהֵי כָּל־נֶחָמָה	'e·lo·**hei** kol- ne·cha·mah	God of all Comfort (2 Cor. 1:3).
אֲבִי־כֹל	'a·vi-khol	Father of all (Eph. 4:6).
אֱלֹהִים	'e·lo·**him**	God (2 Cor. 9:7).
אֱלֹהֵי אֲבֹתֵינוּ	'e·lo·**hei** 'a·vo·**tei**·nu	God of our fathers (Acts 7:32; cp. Deut. 26:7; 1 Chron. 12:17).
אֱלֹהֵי אַבְרָהָם	'e·lo·**hei** 'av·ra·**ham**	The God of Abraham (Acts 7:32; cp. Ex. 3:15).
אֱלֹהֵי יִצְחָק	'e·lo·**hei** yits·**chaq**	The God of Isaac (Acts 7:32; cp. Ex. 3:15).
אֱלֹהֵי יַעֲקֹב	e·lo·**hei** ya·a·kov	The God of Jacob (Acts 7:32; cp. Ex. 3:15).
אֱלֹהֵי הַשָּׁלוֹם	'e·lo·**hei** hash·sha·lom	The God of Peace (Heb. 13:20).
אֱלֹהֵי הַכָּבוֹד	'e·lo·**hei** hak·ka·vod	God of Glory (Acts 7:2; cp. Psa. 29:3).
אֱלֹהִים חַיִּים	'e·lo·**him** chai·yim	The Living God (2 Cor. 3:3; 6:16; cp. Jer. 10:10).

Hebrew	Transliteration	Definition
אֵל יִשְׂרָאֵל	'el yis·ra·'el	The God of Israel (Matt. 15:31; cp. Ps. 68:36).
יְהוָה אֱלֹהִים	'a·do·nai 'e·lo·him	The LORD God (Acts 3:22; cp. Gen. 2:4, etc.).
יְהוָה אֱלֹהֵי יִשְׂרָאֵל	'a·do·nai 'e·lo·hei yis·ra·'el	The Lord God of Israel (Luke 1:68; cp. Isa. 17:6).
יְהוָה צְבָאוֹת	'a·do·nai tse·va·'ot	The LORD of armies (or hosts) (2 Cor. 6:18; James 5:4; cp. 1 Sam. 1:11).
יְהוָה אֱלֹהֵי צְבָאוֹת	'a·do·nai 'e·lo·hei tse·va·'ot	Lord God Almighty; Lord God of Hosts (Rev. 15:3).
אֵל שַׁדַּי	'el shad·dai	*El Shaddai.* The All Sufficient God; *Shad* means "breast" in Hebrew (Rev. 1:8; cp. Gen. 17:1).
הַגְּבוּרָה	ha·ge·vu·rah	The Power (Mark 14:62).
הַיּוֹצֵר	hai·yo·tser	The Creator (Rom. 1:25; 1 Peter 4:9).
אֵל עֶלְיוֹן	'el 'el·yon	*El Elyon.* The Most High God. (Heb. 7:1; cp. Gen. 14:20; Psalm 9:2).
הַגָּאוֹן	hag·ga·'on	The Exaltation; The Excellency (2 Peter 1:17; cp. Job 37:4; Isa. 2:19).
הַגְּדֻלָה בַּמָּרוֹם	ha·ge·du·lah bam·ma·rom	The Majesty on High (Heb. 1:3; cp. 1 Chron. 29:11).
מֶלֶךְ הַקְּדוֹשִׁים	me·lekh haq·qe·do·shim	King of saints (Rev. 15:3).
מֶלֶךְ הַגּוֹיִם	me·lekh hag·goy·im	King of nations (Rev. 15:3; cp. Jer. 10:7).
הַשֹּׁפֵט	hash·sho·fet	The Judge (James 4:12; cp. Judges 11:27).
אֱלֹהִים אֶחָד וְהֶחָכָם	'e·lo·him 'e·chad ve·he·cha·kham	The Only Wise God (1 Tim. 1:17).
מֶלֶךְ הַמְּלָכִים	me·lekh ha·me·la·khim	King of Kings (1 Tim. 6:15; Rev. 17:14; 19:16).
אֲדֹנֵי הָאֲדֹנִים	'a·do·nei ha·'a·do·nim	Lord of Lords (1 Tim. 6:15; Rev. 17:14; 19:16).
הַמְבֹרָךְ	ham·vo·rakh	Potentate (1 Tim. 6:15).
אֵשׁ אֹכְלָה	'esh 'okh·lah	Consuming Fire (Heb. 12:29; cp. Deut. 4:24).
הַשָּׁמַיִם	hash·sha·mai·yim	The Heaven (Matt. 21:25).

B'rit Chadashah Names for Jesus

Hebrew	Transliteration	Definition
יֵשׁוּעַ	ye·**shu**·a'	Yeshua; Jesus (Matt. 1:21; Luke 2:21).
יֵשׁוּעַ בֶּן־יוֹסֵף	ye·**shu**·a' ben yo·**sef**	Jesus son of Joseph (John 1:45).
יֵשׁוּעַ הַנָּצְרִי	ye·**shu**·a' han·**nots**·ri	Jesus of Nazareth (Mk. 1:24; 10:47; 14:67; 16:6; Lk. 4:34; 18:37; 24:19; John 1:45; 18:5, 7; 19:19; Acts 2:22; 6:14; 10:38; 22:8; 26:9; Matt. 26:71).
הַמָּשִׁיחַ	ham·ma·**shi**·ach	The Annointed. The Messiah (John 1:41). Occurs over 500 times in the *B'rit Chadashah*.
הַמָּשִׁיחַ יֵשׁוּעַ	ham·ma·**shi**·ach ye·**shu**·a'	Jesus the Messiah; Jesus Christ (Matt. 1:1, 18; Mk. 1:1; Jn. 1:17; 17:3; Acts 2:38; Rom. 1:1, 3, 6; 1 Co. 1:1ff; 2 Co. 1:1ff, Eph. 1:1ff; Col. 1:1ff; etc.).
בֶּן־דָּוִד	ben da·**vid**	Son of David (Matt. 1:1, 20; 9:27; 12:23; 15:22; 20:30f; 21:9, 15; 22:42; Mk. 10:47f; 12:35; Lk. 3:31; 18:38f).
בֶּן־אַבְרָהָם	ben 'av·ra·**ham**	Son of Abraham (Matt. 1:1; Luke 3:34; 19:9).
בֶּן יָחִיד	ben ya·**chid**	Only Begotten Son (John 1:14, 18; 3:16, 18; Heb. 11:17; 1 John. 4:9).
בְּנִי יְדִידִי	be·ni ye·di·**di**	My Beloved Son (Matt. 3:17; 17:5; Mk. 1:11; 9:7; Lk. 3:22; 1 Co. 4:17; 2 Tim. 1:2; 2 Pet. 1:17).
בֶּן־הָאֱלֹהִים	ben ha·'e·lo·**him**	The Son of God (Dan. 3:25; Matt. 4:3, 6; 14:33; 26:63; 27:40, 43, 54; Mk. 1:1; 3:11; 15:39; Lk. 1:35; 22:70; Jn. 1:34, 49; 5:25; 9:35; 10:36; 11:4, 27; 19:7; 20:31; Acts 8:37; 9:20; Rom. 1:4; 2 Co. 1:19; Gal. 2:20; Eph. 4:13; Heb. 4:14; 6:6; 7:3; 10:29; 1 Jn. 3:8; 4:15; 5:5, 10, 12, 20; Rev. 2:18).
שֹׁרֶשׁ דָּוִד	sho·resh da·**vid**	Root of David (Rev. 5:5; 22:16).
זֶרַע אַבְרָהָם	ze·ra' 'av·ra·**ham**	The Seed of Abraham (Gal. 3:16).
בֶּן־הָאָדָם	ben ha·'a·**dam**	The Son of Man (Matt. 8:20; 9:6; 26:2, 24, 45, 64; Mk. 2:10, Lk. 5:24; 6:5; 24:7; Jn. 1:51; 3:13f; 5:27; 6:27, 53, 62; 8:28; 12:23, 34; 13:31; Acts 7:56; Heb. 2:6; Rev. 1:13; 14:14; cp. Dan. 7:13).
בֶּן־הָאָב	ben ha·'**av**	Son of the Father (2 John 1:3).
בֶּן־עֶלְיוֹן	ben 'el·**yon**	Son of the Highest (Luke 1:32).
אֱלֹהִים בֶּן יָחִיד	'e·lo·**him** ben ya·**chid**	The Only Begotten God (John 1:18).
הַבְּכוֹר	ha·be·**khor**	The Firstborn (Col. 1:15; Heb. 1:6).

Hebrew	Transliteration	Definition
צֶלֶם אֱלֹהִים	tse·lem ʾe·lo·**him**	The Image of God (Col. 1:15).
הָאָמֵן	ha·ʾa·**men**	The Amen (Rev. 3:14).
עֵד הָאֱמֶת וְהַצֶּדֶק	ʿed ha·ʾe·met ve·ha·**tse**·deq	The True and Righteous Witness (Rev. 3:14).
רֵאשִׁית בְּרִיאַת הָאֱלֹהִים	re·shit be·ri·ʾat ha·ʾe·lo·**him**	The Beginning of the Creation of God (Rev. 3:4).
הָעֵד הַנֶּאֱמָן	ha·ʿed han·ne·ʾe·**man**	The Faithful Witness (Rev. 1:5).
הַבְּכוֹר הַקָּם מִן־הַמֵּתִים	ha·be·khor haq·qam min-ham·me·**tim**	First Begotten from the dead (Rev. 1:5).
עֶלְיוֹן לְמַלְכֵי־אֶרֶץ	ʿel·**yon** le·mal·khei-ʾa·rets	Prince of the kings of the earth (Rev. 1:5).
הָאָדָם הָרִאשׁוֹן	ha·ʾa·**dam** ha·ri·shon	The First Adam (1 Cor. 15:45).
הָאָדָם הָאַחֲרוֹן	ha·ʾa·**dam** ha·ʾa·cha·ron	The Last Adam (1 Cor. 15:45).
רַבִּי	**rab**·bi	Rabbi; "my great Master" (Matt. 23:8).
מֶלֶךְ יִשְׂרָאֵל	**me**·lekh yis·ra·ʾel	King of Israel (Mark 15:32).
מֶלֶךְ הַיְּהוּדִים	**me**·lekh hai·ye·hu·dim	The King of the Jews (Matt. 2:2; 27:11, 29, 37; Mk. 15:2, 9, 12, 18, 26; Lk. 23:3, 37; Jn. 18:33, 39; 19:3, 19, 21).
הַדָּבָר	had·da·**var**	The Word (John 1:1).
דְּבַר הָאֱלֹהִים	de·var ha·ʾe·lo·**him**	The Word of God (Rev. 19:13).
דְּבַר הַחַיִּים	de·var ha·**chai**·yim	The Word of Life (1 Jn. 1:1).
הַתְּקוּמָה וְהַחַיִּים	hat·te·qu·**mah** ve·ha·**chai**·yim	The Resurrection and the Life (John 11:25).
יהוה	ʾa·do·**nai**	I AM (John 8:58; cp. Exodus 3:14).
אֶהְיֶה אֲשֶׁר אֶהְיֶה	ʾeh·**yeh** ʾa·sher ʾeh·**yeh**	I AM THAT I AM. *Ehyeh Asher Ehyeh* (John 8:58; cp. Exodus 3:14).
הָאָדוֹן	ha·ʾa·**don**	The Lord (Rom. 10:9).

Hebrew	Transliteration	Definition
הָאֱלֹהִים	ha·'e·lo·**him**	God (John 1:1).
עִמָּנוּאֵל	'im·ma·nu·'**el**	God with us (Matt.1:23; cp. Isa. 7:14).
הוּא הַבָּא	hu hab·**ba**	The One who comes (Luke 7:19).
מוֹשִׁיעַ הָעוֹלָם	mo·**shi**·a' ha·'o·**lam**	The Savior of the world (John 4:42; Phil. 3:20; 1 Tim. 4:10; cp. Isa. 45:15, Jer. 14:8).
הַגֹּאֵל	hag·go·'**el**	The Redeemer; Kinsman Redeemer (John 4:42; cp. Isa. 49:7).
הַמּוֹשִׁיעַ לְכָל-אָדָם	ham·mo·**shi**·a' le·khol·'a·**dam**	The Savior of all men (1 Tim. 4:10; cp. Isa. 45:15, Jer. 14:8).
הַפַּלֵּט	hap·pa·**lat**	Deliverer (Rom. 11:26; cp. Psa. 18:2, 2 Sam. 22:2).
הַנָּבִיא	han·na·**vi**	The Prophet (John 1:25, 6:14; Matt. 13:57, cp. Deut. 18:15).
יֵשׁוּעַ מִנְצֶרֶת	ye·**shu**·a' mi·ne·**tse**·ret	Jesus of Nazareth (Matt. 21:11).
קָדוֹשׁ	qa·**dosh**	The Holy One (Acts 3:14; cp. Isa. 40:25).
קְדוֹשׁ הָאֱלֹהִים	qe·**dosh** ha·'e·lo·**him**	The Holy One of God (Luke 4:34).
צַדִּיק	tsad·**diq**	The Just; The Righteous (Acts 3:14; cp. Zeph. 3:5).
שַׂר	sar	Prince (Acts 5:31).
שַׂר הַחַיִּים	sar ha·**chai**·yim	The Prince of Life (Acts 3:15).
הֶחַי	he·**chai**	The Living One (Luke 24:5).
שֹׁפֵט הַחַיִּים וְהַמֵּתִים	sho·fet ha·**chai**·yim ve·ham·me·**tim**	The Judge of the living and the dead (Acts 10:42, cp. Psa. 50:6, 75:7).
אֶבֶן מָאֲסוּ	'e·ven ma·'a·**su**	The Rejected Stone (Mark 12:10; cp. Psa. 118:22).
רֹאשׁ פִּנָּה	rosh pin·**nah**	Chief Stone; Cornerstone (Mark 12:10; Psa. 118:22).
הָרֹעֶה	ha·ro·'**eh**	The Shepherd (John 10:11; 1 Peter 5:4; cp. Zech. 13:7).
הָרֹעֶה הַטּוֹב	ha·ro·'**eh** ha·**tov**	The Good Shepherd (John 10:11, 14; Heb. 13:20).
רֹאשׁ הָעֵדָה	rosh ha·'e·**dah**	Head of the Congregation; Chief Shepherd (1 Pet. 5:4; Col. 1:18).

Hebrew	Transliteration	Definition
הַמַּשְׁגִּיחַ נַפְשֹׁתֵיכֶם	ham·mash·**gi**·ach naf·sho·**tei**·khem	Watcher of our souls (1 Peter 2:25; cp. Song 2:9).
שֶׂה	seh	Lamb (Rev. 5:12).
שֵׂה הָאֱלֹהִים	seh ha·'e·lo·**him**	Lamb of God (John 1:29, 36).
פִּסְחֵנוּ	pis·**che**·nu	Our Passover (1 Cor. 5:7).
הָאַרְיֵה מִשֵּׁבֶט יְהוּדָה	ha·ar·**yeh** mish·**she**·vet ye·hu·**dah**	The Lion of Judah (Rev. 5:5; cp. Gen. 49:9).
מַלְאָךְ מֵלִיץ	mal·**akh** me·**lits**	Advocate; Intercessor (1 John 2:1; cp. Job 33:23).
מֵלִיץ אֶחָד	me·**lits** 'e·chad	One Mediator (1 Tim. 2:5).
אוֹר הָעוֹלָם	'or ha·'o·**lam**	Light of the World (John 8:12; cp. Psa. 27:1).
נֶאֱמָן וְיָשָׁר	ne·'e·**man** ve·ya·**shar**	Faithful and True (Rev. 19:11).
עֶבֶד הַקָּדוֹשׁ	'e·ved haq·qa·**dosh**	Holy Servant (Acts 4:27).
כּוֹכַב הַשָּׁחַר	ko·khav hash·sha·**char**	Morning Star (Rev. 22:16; cp. Rev. 2:28).
אוֹר־בֹּקֶר מִמָּרוֹם	'or-**bo**·ker mim·ma·**rom**	Sunrise from on high (Luke 1:78).
הַכֹּהֵן הַגָּדוֹל	hak·ko·**hen** hag·ga·**dol**	The Great High Priest (Heb. 3:1; 4:14).
הַדֶּרֶךְ	had·**de**·rekh	The Way (John 14:6).
הָאֱמֶת	ha·'e·met	The Truth (John 14:6).
הַחַיִּים	ha·**chai**·yim	The Life (John 14:6).
הַשַּׁעַר	ha·sha·**ar**	The Door (John 10:9).
אָלֶף וְתָו	'a·leph ve·**tav**	Alpha and Omega (Rev. 1:8, 11; 21:6; 22:13).
רֹאשׁ וָסוֹף	rosh va·sof	Beginning and the Ending (Rev. 1:8).
הָרִאשׁוֹן וְהָאַחֲרוֹן	ha·ri·**shon** ve·ha·'a·cha·**ron**	The First and the Last (Rev. 1:11, 17; 2:8; 22:13).
הַבְּכוֹר	hab·**khor**	The Firstborn (Col. 1:18).
רֹאשׁ לְכָל־הָעֵדָה	rosh le·**khol** ha·'e·**dah**	Head over all things to the church (Eph. 1:22).

Hebrew	Transliteration	Definition
נַחֲלָה בַכֹּל	na·cha·**lah** va·**kol**	Heir of all things (Heb. 1:2).
צֶלֶם אֱלֹהִים	tse·lem ʼe·lo·**him**	Image of God (Col. 1:15).
סוֹד הָאֱלֹהִים	sod ha·ʼe·lo·**him**	The Mystery of God (Col. 2:2).
קֶרֶן יְשׁוּעָה	**qe**·ren ye·**shu**·ʻah	Horn of Salvation (Luke 1:69; cp. 1 Sam. 2:10).
גְּבוּרַת אֱלֹהִים	ge·vu·**rat** ʼe·lo·**him**	The Power of God (1 Cor. 1:24).
חָכְמַת אֱלֹהִים	**chokh**·mat ʼe·lo·**him**	The Wisdom of God (1 Cor. 1:24).
יָדִיד	ya·**did**	The Beloved (Matt. 12:18).
חָתָן	cha·**tan**	Bridegroom (John 3:29).
לֶחֶם אֱלֹהִים	le·chem ʼe·lo·**him**	Bread of God (John 6:33).
לֶחֶם שָׁמַיִם	le·chem sha·**mai**·yim	Bread of Heaven (John 6:32).
הַגֶּפֶן אֱמֶת	hag·**ge**·fen ʼe·**met**	The True Vine (John 15:1).
הַתְּקוּמָה וְהַחַיִּים	ha·te·qu·**mah** ve·ha·**chai**·yim	The Resurrection and the Life (John 11:25).
אִישׁ מַכְאֹבוֹת	ʼish makh·ʼo·**vot**	Man of Sorrows (Isa. 53:3).
בֶּן־אֱלֹהִים חַיִּים	ben ʼe·lo·**him** **chai**·yim	Son of the Living God (Matt. 16:16; John 6:69).
כֹּל בַּכֹּל	kol ba·**kol**	All in all (Eph. 1:23).
צֶמַח צְדָקָה	tse·**mach** tse·da·**qah**	Branch of Righteousness (Jer. 33:15; cp. Isa. 4:2).
אֲדוֹן הַכָּבוֹד	ʼa·**don** hak·ka·**vod**	Lord of Glory (1 Cor. 2:8; cp. Psa. 24:8; Isa. 40:5).
מוֹשֵׁל	mo·**shel**	Ruler; Governor (Matt. 2:6).
הַדָּבָר אֱלֹהִים	had·da·**var** ʼe·lo·**him**	The Word of God (John 1:1, 14; cp. Gen 1).
מְשִׁיחַ הָאֱלֹהִים	ma·**shi**·ach ha·ʼe·lo·**him**	The Messiah of God (Luke 9:20);
הָאֱלֹהִים הַמְבֹרָךְ לְעוֹלָם וָעֶד	ha·ʼe·lo·**him** ham·vo·**rakh** le·ʻo·**lam** va·**ed**	God Blessed forever (Rom. 9:5).

B'rit Chadashah Names for the Holy Spirit

Hebrew	Transliteration	Definition
רוּחַ אֱלֹהִים	ru·ach 'e·lo·**him**	The Spirit of God (Matt. 3:16; 12:28; Rom. 8:9, 14; 15:19; 1 Co. 2:11, 14; 3:16; 7:40; 12:3; Eph. 4:30; 1 Jn. 4:2).
רוּחַ הַקֹּדֶשׁ	ru·ach haq·qo·**desh**	The Holy Spirit; the Holy Ghost (Luke 3:16; 11:13; Eph. 1:13; 4:30; 1 Thess. 4:8; Titus 3:5; 1 Cor. 6:9; Jude 1:20). Occurs more than 90 times in the *B'rit Chadashah*.
רוּחַ הַקֹּדֶשׁ כַּאֲשֶׁר דִּבֶּר	ru·ach haq·qo·**desh** ka·'a·**sher** dib·**ber**	The Holy Spirit Of Promise (Eph. 1:13).
רוּחַ יְהוָה	ru·ach 'a·do·**nai**	The Spirit of Adonai (Acts 5:9).
רוּחַ אֱלֹהִים חַיִּים	ru·ach 'e·lo·**him** chai·yim	Spirit of the Living God (2 Cor. 3:3).
רוּחַ אֲדֹנָי יְהוָה	ru·ach 'a·do·**nai** 'a·do·**nai**	Spirit of the LORD God (Luke 4:18; cp. Isa. 61:1).
הָרוּחַ	ha·**ru**·ach	The Spirit (Acts 2:4; Rom. 8:1; 1 Cor. 2:4, 10; 1 Cor. 2:11-12; 2 Cor. 1:22; 3:6; Gal. 3:2).
רוּחַ עוֹלָם׃	ru·ach 'o·**lam**	The Eternal Spirit (Heb. 9:14).
רוּחַ הָאֱמֶת	ru·ach ha·'e·**met**	The Spirit of Truth (John 15:26).
הַמֵּלִיץ	ham·me·**lits**	The Comforter; Helper (John 14:26; 15:26).
רוּחַ יֵשׁוּעַ	ru·ach ye·shu·a'	The Spirit of Yeshua (Acts 16:7).
רוּחַ יֵשׁוּעַ מְשִׁיחֵנוּ	ru·ach ye·shu·a' me·shi·**che**·nu	The Spirit of Yeshua our Messiah (Phil. 1:19).
רוּחַ הַמָּשִׁיחַ	ru·ach ham·ma·**shi**·ach	The Spirit of the Messiah (Rom. 8:9).
רוּחַ הַחָכְמָה	ru·**ach** ha·chokh·mah	The Spirit of Wisdom (Eph. 1:17).
רוּחַ הֶחָזוֹן	ru·**ach** he·cha·zon	The Spirit of Revelation (Eph. 1:17).

רוח אלהים

Spirit of God

Glossary

OF HEBREW TERMS

Glossary Introduction

Transliterations

Hebrew-to-English glossaries tend to use transliteration schemes that are either overly academic (and thus difficult for the non-specialist) or else simplistic to the point of being misleading. It is our hope that this glossary will provide a balance between these two extremes.

Glossary Format

In this glossary we first list the Hebrew text (in Hebrew-alphabetical order), then the transliteration, and then the definition of the word. Transliterations use dots to separate syllables with the accented syllable in **boldface**. Parts of speech are given in *italics*. Common English spellings are sometimes provided in the definition. If relevant, English Bible scripture references are provided in parentheses. For example,

Hebrew	Transliteration	Definition
אַבָּא	ab·ba	*n. Aramaic.* Abba. "Daddy" or "dear Father"; term of endearment (Mark 14:26; Rom. 8:15; Gal. 4:6).

Vowel Sounds

Hebrew vowel sounds are represented with the following English letters:

a	=	"a" as in *aqua*	o	=	"o" as in yell*o*w
e	=	"e" as in th*ey*	u	=	"u" as in bl*u*e
ei	=	"ei" as in *ei*ght	ai	=	"ai" as in *ai*sle
ey	=	"ey" as in ob*ey*	oy	=	"oy" as in *oi*l
i	=	"i" as in mach*i*ne	uy	=	"uy" as in g*ooey*

Note: The sheva will be usually be transliterated using an "e" when it is vocal.

Consonant Sounds

Hebrew consonants are represented using standard English letters. The following exceptions, however, should be noted:

ch	=	"ch" as in Ba*ch*
kh	=	"ch" as in Ba*ch*
ts	=	"ts" as in nu*ts*
'	=	"guttural" Ayin
'	=	"guttural" Aleph

Note: Sometimes letters with a dagesh (·) will double their consonantal value; other times they will not, depending on the more commonly accepted English transliteration.

Hebrew	Transliteration	Definition
אָב	'av	*n.* Av. Father. Also the name for the 11th month of the Hebrew civil calendar. The plural is "*avot*" and generally refers to the ancient patriarchs.
אַבָּא	'ab·ba	*n. Aramaic.* Abba. "Daddy" or "dear Father"; term of endearment (Mark 14:26; Rom. 8:15; Gal. 4:6).
אֲבַדּוֹן	'a·vad·don	*n.* Abbadon. Destruction. Also the King of the bottomless pit mentioned in Rev. 9:11.
אַב הָרַחֲמִים	'av ha·ra·cha·mim	*n. Merciful Father.* Name of a prayer recited before *Sefer Torah* (Torah Scroll) is returned to the ark.
אָבוֹת	'a·vot	*n.* Avot. *Ethics of the Fathers,* one of sixty-three tractates of the *Mishnah.* "*Avot*" also refers to the opening blessing in the *Shemoneh Esreh.*
אָבִיב	'a·viv	*n.* Abib. The month Nisan. Meaning ears of grain, namely, barley (Ex. 13:4). Spring; springtime. *See* the Jewish Calendar at the end of this section.
אָבִינוּ מַלְכֵּנוּ	'a·vi·nu mal·ke·nu	*n.* Avinu Malkenu. *Our Father Our King,* a prayer recited during the High Holidays and thought to have been written by Rabbi Akiva.
אָבִינוּ שֶׁבַּשָּׁמַיִם	'a·vi·nu sheb·ba·sha·ma·yim	*phr.* "Our Father, Who art in Heaven," the first words of the Lord's Prayer (Matt 6:9; Luke 11:2).
אֲבִיר יַעֲקֹב	'a·vir ya·'a·qov	*n.* "Mighty One of Jacob" (Gen. 49:24; Deut. 10:17; Psa. 132:2, 5; Isa. 1:24, 49:26, 60:1). Title for God. *See* the Names of God.
אֲבֵלוּת	'a·ve·lut	*n.* Avelut. Mourning, esp. the year of mourning for a parent. Divided into periods: from death to burial (*aveilut*); seven days after burial (*shivah*), the first 30 days after death (*sheloshim*), and the first year after death. Upon a parent's death, a child recites the mourner's *Qaddish* for eleven months.
אֶבֶן פִּנָּה	'e·ven pin·nah	*n.* Cornerstone. *Rosh Pinnah* is the head or chief cornerstone (Psalm 118:22, Mark 12:10).
אַבְרָם	'av·ram	*n.* Abram. "Exalted father" or "Father is lofty." The original forebear of the Jewish people.
אַבְרָהָם	'av·ra·ham	*n.* Abraham. "Father of multitudes." Son of Terah, and renamed in Genesis 17. Abraham comes from *av* and *hamon,* the nations.
אַבְרָהָם אָבִינוּ	'av·ra·ham 'a·vi·nu	*n. phr.* "Our father Abraham." (Luke 1:73; Gal. 3:7).
אַבְשָׁלוֹם	'av·sha·lom	*n.* Absalom. "Father of peace" (from *av* and *shalom*). King David's son by Ma'achah (2 Sam. 3:3).
אַגָּדָה	'ag·ga·dah	*n.* Aggadah. Legend or narratives, primarily from the Talmud (cp. *halakhah*). Aggadic literature is edifying in nature.

אִגֶּרֶת / אִגְּרוֹת	'ig·**ge**·ret / 'ig·**rot**	*n.* Letter(s). In the *B'rit Chadashah*, there are eight "general" letters to Messianic Jewish communities and thirteen letters from Rav Sha'ul (Paul), the emissary to the Gentiles.
אִגְּרוֹת מְשִׁיחִי	'ig·**rot** me·shi·**chi**	*n. pl.* Messianic letters; letters directed to the Messianic communities in the *B'rit Chadashah*.
אֲדוֹן	'a·**don**	*n. Adon.* Lord; mister; sir. Also a name for God, e.g., Isa. 10:33. *See* the Names of God.
אֲדוֹן עוֹלָם	'a·**don** 'o·**lam**	*n. Eternal Lord*, a prayer that is part of the Siddur. *Adon Olam* means "Master of the Universe."
אַדִּיר הוּא	'ad·**dir** hu	*n. Glorious Mighty is He.* Song sung at the end of Passover Seder. *Adir* means mighty or glorious.
אָדָם	'a·**dam**	*n. Adam.* Man. First human being created by God, and created *betselem Elohim*, "in the image of God." *Adam Harishon* is the First Adam. *Ben Adam* means "son of man" and is a general term for human being.
אֲדָמָה	'a·da·**mah**	*n.* Soil, earth, ground (as general, tilled, yielding sustenance); earth substance; ground as earth's visible surface; land (Gen. 4:11).
אֲדֹנָי	'a·do·**nai**	*n. pl.* Lord; God; name used as a substitute for the sacred Tetragrammaton; emphatic plural form of *Adon* (Isa. 6:1). Occurs 300 times in the *Tanakh*. *See* the Names of God.
אֲדֹנָי אֶחָד	'a·do·**nai** 'e·**chad**	*phr.* "Adonai is one." From the core utterance of the Shema (Deut. 6:4). *Adonai Echad.*
אַדִּירֵנוּ	'a·di·**re**·nu	*n.* Our Majestic One.
אֲדָר	'a·**dar**	*n. Adar.* Twelfth month of the Jewish calendar, sixth month of the Hebrew Civil calendar. Corresponding approximately to March.
אֲדָר שֵׁנִי	'a·**dar** she·**ni**	*n. Adar II.* Month added in a Jewish Leap Year (see the section on the Jewish calendar).
אַהֲבָה	'a·ha·**vah**	*n.* Love (Prov. 10:12).
אַהֲבַת עוֹלָם	a·ha·**vat** o·**lam**	*phr.* "Everlasting Love" (Jer. 31:3).
אַהֲבָה רַבָּה	'a·ha·**vah** rab·**bah**	*n. Great Love*; initial words of a common prayer preceding recitation of the *Shema*.
אַהֲבַת הַשֵּׁם	'a·ha·**vat** ha·**shem**	*phr.* "The love of God."
אַהֲבַת הָאֱמֶת	'a·ha·**vat** ha·'**e**·met	*phr.* "The love of the truth."
אַהֲבַת יִשְׂרָאֵל	'a·ha·**vat** yis·ra·'**el**	*phr.* "Love of Israel" or of one's fellow Jew. Love of the Jewish people.
אֹהֶל	'o·hel	*n.* Tent.
אֹהֶל מוֹעֵד	'o·hel mo·'**ed**	*n.* Tent of Meeting. Also called the *Mishkan* or Tabernacle.

אַהֲרֹן	'a·ha·**ron**	n. Aaron. The elder brother of Moses (Ex. 4:14. et. al.). *Aharon* means "light bearer."
אוֹהֵב יִשְׂרָאֵל	'o·hev yis·ra·'**el**	n. Friend of Israel. *Ohev Yisrael* means one who loves or cherishes Israel or the Jewish people.
אוֹיֵב	'o·**yev**	n. Enemy, especially of Adonai or His purposes (Ex. 15:16, Psalm 3:7).
אוֹר	'or	n. Or. Light. Daylight.
אוֹר אֱמֶת	'or 'e·met	n. True Light; a title for the Messiah (John 1:9).
אוֹר הַחַיִּים	'or ha·**chai**·yim	n. The light of life (John 8:12), a promise that the *talmidim* of Yeshua would experience His Light.
אוֹר הָעוֹלָם	'or ha·'o·**lam**	n. Light of the world. A title for Yeshua the Messiah (John 8:12).
אוּרִים וְתֻמִּים	'u·**rim** ve·tu·**mim**	n. phr. Urim and Tummim; "light and perfection"; two stones contained in the breastplate of the high priest (Ex. 28:30); used for oracular purposes in ancient Israel.
אוֹת / אוֹתוֹת	'ot / 'o·**tot**	n. Sign/s; miracle/s; wonder/s (Matt. 24:24).
אָח / אַחִים	'ach / 'a·**chim**	n. Brother / brothers. "*Achdut*" means brotherhood or unity and comes from *'echad*.
אֶחָד	'e·**chad**	adj./n. Echad. One.
אַחְדוּת	ach·**dut**	n. Oneness; unity; brotherhood; fellowship.
אָחוֹת / אֲחָיוֹת	'a·**chot** / 'a·cha·**yot**	n. Sister/s.
אַחֲרוֹן	'a·cha·**ron**	adj./ n. "Last." The *acharonim* is a term for "latter" rabbinic authorities (as distinguished from the *Rishonim*, early authorities).
אַחֲרִית הַיָּמִים	'a·cha·**rit** ha·ya·**mim**	n. phr. "Last days" or time preceding the great Day of the Lord. When the *olam hazeh* (present age) is coming to a close and the *olam habah* (world to come) is about to begin (Gen. 49:1; Isa 2:2; Mic. 4:1; Act 2:17; Heb. 1:2; James 5:3; 2 Pet. 3:3).
אִיּוֹב	'iy·**yov**	n. Job. Book of the *Ketuvim* dealing with ultimate mysteries regarding evil and God's existence. *Iyyov* means "persecuted" or "hated."
אֵיכָה	'ei·**khah**	n. Echah. Lamentations. One of the five scrolls. Jeremiah's acrostic lament over Jerusalem's destruction. Part of the *Ketuvim* in the *Tanakh*.
אֵין כֵּאלֹהֵינוּ	'ein ke·lo·**hei**·nu	n. *There is none like our God*, a chant sung on Sabbaths and festivals.
אִיָּר	'iy·**yar**	n. 8th month of the Hebrew calendar. *See* Jewish Calendar.

אִישׁ	'ish	*n.* Man. Human being. Man, as opposed to a woman (Gen. 2:24).
אִישׁ אֱלֹהִים	'ish 'e·lo·**him**	*n.* Man of God; prophet.
אֵל	'el	*n.* Name for God; "Strength." Used 250 times in the *Tanakh*. *See* the Names of God.
אֶל־הָרוֹמִיִּים	'el-ha·ro·miy·**yim**	*n.* Paul's letter to the *qehillah* (congregation) in Rome. This letter is perhaps Paul's greatest doctrinal work, expounding all of the key doctrines of the gospel of God (*besorat haelohim*) in a masterfully written summary.
אֱלֹהִים	'e·lo·**him**	*n.* God; gods. The plural form of *'el*, meaning "strong one." Occurs 2,570 times in the *Tanakh*. (Isa. 54:5; Jer. 32:27; Gen. 1:1; Isa. 45:18; Deut. 5:23; 8:15; Ps. 68:7). First name of God in *Tanakh*. *See* the Names of God.
אֱלֹהִים אָבִינוּ	'e·lo·**him** 'a·**vi**·nu	*n. phr.* "God our Father" (John 8:42).
אֵל מֶלֶךְ נֶאֱמָן	'el **me**·lekh ne·'e·**man**	*n. phr.* "God is a faithful king;" the phrase spoken before the recitation of the *Shema*; a supposed acronym for "Amen."
אֱלוּל	'e·**lul**	*n.* 6th month of the Jewish calendar. *See* the Jewish calendar.
אֵלִיָּהוּ הַנָּבִיא	'e·li·**ya**·hu han·na·vi	*n.* Elijah the prophet; Mal. 3:23, 4:5 says he will herald "the great and terrible day of Adonai." Jewish tradition regards him as the forerunner of the Messiah. *Eliyahu* means "My God is Yah."
אֱלִישֶׁבַע	'e·li·she·**va'**	*n.* Elizabeth. Luke 1:15. *Elisheva* means "Oath of God."
אֱלִישָׁע	'e·li·**sha'**	*n.* Elisha. Elijah's talmid and successor (1 Kings 19:16); *Elisha* means "God is Salvation."
אֶלֶף	'e·leph	*n.* Thousand.
אָלֶף	'a·leph	*n.* Aleph or Alef. 1st letter of the Hebrew alphabet. A silent (guttural) letter. Originally represented by a pictograph meaning "ox," "strength," or "leader." *Gematria* value is 1.
אָלֶף־בֵּית	'a·leph-**bet**	*n.* Hebrew alphabet. *Binah* means understanding.
אָלֶף וְתָו	'a·lef ve·**tav**	*n.* Aleph and Tav. The First and the Last. The Alpha and Omega. Title for Yeshua the Messiah (Rev. 21:6).
אִם יִרְצֶה הַשֵּׁם	'im·yir·**tseh** ha·**shem**	*phr.* "God willing." Lit. "if it please God." Abbreviated in English as **IY"H** or **IYH**.
אֵם / אִמָּהוֹת	'em / 'im·ma·**hot**	*n.* Mother/s.
אִמּוֹת קְרִיאָה	'im·mot qe·ri·**ah**	*n. pl.* "Mothers of Reading"; *matres lectiones*. The letters Yod, Hey, Vav, and sometimes Aleph when used as vowels rather than consonants.

אִמָּא	ʼim·ma	*n. Aramaic.* Mother. Mommy.
אֲמוֹרָאִים	ʼa·mo·ra·ʼim	*n. pl.* Amoraim. Sages of the Talmud from roughly 200-500 A.D. who expounded the *Mishnah* (compiled by Judah the Prince) and the teachings of the *Tannaim*.
אֱמוּנָה	ʼe·mu·nah	*n.* Faith. Firmness; Steadiness; Fidelity; Steadfastness (Ex. 17:2. Deut. 32:4).
אָמֵן	ʼa·men	*excl.* Amen. "Let it be so!"
אֱמֶת	ʼe·met	*n.* Emet. Truth. Firmness; Stability.
אָנָה	ʼa·nah	*excl.* Please.
אֲנַחְנוּ	ʼa·nach·nu	*pn.* We (1st pers. plural).
אֲנִי	ʼa·ni	*pn.* I (1st pers. singular).
אֲנִי מַאֲמִין	ʼa·ni ma·ʼa·min	*n. phr.* "I believe"; the opening phrase for the thirteen principles of faith as set down by *Rambam* or Moses Maimonides (1135-1204). These thirteen principles constitute a sort of "creed" for many devout Jews.
אָנֹכִי	ʼa·no·khi	*pn.* I (1st pers. pronoun: poetic, biblical).
אִסִּיִּים	ʼis·si·im	*n. pl.* Essenes; Jewish ascetic set in the days of the second Temple period.
אֵפוֹד	ʼe·fod	*n.* Ephod. Garment worn by the high priest.
אֲפִיקוֹמָן	ʼa·fi·ko·man	*n.* Afikomen. Piece of matzah hidden during the Passover meal and eaten later.
אֶפְרַיִם	ʼef·ra·yim	*n.* Ephraim, one of the two sons of Joseph the son of the Patriarch Jacob, hence a half-tribe (as was Manasseh).
אַרְבַּע	ʼar·baʻ	*adj./n.* Four.
אַרְבַּע הַקֻּשְׁיוֹת	ʼar·baʻ haq·qush·yot	*n.* The four questions asked during the Passover seder.
אַרְבַּע כַּנְפוֹת	ʼar·baʻ kan·fot	*n. phr.* "Four corners"; Tallit Katan; worn under an upper garment throughout the day; Tsitsit.
אַרְבַּע כּוֹסוֹת	ʼar·baʻ ko·sot	*n. phr.* "Four cups" or glasses of wine drunk on Passover.
אַרְבַּע מִינִים	ʼar·baʻ mi·nim	*n. phr.* The four plant species used on Sukkot: the "*Etrog*" (citron fruit), the "*Lulav*" (branch of the date palm), "*Hadasim*" (three myrtle branches), and the "*Aravot*" (two willow branches).
אַרְבָּעִים	ʼar·ba·ʻim	*adj./n.* Forty.

אֲרוֹן הַקֹּדֶשׁ	'a·**ron** haq·**qo**·desh	*n.* Aron Hakodesh. Cabinet in which the Torah scrolls are kept in the synagogue. The Aron Hakodesh acts as a reminder of the Biblical Ark of the Covenant in which the two stone Tablets were placed.
אֲרִי	'a·**ri**	*n.* Lion. *Ariel* means "Lion of God."
אֲרֹן הָעֵדֻת	'a·**ron** ha·'e·**dut**	*n.* Ark of the Testimony (Ex. 25:6).
אֲרָמִית	'a·ra·**mit**	*n.* Aramaic (language).
אֶרֶץ	'e·rets	*n.* Land.
אֶרֶץ הַקֹּדֶשׁ	'e·rets haq·**qo**·desh	*n.* The Holy Land; Israel.
אֶרֶץ יִשְׂרָאֵל	'e·rets yis·ra·'**el**	*n. phr.* "Land of Israel."
אִשָּׁה	'i·**sha**	*n.* Woman.
אָשָׁם	'a·**sham**	*n.* Guilt offering. *Ashmanu* means "we have sinned" and is recited during Yom Kippur. (Lev. 7:5). The guilt offering is made by one who has unintentionally sinned.
אַשְׁכְּנַז	'ash·ke·**naz**	*n.* Ashkenaz; referring to European Jews in the Diaspora. Cp. *Sepharad.* (Gen 10:3). The name Ashkenaz has since the 10th century been identified with Germany. As the German and French Jews of the medieval period formed a uniform group in culture and religious customs, they were all referred to as *Ashkenazim* in contradistinction to the *Sephardim* or Spanish-Portuguese Jews. Many Ashkenazim moved to the United States to escape European anti-Semitism.
אָשֵׁר	'a·**sher**	*n.* Asher. 1. "Happy." Jacob's 8th son. Mother Zilpah. (Gen. 30:13). 2. One of the 12 tribes of Israel.
אַשְׁרֵי	'ash·**rei**	*n. phr.* "Happy is the one who"; part of a hymn commonly recited in the Shacharit and Minchah services at the synagogue.
אֵשֶׁת חַיִל	'e·shet **chai**·yil	*n. phr.* "Woman of valor." Ideal woman (Prov. 31).
אַתְּ / אַתָּה	'at / 'at·**tah**	*pn.* You (2nd pers. sing. pronoun; fem. / masc.).
אֶתְנַח	'et·**nach**	*n.* Disjunctive accent in the *Tanakh.*
אֶתְרוֹג	'et·**rog**	*n.* One of the *arba mimim* (four spices) used during the festival of *Sukkot* (Lev. 23:40). Citron.

בּ

Hebrew	Transliteration	Definition
בָּבֶל	ba·**vel**	*n.* Babylonia (modern day Iraq); Abraham left Sumerian city of Ur (in southern Babylonia) for the Promised Land. After the fall of Jerusalem in the year 70, Bavel became a center of Jewish scholarship devoted to the study and interpretation of the Torah.
בְּבַקָשָׁה	be·vak·qa·**sha**	*interj.* Please! Also, You're welcome.
בַּיִת / בָּתִּים	**bay**it / ba·tim	*n.* House / houses.
הַבַּיִת הָרִאשׁוֹן	ha·**bay**it ha·ri·shon	*n.* The first Temple.
בְּדִיקָה	be·di·**qah**	*n.* The careful inspection to which a human being or an object is submitted in keeping with religious requirements.
בְּדִיקַת חָמֵץ	be·di·**qat cha**·mets	*n.* Search for chamets (leaven) as part of the preparation for *Pesach*; the *yester ha ra'* (evil impulse) has long been associated with chamets.
בִּטָּחוֹן	bit·ta·**chon**	*n.* Trust in God.
בִּימָה	**bi**·mah	*n.* Platform; pulpit; elevated platform in middle of synagogue.
בִּינָה	**bi**·nah	*n.* Understanding; Insight. cp. *da'at* and *chokhmah*.
בֵּית / בֵית	beit	*n.* Bet / Vet. Second letter of the Aleph-Bet having a "b" as in *boy* sound (without the dagesh, "v" as in *vine*). Originally represented by a pictograph meaning "tent," "house," or "in." Gematria = 2.
בֵּית־אָב	beit-'**av**	*n.* Family; Clan. Lit. "House of the father."
בֵּית־הַבְּחִירָה	beit-ha·be·chi·**rah**	*n.* The Temple in Jerusalem.
בֵּית־דִּין	beit-**din**	*n.* Court; House of Justice. Religious court.
בֵּית־חוֹלִים	beit-cho·**lim**	*n.* Hospital.
בֵּית כְּנֶסֶת	beit ke·**nes**·et	*n.* Synagogue.
בֵּית לֶחֶם	beit **le**·chem	*n.* Bethlehem. The birthplace of Yeshua and King David. "House of bread." (Gen 35:19; Mic 5:2; Matt 2:1; Luke 2:4).
בֵּית מִדְרָשׁ	beit mid·**rash**	*n.* School; *shul*; place of study, esp. For Talmud studies (cp. *shas*).
בֵּית הַמִּקְדָשׁ	beit ham·miq·**dash**	*n.* Sanctuary; Temple in Jerusalem.

בֵּית־סֵפֶר	beit **se**·fer	n. School.
בֵּית־עֲנְיָה	beit **'an**·yah	n. Bethany. A city in Israel. "House of poverty."
בֵּית תְּפִלָּה	beit te·fil·**lah**	n. House of Prayer. Synagogue.
בִּכּוּרִים	bik·ku·**rim**	n. First Fruits; the term *bekhorim* means first born. See the entry on *Chag Habikkurim*.
בִּלְהָה	**bil**·hah	n. Bilhah. Rachel's handmaid whom she gave to Jacob as a concubine, mother to two of Jacob's children, Dan and Naphtali. One of the four Matriarchs of the 12 tribes of Israel. Bilhah means "troubled."
בְּלִיַּעַל	bli·ya·**'al**	n. compound. Belial. "without (bli) profit (ya'al)"; another title for haSatan, the devil (Deut. 13:13; Jdg. 19:22; 1 Sam. 1:16; 1 Ki. 21:10; 2 Cor. 615).
בִּלְעָם בֶּן־בְּעוֹר	**bil**·'am ben be·**'or**	n. Balaam, son of Beor. Midianite prophet hired by King Balak of Moab to curse Israel. (Numbers 22–25, 31; Psalm 106; 2 Pet. 2:15).
בָּלָק בֶּן־צִפּוֹר	ba·**laq** ben-tsip·**por**	n. Balak son of Zippor, king of Moab who hired Balaam to curse Israel. (Num. 22-24; Rev. 2:14).
בְּמִדְבַּר	be·mid·**bar**	n. Numbers; 4th book of Torah, so named (in English) because of the account of the census of the people in chapters 1, 3, 4 and 26. *Bemidbar* means "in the wilderness."
בְּנֵי בְלִיַּעַל	be·**nei** bli·ya·'al	n. pl. Base fellows. Evil people. Children of the devil.
בִּנְיָמִין	bin·ya·**min**	n. Benjamin; 12th son of Jacob. one of the twelve tribes of Israel. *Binyamim* means "son of (the) right (hand)." (Gen. 35:18; Rom. 11:1).
בְּנֵי נֹחַ	be·**nei** no·**ach**	n. pl. Descendants of Noah; given *Sheva' mitzvot* sometimes called the Noahide Precepts (against idolatry, murder, theft, blasphemy, incest, eating blood, and duty of promoting justice).
בְּנֵי־יִשְׂרָאֵל	be·**nei** yis·ra·**'el**	n. pl. Children of Israel; Israel.
בִּנְיַן יְרוּשָׁלַיִם	bin·yan ye·ru·sha·**lai**·yim	n. "Rebuilding of Jerusalem," the 14th blessing of the *Shemoneh Esreh*.
בְּנִי יְדִידִי	be·**ni** ye·di·**di**	n. Beloved Son. Title for Yeshua the Messiah (Matt. 3:17).
בֵּן	ben	n. Son; member of; a tribe, etc.
בֶּן־אָדָם	ben '·a·**dam**	n. Human being; person; man.
בֶּן־בְּרִית	ben be·**rit**	n. Participant in the covenant; Jew; ally.
בֶּן־חַיִל	ben **chai**·yil	n. Hero; strong man; cp. *Eshet chayil*.

בֶּן יָחִיד	ben ya·**chid**	*n.* Only begotten Son; unique son (John 1:14).
בָּנִים לֵאלֹהִים	ba·**nim** le·lo·**him**	*n. pl.* Sons of God; children of God (John 1:12).
בְּסֵדֶר	be·**se**·der	*idiom.* OK. In order.
בְּסִיַעְתָּע דִשְׁמַיָא	be·si·**ya**'·ta dish·**mai**·ya	*n. phr. Aramaic.* "With the help of Heaven"; or, "With God's help." Abbreviated as **BS"D.**
בְּעֶזְרַת הַשֵּׁם	be·'ez·**rat** hash·shem	*phr.* "With the Help of God"; phrase said before making any future undertaking. Abbr. **B"H.**
בַּעַל	ba·'al	*n.* Master; owner; husband; (spurious) Lord; The Baal Shem Tov (Master of the Good Name) is the founder of *Chassidism.*
בַּעַל-זְבוּב	ba·'al-ze·**vuv**	*n.* Beelzebub; Philistine god (2 Kings 1:2). "Lord of the flies." Derogatory name for Satan.
בַּעַל נֵס	ba·'al nes	*n.* Miracle worker. Wonder worker.
בַּעַל תְּקִיעָה	ba·'al te·**qi**·ah	*n.* The one who blows the Shofar during High Holiday services; Shofar blower.
בַּעַל תְּשׁוּבָה	ba·'al te·shu·**vah**	*n.* Newly religious Jew; penitent; a Jew who returns to the way of the Torah.
בִּקּוּר חוֹלִים	bi·**qur** cho·**lim**	*n.* Visiting the sick.
בַּר	bar	*n. constr.* Son of (Aramaic).
בַּר מִצְוָה	bar mits·**vah**	*n.* Son (bar) of the commandment; man of duty. Normally at the age of 13, the Jewish boy reaches maturity and is thereafter considered responsible for his religious acts. A Bar Mitzvah can be called up to the read the Torah, use *Tefillin* in weekday prayers each morning, and be counted as one of the ten men necessary for *minyan,* the minimum number required for congregational worship service.
בְּרֵאשִׁית	be·re·**shit**	*n.* Genesis; first book of Torah. *Bereshit* means "in the beginning."
בְּרִיאָה	be·ri'·**ah**	*n.* Creation.
בָּרוּךְ	ba·**rukh**	*adj.* Blessed.
בָּרוּךְ הַבָּא	ba·**rukh** hab·**ba**	*phr.* "Welcome!"
בָּרוּךְ הַשֵּׁם	ba·**rukh** ha·**shem**	*phr.* "Thank God!" Abbreviated as **B"H.**
בָּרוּךְ שֶׁאָמַר	ba·**rukh** she·'a·**mar**	*n.* The *Barukh She'amar* is normally included as part of the core service in the synagogue.
בְּרִית	be·**rit**	*n.* Covenant.
בְּרִית מִילָה	be·**rit** mi·**lah**	*n.* Circumcision.

בְּרִית חֲדָשָׁה	be·rit cha·da·**shah**	*n.* New Testament. *B'rit Chadashah* means "New Covenant." Like the *Tanakh*, it can be divided into three main parts: *Gospels/Acts* (corresponding to *Torah*), Letters (corresponding to *Ketuvim*), and Revelation (corresponding to *Nevi'im*).
בְּרִית יְשָׁנָה	be·rit ye·sha·**nah**	*n.* Old Testament; better to use the acronym *Tanakh* among practitioners of Judaism.
בְּרָכָה / בְּרָכוֹת	be·ra·chah / be·ra·**khot**	*n.* Blessing(s). Formula of thanksgiving in Jewish prayers.
בִּרְכוֹת הַשַּׁחַר	bir·**khot** hash·sha·**char**	*n.* Morning prayers / blessings.
בִּרְכוֹת הַתּוֹרָה	bir·**khot** hat·to·**rah**	*n.* Blessings before reading the Torah.
בָּרְכוּ	ba·re·**chu**	*n.* The call to worship in the synagogue; The opening word of a well-established formula, preceding the *Shema* and the *Shemoneh Esreh*.
בִּרְכַּת הוֹרִים	bir·**khat** ho·**rim**	*n.* Parental blessing.
בִּרְכַּת הַמִּינִים	bir·**khat** ham·mi·**nim**	*n.* "Against Heretics," the 12th so-called blessing of *Shemoneh Esreh*, originally directed against Jewish believers in Yeshua the Messiah of Israel.
בִּרְכַּת הַמָּזוֹן	bir·**khat** ham·ma·**zon**	*n.* Grace after meals; bentch (*Yiddish*).
בִּרְכַּת הַנֵּרוֹת	bir·**khat** han·nei·**rot**	*n.* Blessing of the lights; said by the woman of the house as she lights the Sabbath candles.
בִּרְכַּת כֹּהֲנִים	bir·**chat** ko·ha·**nim**	*n.* Priestly blessing. Also called the "Aaronic" blessing. (Num. 6:24-6).
בְּשׂוֹרָה	be·so·**rah**	*n.* Tidings; News; Message.
בְּשָׂמִים	be·sa·**mim**	*n.* Spices used for the *Havdalah* ceremony.
בָּשָׂר	ba·**sar**	*n.* Flesh; meat; body.
בָּשָׂר אֶחָד	ba·**sar** 'e·**chad**	*phr.* "One flesh." (Gen. 2:24); describing the unity of a man and woman through marriage.
בָּשָׂר וָדָם	ba·**sar** va·**dam**	*adj./n.* Flesh and blood; mortal.
בְּשׂוֹרַת הַגְּאֻלָּה	be·so·**rat** hag·ge·'u·**lah**	*n.* Good News of Redemption. Gospels. The four portraits of the Messiah of Israel as given by His messengers. *Basorah* means "good news" and *Geulah* means "redemption."
בַּת / בָּנוֹת	bat / ba·**not**	*n.* Daughter; a *bat mitzvah* is a girl who has reached the age of accountability in Judaism
בַּת-קוֹל	bat·**qol**	*n.* Voice from heaven. *Bat Qol* has been defined as a mysterious voice by which God on occasion communicated to men.
בַּת-שֶׁבַע	bat·**she**·va'	*n.* Bathsheba. "Daughter of an oath."

Hebrew	Transliteration	Definition
גָּאוֹן גְּאוֹנִים	ga·'on / ge·'o·nim	*n.* Gaon. Head of Babylonian academy; hence, Torah scholar; genius; glory; pride.
גְּאֻלָּה	ge·'ul·lah	*n.* Redemption; ransom; freedom. Also refers to the 7th blessing in the *Shemoneh Esreh*.
גִּבּוֹר	gib·bor	*adj.* Mighty. *El Gibbor* is one of the Names of God. *See* the Names of God.
גְּבוּרוֹת	ge·vu·rot	*n.* 2nd blessing of *Shemoneh Esreh* proclaiming God's might.
גְּבוּרָה	ge·vu·rah	*n.* Courage; Strength; fortitude.
גֶּבֶר	ge·ver	*n.* Man; male.
גַּבְרִיאֵל	gav·ri·'el	*n.* Gabriel. Angel sent to Daniel. (Dan. 8:16).
גָּד	gad	*n.* Gad. One of the 12 tribes of Israel (Gen 30:11).
גָּדוֹל	ga·dol	*adj.* Great; big; large.
גִּדְעוֹן	gid·'on	*n.* Gideon, judge of Israel (Judges 6:11).
גְּדֻלָּה	ge·dul·lah	*n.* Greatness.
גּוֹג וּמָגוֹג	gog u·ma·gog	*n.* Gog and Magog (Ezekiel 38-9).
גּוֹי / גּוֹיִם	goy / goy·im	*n.* Gentile; nation.
גֵּט	get	*n.* Divorce (rabbinical Judaism); Bill of divorcement.
גֵּיהִנֹּם	gei·hi·nom	*n.* Gehenna (Jer. 32:35); vision of Hell.
גִּילָה	gi·lah	*n.* Joy.
גֵּר / גֵּרִים	ger / ge·rim	*n. pl.* Proselytes; from *ger*, stranger. *Ger Tsedek* is a righteous convert.
גָּלוּת	ga·lut	*n.* Galut. Exile; banishment; Diaspora.
גָּלִיל	ga·lil	*n.* Galilee; Northern hill country of Israel.
גְּלִילָה	ge·li·lah	*n.* Gelilah: tying up and covering the Sefer Torah as an honor in the synagogue.

גִּימַטְרִיָּא	gi·**mat**·riy·ya	*n.* Gematria. Numeric equivalents of Hebrew letters.
גֹּלֶם	**go**·lem	*n.* Psalm 139:16; robot; automaton.
גְּמִילוּת חֲסָדִים	ge·mi·**lut** cha·sa·**dim**	*n.* Practice of kindness; benevolence.
גִּמֶל	**gi**·mel	*n.* Gimmel. 3rd letter of the Hebrew alphabet having a sound of "g" as in *girl*. Originally represented by a pictograph meaning "foot," "camel," or "pride." Gematria = 3.
גְּמָרָה	ge·**ma**·rah	*n.* Gemara; 2nd part of Talmud (amplification of Mishnah); *Yam ha-Talmud*: ocean of Talmud.
גַּן עֵדֶן	gan 'e·den	*n.* Paradise; Garden of Eden.
גַּנָּב	gan·**nav**	*n.* Ganav; Thief (Rev. 16:15).
גְּנִיזָה	ge·ni·**zah**	*n.* Genizah: repository for discarded sacred writings (usually a storeroom in a synagogue).
גֶּפֶן	**ge**·fen	*n.* Vine.
גֶּפֶן אֱמֶת	**ge**·fen 'e·**met**	*n.* True Vine (John 15:1). *See* the Names of God.
גֶּרֶשׁ / גֵּרְשַׁיִם	**ge**·resh / ger·**shai**·yim	*n.* The apostrophe character used to indicate that the Hebrew characters are to be understood as an abbreviation or in a non-standard manner, as in Gematria or abbreviated phrases.
גֶּשֶׁם	**ge**·shem	*n.* Rain.
גַּת־שְׁמֵנָה	gat-she·mei·**nah**	*n.* Gethsemane. The garden where Jesus prayed and was apprehended by the Temple police.

Hebrew	Transliteration	Definition
דְּבִיר	de·**vir**	*n.* Holy of Holies.
דִּבְרֵי הַיָּמִים	div·**rei** hai·ya·**mim**	*n.* Chronicles, book of the *Ketuvim* in the *Tanakh*. Chronicles documents the history of Judah (i.e., the southern kingdom), and in particular emphasizes the role of King David as the establisher of Temple worship. *Divrei Hayamim* means the "things or words of the days."
דָּבָר	da·**var**	*n.* Word; thing; saying; *Davar Adonai* is the word of the Lord. בְּרֵאשִׁית הָיָה הַדָּבָר. (John 1:1).
דְּבָרִים	de·va·**rim**	*n.* Deuteronomy. Renewal of the Mosaic covenant with blessings for obedience and consequences for disobedience. *Devarim* means "words" and is referred by Jews as the "repetition" of the Torah.
דְּבַר תּוֹרָה	de·**var** **to**·rah	*n.* Devar Torah: a word of Torah; a brief sermon or speech on a religious topic.
דִּבֵּר / דִּבְּרוֹת	di·**ber** / dib·be·**rot**	*n.* Word; commandment.
דְּבֵקוּת	de·ve·**qut**	*n.* Devekut. Attachment or devotion to God (from the Chassidic movement).
דָּגֵשׁ	da·**gesh**	*n.* Dagesh; emphasis; stress. Any Hebrew letter (*except* the gutturals א, ה, ח, ע and ר) can have a dot inside of it called a "dagesh mark." The presence of a dagesh mark may affect the way in which a word is divided into syllables and pronounced. "Begedkephat" letters may take a dagesh *lene* (weak stress) or dagesh *forte* (strong stress).
דּוֹד	dod	*n.* Lover; Uncle.
דָּוִד	da·**vid**	*n.* David; King David. הַמֶּלֶךְ דָּוִד (King David).
דַּיָּן	**dai**·yan	*n.* Judge, esp. Rabbinical judge of a *beit din* (religious court). A *din* is a regulation.
דָּוִד הַמֶּלֶךְ	da·**vid** ham·**me**·lekh	*n.* King David.
דִּינֵי שָׁמַיִם	di·**nei** sha·**mai**·yim	*n. pl.* Laws of Heaven.
דּוּכָן	**du**·khan	*v. Yiddish.* Duchen: to recite the Aaronic blessing (*birkhat kohanim*) from the platform in front of the Holy Ark. In Hebrew, *dukhan* means "platform."
דַּוְקָה	**dav**·qah	*excl.* Davka. Exclamation of surprise with ironic twist; "of all things!," "would you believe?"

דָּנִיֵּאל	da·ni·'el	*n.* 1) Daniel; book of the *Ketuvim* in the *Tanakh*. 2) Adonai's messenger to the exiles who received portentous visions for the future. *Dani'el* means "God is Judge."
דֶּלֶת	**de·**let	*n.* Door.
דָּלֶת	**da·**let	*n.* Dalet. 4th letter of the Hebrew alphabet having a sound of "d" as in *door*. Originally represented by a pictograph meaning "tent door," or "pathway." Gematria = 4.
דָּם	dam	*n.* Blood.
דִּין	din	*n.* Justice. Refers to the 11th blessing of the *Shemoneh Esreh*.
דַּעַת	**da·**'at	*n.* Knowledge; cp. *binah* and *chochmah*. Also refers to the 4th blessing of Shemoneh Esreh.
דַּף יוֹמִי	daf yo·**mi**	*n.* Daf Yomi. Page a day of Talmud; "Daily Page"; the prescribed page of Talmud studied every day by some Orthodox Jews.
דִּקְדּוּק	diq·**duq**	*n.* Grammar.
דְּרוּשׁ	de·**rush**	*n.* Sermon; homiletical interpretation.
דְּרָשׁ	de·rash	*n.* Interpretation; exegesis.
דְּרָשָׁה	de·**ra·**shah	*n.* Drasha. Sermon; learned address.
דֶּרֶךְ אֶרֶץ	**de·**rekh 'e·rets	*phr.* "The way of the land"; correct behavior; good manners; consideration for others.
דַּרְכֵי אֱמוֹרִי	dar·**khei** 'e·mo·**ri**	*n. pl.* Amorite customs; witchcraft; impure mysteries; heathen customs.
דָּת	dat	*n.* Religion.
דָּתִי	da·**ti**	*adj.* Religious.

Hebrew	Transliteration	Definition
הֵא	hey	*n.* Hey. 5th letter of the alphabet having a guttural sound of "h" as in *hay*. Originally represented by a pictograph meaning "behold!" Gematria = 5.
הָאָדָם הָאַחֲרוֹן	ha·'a·**dam** ha·'a·cha·**ron**	*n.* The Second Adam. Title for Yeshua the Messiah (1 Cor. 15:45).
הַבְדָּלָה	hav·**da**·lah	*n.* Havdalah; "distinction;" ceremony marking end of Shabbat; four benedictions: wine, spices, light, etc. *See* Lesson Twelve.
הֶבֶל	**he**·vel	*n.* 1. Abel. Third son of Adam and Eve. 2. Vanity; vapor; breath (Eccl. 1:2).
הֲבֵל הֲבָלִים	ha·**vel** ha·va·**lim**	*n. phr.* "Vanity of vanities" (Eccl. 1:2).
הַגְבָּהָה	hag·ba·**hah**	*n.* Hagbaha: The honor of raising the *Sefer Torah* (briefly) for the congregation to see.
הַגָּדָה	hag·**ga**·dah	*n.* Telling; story; narrative.
הַגָּדָה שֶׁל פֶּסַח	hag·**ga**·dah shel **pe**·sach	*n.* Passover *Haggadah*; recital part of the *seder*.
הַגְּדֻלָּה בַּמָּרוֹם	ha·ge·dul·**lah** bam·ma **rom**	*n. phr.* "The Greatness on High", a euphemism for YHVH (Heb. 1:3).
הַדָּבָר	had·da·**var**	*n.* The Word (of Adonai). בְּרֵאשִׁית הָיָה הַדָּבָר (John 1:1, 14).
הַדְלָקַת הַנֵּרוֹת	had·**la**·qat ha·ne·**rot**	*n. phr.* Lighting of the candles (on Shabbat).
הֲדַסָּה	ha·**das**·sah	*n.* Hadassah, the Hebrew name for Esther (Esther 2:7). *Hadassah* means "myrtle."
הוֹד	hod	*n.* Glory; Splendor; Majesty.
הוֹדָאָה	ho·da·'**ah**	*n.* "Thanksgiving," the 18th blessing of the *Shemoneh Esreh*.
הוֶֹה	ho·**veh**	*n.* Present (tense); derived from the root היה, meaning to be; to exist.
הֲוָיָה	ha·va·**yah**	*n.* Being; existence. *Shem Havayah* is the Name of God.
הוֹרִים	ho·**rim**	*n. pl.* Parents.
הוֹשֵׁעַ	ho·**she**·a'	*n.* Hosea, one of the 12 "Minor" prophets and part of the *Nevi'im*. Adonai's messenger to the northern kingdom during her declining years regarding the love of God despite Israel's failures. *Hoshea'* means "Adonai is Deliverer."

הוֹשַׁעְנָא	ho·sha·'·na	*phr.* Hosanna; from an abbreviation of "O save!" (Psalm 118:25: הוֹשִׁיעָה נָּא)
הוֹשַׁעְנָא רַבָּה	ho·sha·'·na rab·bah	*n.* Hoshana Rabba; Great Hoshana; The 7th day of *Sukkot* special service.
הֲלָכָה	ha·la·khah	*n.* Halakha; Talmudic law regarding rules of conduct; (usually contrasted with *Aggadah*).
הִלֵּל	hil·lel	*n.* Hillel. Jewish student center. Named after the great Rabbi Hillel.
הַלֵּל	hal·lel	*n.* Praise; Praise songs. (Psalms 113-118).
הַלְלוּיָה	ha·le·lu·yah	*phr.* "(you [pl.]) praise the LORD!"
הַמָּשִׁיחַ בֶּן־אֵל חַי	ham·ma·shi·ach ben-'el chai	*phr.* The Son of the Living God; John 6:69.
הִנֵּה	hin·nei	*excl.* Behold! Look!
הִנְנִי	hi·ne·ni	*phr.* "Here I am." הִנְנִי שְׁלָחֵנִי ("Here I am, send me," Isa. 6:8).
הַפְטָרָה	haf·ta·rah	*n.* Haftarah; concluding prophetic section after reciting the Torah on Shabbat or festivals.
הַקָּדוֹשׁ בָּרוּךְ הוּא	haq·qa·dosh ba·ruch hu	*phr.* Name for God: "The Holy One, blessed be He."
הַקָּפוֹת	haq·qa·fot	*n.* The procession around the synagogue of the Sefer Torah during the holiday of *Simchat Torah*.
הַר	har	*n.* Mountain.
הַר הַבַּיִת	har ha·bai·yit	*n.* The Temple Mount.
הָרַחֲמָן	ha·ra·cha·man	*n.* God the merciful One. *See* the Names of God.
הַר סִינַי	har si·nai	*n.* Mount Sinai. The place where Moses was given the Torah from Adonai (Ex. 19:20).
הָרֹעֶה הַטּוֹב	ha·ro·'eh ha·tov	*n.* The Good Shepherd (John 10:11); Title of Yeshua the Messiah.
הַר מְגִדּוֹ	har me·gid·do	*n.* Armageddon. "Hill of Megiddo" (Rev. 16:16).
הִשָּׁאֲרַת הַנֶּפֶשׁ	hash·'a·rat ha·ne·fesh	*n.* Immortality.
הַשְׁגָּחָה	hash·ga·chah	*n.* Providence; God's overarching rule and sovereign purposes; predestination.
הַשִּׁילוּשׁ הַקָּדוֹשׁ	hash·shi·lush haq·qa·dosh	*n.* The Holy Trinity (The Trinity is a Jewish concept!). *See* the Names of God.

Hebrew	Transliteration	Definition
הַשְׂכָּלָה	has·ka·**lah**	*n.* Haskalah; Enlightenment; Jewish education movement.
הַשֵּׁם	hash·**shem**	*n.* HaShem. The Name (of God). Substitute name for YHVH.
הִתְגַּלּוּת	hit·ga·**lut**	*n.* 1) Revelation; Disclosure; 2) In the *B'rit Chadashah*, the revelation of Yeshua the Messiah as given to His emissary *Yochanan* (John).
הַתִּקְוָה	ha·tik·**vah**	*n.* "The hope"; national anthem of Israel.

Hebrew	Transliteration	Definition
וְ	ve	*conj.* Used as a general conjunction meaning "and" and also as a grammatical reversative.
וִדּוּי	vid·**duy**	*n.* Confession.
וָו	vav	*n.* Vav. 6th letter of the Hebrew alphabet having a sound of "v" as in *v*ine. Originally represented by a pictograph meaning "nail," "peg," or "add." Gematria = 6.
וַיִּקְרָא	vai·yiq·**ra**	*n.* Leviticus; Detailed instructions for the ancient priesthood regarding how Israel might approach God by means of the rituals in the *mishkan* (Tabernacle). *Vaiyiqra* means "And He called."

Hebrew	Transliteration	Definition
זֹהַר	**zo**·har	*n.* Zohar; "Splendor"; A work written by Rabbi Shimon bar Yokhai (2nd century) and his students; mystical commentary on the Torah and the main text of the *Qabbalah*.
זַיִן	**za**·yin	*n.* Zayin. 7th letter of the Hebrew alphabet having a sound of "z" as in *zebra*. Originally represented by a pictograph meaning "plow" or "weapon." Gematria = 7.
זַיִת	**za**·yit	*n.* Olive. Olive tree.
זָכָר	za·**khar**	*adj.* Male (gender). Masculine (grammar).
זֵכֶר לִיצִיאַת מִצְרַיִם	**ze**·kher li·tsi·**at** mits·**rai**·yim	*n.* Exodus memorial; remembering the Exodus from Egypt.
זִכָּרוֹן	zik·ka·**ron**	*n.* Remembrance.
זְכַרְיָה	ze·**khar**·yah	*n.* 1) Zechariah, one of the Minor Prophets in the Nevi'im. 2) A prophet to the restored remnant who speaks of the Messiah's two comings and God's faithfulness to Israel. *Zecharyah* means "God has remembered."
זִלְפָּה	**zil**·pah	*n.* Zilpah. The Syrian woman given by Laban to Leah as a handmaid, a concubine of Jacob, mother of Asher and Gad. *Zilpah* means "weary."
זְמִירוֹת	ze·mi·**rot**	*n. pl.* Zemirot; Table songs for Shabbat.
זְמָן	ze·**man**	*n.* Time; season.
זְנוּת	ze·**nut**	*n.* Zenut. Sexual immorality; prostitution.
זָקֵן	za·**qen**	*n.* Elder; learned man.
זְקֵנִים	ze·qe·**nim**	*n. pl.* Elders.
זָר	zar	*adj.* Strange; foreign; stranger; 'avodah zarah is idolatry.

Hebrew	Transliteration	Definition
חָבִיב	cha·**viv**	*adj.* / *n.* Dear; Beloved.
חֲבִיבוּת	cha·vi·**vut**	*n.* Love; friendliness.
חֲבַקּוּק	cha·vaq·**quq**	*n.* 1) Habakkuk. Eighth book of the Minor Prophets in the Nevi'im. 2) A messenger to Judah regarding her judgment by the Chaldeans. *Chavaquq* means "Embracer."
חָבֵר	cha·**ver**	*n.* Friend; comrade; *Chaverut* means friendship.
חֶבְרָה	chev·**rah**	*n.* Society; association.
חֲבֵרוּת	cha·ve·**rut**	*n.* Friendship.
חַג	chag	*n.* Festival; see the Jewish calendar for a list of the *chagim*.
חַגַּי	chag·**gai**	*n.* Haggai. Tenth book of the Minor Prophets. Haggai ministered to the exiles and spoke of the rebuilding of the Temple and the coming kingdom of Messiah Yeshua. *Chagai* means "Festive."
חַג הַבִּכּוּרִים	chag hab·bik·ku·**rim**	*n.* Feast of Firstfruits; *Chag Habikkurim* is on the 18th of Nisan, the first day following the Shabbat of *Pesach* and is a symbol of the resurrection of the Messiah Yeshua from the dead.
הַג שָׂמֵחַ	chag sa·**me**·ach	*phr.* "Happy Holiday!" Said to express best wishes on a Jewish holiday.
חַגִּים וּזְמַנִּים	chag·**gim** uz·man·**nim**	*n.* Feasts and Festivals. See *Calendar* for a list of the Jewish holidays.
חֶדֶר	**che**·der	*n.* Room; Jewish (elementary) school.
חֹדֶשׁ / חֲדָשִׁים	**cho**·desh / cho·da·**shim**	*n. pl.* Month(s); see *Calendar* for a list of the Jewish months; *Rosh Chodesh* is the first of the month. The names of the months are Babylonian in origin.
חֲדָשָׁה	cha·da·**shah**	*n.* News. *adj.* New.
חַוָּה	chav·**vah**	*n.* Eve. Gen 3:20; The primordial mother and first created female human being by Adonai.
חוֹטֵא	cho·**te**	*n.* Sinner.
חוּמָשׁ	**chu**·mash	*n.* Chumash; Pentateuch; the first five books of Moses, usually bound in a codex (book) form and accompanied with Rashi commentary.

חָזוֹן	cha·**zon**	Revelation; vision; prophecy.
חָזוּת	cha·**zut**	*n.* Prophecy.
חֲזִיר	**cha**·zir	*n.* Pig; swine; glutton.
חַזָּן	**cha**·zan	*n.* Cantor. Singer or chanter of the Torah and *berachot* in the synagogue.
חַזָּנוּת	cha·za·**nut**	*n.* Cantillation; Singing prayers or chanting *Torah* or *Tanakh*
חֲזַק	cha·**zaq**	*phr.* "Well done!" – said on completing a book of Scripture; also: "Courage!"
חֲזַק וֶאֱמַץ	cha·**zaq** ve·'e·**mats**	*phr.* "Be strong and of good courage!"
חֵטְא	chet	*n.* Sin; missing the mark.
חֲטָף	cha·**taf**	*n.* Chataf; compound.
חַי	chai	*adj.* 1) Alive; living; Fresh; new; creation. 2) *n.* A pendant with these letters worn as jewelry.
חַיִּים	**chai**·yim	*n.* Life.
לְחַיִּים	le·**chai**·yim	*phr.* "To Life!"
חֵית	chet	*n.* Chet. 8th letter of the Hebrew alphabet having a guttural sound of "ch" as in Ba*ch*. Originally represented by a pictograph meaning "tent wall" or "fence." Gematria = 8.
חָכָם	cha·**kham**	*n.* Wise man; learned man; Torah scholar.
חָכְמָה	**chokh**·mah	*n.* Wisdom; cleverness; cp. *binah* and *da'at*.
חָכְמַת שְׁלֹמֹה	**chokh**·mat she·**lo**·mo	*n.* The Wisdom of Solomon. Book of the Apocrypha.
חֹל	chol	*adj.* Profane; ordinary; a *yom chol* is an ordinary day, as opposed to a sacred day
חַלָּה	**chal**·lah	*n.* Challah. Shabbat bread.
חֹל הַמּוֹעֵד	chol ha·mo·**'ed**	*n.* Intermediate day during a festival; "semi-festival" days.
חִלּוּל הַשֵּׁם	chi·**lul** ha·**shem**	*n.* Bringing God's Name into disgrace; scandal; this is the opposite of *qiddush hashem*, martyrdom.
חָמֵץ	cha·**mets**	*n.* Leavened bread; yeast.

חָמֵשׁ מְגִלּוֹת	cha·**mesh** me·gil·**lot**	*n.* The Five Scrolls (often referred to as simply *megillot*) containing *Song of Songs, Ruth, Lamentations, Ecclesiastes,* and *Esther.*
חֲמִשָּׁה חֻמְשֵׁי תּוֹרָה	cha·mish·**shah** chum·**shei** to·rah	*n.* The five books of the *Torah.* Five fifths of the Torah. *Chumash.*
חֲמִשִּׁים	cha·mish·**shim**	*n./adj.* Fifty.
חֲנוֹךְ	cha·**noch**	*n.* Enoch, who, along with Elijah, was "translated" into heaven and never physically died (see Gen. 5:24 and 2 Kings 2:11).
חֵן	chen	*n.* Grace; Favor; loveliness.
חַנּוּן	chan·**nun**	*adj.* Gracious.
חֲנֻכָּה	cha·**nuk**·kah	*n.* Chanukah. "Dedication." Often called Festival of Lights. Begins on Kislev 25 and lasts for eight days. The holiday recognizes the Maccabean victory of a small army over the Assyrian-Greek forces in 164 B.C.E. and the rededication of the Temple. The celebration is marked by lighting candles in a *chanukiyah,* spinning dreidels, eating latkes, and retelling the story of the power of the spirit.
חֲנֻכִּיָּה	cha·nu·**kiy**·yah	*n.* Chanukiyah; The eight-branched menorah, with a place for a ninth candle (shamash) that lights the others, especially designed for Chanukah.
חֲנֻכַּת הַבַּיִת	cha·nuk·kat ha·**bai**·yit	*n.* Dedication of a house, especially by nailing up a *mezuzah* on the doorpost and reciting the appropriate blessing.
חַס וְשָׁלוֹם	chas ve·sha·**lom**	*excl.* "God forbid!" "Perish the thought!" Lit. "Mercy and peace!"
חֶסֶד	**che**·sed	*n.* Grace; favor; lovingkindness; generous deed.
חֶסֶד שֶׁל אֱמֶת	**che**·sed shel 'e·**met**	*n phr.* Unselfish act of kindness, especially towards the dead who can never repay.
חָסִיד	chas·**sid**	*n.* Chassid. Pious man.
חֲסִידוּת	chas·si·**dut**	*n.* Piety; Chassidism.
חֲסִידֵי אֻמּוֹת הָעוֹלָם	cha·si·**dei** 'u·mot ha·'o·**lam**	*phr.* "Benevolent Gentiles." Non-Jews who have protected and helped the Jewish people, especially in times of persecution or suffering, such as the Holocaust.
חֲסִידִים	chas·si·**dim**	*n.* Chassidim. Modern movement from the teachings of Rabbi Israel Baal Shem Tov (1700-1760) stressing personal heartfelt experience of God. The *yetser ha ra* (evil impulse) must be mastered by *chokhmah, binah,* and *da'at.*

חֻפָּה	chup·pah	*n.* Chuppah. Wedding canopy. Used during the wedding ceremony and forming a sacred space in the center of the *Bimah*. It symbolically represents the bridal chamber, where the couple would go after the wedding to consummate the marriage.
חֲרֵדִי	cha·re·**di**	*n.* Ultra-Orthodox Jew.
חֵרוּת	che·**rut**	*n.* Liberty; freedom. *Pesach* is sometimes called *Chag ha cherut.*
חֵרֶם	che·**rem**	*n.* Ban; destruction; object consecrated to te Temple; excommunication.
חֲרֹסֶת	cha·**ro**·set	*n.* Sweet spread eaten at *Pesach* during seder. A mixture of apples, raisons, nuts, and wine served at the seder to represent mortar on the seder plate.
חֶשְׁבּוֹן הַנֶפֶשׁ	chesh·bon ha·**ne**·fesh	*n.* Soul-searching; self-accounting; traditionally associated with the *teshuvah* season between *Rosh Hashanah* and *Yom Kippur.*
חֻצְפָּה	**chuts**·pah	*n.* Nerve; Gall; brazen effrontery; cheek.
חֶשְׁוָן	**chesh**·van	*n.* Second month; *See* Jewish calendar.
חֹשֶׁךְ	**cho**·shekh	*n.* Darkness; (John 1:5).
חֹשֶׁן	**cho**·shen	*n.* Breastplate (of the high priest), worn over the *ephod* containing the *Urim and Tummin.* This breastplate is also called *Choshen mishpat* (breastplate of judgment).
חָתָן	cha·**tan**	*n.* Bridegroom.
חָתָן בְּרֵאשִׁית	cha·**tan** be·rei·**shit**	*n.* "Bridegroom of Genesis"; honor of being called up to open the Torah reading cycle on *Simchat Torah*, usually given to a strong member of the synagogue.
חָתָן תּוֹרה	cha·**tan** **to**·rah	*n.* Bridegroom of Torah; honor of being called up to close the Torah reading cycle at the synagogue.
חֲתוּנָה	cha·tu·**nah**	*n.* Jewish wedding. *Chatan* is the groom; *Kalah* is the bride; *Edim* are witnesses.

Hebrew	Transliteration	Definition
טְבִילָה	te·vi·**lah**	*n.* Tevilah. Baptism; Immersion. The act of taking a ritual bath in a *miqveh* of running water, usually to cleanse from impurity (e.g., after menstruation). Complete immersion is also normally required for proselytes on being accepted into Judaism.
טֵבֵת	te·vet	*n.* Tevet. 10th month of the Jewish calendar. See Calendar.
טָהוֹר	ta·**hor**	*adj.* Clean; pure; innocent. (Psalm 51:10). *Lev tahor* is a clean or pure heart. The red heifer is said to cleanse from tumah (Num. 19:2).
טָהֲרוֹת	ta·ho·**rot**	*n.* Uncleanliness; ceremonial defilement.
טוֹב	tov	*adj./n.* Good; right; pleasant; happy.
ט״וּ בִּשְׁבָת	tu bish·vat	*n.* Tu Bishvat; 15th day of Shevat; New Year for trees; Israeli Arbor Day; usually marks first day of spring in Israel. (Note the use of the *gerashim* to indicate the number 15).
טוּמְאָה	tum·'**ah**	*n.* Impurity; filth. Ceremonial defilement.
טֵית	tet	*n.* Tet. 9th letter of the Hebrew alphabet having a sound of "t" as in *t*all. Originally represented by a pictograph meaning "basket" or "snake." Gematria = 9.
טַלִּית	tal·**lit**	*n.* Tallit. Prayer shawl worn during Shacharit services. (Num. 15:38-39). Includes "fringes" or tsitsit.
טַלִּית קָטָן	tal·lit qa·**tan**	*n.* Four-cornered garment worn under a shirt with tassels (tsitsit). Also known as *arba kanfot*.
טָעִים	ta·**im**	*adj.* Tasty.
טַעַם / טַעֲמִים	ta·'**am** / ta·'a·**mim**	*n.* Accent mark(s); Stress; Accent marks were probably introduced by Ezra the Scribe and made part of the Masoretic text by Aaron Ben Asher.
טַעֲמֵי הַמִּקְרָא	ta·'a·**mei** ham·miq·**ra**	*n. pl.* Bible accent marks; trope; cantillation signs; placed above or below the words of the *Tanakh*. Serve as musical notes, tone syllable identifiers, and marks of punctuation (e.g., pausal, disjunctive).
טְרֵפָה	te·re·**fah**	*adj./n.* Treyf; Non-Kosher; literally "torn." Since meat torn by wild animals is forbidden under the Jewish dietary laws, treyf means "non-kosher" or "not fit" to be eaten by Jews.

Hebrew	Transliteration	Definition
יִגְדַּל	yig·**dal**	*n.* Yigdal. Poem recited during the Shacharit service. Summarizes the 13 principles of faith of Moses Maimonides "Ani Ma'amin."
יָהּ	yah	*n.* God. *See* Names of God.
יְהוּדָה	ye·**hu**·dah	*n.* Judah. The fourth son of Jacob and patriarch of the tribe Judah. Also the name for the southern kingdom of ancient Israel.
יַהֲדוּת	ya·ha·**dut**	*n.* Judaism; Jewry.
יְהוּדִי	ye·hu·**di**	*adj.* Jewish; Judean; Jew.
יְהוֹשֻׁעַ	ye·**ho**·shu·a'	*n.* Joshua: Book of the *Nevi'im* in the *Tanakh*. The name *Yehoshua* means "the Lord saves."
יְיָ	'a·do·**nai**	*n.* God. Substitute for YHVH.
יוֹאֵל	yo·'**el**	*n.* Joel. 1) 2nd book of the Minor Prophets in the *Nevi'im*. 2) Adonai's messenger to Judah during her declining years regarding the great Day of the Lord and the judgment of the nations. *Yo'el* means "Adonai is God."
יוֹבֵל	yo·**vel**	*n.* Jubilee. 50th year as sabbatical for the land and the liberation from all obligations.
יוֹד	yod	*n.* Yod. 10th letter of the Hebrew alphabet having a sound of "y" as in *yes*. Sometimes functions as a "consonantal vowel." Originally represented by a pictograph meaning "arm and hand" or "deed." Gematria = 10. Sometimes pronounced "Yud."
יוֹחָנָן	yo·cha·**nan**	*n.* John. *Yochanan*. "God gives grace." Name of a *shaliach* of Yeshua.
יוֹם	yom	*n.* Day.
יוֹם הָעַצְמָאוּת	yom ha·'ats·ma·'**ut**	*n.* Israeli Independence Day, Iyyar 5th (on May 14th 1948, Israel was declared a nation).
יוֹם כִּפּוּר	yom kip·**pur**	*n.* Day of Atonement. Yom Kippur; 10th Tishri; Climax of the ten day period of repentance (Days of Awe) that begins with Rosh Hashannah and ends with the Day of Judgment.
יוֹם רִאשׁוֹן	yom ri·**shon**	*n.* Sunday; the first day of the week. See Jewish calendar.
יוֹחָנָן הַמַּטְבִּיל	yo·cha·non ham·mat·**bil**	*n.* John the Baptist.
יוֹם טוֹב	yom **tov**	*n.* Holiday; Jewish religious day or festival. See Calendar. Cp. *Yom Chol.*

יוֹנָה	yo·nah	n. 1) Jonah, book of the *Nevi'im* in the *Tanakh*. 2) A messenger to the northern Kingdom, Jonah tells the story of God's love for the goyim -- and Israel's mission to be a light unto the nations. *Yonah* means "dove."
יְסוֹד	ye·sod	n. Ground. Foundation; *Hayasod* means "the foundation."
יוֹסֵף	yo·sef	n. Joseph. "Adonai will add." 1) The eldest son of Jacob by Rachel and the father of Manasseh and Ephraim (Gen. 30:24). A portrait of Messiah.
יָמִים נוֹרָאִים	ya·mim no·ra·'im	n. pl. Days of Awe; Ten days from *Rosh Hashanah* to *Yom Kippur* marking personal and corporate *teshuvah*.
יִזְכֹּר	yiz·kor	n. Memorial prayer; a memorial service in the synagogue.
יְחֶזְקָאל	ye·chez·qi·'el	n. 1) Ezekiel, part of the Nevi'im in the *Tanakh*; 2) Adonai's messenger to the exiles about the judgment on Jerusalem. *Yechezkiel* means "God Strengthens."
יָחִיד	ya·chid	adj. Individual; unique; one of a kind. Yeshua the Messiah is called *Ben Yachid* (John 1:14).
יַיִן	ya·yin	n. Wine.
יָם	yam	n. Sea; Ocean; Lake
יַם־סוּף	yam suf	n. Red Sea. Sea of Reeds. (Ex. 13:18). *Suf* means reed, rush, or water plant.
יַעֲקֹב	ya·'a·qov	n. Jacob. The son of Isaac, grandson of Abraham, and the father of the 12 patriarchs of the tribes of Israel. *Ya'aqov* means "heel holder" or "supplanter"; later he was renamed "Israel" ("God prevails") by Adonai (Gen. 32:28).
יֹפִי	yo·fi	Excl. Excellent! Very good!
יְצִיאַת מִצְרַיִם	ye·tsi·'at mits·rai·yim	n. The Exodus from Egypt.
יִצְחָק	yits·chaq	n. Isaac. The son of Abraham by Sarah his wife (Gen. 17:9) and the father of Jacob and Esau. One of the three patriarchs of national Israel. *Yitschaq* means "he laughs."
יֵצֶר	ye·tser	n. Inclination; Impulse.
יֵצֶר טוֹב	ye·tser tov	n. Good impulse; feeling to do good.
יֵצֶר רָע	ye·tser ra'	n. Evil impulse; inclination to do evil or perform wicked acts.

יְרֵא שָׁמַיִם	ye·re sha·**mai**·yim	*n.* God-fearing man.
יִרְאָה	yir·**'ah**	*n.* Fear; reverence.
יִרְאַת הַשֵּׁם	yir·**'at** hash·shem	*n.* Fear of God; piety.
יִרְאַת שָׁמַיִם	yir·**'at** sha·**ma**·yim	*n.* Fear of Heaven; piety.
יְרוּשָׁלַיִם	ye·ru·sha·**lai**·yim	*n.* Jerusalem. Also known as the City of David, Zion, Salem, Ariel, Jebus, the "City of God," the "holy city," comes to designate heaven itself (Heb. 12:22-23). *Jerusalem* means "foundation of peace."
יָרֵחַ	ya·**re**·ach	*n.* Moon.
יְרֵחוֹ	ye·re·**cho**	*n.* Jericho. First city conquered by Joshua upon entrance to the promised land.
יִרְמְיָהוּ / יִרְמְיָה	yir·me·**ya**·hu / yir·me·**yah**	*n.* 1) The book of Jeremiah, part of the *Nevi'im* in the *Tanakh.* 2) Adonai's messenger to Judah during her final years before falling to the Babylonians. *Yirmeyahu* means "Adonai will Lift Up."
יֵשׁוּעַ	ye·**shu**·a'	*n.* Jesus. The proper name for YHVH in the flesh; the Messiah and rightful King of the universe. *Yeshua* means "YHVH saves" (Matt. 1:21).
יֵשׁוּעַ בֶּן־דָּוִד	ye·**shu**·a' ben-da·vid	*n.* Yeshua, Son of David. Title for the Messiah. *See* the Names of God.
יְשׁוּעָה	ye·shu·**'ah**	*n.* Help; deliverance; victory.
יְשַׁעְיָה	ye·sha'·**yah**	*n.* Isaiah. Alternate name for *Yesha'yahu.*
יְשַׁעְיָהוּ	ye·sha'·**ya**·hu	*n.* 1) The book of Isaiah, part of the *Nevi'im* in the *Tanakh.* 2) Adonai's messenger to Judah during her declining years regarding the coming Messiah and Israel's true King. *Yesha'yahu* means "Adonai is Salvation."
יְשִׁיבָה	ye·**shi**·vah	*n.* Yeshiva; oldest institute of Jewish learning. Rabbinical seminary.
יִשְׂרָאֵל	yis·ra·**'el**	*n.* Israel. The name given to Jacob by the Angel of the LORD at Peniel ("God prevails") by Adonai (see Gen. 32:28). The land of Israel is *Erets Yisrael.*
יְשֻׁרוּן	ye·shu·**run**	*n.* Jeshurun; Poetic name for Israel (Deut. 32:15).
יִשָּׂשכָר	**yis**·sa·char	*n.* Issachar. One of the twelve tribes of Israel (Gen. 30:18). (The second Sin is silent.)
יִשְׁתַּבַּח	**yish**·ta·bach	*n.* From *Shacharit* services; poem of praise; part of *Barukh She'amar.*

כ

Hebrew	Transliteration	Definition
כָּבוֹד	ka·**vod**	*n.* Glory; honor; wealth. The *shoresh* (root) with its derivatives occurs 376 times in the *Tanakh*.
כִּבּוּד אָב וָאֵם	kib·**bud** ʼav va·ʼem	*n. phr.* Honoring parents. Honoring father and mother.
כֹּהֵן	ko·**hen**	*n.* Kohen. Priest. The priest and his descendants, traditionally considered to be directly descended from Aaron, but first used in the *Tanakh* in reference to *Melchi-Tsedeq* (Gen. 14:18).
כֹּהֵן גָּדוֹל	ko·**hen** ga·**dol**	*n.* High Priest. *Kohen Gadol*. The Kohen Gadol wore the "robe of the ephod," the "breastplate of judgment" (with the Urim and Thummim), and the "mitre," or upper turban, with a gold plate in front engraved with "Holiness to the Lord," fastened to it. To the high priest alone it was permitted to enter the *Qodesh Haqodashim* (Holy of Holies), which he did only once a year, on *Yom Kippur*.
כְּהֻנָּה	ke·hun·**nah**	*n.* Priesthood; office.
כֹּהֲנִים	ko·ha·**nim**	*n. pl.* Kohenim. Priests.
כּוֹלֵל	ko·**lel**	*n.* Kolel. Community.
כַּוָּנָה	ka·van·**nah**	*n.* Kavannah. Intention; Inner disposition; Chief requirement for prayer and worship, as well as for acts of *mitzvot*. Inner concentration during prayer; heartfelt direction in prayer.
כּוּתִים	ku·**tim**	*n. pl.* Samaritans; Also: those who oppose Jewish teachings.
כֹּל	kol	*adj.* All; everything.
כָּל-	kol	*adj. (construct form)* All; everything.
כָּל הַכָּבוֹד	kol hak·ka·**vod**	*phr.* "All the glory!" Used idiomatically to express praise or congratulations for an achievement.
כַּלָּה	**kal**·lah	*n.* Bride; Engaged girl.
כֹּל-יָכֹל	kol-ya·**khol**	*adj.* Omnipotent. "Able to do all."
כָּל נִדְרֵי	kol **nid**·rei	*n.* Kol Nidre; Disavowal of any oaths made under coercion; recited on eve of *Yom Kippur*. The prayer asks for release from all vows made henceforth as a historical protective device for Jews forced to make vows to other religions in order to save their lives.

כְּלֵי קֹדֶשׁ	ke·lei **qo**·desh	*n. pl.* Sacred objects used in the Temple; generally any sacred objects (e.g., *Sefer Torah, Siddur*, etc.)
כֵּן	ken	*part.* Yes.
כְּנֵסִיָּה	ke·ne·si·yah	*n.* Church; assembly; meeting.
כְּנֶסֶת	ke·**nes**·set	*n.* Knesset (Israel's Parliament); Assembly; Congress.
כְּנֶסֶת הַגְדֹלָה	ke·**nes**·set hag·ge·do·**lah**	*n. Great Knesset;* Great Assembly; Sanhedrin.
כְּנַעַן	ke·na·**an**	*n.* Canaan.
כֵּס	kes	*n.* Throne; Chair.
כִּסֵּא	ki·se	*n.* Throne.
כִּסֵּא הַכָּבוֹד	ki·**se** hak·ka·**vod**	*n.* Throne of God.
כִּסְלֵו	kis·**lev**	*n.* Kislev; 3rd month of the Hebrew civil calendar. See Hebrew calendar.
כֶּסֶף	**ke**·sef	*n.* Money; Silver. Mammon.
כַּף / כַך	kaf / khaf	*n.* Kaf / Khaf. 11th letter of the Hebrew alphabet having the a sound of "k" as in *kite* (without the dagesh, "ch" as in ba*ch*). Originally represented by a pictograph meaning "palm" (of a hand) or "open." Gematria = 20. Transliterated as "k(h)." Khaf also has a sofit (final) form (ך).
כִּפָּה	kip·**pah**	*n.* Kippah. Skullcap; Worn as a sign of respect and religious observance in the synagogue. Also known as a *yarmulke* (Yiddish).
כִּפּוּר	kip·**pur**	*n.* Atonement; Forgiveness.
כַּפָּרָה	kap·pa·**rah**	*n.* Forgiveness. *Yom Kippur* custom is based on the idea of ransom, one life for another. After reciting from the Book of Job (33:23-24), a rooster (for men) or a hen (for women) is swung three times over the heads of the penitent and the following is said: "This is in exchange for me you, this is instead of you, this is *kapparah* for you. This rooster will go to its death, but you will go forward to a good life and into *shalom*."
כְּפַר-נַחוּם	ke·far-na·**chum**	*n.* Capernaum. In the *B'rit Chadashah*, the city where Yeshua did much of His ministry. "Village of Nachum."
כַּפֹּרֶת	kap·**po**·ret	*n.* Cover upon the Holy Ark; cover; curtain.

Hebrew	Transliteration	Definition
כְּרוּב / כְּרוּבִים	ke·**ruv** / ke·ru·**vim**	n. Cherub/ Cherubim. Heavenly creatures (angels) who guarded the way to the Tree of Life in the Garden of Eden (Gen. 3:24)
כְּשָׁפִים	ke-sha·**fim**	n. Witchcraft; superstitious practices.
כָּשֵׁר	ka·**sher**	adj. Kosher; Good; Approved; Ritually correct; Conforming to Jewish dietary laws.
כַּשְׁרוּת	kash·**rut**	n. Dietary laws; also: keeping kosher; kosher foods in general.
כְּתַב יָד	ke-tav **yad**	n. Handwriting.
כְּתַב הַקֹּדֶשׁ	ke-tav haq·**qo**·desh	n. Holy writings; Scriptures.
כְּתַב רָהוּט	ke-tav ra·**hut**	n. Cursive writing.
כִּתְבֵי הַקֹּדֶשׁ	kit·vei haq·**qod**·desh	n. The Holy Bible. Tanakh.
כְּתָב מְרֻבָּע	ke-tav me-ru·**ba'**	n. Hebrew square script.
כְּתֻבָּה	ke-tu·**bah**	n. Marriage contract. Traditional Jewish marriage contract, which spells out the contractual responsibilities of the groom to the bride, often written in beautiful Hebrew calligraphy.
כָּתוּב	ka·**tuv**	n. Biblical verse; pasuq.
כְּתוּבִים	ke-tu·**vim**	n. Ketuvim. Writings; 3rd major part of Tanakh. The word Ketuvim is the plural form of Ketav, or writing. The Ketuvim, or Hebrew literary books, are subdivided into three major parts: Wisdom Literature, Megillot (scrolls), and Histories (which, somewhat strangely, includes Daniel, a prophetic book).
כְּתוּבִים אַחֲרוֹנִים	ke-tu·**vim** a-cha-ro·**nim**	n. Apocrypha. Books such as Ecclesiasticus by Ben Sira, discovered in a Genizah. Also called Sefarim Chitsonim (outside books), that is, books excluded from the Tanakh.
כֹּתֶל מַעֲרָבִי	ko·**tel** ma·'a·ra·**vi**	n. West Wall; Kotel. "Wailing Wall"; Remnant of the western wall of the Temple in Jerusalem. Part of the wall enclosing Herod's Temple is still standing in the old section of Jerusalem. This part of the wall has been regarded as sacred ever since the Talmudic period and has served as a place of pilgrimage for Jews from all parts of the world.
כֶּתֶר	**ke**·ter	n. Crown; Diadem.
כֶּתֶר תּוֹרָה	**ke**·ter **to**·rah	n. Crown of Torah; artistic silver crowns used to adorn the Sefer Torah in the synagogue.

Hebrew	Transliteration	Definition
לְ-	le-	*prep.* To; unto; for; marks grammatical object.
לֵאָה	**le·**'ah	*n.* Leah. The daughter of Laban, first wife of Jacob, and mother of Reuben, Simeon, Levi, Judah, Issachar, Zebulun, and Dinah. One of the four Matriarchs of the 12 tribes of Israel.
לָבָן	la·van	*n.* Laban. The son of Bethuel, brother of Rebekkah, and father of Leah and Rachel (Gen. 24:29).
ל״ג בְּעֹמֶר	lag be·**'o·**mer	*n.* 32nd day of counting the Omer (from Pesach to Sukkot). Semi-holiday en route to Sukkot.
ל״ו צַדִּיקִים	**la·**med vav tsad·di·**qim**	*n.* Lamed-Vav Tsaddikim. 36 hidden saints held to keep God from destroying the world on account of their virtue and faith. Note the use of the *gereshim.*
לֹא	lo	*adv.* Not; no.
לֹא עָלֵינוּ	lo '**a·lei·**nu	*phr.* "Not upon us!" May it not happen to us!
לֵב	lev	*n.* Heart; core; center.
לֵבָב	le·vav	*n.* Heart.
לָבָן	la·**van**	*n./adj.* White.
לְבָנוֹן	**le·**va·non	*n.* Lebanon.
לֵוִי	le·**vi**	*n.* Levi. 3rd son of Jacob and patriarch of the tribe of Levi (Gen. 29:34).
לוּחַ שָׁנָה	**lu·**ach sha·**nah**	*n.* Calendar.
לְוִיִּים	le·viy·**yim**	*n. pl.* Levites.
לוּלָב	lu·**lav**	*n.* Lulav. Palm branch used in *Sukkot.*
לֶחֶם	**le·**chem	*n.* Bread.
לֶחֶם הַחַיִּים	**le·**chem ha·**chai·**yim	*n.* Bread of Life. A title for Yeshua the Messiah (John 6:48).
לֶחֶם חַיִּים	**le·**chem **chai·**yim	*n.* Living Bread. A title for Yeshua the Messiah (John 6:51).
לֶחֶם הַפָּנִים	**le·**chem ha·pa·**nim**	*n.* Bread of Presence; Showbread in the Sanctuary.

מל

לַיְלָה	lai·lah	*n.* Night.
לַיְלָה טוֹב	lai·lah tov	*phr.* "Good Night!"
לֵיל מְנוּחָה	leil me·nu·chah	*n.* Good Night! "Restful night!"
לִילִית	li·lit	*n.* Lilith; queen of demons.
לְכָה דוֹדִי	le·khah do·di	*n.* Lechah Dodi; Song/poem; welcome the Shabbat.
לָמֶד	la·med	*n.* Lamed. 12th letter of the Hebrew alphabet having a sound of "l" as in *look*. Originally represented by a pictograph meaning "staff," "goad," or "control." Gematria = 30.
לַמְדָן	lam·dan	*n.* Learned man.
לָמָּה	lam·mah	*part.* Why?
לָמוּד	la·mud	*adj.* Learned; skilled.
לְמַעַן	le·ma·'an	*conj.* For the sake of.
לְמַעַן הַשֵּׁם	le·ma·'an hash·shem	*n. phr.* "For the sake of God."
לִפְנֵי	lif·nei	*prep.* Before.
לִפְנֵי וְלִפְנִים	lif·nei ve·lif·nim	*n.* In the presence of the Holy of Holies.
לְשֵׁם שָׁמַיִם	le·shem sha·mai·yim	*phr.* "For the sake of heaven"; for pure motives. For the Name of God; in honor of God.
לַשָּׁנָה הַבָּאָה	la·sha·nah ha·ba·'ah	*phr.* "Next year in Jerusalem."
לָשׁוֹן	la·shon	*n.* Tongue; speech; language.
לְשׁן הַקֹּדֶשׁ	le·shon haq·qo·desh	*n.* Hebrew. The holy tongue or language
לְשׁן הָרַע	le·shon ha·ra'	*n.* Evil gossip; Slander.

Hebrew	Transliteration	Definition
מְאֹד	me·'od	*adv.* Very; much; entirely.
מֵאָה	me·ah	*n.* Hundred; century.
מַאֲמִין	ma·'a·min	*n.* Believer.
מַבּוּל	mab·bul	*n.* Flood.
מִגְדַּל בָּבֶל	mig·dal ba·vel	*n.* Tower of Babel.
מַגִּיד	mag·gid	*n.* Preacher.
מְגִלּוֹת יָם הַמֶּלַח	me·gil·lot yam ham·me·lach	*n.* The Dead Sea Scrolls (DSS).
מְגִלַּת אֶסְתֵּר	me·gil·lat es·ter	*n.* Esther; one of the five scrolls (part of the *Ketuvim*). The story of God's providence in the affairs of the Jews during the time of Xerxes (486-465 B.C.), ruler of Persia. Read during *Purim*.
מָגֵן	ma·gen	*n.* Shield; Protection.
מָגֵן דָּוִד	ma·gen da·vid	*n.* Shield of David. The Star of David (as seen on the Israeli flag, jewelry, etc.).
מִדְבַּר סִינַי	mid·bar si·nai	*n.* The wilderness of Sinai.
מִדָּה כְּנֶגֶד מִדָּה	mid·dah ke·ne·ged mid·dah	*n.* Measure for measure; the punishment fits the crime.
מִדּוֹת	mid·dot	*n.* Rules of interpretation; Rabbinic hermeneutics.
מִדְיָן	mid·yan	*n.* Midian.
מַדְרֵגָה	mad·re·gah	*n.* Spiritual level.
מִדְרָשׁ	mid·rash	*n.* Midrash; Interpretation; exegesis; investigation.
מַה טֹּבוּ	mah to·vu	*n.* Mah Tovu; In the Siddur, speaks of how good it is for brothers to dwell in unity.
מַה נִּשְׁתַּנָּה	mah nish·ta·nah	*n.* Why (is this night) different (from all other nights)? From the four questions asked at a Passover seder, traditionally by the youngest child.
מוֹהֵל	mo·hel	*n.* Circumciser.
מוּסָף	mu·saf	*n.* Musaf. An additional service, usually associated with special Shabbats and festivals.

מוֹסָד	mo·**sad**	*n.* Institution; also, Israeli secret service.
מוּסָר	mu·**sar**	*n.* Musar. Reproof; Correction; Moral Discipline; Ethics.
מוֹעֵד	mo·**ed**	*n.* Appointed time; festival; gathering; set time.
מוֹעֲדִים	mo·a·**dim**	*n. pl.* Feasts; appointed times. See the Jewish calendar for a list of *mo'adim.*
מוֹעֲדִים לְשִׂמְחָה	mo·a·**dim** le·sim·**chah**	*phr.* "A happy holiday!"
מוֹפֵת	**mo**·fet	*n.* Miracle; sign.
מוֹרָא שָׁמַיִם	mo·**ra** sha·**mai**·yim	*n.* Fear of God.
מוֹרֶה	mo·**reh**	*n.* Teacher (masculine).
מוֹרֶה נְבוּכִים	mo·**reh** ne·vu·**khim**	*n.* Guide for the Perplexed. Work of (Aristotelian) Jewish philosophy by Moses Maimondes (1135-1204) [also known as Rambam] that attempted to reconcile Jewish faith and reason.
מוֹשִׁיעַ	mo·**shi**·a'	*n.* Savior.
מוֹשָׁעָה	mo·**sha**·'ah	*n.* Salvation.
מָוֶת	ma·**vet**	*n.* Death.
מִזְבֵּחַ	miz·**bei**·ach	*n.* Altar; place of sacrifice.
מְזוּזָה	me·zu·**zah**	*n.* Mezuzah; scroll (with the Shema written on it) placed on doorpost.
מָזוֹן	ma·**zon**	*n.* Food.
מַזָּל טוֹב	ma·zal **tov**	*n.* Good luck; congratulations!
מִזְמוֹר	miz·**mor**	*n.* Song; hymn; psalm.
מַזִּיק	ma·**ziq**	*n.* Demon; one who harms.
מַחְזוֹר	mach·**zor**	*n.* "Cycle." Prayerbook for the festivals.
מְחַיֶּה	me·**chai**·yeh	*n. Yiddish.* A delight; a joy; "rapture."
מֵחַיִל אֶל חַיִל	me·**cha**·yil 'el **cha**·yil	*phr.* "From strength to strength."
מְחִילָה	me·chi·**lah**	*n.* Forgiveness.

לוֹן

מַחֲלֹקֶת	mach·**lo**·qet	n. Disagreement; Legal and spiritual disagreement between the sages regarding *Talmud*, Bible, etc.
מִיכָאֵל	mi·kha·'el	n. Michael. "Who is like God." Archangel mentioned in Daniel 10:21, Rev. 12:7.
מִיכָה	mi·khah	n. 1) Micah. 6th of the Minor Prophets and part of the Nevi'im. 2) A messenger to Judah during her declining years, Micah warns of judgment and foretells the Messianic kingdom. *Mikhah* means "Who is like Adonai?"
מַיִם	**mai**·yim	n. Water.
מַיִם חַיִּים	**mai**·yim **chai**·yim	n. Fresh water. Also: Living water: a title for Yeshua the Messiah (John 6).
מַכְפֵּלָה	makh·pe·**lah**	n. Machpelah. The location of a burial cave for the patriarchs, near Hebron (Gen. 23:9).
מִכְשׁוֹל	mikh·**shol**	n. Stumbling-block; difficulty.
מַלְאָךְ	mal·'**akh**	n. Angel; Messenger.
מַלְאָךְ הַמָּוֶת	mal·'akh ham·ma·**vet**	n. Angel of Death.
מַלְאָךְ מֵלִיץ	mal·'akh me·**lits**	n. Advocate (1 John 2:1).
מְלָאכָה	me·la·**khah**	n. Work; service.
מַלְאָכִי	mal·'a·**khi**	n. 1) Malachi; one of the Minor prophets in the Nevi'im; 2) A prophet to the restored remnant who speaks of the Lord's love for His erring people and warns of judgment. *Malakhi* means "Messenger of Adonai."
מַלְאָכִים	mal·'a·**khim**	n. Angels; Messengers.
מִלָּה	mil·**lah**	n. Word.
מִלִּים	mil·**lim**	n. pl. Words.
מִלּוֹן	mil·**lon**	n. Dictionary; Lexicon.
מַלְכוּת הָאֱלֹהִים	mal·khut ha·'e·lo·**him**	n. The kingdom of God (John 3:5).
מַלְכוּת הַשָּׁמַיִם	mal·khut hash·sha·**mai**·yim	n. Kingdom of heaven (Matt: 4:17).
מְלָכִים	me·la·**khim**	n. Kings. The book of Kings, part of the Nevi'im in the Tanakh. English Bibles divide Kings into 1st and 2nd Kings.

מֶלֶךְ	me·lekh	*n.* King.
מֶלֶךְ הַיְהוּדִים	me·lekh hai·ye·hu·**dim**	*n.* King of the Jews; Title for Yeshua the Messiah (Matt. 27:37).
מֶלֶךְ מַלְכֵי הַמְּלָכִים	me·lekh mal·**khei** ham·me·la·**khim**	*n.* King of the king of kings. A Title for God.
מֹלֶךְ	mo·lekh	*n.* Molech; Canaanite deity worshipped with human sacrifices
מַלְכִּי־צֶדֶק	mal·ki·**tse**·deq	*n.* Melchizedek. King of Righteousness, King of Salem; Gen. 14:18-20; Psalm 110:4; Heb. 5:6.
מְלַמֵּד	me·la·**med**	*n.* Teacher, usually of religion.
מֵם	mem	*n.* Mem. 13th letter of the Hebrew alphabet having a sound of "m" as in *mom*. Originally a pictograph representing water or chaos. Gematria = 40. Mem also has a sofit (final) form.
מָמוֹן	mam·**mon**	*n.* Mammon; money.
מַמְזֵר	mam·**zer**	*n.* Mamzer. Illegitimate child; bastard.
מַמָּשׁ	mam·**mash**	*n.* Essential thing; reality; concreteness; 2) *adv.* Really; truly ("It was *mamash* a miracle!")
מָן	man	*n.* Manna.
מִן הַשָּׁמַיִם	min hash·sha·**mai**·yim	*phr.* "Heaven-sent."
מִנְהָג	min·**hag**	*n.* Custom; manner; conduct; practice.
מְנוֹרָה	me·no·**rah**	*n.* Menorah; Candlestick. Lampstand. Seven-branched candelabrum that stood in the Temple.
מְנַשֶּׁה	me·**nash**·sheh	*n.* Manasseh. Son of Joseph, grandson of Jacob (Gen. 45:51). A half-tribe, as was Ephraim.
מִנְיָן	min·**yan**	*n.* Minyan. A group of ten bar mitzvah adults necessary for the prayer service.
מָסוֹרָה	ma·so·**rah**	*n.* Massorah; the work of scribal transmission of the *Tanakh* (Masoretic text)
מַסֹרֶת	ma·so·**ret**	*n.* Tradition.
מְסִירוּת	me·si·**rut**	*n.* Devotion.
מְסִירוּת נֶפֶשׁ	me·si·rut **ne**·fesh	*n.* Sacrifice. Unselfish act. Sacrifice of the soul.
מִסְפָּר	mis·**par**	*n.* A number.

מִסְפָּרִים	mis·pa·**rim**	*n. pl.* 1) Numbers; *2)* Numerology; study of numbers and their significance in the Hebrew text.
מָעוֹז צוּר	ma·'oz **tsur**	*n.* "Rock of Ages"; sung after kindling of Chanukkah lights.
מַעֲרִיב	ma·'a·**riv**	*n.* Evening prayer; service for evening prayers.
מַעֲשֶׂה	ma·'a·**seh**	*n.* Deed; Act; Work; Practice.
מַעֲשֵׂה בְרֵשָׁאִית	ma·'a ·seh ve·re·**shit**	*n.* Creation.
מַעֲשֵׂי הַשְּׁלִיחִים	ma·'a·sei hash·she·li·**chim**	*n.* Acts of the Apostles. The works of the *Ruach Haqodesh* (Holy Spirit) in the early church as reported by Luke (Luke 1:3. Acts 1:1). *Ma'asei Hashelichim* means "deeds of the sent ones" in Hebrew.
מַעֲשָׂם טוֹבִים	ma·'a·**sim** to·**vim**	*n. pl.* Good works.
מַעֲשֵׂר	ma·'a·**ser**	*n.* Tithe; tenth.
מַפִּיק	map·**piq**	*n.* Mappiq; Dagesh in final hey.
מַפְטִיר	maf·**tir**	*n.* Maftir. Concluding section of a Torah reading.
מְפָרְשֵׁי הַמִּקְרָא	me·far·**shei** ha·miq·**ra**	*n.* Bible Commentators.
מַפְתֵּחַ	maf·te·**ach**	*n.* Index (of a book).
מַצָּה	**mats**·tsah	*n.* Matzah; unleavened bread. See *Pesach.*
מִצְוָה	**mits**·vah	*n.* Precept; Command; deed of piety or charity.
מִצְוַת עֲשֵׂה	mits·vat 'a·**seh**	*n.* Positive commandment (of the 613 commandments of the *Tanakh*).
מִצְוַת לֹא־תַעֲשֶׂה	mits·vat lo-ta·'a·seh	*n.* Negative commandment (of the 613 commandments of the *Tanakh*); prohibition.
מִצְוֹת	mits·**vot**	*n. pl.* Commandments.
מַצְפּוּן	mats·**pun**	*n.* Conscience; what is hidden.
מִצְרַיִם	mits·**ra**·yim	*n.* Egypt.
מִקְדָּשׁ	miq·**dash**	*n.* Temple; Sanctuary.
מִקְוֶה	miq·**veh**	*n.* Mikveh; purifying bath to remove ceremonial uncleanness; baptismal pool.

מַקָּף	maq·**qaf**	*n.* Hyphen.
מִקְרָא	miq·**ra**	*n.* Bible; reading; recital.
מִקְרָא קֹדֶשׁ	miq·**ra** **qo**·desh	*n.* Biblical holiday.
מִרְיָם	mir·**yam**	*n.* Mary. Miriam. Mother of Yeshua the Messiah (Matt. 1:16).
מָרַן אֲתָא	ma·ran ʼa·**ta**	*Excl. Aramaic.* Maranatha! "Our Lord, come!"
מָרְדְּכַי	**mor**·do·khai	*n.* Mordecai; cousin and adoptive father of queen Esther; son of Jair of the tribe of Benjamin; deliverer under Divine providence of the children of Israel from the destruction plotted by Haman the chief minister of Ahasuerus (Esther 2:7).
מָרוֹר	ma·**ror**	*n.* Maror. Bitter herbs; usually horseradish during a Seder.
מַרְקוֹס	mar·**qos**	*n.* Mark. Emissary of Yeshua the Messiah and author of the gospel of Mark.
מְשֻׁגָּע	me·shug·**ga**ʻ	*adj.* Crazy; mad; insane.
מֹשֶׁה	**mo**·sheh	*n.* Moses. Deliverer of Israel from Egypt, agent through whom Israel received the Torah. (Ex. 2:10).
מֹשֶׁה רַבֵּנוּ	**mo**·sheh ra·**be**·nu	*n.* Moses our Teacher. Honorary title given to Moses.
מָשִׁיחַ	ma·**shi**·ach	*n.* Messiah; The Anointed. Yeshua ben Yosef is the promised Mashiach of Israel.
מָשִׁיחַ בֶּן־דָּוִד	ma·**shi**·ach ben-da·**vid**	*n.* Mashiach ben David. The final deliverer of the Jewish people. Descendant of King David, of the tribe of Judah. Yeshua the Messiah in His second coming.
מָשִׁיחַ בֶּן־יוֹסֵף	ma·**shi**·ach ben-yo·**sef**	*n.* Mashiach ben Yosef. The Messiah from the house of Joseph. One of two Messianic figures which are described in the written and oral traditions of Judaism. *Mashiach ben Yosef* is considered to be a forerunner and harbinger of the final deliverer, *Mashiach ben David.* Christians see Yeshua as the fulfillment of both portraits of Messiah in the *Tanakh* and the oral tradition. Yeshua the Messiah in His first coming as suffering Servant.
מַשְׂכִּיל	mas·**kil**	*adj.* Enlightened.
מִשְׁכָּן	mish·**kan**	*n.* Tabernacle; tent.
מָשָׁל	ma·**shal**	*n.* Proverb; Saying.

מִשְׁלֵי	mish·**lei**	*n.* Proverbs of Solomon; part of the *Ketuvim* of the *Tanakh*. *Mishlei* means "proverbs" or "parables."
מְשֻׁמָּד	me·shum·**mad**	*n.* Apostate (from Judaism). *Shemad* means one who has converted or been baptized.
מִשְׁנָה	mish·**nah**	*n.* Mishnah; earlier part of the Talmud; divided into six orders or parts (*sedarim*) of sixty three tractates.
מִשְׁפָּחָה	mish·pa·**chah**	*n.* Family. By extension, a close association.
מִשְׁפָּט	mish·**pat**	*n.* Justice; Judgment.
מַתִּי	mat·**tai**	*n.* Matthew. Emissary of Yeshua the Messiah and author of the gospel of Matthew.
מַתִּתְיָהוּ	mat·tit·ya·hu	*n.* Matthew. Alternate spelling. Emissary of Yeshua the Messiah and author of the gospel of Matthew. *Mattityahu* means "gift of God."
מַתָּן	mat·**tan**	*n.* Gift.
מַתָּן תּוֹרָה	mat·**tan** to·rah	*n.* Mattan Torah. The giving of the Torah at Sinai. Normally celebrated at *Shavu'ot*.

Hebrew	Transliteration	Definition
נֶאֱמָן	ne·'e·**man**	*adj.* Trustworthy; reliable; faithful.
נֶאֱמָנוּת	ne·'e·ma·**nut**	*n.* Trust; faith.
נְבוּאָה	ne·vu·**ah**	*n.* Prophecy.
נִבּוּל פֶּה	nib·**bul** peh	*n.* Foul language.
נִבְחָר	niv·**char**	*adj.* Elect; Chosen.
נָבִיא	na·vi'	*n.* Prophet.
נְבִיאִם	ne·vi·'**im**	*n.* Prophets. Second main division of the *Tanakh*. The *Nevi'im*, or Hebrew prophetical books, are subdivided into two major parts: four books of the "Former" prophets and 15 books of the "Latter" prophets. Weekly readings are called *Haftarah* portions.
נְבִיאִם רִאשׁוֹנִים	ne·vi·'im ri·sho·**nim**	*n.* Former Prophets. Joshua, Judges, Samuel, and Kings. Part of the *Nevi'im* of the *Tanakh*.
נְבִיאִם אַחֲרוֹנִים	ne·vi·'im 'a·cha·ro·**nim**	*n.* Latter Prophets. Part of the *Nevi'im* of the *Tanakh* consisting of the three main prophets (Isaiah, Jeremiah, and Ezekiel) and the Twelve Minor prophets (*trei asar*).
נֶגֶב	**ne**·gev	*n.* Negev; South; southern region of Israel.
נָגִיד	na·**gid**	*n.* Nagid. Prince; Leader.
נִגּוּן	nig·**gun**	*n.* Niggun; Traditional musical theme for a given service or festival.
נְדָבָה	ne·da·**vah**	*n.* Donation (as to a synagogue).
נוּ	**nu**	*part.* "Well?" "So?"
נָצְרִי	nots·**ri**	*n./adj.* Christian.
נוֹרָא	no·**ra**	*adj.* Feared; Terrible; the High Holidays are called Hayamim Hanora'im, the Days of Awe.
נוּן	nun	*n.* Nun. 14th letter of the Hebrew alphabet having a sound of "n" as in *n*ow. Originally a pictograph representing seed or fish. Gematria = 50. Nun also has a sofit (final) form.

נָזִיר	na·**zir**	*n.* Nazarite; One dedicated to God by vow involving abstinence from intoxicants and from cutting the hair.
נֹחַ	**no**·ach	*n.* Noah.
נָחוּם	na·**chum**	*n.* 1) Nahum, book of the *Nevi'im* in the *Tanakh*. 2) A messenger to Judah during her declining years, Nahum foretells the doom of the Assyrian empire. *Nachum* means "Consolation," or "Comforter."
הַיָּמִים הַנּוֹרָאִם	hai·ya·**mim** han·no·ra·'**im**	*n.* Days of Awe; High Holidays. 10 days from *Rosh Hashanah* to *Yom Kippur*.
נָחוֹר	na·**chor**	*n.* Nahor. Grandfather of the patriarch Abraham (Gen 11:22); 2) Son of Terah and brother of the patriarch Abraham (Gen 11:26).
נְחֶמְיָה	ne·chem·**yah**	*n.* Nehemiah: book of the *Ketuvim* in the *Tanakh*. *Nechemyah* means "consolation of God."
נֹחַם	**no**·cham	*n.* Sorcery; magic.
נָחָשׁ	na·**chash**	*n.* Snake; Serpent.
נְחֻשְׁתָּן	ne·chush·**tan**	*n.* The Brass Serpent.
נַחַת	**na**·chat	*n.* Nachat; Fulfillment; Joy and Pride over something.
נְטִילַת יָדַיִם	ne·ti·**lat** ya·**da**·yim	*n.* Handwashing.
נִיבִים עִבְרִיִּים	ni·**vim** 'iv·ri·**yim**	*n.* Hebrew expressions, such as "barukh hashem," "be'ezrat hashem," "chas veshalom," etc.
נְסִיעָה טוֹבָה	ne·si·'**ah** to·**vah**	*phr.* "Safe Journey!"
נִיסָן	ni·**san**	*n.* Nisan; Name of the 7th month.
נֵס	nes	*n.* Miracle.
נִסִּים	nis·**sim**	*n.* Miracles.
נָכוֹן	na·**chon**	*adj.* Right; Correct.
נְכוֹנוּת	ne·kho·**nut**	*n.* Truth; Correctness; Willingness.
נָעִים	na·'**im**	*adj.* Pleasant; Agreeable; lovely.
נָפִיל	na·**phil**	*n.* Giant.
נִפְלָא	nif·**lah**	*adj.* Wonderful.

נְפִלִים	ne·phi·**lim**	*n.* Nephilim. Giants (Gen 6:4). The word may also be derived from a root signifying "wonder," and hence "monsters."
נַפְתָּלִי	naf·ta·li	*n.* Naphtali. (1) Tribe of Israel descended from a son of the Patriarch *Ya'aqov*.
נֶפֶשׁ	**ne**·fesh	*n.* Self; Soul; Spirit; essence; innermost part.
נֶפֶשׁ חַיָּה	ne·fesh chai·**yah**	*n.* Living Creature.
הַשְׁאָרַת הַנֶפֶשׁ	hash·'a·rat ha·**ne**·fesh	*n.* Immortality.
נֵצַח	**ne**·tsach	*n.* Eternity; Steadfastness.
נִצְחִי	nits·**chi**	*adj.* Eternal.
נַצְרוּת	nats·**rut**	*n.* Christianity.
נֵצֶר	**ne**·tser	*n.* Branch (Isaiah 11:2); descendant.
נָצְרִי	nats·**ri**	*adj.* Christian (lit. from Nazareth).
נָצֶרֶת	na·**tse**·ret	*n.* Nazareth; Town in the Galil where Yeshua the Messiah grew up.
נְקֵבָה	ne·qe·**vah**	*adj.* Feminine; female.
נְקֻדָּה	ne·qud·**dah**	*n.* Vowel point; dot; point.
נַקְדִּימוֹן	naq·di·**mon**	*n.* Nicodemus. *Parush*, member of the Sanhedrin and "teacher in Israel" John 3:1.
נִקּוּד	niq·**qud**	*n.* Niqqud. Punctuation (plural is *niqqudot*).
נֵר	ner	*n.* Candle; Light; Lamp.
נֵר תָּמִיד	ner ta·**mid**	*n.* Ner Tamid; Perpetual Lamp; Ex. 27:20; Lev 24:2: lamp burning in the *Mishkan* (tabernacle); now used as a continual light placed before the *aron qodesh* in the synagogue.
נִשּׂוּאִין	ni·su·'**in**	*n.* Marriage; Jewish wedding.
נְשִׂיאַת כַּפַּיִם	ne·si·'**at** kap·**pa**·yim	*n.* Lifting up the hands (priest's blessing); Aaronic blessing.
נְשָׁמָה	ne·sha·**mah**	*n.* Soul; Breath of life; spirit; living being
נְשָׁמָה יְתֵרָה	ne·sha·**mah** ye·te·**rah**	*n.* Sabbath soul. Extra blessing given during Sabbath observance.

Hebrew	Transliteration	Definition
סַבְלָנוּת	sav·la·**nut**	*n.* Patience.
סֵבֶר	se·ver	*n.* Hope.
סֶגּוֹל	se·**gol**	*n.* Segol. Hebrew vowel mark.
סִדּוּר	sid·**dur**	*n.* Siddur. Prayer book. Arrangement of the book begins with *Shacharit*, *Minchah*, and *Ma'ariv* services, then Shabbat and festival services.
סְדֹם	se·**dom**	*n.* Sodom. City near the Dead Sea destroyed by God (Gen. 10:19, 19).
סֵדֶר	se·der	*n.* Seder. Order; Arrangement; ceremonies of the Passover meal.
סֵדֶר לֵיל פֶּסַח	se·der leil pe·sach	*n.* Passover Seder.
סִדְרָה	**sid**·rah	*n.* Sidrah. "Order." Bible-portion; Parasha; One of 54 divisions of the Torah which are read at the synagogue consecutively until the entire *Torah* is completed.
סוֹד	sod	*n.* Secret.
סוֹף	sof	*n.* End. Finish; אֵין סוֹף (*Ein Sof*) means "without end" and is a Kabbalistic Name for God.
סוֹף פָּסוּק	sof pa·**suq**	*n.* End of verse marker that looks like a colon in the Masoretic text of the *Tanakh*.
סוּף	suf	*n.* Reed. *Yam Suf* is the Sea of Reeds.
סוֹפִית	so·**fit**	*adj.* / *n.* Final (letter); ending letterform of the five Hebrew letters Kaf, Mem, Nun, Pey, and Tsade.
סוֹפֵר	**so**·fer	*n.* Scribe; writer.
סוֹפְרִים	so·fe·**rim**	*n. pl.* Scribes.
סִיּוּם	siy·**yum**	*n.* Siyyum. Celebration over the completion of a *Sefer Torah* scroll.
סִיוָן	si·van	*n.* Sivan. Month of Jewish calendar.
סִינַי	si·**nai**	*n.* Sinai; mountain in the desert between Egypt and Israel where Israel received the Torah from God through Moses.
סִיַעְתָּא דִשְׁמַיָּא	si·**ya**'ta dish·**mai**·ya	*n. phr.* [Aramaic] "Help from Heaven." Abbreviated as **S"D**.

מְלוֹ

סֻכָּה	**suk·**kah	*n.* Sukkah; Hut; Tent; Tabernacle. Temporary structure built for the celebration of *Sukkot* in recognition of the temporary dwellings built by the Jews as they journeyed from Egypt to Canaan.
סֻכּוֹת	suk·**kot**	*n.* Sukkot. Feast of Tabernacles; Fall festival; celebrating the forty years when the people of Israel lived in booths or tents in the desert. Sukkot is one of three pilgrim festivals when Jews were expected to go up to Jerusalem.
חַג הַסֻּכּוֹת	chag has·suk·**kot**	*n.* Feast of Tabernacles. Feast of Booths. See entry for Sukkot, above.
סֶלָה	se·**lah**	*interj.* Selah. Perhaps related to shoresh meaning to lift up (as voices) before a pause. Psalm 3:2, etc.
סִלּוּק	sil·**luq**	*n.* Silluq; Cantillation sign; accent mark in the Masoretic text used for chanting *Tanakh.*
סְלִיחָה	se·li·**chah**	*n.* Forgiveness.
סְלִיחוֹת	se·li·**chot**	*n.* Prayers for forgiveness, esp. said during the "Days of Awe," from *Rosh Hashanah* to *Yom Kippur.*
סְמִיכָה	se·mi·**khah**	*n.* Semikhah. 1) Laying on our hands (upon the head of the sacrifice); 2) Ordination (as of a Rabbi).
סָמֶךְ	**sa·**mekh	*n.* Samekh. 15th letter of the Hebrew alphabet having a sound of "s" as in *s*on. Originally a pictograph representing a staff. Gematria = 60.
סַנהֶדְרִין	san·hed·**rin**	*n.* Sanhedrin. High court of law.
סִפּוּר	sip·**pur**	*n.* Story; Narrative.
סְפִירַת הָעֹמֶר	se·fi·**rat** ha·'o·mer	*n.* Count of the omer for 49 days between *Pesach* and *Shavu'ot* (Lev. 23:16).
סֵפֶר	**se·**fer	*n.* Book. The Jews are sometimes referred to as *Am hasefer*: People of the book.
סֵפֶר תּוֹרָה	**se·**fer **to·**rah	*n.* Sefer Torah. Torah scroll kept in the *aron qodesh* of the synagogue.
סְפָרַדִּי	se·fa·rad·**di**	*n.* Sephardic. Spanish.

Hebrew	Transliteration	Definition
עֶבֶד	'e·ved	*n.* Slave. Servant.
עֶבֶד הַשֵּׁם	'e·ved ha·shem	*n.* Servant of God.
עַבְדוּת	'av·dut	*n.* Slavery; service.
עֲבוֹדָה	'a·vo·dah	*n.* Work; Labor; Worship; Specifically the sacrificial Temple service as performed by the *kohen gadol* (high priest).
עֲבוֹדָה זָרָה	'a·vo·dah za·rah	*n.* Idolatry; in the *Mishnah*, the 8th tractate in the order of Neziqin, dealing with regulations related to idols and idolatry.
עֲבֵרָה	'a·ve·rah	*n.* Sin; Transgression.
עִבְרִי	'iv·ri	*n./ adj.* Hebrew; Jew.
עִבְרִים	'iv·rim	*n. pl.* Hebrews (as a people).
עִבְרִית	'iv·rit	*n.* Hebrew (language).
עַד	'ad	*n.* Eternity.
עֵד	'ed	*n.* Witness.
עֵדוּת	'e·dut	*n.* Testimony; Witness.
עֵדִים	'e·dim	*n. pl.* Witnesses.
עֵדֶן	'e·den	*n.* Delight; Pleasure; Luxury; *Gan Eden* is the Garden of Eden representing paradise.
עוֹבַדְיָה	'o·vad·yah	*n.* Obadiah; Shortest of the prophetic books in the Nevi'im of the Tanakh. *'Ovadyah* means "servant of Adonai."
עוֹז	'oz	*n.* Strength.
עוֹזֵר	'o·zer	*n.* Helper.
עוֹלֶה	'o·leh	*n.* Immigrant to Israel (lit. "one who ascends").
עוֹלָה	'o·lah	*n.* Burnt offering.

עוֹלָם	'o·**lam**	*n.* Eternity; world. Also: everlastingness.
עוֹלָם הָאֱמֶת	'o·**lam** ha·'e·**met**	*n.* The world to come, in which truth will prevail.
עוֹלָם הַזֶּה	'o·**lam** haz·**zeh**	*n. phr.* This present age; this world.
עוֹלָם הַבָּא	'o·**lam** hab·**bah**	*n. phr.* The world to come.
עֲזָאזֵל	'a·za·**zel**	*n.* Azazel. Name of the place where the scapegoat was sent on *Yom* Kippur.
עֶזְרָא	'ez·**ra**	*n.* Ezra; book of the *Ketuvim* in the *Tanakh*. *Ezra* means "help" or "aid."
עֶזְרָתָה	'ez·ra·tah	*n.* Help; aid.
עַיִן	'a·yin	*n.* Ayin. 16th letter of the Hebrew alphabet. Ayin is a guttural letter. Originally a pictograph representing an eye. Gematria = 70.
עַיִן־הָרָע	'a·yin ha·**ra**'	*n.* Evil Eye. Stinginess.
עַיִן טוֹבָה	'a·yin to·**vah**	*n.* Good Eye; Generosity; good will.
עַיִן רָעָה	'a·yin **ra**·'ah	*n.* Evil eye; ill-will.
עִיר	'ir	*n.* City.
עִיר הַקֹּדֶשׁ	'ir haq·**qo**·desh	*n.* The Holy City; Jerusalem.
עַל הַנִּסִּים	'al han·nis·sim	*n.* Al-Ha-Nissim. Passages added to *Chanukkah* and *Purim* prayers. "For the miracles"
עָלָיו הַשָּׁלוֹם	'a·**lav** hash·sha·lom	*phr.* "May he rest in peace" – said when referring to a dead man. Abbreviated as **A"H**.
עָלֶיהָ הַשָּׁלוֹם	'a·**ley**·ha hash·sha·lom	*phr.* "May she rest in peace" – said when referring to a dead woman. Abbreviated as **A"H**.
עֲלִיָּה	'a·li·**yah**	*n.* Aliyah. 1) Going up; Ascent; being called to the Torah reading; 2) Immigration to Israel.
עֶלְיוֹן	'el·**yon**	*n.* The Most High; God; Upper; Highest. *See* the Names of God.
עֶלְיוֹנוּת	'el·yo·**nut**	*n.* Supremacy.
עָלֵינוּ	'a·**lei**·nu	*n.* Aleinu. Closing prayer of the three daily services (popular since the 13th century).
עַם	'am	*n.* People; Nation.
עַם הָאָרֶץ	'am ha·'**a**·rets	*n.* Inhabitants; crowd; common people; ignorant people.

עָמוֹס	‘a·**mos**	n. Amos. Earliest (chronologically) of the "Minor Prophets" in the *Tanakh*. *Amos* means "to be burdened or troubled." His main center of activity was in the northern kingdom.
עֲמִידָה	‘a·mi·**dah**	n. Amida. *Shemoneh Esreh*. Prayer of the Eighteen Benedictions. "Standing" prayer.
עֹמֶר	‘**o**·mer	n. Omer (measure of grain).
עֹנֶג	‘**o**·neg	n. Oneg. Pleasure; Delight; Party.
עֹנֶג שַׁבָּת	‘**o**·neg shab·**bat**	n. Shabbat party.
עֵץ	‘ets	n. Tree.
עֵץ הַחַיִּים	‘ets ha·**chai**·yim	n. Tree of Life (Gen. 2:9).
עִקְבוֹת מְשִׁיחָא	‘iq·**vot** me·shi·**cha**	n. Prelude to the Messiah. "Footsteps of the Messiah."
עֲקֵדָה	‘a·qe·**dah**	n. Akedah. Sacrifice of Isaac by his father Abraham (Gen. 22:1-19).
עֲקֵדַת יִצְחָק	‘a·qe·**dat** yits·**chaq**	n. The binding of Isaac.
עֶרֶב	‘**e**·rev	n. Evening.
עֶרֶב טוֹב	‘**e**·rev **tov**	*Phr.* "Good evening!"
עַרְבִית	‘ar·**vit**	n. Evening prayers; see also *Ma‘ariv*.
עֶרֶב שַׁבָּת	‘**e**·rev shab·**bat**	n. Erev Shabbat. Friday up to sundown.
עָרֵי יִשְׂרָאֵל	‘a·**rei** yis·ra·’**el**	n. Cities of Israel.
עָרֵי מִקְלָט	‘a·**rei** miq·**lat**	n. Cities of Refuge.
עֵשָׂו	‘e·**sav**	n. Esau. The eldest son of Isaac and Rebecca and twin brother of Jacob; sold the birthright for food when he was hungry and the divine blessing went to Jacob; progenitor of the Edomites. Esau means "hairy."
עֶשֶׂר סְפִירוֹת	‘e·ser se·fi·**rot**	n. Ten Sefirot. Ten divine emanations or manifestations of God of Jewish mysticism.
עֲשָׂרָה בְּטֵבֵת	‘a·sa·**rah** be·**te**·vet	n. Tenth of Tevet. Fast day commemorating the siege of Jerusalem by Nebuchadnezzar in 586 BC.
עֲשֶׂרֶת הַדִּבְּרוֹת	‘a·**se**·ret had·di·be·**rot**	n. Ten Commandments (Ex. 20:2-17; Deut. 5:6-21).

עֲשֶׂרֶת הַשְּׁבָטִים	ʻa·se·ret hash·she·va·**tim**	*n.* Ten Tribes (of the northern kingdom of Israel). In the Apocrypha, it is written that the ten tribes moved to a far away country and resettled there (2 Esdras 13:41-47). These are sometimes referred to as the "lost tribes."
עֲשֶׂרֶת יְמֵי תְשׁוּבָה	ʻa·se·ret ye·**mei** te·shu·**vah**	*n.* Ten days of repentance. Penitential season. Time from the 1ˢᵗ of Tishri (*Rosh Hashanah*) and ending with the close of *Yom Kippur*. These days are also known as *Yamim Nora'im*, the Days of Awe.
עַתִּיק יוֹמִין	ʻat·tiq yo·**min**	*n. Aramaic.* Ancient of Days. Name for God (Dan. 7:9, 13, 22).

Hebrew	Transliteration	Definition
פֵּא / פָּא	pey / fey	*n.* Pey / Fey. 17th letter of the Hebrew alphabet having a "f" as in *food* sound (with a dagesh, "p" as in *park*). Originally represented by a pictograph meaning "mouth," "work," or "speech." Gematria = 80. Fey also has a sofit (final) form (ף).
פֵּאוֹת	pe·'ot	*n. pl.* Peot. Earlocks.
פֵּאוֹת הָרֹאשׁ	pe·'ot ha·rosh	*n. pl.* Earlocks (Lev. 19:27-8).
פִּדְיוֹן	pid·yon	*n.* Redemption; Rescue; Ransom.
פִּדְיוֹן הַבֵּן	pid·yon ha·ben	*n.* Ceremony of redeeming the firstborn, 31st day after the birth (Ex. 13:13; Num. 18:16).
פִּדְיוֹן שְׁבוּיִים	pid·yon she·vu·yim	*n.* Ransom of captives.
פּוּרִים	pu·rim	*n.* Purim. "Lots." Festival that celebrates the survival of the Jewish people in the time when Haman the Agagi attempted to kill them (as described in *Esther*).
פֶּלֶא	pe·le	*n.* Wonder; Miracle.
פִּלְפּוּל	pil·pul	*n.* Debate, esp. regarding Halakha or legal matters. *Pilpel* means "pepper."
פָּנִים	pa·nim	*n. sing. pl. constr.* Face; Features; Countenance
פָּסוּק	pa·suq	*n.* Pasuq. Verse. Bible verse. Cp. *Pereq.*
פְּסוּקֵי דְזִמְרָה	pe·su·qei de·zim·rah	*n.* Verses of Song; praise sung or chanted before prayer in the Shacharit service.
פֶּסַח	pe·sach	*n.* Pesach; Passover; The feast of Passover, celebrating the Exodus of the Jewish nation from Egypt under the leadership of Moses. *Pesach,* along with *Shavu'ot* and *Sukkot,* one of the three pilgrim festivals (*shalosh regalim*) when Jews were to come to Jerusalem.
פִּקּוּחַ נֶפֶשׁ	piq·qu·ach ne·fesh	*n.* Saving of life.
פַּרְדֵּס	par·des	*n.* Orchard; "Garden of knowledge." An acronym for *Peshat, Remez, Drash,* and *Sod,* indicating the four traditional levels of interpretation a given *pasuq* might have.
פָּרוּשׁ	pa·rush	*n.* Pharisee; see entry on *Perushim.*

פְּרוּשִׁים	pe·ru·**shim**	*n. pl.* Pharisees; Perushim; The *Perushim* and the *Tseduqim* were the two main groups of the religious establishment in the time of Yeshua. The Perushim focused on the Torah and what it requires of ordinary people, rather than on the Temple ritual. When the Temple was destroyed in 70 c.e., the Perushim developed their tradition into the basis for Jewish life everywhere; this tradition is the core of the Talmud and of modern religious Judaism.
פָּרֹכֶת	pa·**ro**·khet	*n.* Parokhet; Curtain in the Temple before the Ark of the Law; Curtain, specifically the one dividing the Holy of Holies from the rest of the Temple or Tabernacle. There were actually two such curtains: the first separated the Holy Place from the outer court (Ex. 26:36–37, 36:37–38), whereas the second separated the Holy of Holies from the Holy Place (Ex. 26:31–33, 36:35–36). The curtain covering the Ark of the Torah in a modern synagogue is also called a parokhet.
פִּרְקֵי אָבוֹת	pir·**qei** a·**vot**	*n. Pirke Avot;* Chapters of the Fathers; Ethics of the Fathers; from the *Mishnah.* Collection of maxims of the sages from the Mishnah (Hillel, Akiva, etc.).
פְּרַקְלִית	pe·raq·**lit**	*n.* Paraclete; Attorney; Defender; Counselor.
פָּרָשָׁה	pa·ra·**shah**	*n.* Weekly Torah reading. Cp. *sidrah.*
פָּרָשִׁיּוֹת	pa·ra·shi·**yot**	*n. pl.* Weekly Torah readings.
פָּרָשַׁת הַשָּׁבוּעַ	pa·ra·**shat** hash·sha·**vu**·a'	*n.* Weekly Torah portion; weekly *sidrah.*
פַּרְשָׁן	par·**shan**	*n.* Commentator.
פַּרְשָׁנוּת	par·sha·**nut**	*n.* Exegesis; Commentary.
פְּשָׁט	pe·**shat**	*n.* Literal, plain-sense meaning of a text.
פַּתָּח	pat·**tach**	*n.* Patach; vowel sign.

Hebrew	Transliteration	Definition
צָבָא	tsa·**va'**	*n.* 1) Army; host; multitude; 2) Military service.
צְבָא הַשָּׁמַיִם	tse·va' hash·sha·**mai**·yim	*n.* Host of stars; host of the heavens.
צְבָאוֹת	tse·va·**'ot**	*n. pl.* Armies; hosts; multitudes.
צַבָּר	tsab·**bar**	*n.* Sabra; Israeli-born person.
צִדּוּק	tsid·**duq**	*n.* Justification.
צַדּוּקִים	tsad·du·**qim**	*n. pl.* Sadducees. One of the two main groups in the religious establishment of Yeshua's time (the other being the Pharisees (*Perushim*)). The *Tsaddukim* tended to be more Hellenistic and more willing to cooperate with the Roman conquerors than the *Perushim*.
צָדִי	tsa·**di**	*n.* Tsade. 18th letter of the Hebrew alphabet having a "ts" sound (as in nu*ts*). Originally represented by a pictograph of a prostrate man. Gematria = 90. Tsade also has a sofit (final) form.
צִידוֹן	tsi·**don**	*n.* Sidon. Town on the coast north of Tyre (Matt.11:21).
צַדִּיק	tsad·**diq**	*n.* Pious man; *adj.* just; righteous.
צַדִּיקִים	tsad·di·**qim**	*n. pl.* Righteous people; *Lamed Vav Tsadeqim*.
צַדֵק	tsad·**deq**	*v.* To justify; declare righteous.
צֶדֶק	**tse**·deq	*n.* Justice; honesty.
צְדָקָה	tse·da·**qah**	*n.* Tsedakah; Charity; Benevolence; Justice.
צוּר	tsur	*n.* Rock.
צוּר יִשְׂרָאֵל	tsur yis·ra·**'el**	*n.* Rock of Israel; *see* the Names of God.
צוֹם	tsom	*n.* Fast.

צוֹם גְּדַלְיָה	tsom ge·**dal**·ya	*n.* Fast of Gedaliah; A fast day commemorating the assassination of Gedaliah, governor of Judea after the destruction of the first Temple (586 BC). After his death, the Jews were dispersed; in mourning over the Exile, the Rabbis decreed it to be a public fast day. Occurs the day after *Yom Kippur*.
צִיּוֹן	tsi·**yon**	*n.* Zion; Originally called the City of David, south of the modern Old City of Jerusalem. Later the name came to refer metaphorically to the Temple Mount itself, and by extension, to Jerusalem and the people of Israel.
צִיּוֹנוּת	tsi·yo·**nut**	*n.* Zionism.
צִיצִית	**tsi**·tsit	*n.* Tsitsit. Fringes. Ritual fringes on the Tallit or Tallit Katan tied with special knots to remind us of the mitzvot and our responsibility to keep them. The Torah attaches great importance to the wearing of tsitsit as a visible reminder of the obligation to keep the divine mitzvot (Num. 37:29). The tsitsit is made of eight threads with five knots. In orthodox circles, the tsitsit are kissed during recitation of some prayers and blessings.
צֶלָב	tse·**lav**	*n.* Cross.
צֶלֶם	**tse**·lem	*n.* Image; Likeness. (Gen. 1:26: "Let us make man in our image...").
צָמִית	tsa·**mit**	*adj.* Everlasting; eternal.
צְמִיתוּת	tse·mi·**tut**	*n.* Eternity.
צְנִיעוּת	tse·ni·'**ut**	*n.* Modesty; piety; opposite of shamelessness.
צְפַנְיָה	tse·**fan**·yah	*n.* Zephaniah, book of the *Nevi'im* in the *Tanakh*. *Tsefanyah* means "Adonai has hidden."
צָרוֹת	tsa·**rot**	*n. pl.* Troubles; (Yiddish: "*Tsuris*"); heartache; oiy; woe.

Hebrew	Transliteration	Definition
קִבּוּץ	qib·**buts**	*n.* Kibbutz. 1) Gathering; collection; group; collective.
קַבָּלָה	qab·ba·lah	*n.* Kabbalah. Reception; Acceptance; The Kabbalah codifies Jewish mystical teachings from the 13th century.
קַבָּלַת־פָּנִים	qab·ba·**lat**-pa·**nim**	*n.* Reception; Welcome.
קַבָּלַת־שַׁבָּת	qab·ba·**lat**-shab·**bat**	*n.* Kabbalat Shabbat. Welcoming of the Shabbat. Opening service on Friday evening preceding the *Ma'ariv* service.
קָדוֹשׁ	qa·**dosh**	*n. / adj.* Saint; holy; sacred.
קְהִלָּה־קְדוֹשָׁה	qe·hil·**lah**-qe·do·**shah**	*n.* A Jewish community.
קִדּוּשׁ	qid·**dush**	*n.* Kiddush. Blessing over the wine on Sabbaths and Festivals.
קִדּוּשׁ הַחֹדֶשׁ	qid·**dush** ha·**cho**·desh	*n.* Fixing the day of the new moon; prayer said on the new moon.
קִדּוּשׁ הַשֵּׁם	qid·dish hash·**shem**	*n.* Sanctifying the Name of God; martyrdom.
קִדּוּשִׁין	qi·du·**shin**	*n.* Marriage ceremony.
קַדִּישׁ	**qad**·dish	*n.* Kaddish; Doxology glorifying God's Name; prayer said for the dead.
קַדֵּשׁ אֶת הַשֵּׁם	qa·**desh** et hash·**shem**	*n.* To sanctify the Name of God by noble deeds or by martyrdom.
קֹדֶשׁ־הַקֳּדָשִׁים	qo·**desh**-haq·qo·da·**shim**	*n.* The Holy of Holies.
קְדֻשָׁה	qe·du·**shah**	*n.* Sanctification; holiness; The Qedushah is also a prayer (requiring a minyan) that repeats the "Holy, Holy, Holy..." verses in the *Tanakh*.
קָדָשִׁים	qa·da·**shim**	*n. pl.* Holy things; sacrifices.
קָהָל / קְהִלָּה	qa·**hal** / qe·hil·**lah**	*n.* Assembly; Community.
קֹהֶלֶת	qo·**he**·let	*n.* Ecclesiastes, one of the five scrolls (part of the *Ketuvim*). Solomon's study of the futility and meaninglessness inherent in natural reasoning "under the sun." Read during *Sukkot* (Tabernacles). *Qohelet* means "one who assembles."

קוֹל	qol	n. Voice.
קוֹף	qof	n. Qof; 19th letter of the Hebrew alphabet having a "k" sound (as in king) or a "q" sound (as in queen). Originally represented by a pictograph of the sun on the horizon. Gematria = 100. Often transliterated using a "k" rather than a "q."
קְטוֹרֶת	qe·to·ret	n. Incense.
קָמֵץ	qa·mets	n. Qamets; (Long) vowel of the "A-Class" with a sound of "ah."
קַנָּא	qan·na	adj. Jealous (Ex. 20:5).
קוֹץ	qots	n. Qots. Serif or stroke on top of a Hebrew letter. This may refer to the "tittle" Yeshua spoke of in Matt. 5:8 and Luke 16:17.
קוֹצוֹ שֶׁל יוֹד	qo·tso shel yod	n. phr. "The Qots of a Yod." The tiniest thing; minutia; The serif mark atop a Yod, the smallest Hebrew letter. See Qots, above.
קִצּוּר שֻׁלְחָן עָרוּךְ	qi·tsur shul·chan 'a·rukh	n. Jewish law code based on the Shulchan Aruch and widely used by earlier American generations to define the duties of being Jewish. a.k.a. "Kitsur."
קָרָאִי	ka·ra·'i	n. Karaite; Member of a Jewish sect that rejects Rabbinical / Talmudic interpretation of the Tanakh.
קָרָאִים	qa·ra·'im	n. pl. Karaites. Sect founded by Anan ben David in the middle of the 8th century.
קָרְבָּן	qor·ban	n. Sacrifice; Offering; Gift. (Matt 5:23).
קָרְבָּנוֹת	qor·ba·not	n. Offerings. Sacrifices.
קֹרַח	qo·rach	n. Korah. Levite who led a rebellion against Moses in the wilderness (Num. 16, 26; Jude 11).
קְרִי	qe·re	n. Qere. Masoretic reading; textual variant. "What is read." Compare Ketiv, "What is written."
קְרִי וּכְתִיב	qe·re u·khe·tiv	n. Qere and Ketiv. Variants to be read are called "Qere"; variants as written are called "Ketiv." The Masorah indicates when to omit reading a word that is written and substitute it with what is read.
קְרִיאָה	qe·ri·'ah	n. Calling (by God); election.
קְרִיאַת הַתּוֹרָה	qe·ri·'at ha·to·rah	n. Torah Reading. Public reading of Torah at the synagogue.
קְרִיאַת־שְׁמַע	qe·ri·'at she·ma'	n. Keriat Shema. The recitation of the Shema (Deut 6:4-9; 11:31-21; and Num. 15:37-41).
קְרִיעָה	qe·ri·'ah	n. Keriah. Rending of the garments as a sign of grieving (2 Sam. 13:31).

ר

Hebrew	Transliteration	Definition
רְאוּבֵן	re·u·**ven**	*n.* Rueben. Tribe of Israel named after the first son of the Patriarch Jacob (Gen. 29:32).
רֹאשׁ	rosh	*n./ adj.* Head; top; chief; principal; beginning.
רֹאשׁ חֹדֶשׁ	rosh **cho**·desh	*n.* New Moon. "Head of the moon."
רֹאשׁ הַשָּׁנָה	rosh hash·sha·**nah**	*n.* Rosh Hashanah; New Years day. The Jewish New Year commemorating the creation of the universe; universal day of judgment. Falling on the first and second days of the month of Tishri when Jews examine their actions of the preceding year. The blowing of the ram's horn is prophetic of the rapture of the *ekklesia* or church.
רִאשׁוֹן	ri·**shon**	*adj.* 1) First; Former; Foremost; 2) *n.* Medieval Torah authorities (cp. *acharonim*) such as Rashi, Maimonides, Yehuda Halevi.
רֵאשִׁית	rei·**shit**	*n.* Beginning; Best; First Fruit.
רַב	rav	*n.* Master; teacher; lord; scholar; rabbi.
רַבִּים	rab·**bim**	*adj.* Much; many.
רִבּוֹן	rib·**bon**	*n.* Master; Sovereign.
רִבּוֹנוֹ שֶׁל עוֹלָם	rib·**bo**·no shel 'o·**lam**	*n.* The Lord; Master of the Universe.
רַבִּי	**rab**·bi	*n.* Rabbi. Title given to a teacher or master.
רְבִיעִי	re·vi·'**i**	*adj.* 4th; the fourth part.
רַבָּנוּת	rab·ba·**nut**	*n.* Rabbinate; Office of a Rabbi.
רַבָּנָן	rab·ba·**nan**	*n. pl.* Talmudic scholars.
רִבְקָה	**riv**·qah	*n.* Rebekah. The daughter of Bethuel, sister of Laban, wife of Isaac, and mother of Esau and Jacob (Gen. 22:23).
רְגָלִים	re·ga·**lim**	*n.* Turn; time; holiday of pilgrimage to Jerusalem (*regalim* means "feet").
רָחוּת	ra·**chut**	*adj.* Fluent.
רוּחַ	**ru**·ach	*n.* Ruach. Wind; Breath; Air; Spirit. *Ruach Haqodesh* is the Holy Spirit. *See* Names of God.

רוּחוֹת	ru·chot	n. pl. Spirits.
רוּחַ הַקֹּדֶשׁ	**ru**·ach haq·**qo**·desh	n. Ruach Hakodesh; Holy Spirit; Divine Spirit; Inspiration; Prophecy. See the Names of God.
רוּחַ רָעָה	**ru**·ach **ra**·ʻah	n. Evil spirit; hatred; malice.
רוּחָנִיּוּת	ru·cha·ni·**yut**	n. Spirituality.
רוּת	rut	n. Ruth. One of the five scrolls (part of the Ketuvim). Recited in the synagogue in Shavu'ot. Rut means "close friend" or "mate."
רוֹמֵם	ro·**mem**	v. To raise; to exalt; to lift up.
רוֹעֶה	ro·ʻ**eh**	n. Shepherd; leader (Psalm 23).
רָחָב	ra·**chav**	n. Rahab. The prostitute in Jericho who hid the Israelite spies in the days of Joshua (Josh. 2).
רַחוּם	ra·**chum**	adj. Merciful.
רָחֵל	ra·**chel**	n. Rachel. The daughter of Laban, wife of Jacob, and mother of Joseph and Benjamin. Rachel means "ewe" (female lamb). One of the four Matriarchs of the 12 tribes of Israel.
רֶחֶם	**re**·chem	n. Womb; bowels of compassion.
רַחֵם	ra·**chem**	n. Compassion; pity; love.
רַחֲמִים	ra·cha·**mim**	n. pl. Compassions; tender mercies; mercy.
רַחֲמָן	ra·cha·**man**	adj. Merciful.
רַחֲמָנָא לִיצְלָן	ra·cha·**ma**·na lits·**lan**	phr. Aramaic. "God forbid!"
רַחֲמָנוּת	ra·cha·ma·**nut**	n. Compassion; Mercy.
רֵישׁ	resh	n. Resh. 20th letter of the Hebrew alphabet having an "r" sound (as in rain). Originally represented by a pictograph of a head or person. Gematria = 200.
רַמְבָּ״ם	**ram**·bam	Acr. Rambam. Acronym for Rabbi Moses Ben Maimon, otherwise known as Maimonides (1135-1204), perhaps the greatest Jewish sage of the Middle Ages. Note the gerashim in this name.
רַע	raʻ	n. Evil; distress; injury.
רַע עַיִן	raʻ ʻa·yin	n. Evil eye; envy; selfishness.

לְוֹן

רֵעַ	**re**·a'	*n.* Neighbor; friend; companion (Lev. 19:18).
רָעָה	**ra**·'ah	*n.* Evil; wickedness; injury.
רֵעוּת	re·'**ut**	*n.* Neighborliness; friendship.
רְפוּאָה	re·fu·'**ah**	*n.* Healing.
רְפוּאָה שְׁלֵמָה	re·fu·'**ah** shle·**mah**	*phr.* "Get well soon," "A complete healing," "A speedy recovery!"
רָפֶה	ra·**feh**	*adj./ n.* Weak; a "Begadkephat" letter without dagesh.
רִקוּדִים	ri·qu·**dim**	*n.* Jewish dances, such as the hora. Jewish folk dancing. Any dances.
רָשָׁע	**ra**·sha'	*n.* Sinner; wicked man.
רַשִׁ״י	**ra**·shi	*n.* Rashi; great French commentator of the *Tanakh* and the Talmud. Rabbi Shelomo Yitshaki (1040-1105). *Chumash* with Rashi constitutes the basic Jewish education for many generations of Jews in the *galut*. Note the *gerashim* used to indicate that this is an abbreviation.

Hebrew	Transliteration	Definition
שָׁאוּל	sha·'ul	n. Saul. "also known as Paul" (Acts 13:9). Messiah's emissary to the gentile world.
שְׁאוֹל	she·'ol	n. Sheol. Hell; Grave; depth.
שְׁאֵלָה	she·'e·lah	n. Question; Request; A question, especially given to a rabbi regarding Jewish observance.
שְׁאֵלוֹת	she·'e·lot	n. pl. Questions, esp. rabbinical questions regarding halakhah.
שָׁבוּעַ	sha·vu·a'	n. Week. See the Jewish Calendar.
שָׁבוּעַ טוֹב	sha·vu·a' tov	phr. "Good week!"
שָׁבוּעוֹת	sha·vu·'ot	n. Shavuot; Pentecost; Feast of Weeks; weeks. The Festival commemorating giving of the Torah at Har Sinai to Israel. Observed on the fiftieth day after the first day of Pesach. Shavu'ot is the concluding festival of the Spring season, a festival of the offering of the first fruits, and a picture of the resurrection of Yeshua the Messiah as the Firstfruits (1 Cor. 15:20).
שְׁבוּעָה	she·vu·'ah	n. Oath.
שֶׁבַח לָאֵל	she·vach la·'el	phr. "Thank God!"
שְׁבָט	she·vat	n. Shevat. 5th month; see the Jewish Calendar.
שְׁבִיעִי	she·vi·'i	adj. Seventh.
שֶׁבַע בְּרָכוֹת	she·va' be·ra·khot	n. Seven blessings; Blessings recited over wine during a wedding ceremony. Also a party for the newlyweds during the first week of marriage.
שִׁבְעָה	shiv·'ah	n. Shivah. Seven-day mourning period. "Sitting Shivah" is a custom of sitting on a low stool during the grieving process. Shivah means "seven."
שִׁבְעָה עָשָׂר בְּתַמּוּז	shiv·'ah 'a·sar be·ta·muz	n. 17th of Tammuz. Fast day commemorating the breaking down of the wall of Jerusalem by Nebuchadnezzar and the cessation of Temple worship during the siege of Titus.
שְׁבָרִים	she·va·rim	n. Shevarim. Along with Teqiah and Teru'ah, a sequence of shofar blasts. Shevarim "fragments" are three broken blasts of the shofar.

שִׁבְעִים פָּנִים לַתּוֹרָה	shiv·'im pa·nim la·to·rah	*phr.* "The Torah has 70 faces." A phrase used to indicate different levels of interpretation of the Torah. See *Pardes*.
שַׁבָּת	shab·bat	*n.* Shabbat; Sabbath; Day of rest. (Ex. 20:8). Observed from sunset Friday evening to sundown Saturday evening, marked by rest, worship, and study. One who traditionally observes the legal requirements for Shabbat is called *Shomer Shabbat*. One of the *aseret hadibrot,* or Ten Commandments (Ex. 20:2-17; Deut. 5:6-21).
שַׁבָּת בְּרֵאשִׁית	shab·bat bre·shit	*n.* The first Sabbath after *Simchat Torah* on which the portion of Bereshit (Genesis) is read.
שַׁבָּת הַגָּדוֹל	shab·bat hag·ga·dol	*n.* Shabbat Hagadol; Sabbath preceding *Pesach.* Called "great" (*gadol*) because it began the story of the passage of the Jews from slavery into freedom, and it was the Shabbat when the Jews of Egypt sprinkled lamb's blood on doorposts to prevent the Angel of Death from stopping by their households during the last plague.
שַׁבַּת שׁוּבָה	shab·bat shu·vah	*n.* Sabbath between *Rosh Hashanah* and *Yom Kippur,* during the Days of Awe.
שַׁבָּת שָׁלוֹם	shab·bat sha·lom	*phr.* "Good Sabbath!"
עֶרֶב שַׁבָּת	'e·rev shab·bat	*n.* Sabbath Eve (Friday evening).
שַׁבָּתוֹן	shab·ba·ton	*n.* 1) Rest; Cessation from work. 2) One of the seven annual Sabbaths.
שַׁבָּת שַׁבָּתוֹן	shab·bat shab·ba·ton	*n.* A high sabbath. "Sabbath of sabbaths."
שֵׁד	shed	*n.* Demon.
שֵׁדִים	she·dim	*n.* Demons.
שִׁדּוּךְ	shi·dukh	*n.* Shidukh; A match or arranged marriage (arranged by the *Shadkhan* or matchmaker).
שִׁדּוּכִים	shi·du·khim	*n. pl.* Arranged marriages.
שַׁדּוּן	shad·dun	*n.* The Almighty; *see* the Names of God.
שַׁדַּי	shad·dai	*n.* Shaddai; Almighty; *see* the Names of God.
שַׁדְכָן	shad·khan	*n.* Marriage broker.
שֶׂה	seh	*n.* Lamb. *Seh Ha'elohim* is the Lamb of God, a title for the Messiah Yeshua (John 1:29).
שֶׁהֶחֱיָנוּ	she·he·che·ya·nu	*n.* Shehecheyanu. Customary blessing said upon any special occasion.

שֵׂה הָאֱלֹהִים	seh ha·'e·lo·**him**	*n.* The Lamb of God (John 1:29); a Title for the Messiah Yeshua. *See* the Names of God.
שְׁוָא	she·**va**	*n.* Sheva (vowel sign).
שְׁוָא נָח	she·va **nach**	*n.* Quiescent Sheva.
שְׁוָא נָע	she·va **na'**	*n.* Vocal Sheva.
שׁוֹאָה	sho·'ah	*n.* Destruction; Catastrophe; also: the Nazi Holocaust.
שׁוּם דָּבָר	**shum** da·var	*phr.* "Nothing."
שׁוֹמֵר	sho·**mer**	*n.* Watchman; Guard.
שׁוֹמֵר שַׁבַּת	sho·mer shab·**bat**	*n.* Sabbath observer; someone who keeps Shabbat laws in a traditional way.
שׁוֹמְרוֹנִי	shom·ro·**ni**	*n. / adj.* Samaritan. The Samaritans, a mixed ethnic group descended from Jews deported by the Assyrians in the 8th century B.C. and other peoples ruled by the Assyrians, followed a religion combining pagan and Jewish elements. By the first century most Jews regarded them as pariahs. Matt. 10:5+.
שׂוֹנֵא	so·**nei**	*n.* Enemy.
שׁוֹפְטִים	sho·fe·**tim**	*n.* Judges: Book of the *Nevi'im* in the *Tanakh.* The story of how Adonai raised up twelve remarkable individuals (called judges or *shofetim*) to deliver Israel from her enemies.
שׁוֹפָר	sho·**far**	*n.* Shofar; Ram's Horn; also trumpet. A hallowed out ram's horn, reminding us of the ram offered by Avraham instead of his son (Gen. 22:13); historically used to herald freedom and assemble the community, it is now used for the month preceding Rosh Hashanah as well as during the *Yamim Noraim* to call toward repentance. It is a symbol of revelation and redemption, as sounded at Sinai (Ex. 19:16, 19).
שׁוֹפָר הַגָּדוֹל	sho·**far** hag·ga·**dol**	*n.* The great shofar.
שׁוּרֵק	shu·**ruq**	*n.* Shuruq; U-class vowel mark with an "oo"sound. Shuruq is a long vowel (וּ).
שׁוּשָׁן פּוּרִים	shu·**shan** pu·**rim**	*n.* Celebration of Purim as a second day after the regular Purim celebration (customary in Jerusalem).
שַׁחַר	sha·**char**	*n.* Dawn; Daybreak; Morning.

שִׁחְרוּר	shich·**rur**	*n.* Liberation; Setting free.
שַׁחֲרִית	sha·cha·**rit**	*n.* Morning Prayer Service performed in the synagogue.
שְׁחִיטָה	she·chi·**tah**	*n.* Ritual slaughtering of animals.
שָׂטָן	sa·**tan**	*n.* Satan; Accuser.
שְׂטָנִי	se·ta·**ni**	*adj.* Satanic.
שִׁין / שִׂין	shin / sin	*n.* Shin / Sin; 21ˢᵗ letter of Hebrew alphabet having the sound of "sh" as in *sh*y (or "s" as in *s*un). Originally a pictograph representing a mouth. Gematria = 300.
שִׁיר	shir	*n.* Song.
שִׁיר הַשִּׁירִים	shir hash·shi·**rim**	*n.* Song of Songs, one of the five scrolls (part of the *Ketuvim*). Written by King Solomon and considered an allegory of the relations between Adonai and Israel (and Messiah's love for the Church). Read during *Pesach* (Passover). *Shir Hashshirim* means "Song of (all) songs."
שִׁיר שֶׁל יוֹם	shir shel **yom**	*n.* Psalm of the day.
שִׁירַת יִשְׂרָאֵל	shi·**rat** yis·ra·**'el**	*n.* Jewish Music; Songs of Israel.
שְׁכִינָה	she·khi·**nah**	*n.* Shekhinah; Divine Presence; Inspiration. Sometimes used to refer to the Presence of God and specifically when it dwelt (rested) between the *Keruvim* (Cherubim) over the Seat of Atonement of the Ark of Testimony in the *Qodesh Haqodeshim* (Holy of Holies).
שֵׂכֶל	**se**·khel	*n.* Common-sense.
שָׁלוֹם	sha·**lom**	*n.* Shalom. Peace; Wholeness; well-being; wellness.
שָׁלוֹם עֲלֵיכֶם	sha·**lom** 'a·lei·**chem**	*n.* Shalom Aleichem. Hymn chanted on Friday nights recited upon returning home from Sabbath-eve services.
שְׁלִיטָ"א	she·li·ta	*acr.* Acronym for a Hebrew phrase "May he live a long and good life, Amen" said by ultraorthodox when mentioning the name of a revered rabbi.
שְׁלֹשִׁים	she·lo·**shim**	*n.* Thirty; Thirty days of mourning as part of the Jewish grieving process.
שֻׁלְחָן	shul·**chan**	*n.* Table.

שֻׁלְחָן הַפָּנִים	shul·chan hap·pa·**nim**	*n.* Table of the Showbread. (Variant of the entry, below).
שֻׁלְחָן לֶחֶם פָּנִים	shul·chan **le**·chem pa·**nim**	*n.* Table of Showbread (Ex. 25:30).
שֻׁלְחָן עָרוּךְ	shul·**chan** ʻa·**ruch**	*n.* Shulchan Aruch. "Prepared Table" by Rabbi Joseph Karo (1488-1575). A practical guide to traditional Jewish observance.
שָׁלִיחַ	sha·**li**·ach	*n.* Messenger; Delegate. Emmisary. A person sent forth as an agent to perform a task for a Principal. In Jewish understanding the identity of the agent becomes that of the Principal when the agent performs the task given to him by the Principal.
שָׁלִיחַ צִבּוּר	sha·**li**·ach tsib·**bur**	*n.* Sheliach Tsibbur; Prayer leader, especially in a congregation.
שְׁלִיחוּת	she·li·**chut**	*n.* Mission; Commission; Message.
שְׁלִישִׁי	she·li·**shi**	*adj.* 3rd
שֶׁלֶם	**she**·lem	*n.* Thanksgiving offering; Peace offering.
שְׁלֹשׁ עֶשְׂרֵה מִדּוֹת	she·losh ʻes·reh mid·**dot**	*n.* The thirteen attributes of God, according to the sages' reflections upon Ex. 34:6-7.
שְׁלֹשׁ רְגָלִים	she·losh re·ga·**lim**	*n.* Three annual pilgrimage festivals: *Pesach*, *Shavu'ot*, and *Sukkot* (Ex. 23:14).
שָׁלֵם	sha·**lem**	*adj.* Whole; Well; Perfected.
שְׁלֹמֹה	she·lo·**moh**	*n.* Solomon. The son of King David by Bathsheba and 3rd king of Israel; author of Proverbs and Song of Songs and Ecclesiastes.
שֵׁם	shem	*n.* Name; also the name of Shem, son of Noah (Gen. 5:32).
שֵׁם הַמְּפֹרָשׁ	shem ha·me·fo·**rash**	*n.* Sacred Name of God; YHVH; Spoken only 10 times once per year, at *Yom Kippur* by the *Kohen Gadol* (Yoma 39b), and in an undertone to conceal it from the rest of the people who might overhear it.
שֵׁם מִשְׁפָּחָה	shem mish·pa·**chah**	*n.* Surname; Family Name.
שֵׁמִיִּים	she·mi·**yim**	*n.* Semites; perhaps descendants from Shem.
שְׁמָד	she·**mad**	*n.* Forced conversion; also: apostasy (from Judaism).
שְׁמוּאֵל	she·mu·**el**	*n.* Samuel. 1) The book of Samuel, part of the *Nevi'im* in the *Tanakh*; 2) Samuel, the great prophet, priest, and judge of Israel.
שְׁמוֹנָה	she·mo·**nah**	*adj. / n.* Eighth.

שְׁמוֹנֶה עֶשְׂרֵה	she·mo·neh ʻes·reh	n. Shemoneh Esreh; Central prayer of the synagogue service. Also called the *Amidah* (standing).
שְׁמוֹת	she·**mot**	n. pl. Names; 1) Exodus. The story of the liberation of the Jewish people from their bondage in Egypt and the giving of the Mosaic covenant to Israel.
שְׁמוֹת הָאֱלֹהִים	she·**mot** ha·ʼe·lo·**him**	n. pl. The names and Titles of God. See Lesson Seventeen.
שִׂמְחָה	sim·chah	n. Joy; Gladness; Happiness; cheerfulness.
שִׂמְחַת תּוֹרָה	sim·chat **to·**rah	n. Simchat Torah; festival of the Torah; "Joy of the Torah." The last day of the festival of *Sukkot* during which the final (weekly) portion of the Torah is concluded and the first one is begun. The festival is marked by rejoicing and congregational dancing around the *Sefrei Torah*.
שְׁמִטָּה	she·mit·**tah**	n. Sabbatical Year; 7th year in the cycle to leave land fallow.
שָׁמַיִם	sha·**mai**·yim	n. Heaven; sky; *Malkhut Shamayim* is the Kingdom of Heaven.
שְׁמֵי הַשָּׁמַיִם	she·mei hash·sha·**mai**·yim	n. Highest Heaven. The third heaven.
שְׁמַע	she·maʻ	n. Shema. "Hear!" The first word in the Jewish confession of faith proclaiming that God is one. (see Deut. 6:4). The Shema is the central prayer in the Jewish prayerbook (*Siddur*) and is often the first verse of Scripture that a Jewish child learns. During its recitation in the synagogue, Orthodox Jews pronounce each word very carefully and cover their eyes with their right hand. Many Jews recite the Shema at least twice daily: once in the morning and once in the evening; it is also sometimes said as a bedtime prayer ("the bedtime Shema"). The complete Shema is composed of three parts.
שְׁמַע יִשְׂרָאֵל	she·maʻ yis·ra·ʼel	n. The Shema, chief confession of the Jewish faith; (Deut. 6:4). See the entry above.
שִׁמְעוֹן	shim·ʻon	n. Simeon. "Heard." The 2nd son of Jacob by his wife Leah and progenitor of the tribe of Simeon. Also the name for Peter in the *B'rit Chadashah* (Matt 4:18).
שֹׁמְרוֹן	shom·ron	n. Samaria. Capital of the Northern Kingdom of ancient Israel. The later Samaritans were a mixed ethnic group descended from Jews deported by the Assyrians in the 8th century B.C. and other peoples ruled by the Assyrians, followed a religion combining pagan and Jewish elements.
שַׁמָּשׁ	**sham**·mash	n. Shammash; 1) Synagogue caretaker or custodian; deacon; 2) Servant candle for Chanukkah menorah.

שֶׁמֶשׁ	she·mesh	*n.* Sun.
שִׁמְשׁוֹן	shim·shon	*n.* Samson. Judge of Israel (Judges 13-16).
שָׁנָה	sha·nah	*n.* Year. See the Calendar.
שָׁנָה טוֹבָה	sha·nah to·vah	*phr.* "Happy New Year!"
שֵׁנִי	she·ni	*adj.* Second; Yom Sheni is Tuesday.
שַׁס	shas	*abbr.* Shas. Talmud. Abbreviation for *Shisha Sidarim*, the six orders of the *Mishnah* that form the basis of the Talmud. *Shas* and *Chumash* with Rashi is considered a good Jewish religious education.
שָׁעָה	sha·'ah	*n.* Hour; Time (as of the clock).
שִׁעוּר	shi·'ur	*n.* Lesson; also: religious class, often informal.
שִׁעוּר בַּיִת	shi·'ur ba·yit	*n.* Homework.
שָׂעִיר לַעֲזָאזֵל	sa·'ir la·'a·za·zel	*n.* Scapegoat. (Lev. 16:8).
שְׁפָטִים	she·fa·tim	*n.* Judgment; punishment.
שִׁקּוּץ	shiq·quts	*n.* Idol; Abomination.
שֶׁקֶל	she·qel	*n.* Shekel; Money; mammon.
שֶׁקֶר	she·qer	*n.* Lie; Falsehood; Deceit.
נְבִיא שֶׁקֶר	ne·vi' she·qer	*n.* False prophet.
שַׁקְרָן	shaq·ran	*n.* Liar. Another Hebrew word for liar is *kozev*.
שַׂר	sar	*n.* Prince; Ruler; Leader; Captain; Minister.
שַׂר-שָׁלוֹם	sar-sha·lom	*n.* Prince of Peace (Isa. 9:6); *see* the Names of God.
שָׂרָה	sa·rah	*n.* Sarah. Princess. Wife of Abraham and matriarch of the Hebrews (Gen. 17:15).
שָׂרַי	sa·rai	*n.* Sarai. "My princess." The original name of Sarah the wife of Abram (Gen. 11:29; 17:15).
שָׁרוֹן	sha·ron	*n.* Sharon. A geographical region of Israel.
שֹׁרֶשׁ	sho·resh	*n.* Shoresh; Root; origin; radical of a verb or word.

Hebrew	Transliteration	Definition
תְּאֵנָה	te·'e·**nah**	*n.* Fig. Fig tree.
תֵּבָה	te·**vah**	*n.* Chest holding the scrolls of the Law in the synagogue; ark.
תֵּבַת נֹחַ	te·vat **no**·ach	*n.* Noah's ark.
תְּבוּנָה	te·vu·**nah**	*n.* Understanding; Intelligence.
תָּג	tag	*n.* Crown; crownlet on Hebrew letters; serif; tittle. The plural is usually rendered *tagin*.
תֹּהוּ	**to**·hu	*n.* Emptiness; Waste.
תֹּהוּ וָבֹהוּ	**to**·hu va·**vo**·hu	*n.* Form and Void; chaos. (Gen. 1:2).
תְּהִלָּה	te·hil·**lah**	*n.* Praise; song of praise.
תְּהִלִּים	te·hil·**lim**	*n.* Psalms. Book of Psalms. Sacred prayerbook and hymnal of the *Tanakh*. Divided into five separate books (Psalms 1-41, 42-72, 73-89, 90-106, and 107-150, respectively). Messianic Psalms include 2, 8, 16, 22, 45, 69, 72, 89, 100, 118, 132. *Tehillim* means "praises."
תָּו	tav	*n.* Tav. 22nd letter of the Hebrew alphabet having the sound of "t" as in *t*all. Originally a pictograph representing a mark or sign or covenant. Gematria = 400. A "Begedkephat letter" (may take a dagesh lene).
תּוֹדָה	to·**dah**	*excl.* Thanks!
תּוֹדָה רַבָּה	to·**dah** rab·**bah**	*phr.* "Thanks very much!"
תּוֹחֶלֶת	to·**che**·let	*n.* Hope; Expectation.
תּוֹכֵחָה	to·kha·**chah**	*n.* Rebuke.
תּוֹלְדוֹת	tol·**dot**	*n.* Descendants; successive generations; lineage, as in the "toldot of Yeshua" (Matt. 1; Luke 3).
תּוֹלְדוֹת יִשְׂרָאֵל	tol·**dot** yis·ra·**'el**	*n.* Jewish history.
תּוֹסֶפְתָּא	to·**sef**·ta	*n.* Tosefta. Supplement to the *Mishnah*. It contains a large collection of tannaitic statements of the traditional law (*Halakhah*).

תּוֹרָה	to·rah	n. Torah. The word *Torah* comes from the root word *yarah* meaning "to shoot an arrow" or "to hit the mark." Properly used, the word means "teaching" or "instruction." In the *Tanakh*, Torah refers to the first five books of Moses. The actual Torah itself is referred to as the *Sefer Torah*, or sacred Torah scroll. The *Chumash* is a book form of the *Torah*, usually subdivided into 54 smaller literary units called *parashiot* (the name of each *parashah* comes from a key word of the section). The word *Torah* is better understood as "teaching" or "understanding" rather than "law."
תּוֹרָה לִשְׁמָהּ	to·rah lish·mah	n. Study of Torah for its own sake.
תּוֹרָה מִסִּינַי	to·rah mi·si·nai	n. Revelation; belief that God revealed both the written and oral Torah to Moses at Mount Sinai.
תּוֹרָה שֶׁבִּכְתָב	to·rah she·bich·tav	n. Written Torah; Written Law; Often used synonymously with the 24 holy writings that make up the *Tanakh*.
תּוֹרָה שֶׁבְּעַל פֶּה	to·rah sheb·ʻal peh	n. Oral Torah; Talmud. Tradition reports that the two forms of Torah, *Torah she-bikhtav* and *Torah she-beʻal peh*, have existed side by side ever since the revelation at *Har Sinai*. The Oral Torah, which was not committed to writing during the centuries preceding the compilation of the *Mishnah*, was transmitted orally by a chain of sages and carriers of tradition. Karaites reject all Oral Torah.
תּוֹרָנִי	to·ra·ni	n. Talmudic scholar.
תְּחִיָּה	te·chi·yah	n. Revival.
תְּחִינָה	te·chi·nah	n. Personal prayers. Personal devotions to God, in addition to the prescribed prayers in the synagogue.
תְּחִיַת הַמֵּתִים	te·chi·yat ha·me·tim	n. Resurrection from the dead.
תְּחִיַת הַמָשִׁיחַ	te·chi·yat ha·ma·shi·ach	n. The resurrection of the Messiah (Matt. 16:21; Acts 2:32).
תְּחִנָּה	te·chin·nah	n. Prayer.
תְּחִנּוֹת	te·chin·not	n. Private devotions to God.
תֵּימָן	tei·man	n. Yemen; South.
תֵּימָנִי	te·ma·ni	adj. Yemenite.
תֹּכֶן הָעִנְיָנִים	to·khen ha·ʻin·ya·nim	n. Table of contents.
תַּכְרִיכִין	takh·ri·khin	n. pl. Burial clothes; Shrouds.

תַּלְמוּד	tal·mud	n. Talmud. An encyclopedic collection of legalistic interpretations consisting of the *Mishnah* (oral law) and *Gemara* (commentary on the *Mishnah*). The Jerusalem Talmud was composed in Israel and compiled at the end of the 5th century C.E.; the (larger) Babylonian Talmud (*Talmud Bavli*) was compiled by the Babylonian Sages and redacted around the year 500 C.E.
תַּלְמוּד תּוֹרָה	tal·mud to·rah	n. 1) Study of Torah (both written and oral Torah); 2) Hebrew school.
תַּלְמִיד	tal·mid	n. Pupil; student; disciple.
תַּלְמִיד חָכָם	tal·mid cha·kham	n. Learned man; scholar.
תַּלְמִידִים	tal·mi·dim	n. pl. Disciples; followers.
תָּם	tam	adj. Pure; perfect; whole; sincere.
תַּמִּים	tam·mim	adj. pl. Pure; perfect; whole; sincere.
תַּמּוּז	tam·muz	n. Tammuz. Name of the 4th month. *See* Hebrew calendar.
תָּמִיד	ta·mid	n. 1) Daily offering in the Temple; 2) Daily prayer service said in the synagogue.
תַּנָּאִים	tan·na·'im	n. Tannaim. Teachers directly mentioned in the *Mishnah* and *Tosefta*. The Tannaitic period began with the death of Hillel and Shammai (1st century A.D.) and ends with Rabbi Judah ha-Nasi, compiler and editor of the *Mishnah* (beginning of the 3rd century). The Tannaim were successors to sages called *Soferim*. The adjective form is *tannaitic*.
תַּנַ"ךְ	ta·nakh	n. Hebrew Bible. The Hebrew Bible is called the *Tanakh* (sometimes transliterated as *Tanak* or *Tanach* in English), an acronym for <u>*T*</u>*orah*, <u>*N*</u>*evi'im*, and <u>*K*</u>*etuvim*. Note the use of the *gerashim* to indicate an acronym.
תַּעֲנִית	ta·'a·nit	n. Fast; Sad fast day.
תַּעֲנִית אֶסְתֵּר	ta·'a·nit 'es·ter	n. Fast of Esther. 13th of Adar, the day preceding Purim.
תַּעֲנִית בְּכוֹרוֹת	ta·'a·nit be·kho·rot	n. Fast of the firstborn.
תְּפִלָּה	te·fil·lah	n. Prayer.
תְּפִלָּה לְחוֹלֶה	te·fil·lah le·cho·leh	n. Prayer for the sick.

תְּפִלִּין	te·fil·**lin**	n. Tefillin; Phylacteries; two black leather boxes containing scrolls with Bible passages on them (Ex. 13:1–16; Deut. 6:4–9, 11:13–21). During synagogue prayers men affix one to their hand and arm and the other to their forehead, in obedience to Deut. 6:8.
תְּפִלַּת הַדֶּרֶךְ	te·fil·**lat** had·**de**·rech	n. Prayer before starting a journey.
תְּפִלַּת הַשַּׁחַר	te·fil·**lat** ha·sha·**char**	n. Morning Prayer.
תְּפִלַּת שֶׁבַע	te·fil·**lat** she·**va'**	n. Tefillat Sheva. Abbreviated Amida with only seven of the 18 blessings said.
תִּקּוּן	tiq·**qun**	n. Improvement; amelioration; correction; repair. *Tiqqun 'Olam* means "repair of the world."
תְּפוּצָה	te·fu·**tsah**	n. Diaspora; Dispersion; Galut.
תְּקִיעָה	te·qi·**ah**	n. Teqiah. Shofar blast. One loud blast from the Shofar. Cp. *Teruah, Shevarim.*
תַּרְגּוּם	tar·gum	n. Targum. Translation. Version. The name given to the Aramaic translation of the Scriptures that was read to the populace in Babylonian periods. Except for some interpolations and paraphrases, the *Targum Bavli*, also known as *Targum Onkelos*, is a very faithful translation. *Targum Yerushalmi* is less faithful to the text.
תַּרְגּוּם הַשִּׁבְעִים	tar·gum ha·shiv·**'im**	n. Septuagint. Greek translation of the *Tanakh* supposedly performed by six scholars from each of the 12 tribes of Israel. Hellenistic version of the *Tanakh* composed for Alexandrian Jews before the start of the common era.
תְּרוּעָה	te·**ru**·'ah	n. Teruah. Nine short blasts on a shofar. Cp. *Tekiah, Shevarim.*
תֶּרַח	**te**·rach	n. Terah. Father of the patriarch Abraham (Gen 11:26).
תְּרֵי עָשָׂר	te·rei a·**sar**	n. Twelve. The Minor Prophets.
תַּרְיַ"ג מִצְווֹת	tar·yag mits·**vot**	n. Taryag Mitzvot. 613 commandments found in the *Tanakh*, 248 positive and 365 negative mitzvot (the *gerashim* indicates an acronym: תַּרְיַ"ג = 613).
תְּשׁוּבָה	te·shu·**vah**	n. Return; reply; repentance.
תְּשׁוּעָה	te·shu·**'ah**	n. Help; Salvation.
תַּשְׁלִיךְ	tash·**likh**	n. Tashlich. A ceremony held near a flowing body of water on the first day of Rosh Hashanah during which individuals empty their pockets and symbolically "cast their sins upon the water." (Micah 7:19).

תַּשְׁמִישֵׁי קְדוּשָׁה	tash·mi·**shi** qe·du·**shah**	*n. pl.* Sacred objects for religious use (e.g., Siddur, Tallit; Qiddush cup, etc.)
תִּשְׁעָה בְּאָב	tish·**ah** be·**av**	*n.* Tish'ah Be'av. 9th day of Av (Zech 8:19) mentioned as the fast of the fifth month commemorating national calamities such as the destruction of both Temples, the fall of Bar Kochba's fortress, the expulsion of the Jews from Spain in 1492. This is a solemn fast day.
תִּשְׁרֵי	**tish**·ri	*n.* Tishri. Name of the 1st month of the Jewish religious calendar (7th month of the civil calendar).
תּוּשְׁלַבַּ"ע	tush·la·**ba**	*Acronym.* Tushlaba. An acronym from the Hebrew phrase: תַּם וְנִשְׁלָם, שֶׁבַח לְאֵל בּוֹרֵא עוֹלָם expressing thanks to God for the completion of a book on a Jewish subject.

Introduction to the Hebrew Calendar
לוּחַ

The Jewish Day

The Jewish day (*yom*) begins at sundown, when three stars become visible in the sky (the rabbis reasoned that the day begins at sunset based on the description of God's activity in creation, "and the evening and the morning were the first day," Gen 1:5).

The Jewish Week

The Jewish week (*shavu'a*) begins on Sunday and ends on Shabbat:

Hebrew	Trans.	Day
יוֹם רִאשׁוֹן	yom ri·**shon**	Sunday
יוֹם שֵׁנִי	yom she·**ni**	Monday
יוֹם שְׁלִישִׁי	yom she·li·**shi**	Tuesday
יוֹם רְבִיעִי	yom re·vi·**'i**	Wednesday
יוֹם חֲמִישִׁי	yom cham·i·**shi**	Thursday
יוֹם שִׁשִּׁי	yom shi·**shi**	Friday
יוֹם שַׁבָּת	yom shab·**bat**	Shabbat

Shabbat

The fourth of the ten *mitzvot* (commandments) is, "Remember the Sabbath day, to keep it holy" (Ex. 20:8, KJV). Shabbat is therefore considered to be the most important day of the week, since the observance of Shabbat is explicitly set forth as one of the Ten Commandments.

During Shabbat, no "work" (defined under 39 main categories associated with the building of the Tabernacle in the desert) is to be performed, since this would violate the idea of "rest" (*shabbaton*) that is to mark the day.

For additional information about Shabbat, including the Shabbat home ceremony, see Lesson Fourteen.

Jewish Months and Year

The Hebrew calendar is based on the time it takes from the appearance of the "new moon" to the appearance of a full moon (normally about 30 days). The appearance of the new moon is called *Rosh Chodesh* (meaning "head of the month") and is observed in synagogues with additional prayers.

In the *Tanakh*, the first month of the calendar is the month of Nissan (when Passover occurs - see Ex. 12:12); however, *Rosh Hashanah* ("head of the year") is in Tishri, the seventh month, and that is when the year number is increased.

Hebrew	Trans.	Time	Festivals	Biblical	Civil
נִיסָן	Ni·san	Mar-Apr	**Pesach** (14th); **Chag Hammatsah** (15th-22nd); Yom Habikkurim (18th); [also Yom Hashoah (27th)].	1	7
אִיָּיר	Iy·yar	Apr-May	Yom Ha'atsmaut (5th); Yom Yerushalayim (28th)	2	8
סִיוָן	Si·van	May-June	**Shavu'ot** (6th)	3	9
תַּמּוּז	Tam·muz	June-July		4	10
אָב	Av	July-Aug	Tish'ah be'av (9th)	5	11
אֱלוּל	E·lul	Aug-Sept		6	12
תִּשְׁרִי	Tish·ri	Sept-Oct	Rosh Hashanah (1st) [trumpets]; Yom Kippur (10th); **Sukkot** (15th–22nd) ; Simchat Torah (22nd)	7	1
חֶשְׁוָן	Chesh·van	Oct-Nov		8	2
כִּסְלֵו	Kis·lev	Nov-Dec	Chanukkah (John 10:22); from Kislev 25 to Tevet 4 (8 days)	9	3
טֵבֵת	Te·vet	Dec-Jan		10	4
שְׁבָט	Shevat	Jan-Feb	Tu Beshvat (15th)	11	5
אֲדָר	A·dar	Feb-Mar	*Fast of Ester* (13th); Purim (14th).	12	6

Note: When there is a leap year, the extra month added after Adar is called *Adar Sheni*, or Adar the second.

Note: The three bold-faced festival names are known as *Shalosh Regalim,* the three "Pilgrim Festivals" (Ex. 23:14), that focus on key national events in Israel's history. The *High Holidays* run from the ten days from Rosh HaShanah to Yom Kippur and focus on individual repentance (*teshuvah*).